Global Perspectives on Sanctions

Global Perspectives on Sanctions

Norm Contestation and its Impact on International Politics

Edited by
Roberto Belloni, Thomas Biersteker and Francesco Giumelli

EDINBURGH
University Press

Edinburgh University Press is one of the leading university presses in the UK. Publishing new research in the arts and humanities, EUP connects people and ideas to inspire creative thinking, open new perspectives and shape the world we live in. For more information, visit www.edinburghuniversitypress.com.

Cover design: www.richardbudddesign.co.uk

Edinburgh University Press Ltd
13 Infirmary Street, Edinburgh EH1 1LT

Typeset in 10.5/13pt Bembo
by Cheshire Typesetting Ltd, Cuddington, Cheshire
Printed and bound by CPI Group (UK) Ltd, Croydon, CR0 4YY

A CIP record for this book is available from the British Library

ISBN 978 1 3995 5000 0 (hardback)
ISBN 978 1 3995 5001 7 (webready PDF)
ISBN 978 1 3995 5002 4 (epub)

Most of the chapters included in this volume were initially discussed at a workshop at the University of Trento made possible by funding from Dipartimenti d'Eccellenza 2018–22.

MIX
Paper | Supporting responsible forestry
FSC www.fsc.org FSC® C013604

This book is printed using paper from well-managed forests, recycling and other controlled sources

Contents

Illustrations

Figures

Tables

The Contributors

John Agbonifo is Professor of Sociology and Sustainable Development, and Director of the Global Affairs and Sustainable Development Institute (GASDI) of Osun State University, Nigeria. His research interest centres on governance, international peace and security, and environmental transformations. He explores the themes from a sub-Saharan African perspective, focusing in particular on sanctions, conflict analysis, peace studies, climate change and extractive industries. His latest publications include 'Nonstate Armed Groups, Leadership, and Sanctions Effectiveness' (*African Security*, 2021) and 'Fuel Subsidy Protests' in *Nigeria: The Promise and Mirage of Empowerment* (2023).

Fariba Alikarami is Postdoctoral Fellow in Sanctions and International Relations at the Graduate Institute of International and Development Studies in Geneva. She earned her PhD in International Relations from the University of Tehran, focusing on the use of sanctions in US foreign policy. She previously served as a visiting researcher on sanctions at Leiden University in the Netherlands and has worked with various public and private institutions, including the Institute of Foreign Policy Studies and the International Relations and Energy Research Institute in Iran. Her research interests include international sanctions, foreign policy and Middle East affairs.

Roberto Belloni is Professor of International Relations at the University of Bologna. Previously he held research and teaching positions at Denver University, Harvard, Johns Hopkins (Bologna Center), Queens Belfast and Trento. He has worked extensively on various aspects of democratisation and peace processes, with particular reference to the Balkans. His recent publications include *Critical Theory and Peace Processes: Gramsci, Civil Society and the Struggle for Hegemony* (2026); *The Rise and Fall of Peacebuilding in the Balkans*

(2020); and *Stabilization as the New Normal in International Interventions: Low Expectations?* (ed. with F. N. Moro, 2020).

Thomas Biersteker is Professor Honoraire at the Geneva Graduate Institute and a Senior Fellow with the Centre for Policy Research of the UN University. He previously taught at Yale University, the University of Southern California and Brown University. Author/editor of eleven other books, including *Targeted Sanctions: The Impacts and Effectiveness of United Nations Action* (2016) and *Informal Governance in World Politics* (2024), his research focuses on international relations theory, global governance and international sanctions. He received his PhD and MS from MIT, his BA from the University of Chicago, and he is the principal developer of the UNSanctionsApp.

Rishika Chauhan is a MacArthur-funded post-doctoral researcher at the Department of War Studies at King's College London. Her research focuses on sanctions and non-proliferation, with an emphasis on Indian and Chinese perspectives. She has held teaching and research positions at the University of Delhi, the Observer Research Foundation, the Indian Pugwash Society, Boston University and Yale-NUS College. She was also a member of the 2024 UK Sanctions Implementation and Strategy Taskforce, constituted by RUSI, London.

Matteo Dian is an Associate Professor at the Department of Political and Social Sciences, the University of Bologna. He earned his PhD at the Scuola Normale Superiore in Florence. His last books are *China's Blueprint for Global Leadership: GSI, GDI, GCI and Xi Jinping's Vision for the International Order* (2025, with Silvia Menegazzi) and *Reluctant Remilitarization: The Transformation of Defence Policy and Armed Forces in Japan, Germany and Italy* (Edinburgh University Press, 2023, with F. Moro and F. Coticchia). His research focuses on IR theory, security in East Asia, Japanese and Chinese foreign policies, and US foreign policy.

Piotr Dutkiewicz (LLM, PhD) is Distinguished Research Professor, Department of Political Science at Carleton University, Canada. Research interests: international relations, world order, Russian and European politics. Professor Dutkiewicz was editor-in-chief of a nineteen-volume series on 'Local and Regional Development in Poland and Eastern Europe' (1986–9) and has edited (or co-edited) ten books; most recently, *Civilizations and World Order* (2022, co-edited with Elena Chebankova); *Hegemony and World Order: Reimagining Power in Global Politics* (Routledge, 2021, co-edited with Tom

Casier and Jan Aart Scholte); and *Eurasia on the Edge* (2018, co-edited with Richard Sakwa and Fyodor Lukyanov).

Francesco Giumelli is Associate Professor of International Relations at the University of Groningen. He previously held research and teaching positions at Metropolitan University Prague and served as Deputy Director of the IR department in Groningen (2017–23). His research focuses on international sanctions, illicit trade and global governance, with particular attention to sanctions evasion and informal practices. His recent publications include *Le Sanzioni Internazionali: Storia, Obiettivi ed efficacia* (2023) and *International Sanctions in Practice: An Interdisciplinary Perspective* (2024, co-edited with Antonio Bultrini, Clara Portela and Mirko Sossai). He chairs the CA21133 GLITSS network on Globalization, Illicit Trade, Sustainability, and Security.

Nasser Hadian Jazy, PhD in Political Science, University of Tennessee, Knoxville, is Professor of Political Sciences, Faculty of Law and Political Sciences, University of Tehran. He was the Director of the Political Development Program at the Center for Strategic Research (1992–5). He was also Visiting Professor and Research Scholar at the Middle East Institute and Middle East and Asian Languages and Cultures Department, Columbia University (2001–4). He is the author of many scientific publications on the issues of Iranian contemporary politics. His areas of scholarly and research interests include Iranian contemporary politics, Iran's nuclear programme and political Islam.

Elin Hellquist is a senior analyst at the Swedish Defence Research Agency (FOI), where she specialises in international military missions and operations. Hellquist's interest in sanctions dates back to her PhD at the European University Institute, where she investigated the meaning of sanctions for the European Union as an international actor. As a postdoctoral researcher at Freie Universität Berlin and Stockholm University, she further explored the relational underpinnings and implications of sanctions, highlighting the significant difference between in-group and out-group measures.

Alexandra Hofer is Assistant Professor in Public International Law at Utrecht University, the Netherlands. Her research has primarily focused on the legality of unilateral sanctions under international law and their utility as an enforcement tool. She frequently conducts interdisciplinary research in international law, integrating international relations and international law to address common issues.

Intigam Mamedov is a postdoctoral research fellow at the Faculty of Humanities, Leiden University, the Netherlands. His research focuses on critical security studies and Russian and post-Soviet politics. Before joining Leiden University, he held research and teaching positions at Northumbria University (UK) and at Lomonosov Moscow State University (Russia).

Phil Orchard is Professor of International Relations at the University of Wollongong and Co-Director of the UOW Future of Rights Centre. He is the author of *Protecting the Internally Displaced: Rhetoric and Reality* (2018) and *A Right to Flee* (2014). His co-edited volumes include *Implementation in World Politics* (2014), *Constructing the Responsibility to Protect* (2020) and, with Antje Wiener, *Contesting the World* (2024) and the *Oxford Handbook on Norms in International Relations* (2025, also with Sassan Gholiagha).

Stefano Palestini is Associate Professor of International Relations at the School of International Studies and at the Department of Sociology and Social Research, Università degli Studi di Trento, Italy. He is also Adjunct Professor at the Institute of Political Science of the Pontificia Universidad Católica de Chile. He holds a PhD in Social and Political Science from the European University Institute. His main research areas are the international and transnational dimension of (de)democratisation, and the politics of transnational governance. His work on the legitimacy of sanctions has been published in *Cooperation and Conflict and International Affairs* among other journals.

Jasmin Ramović is Lecturer in Peace and Conflict Studies in the Politics Department at the University of Manchester. He is interested in interdisciplinary approaches to studying international relations, particularly the intersection of global political economy, peace and conflict studies, and anthropology. His research focuses on local actors in conflict-affected settings, with a specific focus on the economic dimension of their everyday interactions. Ramović is also interested in analysing the state of social contracts in societies divided by violent conflicts, and the role of sanctions in international relations.

María-Cristina Rosas is a Professor and researcher at the Faculty of Political and Social Sciences of the National Autonomous University of Mexico (UNAM). She heads the Olof Palme Center for Analysis and Research on Peace, Security and Development in Mexico. She has served as a consultant to the Mexican Ministry of Foreign Affairs, the governments of Japan, Canada and Sweden, and international organisations in Geneva on trade negotiations. She has authored multiple works on international trade and security, including

The Political Economy of International Security: Sanctions, Carrots and Sticks (2003). Her most recent book addresses intelligence and security in Mexico.

Antje Wiener, FAcSS MAE, holds the Chair of Political Science, especially Global Governance at the University of Hamburg, where she is also Professor of Law. She is a By-Fellow at Hughes Hall, Cambridge and founding editor of *Global Constitutionalism* and the Springer Series on Norm Research in International Relations. Her *Contestation and Constitution of Norms in Global International Relations* (2018) won the International Law Section's Best Book Award in 2020. She has published widely on norms including *Contesting the World* (2024 with Orchard) and the *Oxford Handbook on Norms in International Relations* (2025 with Gholiagha and Orchard).

Wenjie Yu (LLM, PhD) is Associate Professor of International Law and Deputy Director of Foreign-Related Rule of Law Research Centre, at Law School, Southeast University, China. She is co-author of several books on international dispute resolution and international rule of law, including *The Practice of WTO Dispute Settlement: A Perspective with China's Characteristic* (2024) and *The Advancement of the Rule of Law in the International Order* (Nanjing University Press, 2023). Her main research interests focus on international economic law, international dispute resolution, international sanctions and China's foreign-related rule of law.

Acknowledgements

The importance of sanctions as a defining tool of international politics has been increasingly acknowledged since the mid-1990s, attending a significant rise in the adoption of both unilateral and multilateral sanctions which followed the end of the Cold War. The proliferation of sanctions, however, has not been matched by research on how states perceive this tool, on what grounds they may object to it and how they interpret the legitimacy of the norm, of the enforcers and of the measure. We were further intrigued by the stark divergence that emerged following Russia's full-scale invasion of Ukraine in 2022: while the dominant narrative amongst the G7+ countries that applied sanctions on Russia framed the assault as a grave breach of international law demanding a unified global response, many other governments declined to impose sanctions on Moscow, highlighting deep differences in how coercive measures are evaluated, legitimised and contested.

An international workshop held at the Department of Sociology and Social Research at the University of Trento on 15–16 December 2022, titled Non-Western Approaches to Sanctions: Global Perspectives, provided an initial opportunity to discuss these issues with a number of scholars and practitioners. Most of the book's contributors presented an early version of their chapters there. We are grateful to the Department of Sociology and Social Research for generously funding this initiative through the Dipartimenti di Eccellenza 2018–22 budget line. Substantively, this meeting showed the methodological complications with framing the discussion on sanctions as a confrontation between Western and non-Western states, a binary distinction that can reify 'the West' as a category. As a result, we revised our initial hypothesis based on this dichotomy and introduced and drew from the literature on norm contestation in order to explore how states contest (or not) international sanctions regardless of their position within the international system.

A second workshop was held, in a hybrid format, at the Department of Social and Political Sciences at the University of Bologna on 19 June 2023. Thanks are due to Matteo Dian for his efforts to arrange the logistics that made the meeting possible and to the Department's Director, Professor Filippo Andreatta, for his endorsement of the initiative. This second meeting provided the occasion both to expand the conceptual and empirical scope of our analysis through the involvement of other authors and to present and debate revised versions of the initial papers.

We wish to express our gratitude to all colleagues who have contributed their work, time and effort to our project. Thanks are extended to Sam Johnson and Sarah Foyle of Edinburgh University Press for guiding us through the steps of publishing a volume and for coping patiently with the delays that a project of such ambition has entailed. The feedback from the three anonymous reviewers contributed to substantial improvements to the volume, so we are also grateful to them.

Roberto Belloni is especially indebted to the Director of the Department of Sociology and Social Research in Trento, Professor Giuseppe Sciortino, for his personal and institutional support needed to overcome the bureaucratic problems involved in inviting scholars based in sanctioned countries in the so-called Global South for the initial workshop in 2022. He also would like to acknowledge his indebtedness to the Department of Sociology for granting him a sabbatical leave for the 2022–3 academic year and the Robert Schuman Centre for Advanced Studies, European University Institute, for hosting him as a visiting fellow throughout 2022–3. Fiesole proved to be a conducive and stimulating environment to develop initial ideas on this topic. He dedicates this book to Luce for her patience throughout the duration of this project. Luce: by the time you are reading this volume, I hope we are living in a much more peaceful time where war and coercion are replaced by international dialogue, cooperation and mutual accommodation.

Thomas Biersteker would like to acknowledge and thank the participants from across the globe who participated in making Global International Relations a reality in the context of this collaborative project. They overcame the challenges of writing from countries under sanctions, in conditions of exile or facing adverse health situations (among other challenges) to contribute to a collective effort that enhances our understanding of the complexities of the over-used, but often misunderstood, policy instrument of international sanctions. He dedicates this book to those who have struggled over many decades to create intellectual and institutional space for Global International Relations.

Francesco Giumelli would also like to thank the Department of Sociology and Social Research in Trento for welcoming him as Visiting Professor in

May 2022, when the idea of fostering this Global International Relations dialogue first emerged. In particular, Director Giuseppe Sciortino and Roberto Belloni were instrumental in making this possible. He would also like to thank the Department of International Relations and International Organization for its constant support and for fostering a highly inspiring academic community that has sparked numerous research questions on sanctions from various perspectives. This experience strengthened his awareness of the many viewpoints that can give meaning to events and phenomena – an awareness we should always cultivate as we seek to contribute to academic work that is also useful to policymakers and practitioners. Finally, Francesco dedicates this volume to the victims of conflict – especially in Ukraine and in the Palestinian territories – who continue to suffer the consequences of humanity's failure to understand and embrace diversity, the core essence of this volume.

Introduction

Roberto Belloni, Thomas Biersteker and Francesco Giumelli

Introduction

The February 2022 invasion of Ukraine triggered an impressive wave of sanctions against the Russian Federation. However, restrictive measures have been imposed by only a limited number of states, mostly from the Western world and G7 associated countries from Asia such as Japan, South Korea and Singapore. Most states have decided not to adopt sanctions, and despite their support for resolutions criticising the Russian invasion in the United Nations General Assembly, the decision not to adopt sanctions has been often interpreted as either indifference or a sign of implicit support for Russia. The lack of a global front on sanctions, what would then be truly multilateral sanctions, universal in their application (like UN Security Council sanctions), has been explained in the literature mostly by claiming that states lack political will to sanction or wish to remain neutral to the extent possible (see Miliband 2023).

But how do states explain and justify their 'lack of will' or their efforts to remain 'neutral'? How and why do governments, as well as citizens and the private sector, interpret and challenge sanctions and their application? This edited volume intends to contribute to this discussion by investigating contestations of norms with regard to international sanctions. States have frequently contested the norms, rules and procedures governing the global sanction regime, thus affecting the process of adoption and implementation of this policy tool. In this way states have subjected sanctions to processes of interpretation, appropriation, resistance and change.

The sanctions on Russia exemplify this contestation process, but the volume is not limited to the Russian case. By looking at various cases in historical practice and from different geographical vantage points, this volume brings together a collection of reflections on how sanctions have been experienced and understood in different national and regional contexts. The analysis of different contestation strategies and narratives of sanctions contributes to an explanation of why sanctions on Russia have not been imposed, why disagreements have emerged and how states seek to interpret and appropriate sanctions in the development of their own foreign policy. More broadly, the analysis of this process illustrates not only the strengths and weaknesses of sanctions as a regime with its norms, rules and procedures, but also their role as a tool of foreign policy. In this volume, through a rich empirical collection of country and regional case studies, we examine how the utilisation of sanctions in itself has turned into an arena of contestation.

Scholars of international relations and international sanctions from around the world join scholars of norm contestation, international legitimacy and international law to explore sanction contestation by undertaking a multi-perspectivist, empirical and historically grounded set of analyses from European, North American, African, Latin American, Eurasian, Southwest Asian, East Asian, South Asian and Southeast Asian vantage points. They address a number of interrelated questions, including whether the contestation is about the global norms themselves, over who is enforcing them or about how the norms are being enforced through the application of sanctions. Is the reluctance to impose sanctions on Russia due to opposition to norms of non-intervention and the use of force? Or is it because states are protecting their self-interest, or because some states are maintaining space for their possible mediation of the conflict, or because they oppose the self-appointed group of countries imposing sanctions or they object to the use of sanctions in general, or is it because of some combination of these different potential explanations?

In the process of contestation, different key agents (states, their private sectors and their publics) endorse and advance a mix of considerations and arguments. These include cost–benefit calculations related to the impact of sanctions on the target state, bystanders and themselves; doubts about the legality and legitimacy of the measures involved, particularly when they are adopted unilaterally, outside of the UN framework; geopolitical assessments rooted in states' perceptions of their position within the international system and the importance placed on the respect of the institution of sovereignty; cultural understandings of sanctions as inappropriate to support confidence-building and reconciliation processes; value judgements and identity issues raised by the blunt 'us' versus 'them' distinction associated with the use of sanctions, and more.

In brief, this volume contributes to the vast and growing literature on sanctions by connecting the sanctions literature with theoretical perspectives on norm contestation, legitimacy and international law; enhancing the understanding of sanctions by including the plurality of interpretations and narratives that have been formed around this contested space of international politics; providing different perspectives that would facilitate the formulation of multilateral sanctions; and contributing to the development of Global International Relations, taking seriously the perspectives of scholars located across the globe and bringing them into the global conversation about international sanctions. Scholars originally from both sanctions-sending countries (like the US, EU and ECOWAS) and countries under sanctions (like Iran, Russia and Serbia) are included in the volume, even though countries not subjected to sanctions are rare to find since targeted measures were also imposed on targets in the US and in the EU.

Reactive, Proactive and Interpretative Contestation

This edited book examines both the complexity of agents' motivations as well as the strategies they adopt in the process of contestation. Drawing from the theoretical framework developed by Phil Orchard and Antje Wiener (Orchard and Wiener 2024), discussed in more detail in Chapter 1, this book explores three major contestation strategies.

First, **reactive contestation** refers to situations whereby agents engage with a norm to change it, or even to undermine or violate it. Agents challenge the legitimacy as well as the standard of behaviour that the norm seeks to encourage. In practice, reactive contestation may *de facto* lead the agent to side with the sanctioned state in a formal or informal way, as discussed in the conclusion of this book. Second, **proactive contestation** involves the attempt to improve the norm, for example by strengthening procedures of due process and introducing humanitarian carve-outs to ameliorate the impacts of sanctions on the broader population in sanctioned countries. This type of contestation questions the issue of what can be rightfully included within a sanction regime, for example whether sanctions can legitimately target individuals in addition to entire states or the extent to which they can have a non-discriminating impact on the civilian population. Third, **interpretative contestation** reflects the existence of a set of different understandings of the norms underpinning the sanction regime or the practices associated with the use of restrictive measures. These different understandings are influenced especially by states' position within the international system, in particular whether they experienced extended colonial rule. Interpretative contestation is likely to appear in the process of sanction application and, as Orchard and Wiener suggest, may even be inadvertent, since the agent may believe their understanding of the norm and practices associated with it is aligned and compatible with that of other actors.

Reactive, proactive and interpretative contestation can take many forms and may closely overlap with one another. For analytical purposes, however, it is useful to separate them in order to understand better the different arguments agents adopt and their relevance in a particular sanction episode. With regard to reactive contestation, we identify two main empirical manifestations rooted in different interpretations of the normative underpinnings characterising the international system. First, interventionist vs non-interventionist (or sovereigntist) interpretations of the Westphalian state system, and related principles of non-interference in the domestic affairs of sovereign states, influence agents' views with regard to the legitimacy of sanctions. The violation of the norm of territorial integrity of a sovereign state through inter-state aggression, which is a foundational element of the contemporary international system, is perhaps the most significant legitimating factor which may convince agents to adopt sanctions against an aggressor. Indeed, as Palestini (2023) argued, the higher the status of the legitimacy of the norm that is being violated by an international actor, the easier it is to legitimate the sanctions imposed to enforce that norm. However, as the case of Russian aggression in Ukraine confirms, other considerations contribute to shape the perception of both the legitimacy and the legality of sanctions. Support for the norm of non-intervention in general may exceed concerns about territorial integrity and the use of force, particularly if the use of force can be justified in some manner, as Russia has tried to do. As Palestini argues in Chapter 2, one such consideration is the legitimacy of the enforcer, that is, who has the right to impose a particular sanction regime? While sanctions adopted by the United Nations Security Council have a legal validity under international law and are more easily accepted by states as binding, unilateral sanctions do not carry the same normative weight and, as Alexandra Hofer explains in Chapter 4, states may interpret their adoption as a retorsion against a violator. Thus, rather than understanding sanctions as a tool aimed at fostering the kind of conduct intervening states want to reinforce, some states interpret them as a questionable form of 'punishment' and, accordingly, may decide to contest the use of the instrument altogether. This is an additional aspect of legitimacy taken up by Palestini in his chapter, that is, whether sanctions are an appropriate (and proportional) policy tool, given the infractions of norms over which they are applied. The confrontational logic inherent in any sanction regime is said to hinder, rather than favour, the search for stability, negotiated compromise and the restoration of domestic and/or international order. This may hold true for informal multilaterally coordinated sanctions as well (such as those adopted by the G7+), confirming how, once the Security Council *imprimatur* is taken out of the equation, contestation becomes more widespread. A group of states under unilateral international sanctions have lobbied strenuously within the Human Rights Council and at the UN General Assembly for the creation of the office of the special rapporteur on the harmful effects of unilateral coercive measures, or UCMs, in an effort to delegitimise the use of sanctions outside the UN framework.

A second major issue involved in the process of reactive contestation is the legitimacy of sanctions against states vs those against individuals. The imposition of sanctions on individuals is increasingly common and at times more contentious than the imposition of sanctions on states, due to the lack of adequate due process guarantees for individual designations (Biersteker and van den Herik 2026). Even though individual accountability is ever more important within the international system (as confirmed, for example, by the work of the International Criminal Court), both its legitimacy and its legality are far from universally accepted (Welsh, Akande and Rodin 2023).

While reactive contestation appears to challenge both the legality and the legitimacy of many sanctions regimes, and in practice it may align the contesting agent with the sanctioned actor, with proactive contestation, actors engage instead with adjustments to the sanction regime in order to improve it. Their critique is not of the norm itself, but of the impact sanctions have not only on the target state and its population but also on bystanders in neighbouring states or in states closely integrated into global supply chains affected by secondary sanctions. From this perspective, agents may support the introduction of targeted sanctions aimed at minimising the humanitarian costs for the civilian population of the target state. In addition, their contestation may involve efforts to strengthen procedures of due process and the establishment of humanitarian carve-outs when even highly targeted sanctions regimes create unintended challenges for humanitarian actors. Alongside attempts to minimise the humanitarian costs of sanctions, agents may also attempt to improve the effectiveness of sanctions by arguing in favour of the adoption of a particular sanctions regime, for example aimed at weakening the security sector of the target state contemplating nuclear weapons proliferation. In sum, agents accept sanctions as a tool of foreign policy and attempt to modulate their impact in order to make them more effective, less painful for the general population, consistent with the rule of law and supportive of regional security goals.

Finally, interpretative contestation brings to the fore actors' different understandings of states' positions within the international system. As ontological security analysts argue, this understanding is shaped by states' own 'biographical experience' (Steele 2008). First, the post-colonial condition can be the lens through which many states assess the international liberal order. From an anti-colonial perspective, sanctions are seen as an instrument of the strong (Northern, Western) against the weak (Global South, non-West) and, therefore, as a tool of domination and an attempt to control. The fact that most US, EU and even UN sanctions regimes have been imposed on developing countries in the past half a century confirm to post-colonial states the presence of a normative bias against them. In this context, opposition to US/Western sanctions is grounded on a resistance to hegemony and its exercise; an attitude reminiscent of anti-colonial struggles during the Cold War. Paradoxically, however, many post-colonial states have not generally viewed the Russian invasion of Ukraine in anti-colonial terms. From a Ukrainian point of view, it is resisting a revanchist, Russian imperial re-colonisation, but it has not succeeded in advancing this discourse among former colonised states, suggesting the need to further explore the depth and basis of post-colonial argumentations.

A second interpretative type of contestation pits national and global interests against each other. The debate on the relative merits of each position calls into question different interpretations of the current international order. Western states, including the US, have frequently claimed to impose sanctions in the 'interest of the international community'. This claim prompted accusations of using sanctions in the pursuit of Western/American hegemony and employing double standards in international affairs, when Russia is sanctioned for its violations of norms but Israel is not. By contrast, rising powers such as China, India and Russia, among others, have been more explicit in their adoption of sanctions to support and defend their own 'national interests'. All three have used sanctions as counter-measures on others, and their assessment of the national interest may involve a self-conscious reflection of the meaning of national identity and of national harms. Sanctions challenge stratified notions of 'who we are', trigger citizens' interrogations of their place in the world and may lead to citizens' pressure on their government to either adopt or reject a sanction regime. In these circumstances governments can be tempted to use sanctions to capitalise electorally on the situation. Thus, citizens' views are an important but frequently underestimated factor in the sanction debate.

This volume examines different types of sanctions contestation, and their empirical manifestations involving a number of different actors – states, private actors and the general public. Following Orchard and Wiener in Chapter 1, the process of contestation is defined as a neutral one with a range of positive, negative and neutral effects. By focusing on the process of contestation as a normatively neutral process, this volume also seeks to avoid the normative biases involved in the study of views, understandings and strategies emanating from the so-called Global South, sometimes referred to as the 'non-Western world'. The Western/non-Western dichotomy both reifies the 'West' and fails to account for states' behaviour in 'non-Western' regions. For example, as Matteo Dian explains in Chapter 12, similarly to Western states, the BRICS may employ sanctions as an instrument of foreign policy while at the same time adopting different ways to describe them in practice. Thus, the problem is not so much the presence of (presumed) differences between Western and non-Western states, but rather different interpretations and justifications of the application of sanctions.

Norm contestation takes place at different venues, among different actors and over different issues, particularly when it comes to the use of the instrument of sanctions. We integrate the three-fold typology of reactive, proactive and interpretative contestation introduced by Orchard and Wiener in Chapter 1, with Stefano Palestini's useful disaggregation of the legitimacy problem of sanctions. He differentiates between the legitimacy of the norm, the legitimacy of the enforcer and the legitimacy of the measure (Palestini 2023). In the conclusion of this volume, we map the types, locations and different aspects of norm contestation over international sanctions, drawing on the rich empirical content of the chapters included in the volume. Reactive contestation is *often* about norms, proactive is *often* about actors, and interpretative is *often* about instruments. Different chapters, however, highlight reactive contestation over actors enforcing norms or interpretative contestation over the hierarchy of norms being contested, that is, giving priority to some norms over others. Our framework is derived from the following table.

Table I.1 A framework for analysis of global sanctions contestation

Type of contestation	Norms contested (use of force, territorial integrity, sovereign non-interference, human rights)	Actors enforcing (UN, regional organisations, autonomous (G7+) sanctions, etc.) and locations of contestation (in states, private sector or civil society)	Instruments used (sanctions, incentives, diplomacy, threats of or use of force)
Reactive	X		
Proactive		X	
Interpretative			X

Beyond the different types of contestation, we know that different norms are involved in the international sanctions debate over Russia. The norms against inter-state armed aggression and the use of force, support for territorial integrity of UN member states, and non-interference in domestic affairs of sovereign states are all subject to contestation to varying degrees. At the same time, the actors taking it upon themselves to enforce norms in the name of the 'international community' can be contested. This contestation can take place in multiple locations, by states, by their private sectors and by their general publics. Finally, there may be contestation over the instruments themselves, the very use of sanctions. Are sanctions an appropriate foreign policy tool? Do they preclude other options? Are they proportional to the infractions alleged?

Contents of the Volume

The volume is organised around an analytical and conceptual introduction of four chapters, followed by a section on the historical practices of norm contestation over international sanctions with five chapters by scholars from different vantage points on the globe, a shorter section of three chapters focusing more specifically on the contemporary Russia sanctions, and a conclusion.

The first part of the book presents four chapters with analytical, historical, conceptual approaches to norm contestation. The literature on international norms has evolved considerably from the pioneering work of Finnemore and Sikkink (1998) who described the framing and articulation of norms, how norms reached tipping points among state adaptors before becoming internalised in state behaviour. More recent scholarship has considered the performative aspects of international norms, the contestation of norms and their potential erosion (see, for example, Lehti, Pennanen and Jouhki 2020).

Chapter 1 by Phil Orchard of the University of Wollongong in Australia and Antje Wiener of the University of Hamburg in Germany and the University of Cambridge in the UK revisits the typology of norm contestation developed in their 2024 book, *Contesting the World: Norm Research in Theory and Practice*, that distinguishes between reactive, proactive and interpretative types of norm contestation. They apply their framework to the issue of the uneven application of sanctions on Russia since its 2022 invasion of Ukraine. Chapter 2 by Stefano Palestini of the University of Trento in Italy applies a typology of legitimation challenges to sanctions developed in his 2023 *International Affairs* article that differentiates between challenges to the content of norms, to the senders of sanctions or to the decisions to use sanctions to enforce norms. Chapter 3 by Elin Hellquist of the Swedish Defence Research Agency, FOI, engages in a discursive and historical analysis of UN General Assembly debates about the use of sanctions between 1946 and 2023 in order to evaluate changes in both the increasing frequency of sanctions use by the UN and changes in the content of sanctions regimes following the introduction of targeted measures at the end of the 1990s. Finally, Chapter 4 by Alexandra Hofer of the University of Utrecht in the Netherlands considers how the increased use of unilateral and autonomous sanctions measures has raised questions about the legality of the practice. She also considers how the application of targeted sanctions on individuals has raised human rights due process concerns that have affected the legitimacy of the sanctions instrument.

The second part of the book addresses practices of contestation around the globe. Most of the literature on international sanctions is written from the vantage point of the senders of sanctions, not the targets (Biersteker 2018). The sanctions literature and the leading quantitative databases widely used by many sanctions scholars are drawn disproportionately from US, EU and UN sanctions examples. Indeed, there is a distinct US bias in most of the general databases used by quantitative sanctions scholars (Biersteker, Eckert, Tourinho and Hudáková 2018).

Chapter 5 by John Agbonifo from Osun State University in Nigeria addresses the distinctiveness of African approaches to the application of sanctions on members of regional organisations as a means of persuasion, rather than of punishment for non-constitutional changes of government on the African continent. In Chapter 6, Fariba Alikarami and Nasser Hadian Jazy, both of Tehran University in Iran, review Iran's historical experience with sanctions and assess the basis of its narrative and internal discourse about sanctions. They provide a consideration of legal, historical and identity-related perspectives, with special attention to the application of 'maximum pressure' measures by the US. Chapter 7 by Wenjie Yu from Southeast University in China examines China in its dual role of target and source country in the use of sanctions. She shows how Beijing's rhetorical contestation of unilateral sanctions has gone hand in hand with the country's increasing adoption of 'counter-measures' which, because they are adopted against previous illegal actions, are considered as justified under international law. In Chapter 8, Rishika Chauhan from King's College London in the UK reflects on the BRICS countries and describes how discussions of sanctions have consistently come up at their annual summits and have produced three narratives: (1) unilateral sanctions are illegal under international law; (2) sanctions impede the development of the Global South; and (3) cooperation with sanctioned states is justified in terms of the pursuit of national interests. Finally, in Chapter 9 María-Cristina Rosas of UNAM in Mexico discusses the evolution of the sanctions policy in Mexico, emphasises the absence of a strong domestic legal framework for implementation and describes the ambivalence of Mexico's private sector (given its deep integration into the global and regional economy). She argues that this has resulted in variance between the public and private sector positions on the Russia sanctions.

The third part of the book examines sanctions contestation with specific regard to the Russia–Ukraine war. The overwhelming majority of UN member states voted that Russia 'immediately, completely and unconditionally withdraw all of its military forces from the territory of Ukraine within its internationally recognized borders'. Only five states – Belarus, North Korea, Eritrea, Russia and Syria – voted against the resolution, while thirty-five more, including major players such as China and India, abstained. Despite the widespread condemnation of Russian aggression in Ukraine, many states, particularly in the 'Global South', have been reluctant to endorse and adopt the sanctions imposed on Russia.

There are many reasons involved in this choice. Existing military, energy and trade ties to Russia suggest the adoption of a soft stance against Moscow. Not only is Russia the second largest exporter of military equipment globally, but it is also a provider of both nuclear energy and oil products. The Russian State Atomic Energy Corporation (ROSATOM) has built, or is in the process of building, nuclear power plants in a number of states (Armenia, Bangladesh, Belarus, China, India, Iran) and has agreements with a dozen more for future development of nuclear power cooperation efforts (Cohen 2023). Likewise, many states, including Serbia as discussed in Chapter 11, benefit from Russian oil and gas, which continue to be sold abroad despite G7+ sanctions. In addition to military and energy ties, there are other reasons why some states remain neutral with regard to sanctions, as discussed in more detail in the conclusion of this volume.

In Chapter 10, Intigam Mamedov, previously at Moscow State University, now at Leiden University, and Piotr Dutkiewicz from Carleton University in Canada write about the complex contestation within Russia under sanctions. They employ public opinion survey research to analyse how public opinion in Russia is shaped by both Russian government narratives and personal experiences. Russia's 'official narrative' is described, core trends in perceptions of sanctions amongst the Russian public are presented, and other factors that may influence public opinion on sanctions in the country are considered. In Chapter 11, Roberto Belloni from the University of Bologna in Italy and Jasmin Ramović of the University of Manchester in the UK explore the paradoxical situation of Serbia. Despite its status as a candidate for membership in the EU, Serbia has been reluctant to join the EU sanctions on Russia. Serbia's ongoing balancing act between 'West' and 'East' provides it with some distinctive advantages and it appears motivated both by its own experience with sanctions in the 1990s and by its own semi-peripheral position in the international system, which makes the country especially sensitive to status and sovereignty concerns. Finally, in Chapter 12, Matteo Dian from the University of Bologna in Italy argues that ASEAN's decision not to impose sanctions on Russia is associated with its normative opposition to forms of intervention in sovereign affairs (its post-colonial nationalism and long-standing commitment to non-alignment), its varying degrees of dependence on the 'East' vs 'West' and its vulnerability to the global disruptions created by the war.

In the conclusion of the volume the three co-editors, Roberto Belloni (University of Bologna in Italy), Thomas Biersteker (Geneva Graduate Institute in Switzerland) and Francesco Giumelli (University of Groningen in the Netherlands), return to the framework for analysing the normative contestation of international sanctions illustrated in Table I.1 above. They assess the global variation in contestation, drawing on the empirical chapters in the volume, summarise the main findings from the chapters in the book, analyse the variation of the responses to the sanctions against Russia, and assess the strengths and weaknesses of the framework of analysis outlined earlier in this introductory chapter.

References

Biersteker, Thomas. 2018. 'SanctionsApp as Expertise (and Exclusionary Ignorance) in a Global Policy Setting'. In *Assembling Exclusive Expertise: Knowledge, Ignorance and Conflict Resolution in the Global South*, edited by Anna Leander and Ole Weaver. Routledge.

Biersteker, Thomas, Sue E. Eckert, Marcos Tourinho and Zuzana Hudáková. 2018. 'UN Targeted Sanctions Datasets (1991–2013)'. *Journal of Peace Research* 55(3): 404–12.

Biersteker, Thomas J., and Larissa van den Herik. 2026. 'Enhancing the Legitimacy of UN Security Council Sanctions by Strengthening Fair and Clear Procedures'. *Global Governance* 32(1): 29–53.

Cohen, Patricia. 2023. 'Why Russia Has Such a Strong Grip on Europe's Nuclear Power'. *New York Times*, 11 March.

Finnemore, Martha, and Kathryn Sikkink. 1998. 'International Norm Dynamics and Political Change'. *International Organization* 52(4): 887–917.

Lehti, Marko, Henna-Riikka Pennanen and Jukka Jouhki. 2020. *Contestations of Liberal Order: The West in Crisis?* Palgrave.

Miliband, David. 2023. 'The World Beyond Ukraine'. *Foreign Affairs*, May/June.

Orchard, Phil, and Antje Wiener, eds. 2024. *Contesting the World: Norm Research in Theory and Practice*. Cambridge University Press.

Palestini, Stefano. 2023. 'The Politics of Legitimation in Combined Sanction Regimes'. *International Affairs* 99(3): 1087-107.

Steele, Brent J. 2008. *Ontological Security in International Relations: Self-Identity and the IR State*. Routledge.

Welsh, Jennifer, Dapo Akande and David Rodin. 2023. *The Individualization of War: Rights, Liability and Accountability in Contemporary Armed Conflict*. Oxford University Press.

1

Sanctions and Practices of Norm Contestation

Phil Orchard and Antje Wiener

Introduction

Russia's invasion of Ukraine is a clear violation of core international norms. In particular, it violates Article 2(4) of the United Nations (UN) Charter which states that all members of the United Nations 'shall refrain in their international relations from the threat of use of force against the territorial integrity or political independence of any state'. But it is also a clear challenge for the UN as an institution and the role of the UN Security Council. Given that the Russian aggression leads beyond violating a single norm, we therefore identify it as a 'deep contestation' of foundational elements of the UN charter order (UNCO). This observation follows Lake and Wiener who note that

> [D]eep contestation emerges when the fundamental rules of politics, the principles and procedures through which policies get made, come under challenge. Deep contestation signifies that some significant group rejects the foundations of an order others accept or hold dear. Deep contestation is extraordinary politics. . . . Like contestation generally, episodes of deep contestation can strengthen political orders, such as the U.S. Civil War that led to the end of slavery and the passage of the 14th amendment to the U.S. Constitution establishing the principle of equality for all citizens. But deep contestation can also weaken orders, leading societies away from previously shared values in, for instance, racially motivated genocides. In the midst of deep contestation, in the absence of agreement on fundamental rules and norms, which path will be taken is difficult to predict. Questions of access central to normal contestation are themselves contested. Who can speak, under what terms, and what constitutes evidence for and against norms

and practices become part of the 'game' of politics. (Lake and Wiener 2026, 3)

As this chapter argues, we have, over the past two decades, seen the development of a clear toolbox of responses available to the Security Council to respond to atrocity crimes through the Responsibility to Protect (R2P) doctrine. The R2P doctrine specifically links together a set of existing norms around atrocity crimes – genocide, war crimes, crimes against humanity and ethnic cleansing – but also creates two new norms, one focusing on a distinct responsibility for states to protect their own populations and the international community to similarly do so, and a second reflecting that the UN Security Council – and only the Council – has the authority to respond to atrocity crimes through the use of Chapters VI and VII of the UN Charter (Orchard 2020).

While state aggression was not included in the R2P toolkit, the clear and quick evidence of the Russian military engaging in war crimes and crimes against humanity rapidly made the invasion an R2P case, even while Russia itself sought to invoke the language of R2P to justify its claims. Other actors were able to take quick action. These include the International Criminal Court, which rapidly announced an investigation (International Criminal Court 2022) and which has led to arrest warrants being issued by the Court for Russian President Vladimir Putin and Maria Lvova-Belova for the crimes of unlawful deportation and transfer of population (International Criminal Court 2023). The UN Human Rights Council quickly established an Independent International Commission of Inquiry to investigate 'all alleged violations and abuses of human rights and violations of international humanitarian law, and related crimes' in Ukraine, which has issued eight reports. Through the 'United for Peace' procedure, the UN General Assembly has been able to hold an ongoing emergency session to respond to the invasion and has passed a resolution condemning Russia's invasion as illegal and condemning Russia's annexation of Ukrainian territory through its October 2022 annexation declaration. It has also voted to suspend Russia's membership on the Human Rights Council.

But the UN Security Council has been unable to take action. It is clear why this is – the ability of Russia to use its veto against any steps taken by the Council. We have clear signs that absent the veto, the Council would have been more active. This includes its first vetoed resolution, which specifically condemned 'all violations of international humanitarian law and violations and abuses of human rights'.[1] A modified version of this text was then introduced

[1] UN Security Council draft resolution S/2022/155 25 Feb 2022; see also United Nations (2022).

and adopted by the UN General Assembly. There are certain powers that are exclusive to the Council – including its ability to take action to maintain international peace and security through Chapter VII, which includes (through the R2P doctrine) the option to take such measures when a state is manifestly failing to protect its own population from genocide and other atrocity crimes, a responsibility that would certainly extend to the Russian state as the occupying power of territory in eastern Ukraine.

In so doing, the R2P doctrine further extends the issues for which the Council can impose sanctions. As Biersteker and Hudáková (2021, 107) note, the range of issues for which the Council has imposed sanctions include not only armed conflict, but also the 'proliferation of weapons of mass destruction, acts of terrorism, and non-constitutional changes of government' and only sanctions imposed by the Council are legally binding under Chapter VII of the UN Charter (Biersteker et al. 2018, 405). This does not limit the imposition of sanctions – both states and regional organisations including the European Union do impose their own sanctions regimes. Yet, these other mechanisms do not have the legitimacy the Council possesses. As Doxey (1972) argued, authority has been given to the UN to impose sanctions connected to the wider aim of regulating state disputes; the authority the Council has functions because it is also viewed as legitimate.

This is why this particular case is interesting from a norm contestation perspective. The first point to make is that when we focus on sanctions, they are reflecting two somewhat distinct sets of norms. The first is based around the use of sanctions as a specific form of international response to a situation of norm violation. Thus, with respect to Ukraine, the use of sanctions is framed as a response to the violation by Russia of both Article 2(4) and of the norms forbidding atrocity crimes. Here, the use of sanctions is primarily focused on either coercively influencing the target to modify its behaviour; to constrain the target so that it cannot achieve its goal; or to signal more widely that the target's behaviour is not viewed as appropriate (Giumelli 2011, 33–5; Giumelli 2015). Signalling, Hellquist notes (this volume), reflects that sanctions are 'not only for the target, but also for different domestic and international audiences'. The second is whether the application of sanctions by actors other than the UN Security Council is appropriate. As Hofer argues in her chapter, 'States and groups that contest unilateral sanctions rarely object to the norm that the senders are seeking to enforce; rather they dispute the legality and legitimacy of unilateral sanctions as a means of enforcement' (Hofer, this volume).

Because of these two distinct senses of how sanctions are understood, this case is rife for norm contestation. The next section will cover in depth how norm contestations can be understood. But, in brief, on the face of it this appears to be a case of what is referred to as applicatory contestation – here, states have questioned what the applicable action in this situation is, particularly given the absence of direction from the Council, while other states (most notably Russia) have sought to argue that this is not the appropriate response. But applicatory contestations (at least as they are defined) are not meant to affect the validity of the overall norm.

Rather, we can see three alternative types of norm contestations occurring. Contestations, we suggest, need to be viewed overall as a neutral process. How actors, including states, engage in contestation will reflect whether they are seeking to proactively engage with a norm to improve it; reactively engage with a norm to change it and, at the extreme, undermine and violate it; or whether they are engaging in interpretative contestations reflecting a spread of different understandings of the norm (Orchard and Wiener 2024, 4). The remainder of the chapter elaborates on this framework in three further sections. Section one presents the norm contestation approach and details key practices of contestation. Section two addresses the types of contestation we see involved in the case of the Russian invasion, and section three concludes with an outlook for further studies on sanctions based on the norm contestation approach.

The Norm Contestation Approach

Norm contestation views norms as processes, rather than seeing norms as fixed 'things'. That is, 'they are a social phenomenon which carries specific contextualised meanings and therefore is prone to create contestation at best and conflict at worst when dealt with out-of-context' (Wiener 2009, 176). It is perhaps easier to understand this aspect by starting with an alternative understanding of norm emergence, Finnemore and Sikkink's norm life cycle model (1998). For them, norm emergence occurs through three stages, with norm entrepreneurs introducing a new issue or idea which becomes the emerging norm. Early adopting states then take this norm and socialise other states to follow them through a variety of mechanisms including legitimation effects, self-esteem effects and pressure for conformity (Coleman 2013, 166; Finnemore and Sikkink 1998, 901–2). Once the norm passes a tipping point, it is then widely accepted and internalised by actors and achieves a 'taken-for-granted' quality that make conformance with the norm almost automatic' (Finnemore and Sikkink 1998, 904; see also Risse and Sikkink 1999, 15–17). This model, however, has an underlying assumption of stability (Wiener 2014, 23); that there is a single fixed understanding of that norm that actors accept.

Contestation theory, instead, views norms as '"processes", as works-in-progress, rather than as finished products' (Krook and True 2012, 105). Even when norms have acquired a stable quality indicating structural power that is influential for state behaviour (Katzenstein 1996), norms are never fixed. Instead, they are always subject to being critically questioned (Wiener 2014, 1–15) as individual policymakers interpret them in distinct socio-cultural environments. Given that 'conventions, agreements and treaties may trigger different expectations, even among readers of the same text. To understand the impact of individual experience, it is therefore proposed to identify the constitutive input of cultural practices. How to address this by way of empirical research is the main concern . . . Drawing on qualitative foreign policy analysis the suggestion is to focus on the process through which individuals enact meaning-in-use' (Wiener 2009, 180–1). To grasp the effect of norms through practices of 'normal' or 'deep' contestation, it is therefore important to understand that norms have a dual quality, they are 'both structuring and socially constructed through interaction in a context. While stable over particular periods, they always remain flexible by definition' (Wiener 2007, 49).

This is an important distinction, because some strands of scholarship combine contestation with the notion of a fixed norm. Any challenge to the norm, in these cases, is viewed as a sign of degeneration (Panke and Petersohn 2012; McKeown 2009). Deitelhoff and Zimmermann (2020) have sought to argue against such a position by separating out norm change and norm decay. They argue this is possible by arguing two types of contestations can matter. Norm validity contestations, in their view, focus on 'which norms a group of actors want to uphold' and whether existing normative claims are righteous (Deitelhoff and Zimmermann 2020, 56). Norm applicatory contestations instead focus on questions around whether a given norm is appropriate for a given situation, which actions the norm may require in a specific situation, and which norm should be prioritised in a specific situation if a number of norms apply (Deitelhoff and Zimmermann 2020, 57). Thus, validity contestations attack 'the very core of a norm, that is, the basis of its normative obligation', while applicatory contestations do not question that core. Distinguishing between these two types of contestation is useful because it identifies different ways a contestation may occur. But the claim that these types of contestation are both distinct and unique is, in our view, problematic because it presumes that a fixed and stable understanding of a norm exists; a specific behavioural rule that can only be affected by a validity contestation, and not by an applicatory contestation. But applicatory contestations do affect meaning, and Deitelhoff and Zimmermann acknowledge that such contestations can be used as 'a backdoor strategy for watering down norms more generally' and they can support a norm's general legitimacy (Deitelhoff and Zimmermann 2020, 58). They do create new understandings of a norm, even if only at the margins.

Instead, we view contestation as a neutral process because of a range of positive, negative or neutral effects on how a norm is understood. When norm contestation occurs, this can trigger two distinct norm conflicts, based on how agents interact amongst each other and with respect to a specific norm. The first take considers the challenge-change relationship to take place between a given agent (A) and a given norm (N1) which produces a specific understanding of that norm for that agent – this is the A-N1 relationship. While this interaction may be repeated, it is always between one or more agents (A+1) and a given norm and may reflect two types of contestation: one that is deliberate or one that is interpretative. By contrast, the second take considers the challenge-change relation to take place between a variety of agents (A1, A2, and so on) who are part of a conflictive encounter. During that encounter, norms are challenged and changed, and it is this second take that is traditionally viewed as the norm-generative practice, with contestation generating mutually recognised norms or normative meaning in addition to normality.

Contestation lets us highlight new-found understandings of the role of politics at both the global and local levels, as well as new plural understandings of agency in norm generation and resistance (Wiener 2018; True and Wiener 2019). Most importantly, contestation focuses on the multiplicity who can have 'access' to shaping norms and their meaning-in-use through participation in politics. By asking whose norms and whose practices count, this research not only acknowledges the dual nature of norms but introduces a more specific attention to societal agency in the field while also acknowledging north–south and regional power biases that have existed in norms research (Acharya 2004; Acharya 2013; Draude 2019; Wiener 2017a; Wiener 2022).

To identify, locate and evaluate instances of norm contestation and their role on norm(ative) change in the global order, Wiener has introduced the cycle-grid model (see Wiener 2018: 44, Figure 2.1). Rather than focusing on the international (or domestic levels), or a particular phase of a norm life cycle, the model demonstrates that contestations which can reformulate normative meaning can occur *in principle* at any time.

In order to generate conditions that enable affected stakeholders' access to proactive contestation (including, for example, access to formal, social and cultural validation) the model centres on the method of 'zooming in on local contestations that are conditioned by local "normative opportunity structures" on the one hand, and then zooming out onto the global stage to explore potential pathways for staging global multilogues including a majority of affected stakeholders to explore "themes of tension" and "global issues" that are reflected by the global "normative structure of meaning- in-use", on the other' (Wiener 2023, 29). This allows for assessing norm(ative) change in a global context with reference to 'two analytically distinct – local and global – normative structures' (Wiener 2023, 14). The framework applies two central tools from the toolkit of norm research (Orchard and Wiener 2024). First, the norm-typology distinguishes three types of norms according to their moral reach and expected degree of contestation (that is, a fundamental norm with broad moral reach, an organising principle with instructions for negotiation or a standard regulation). And second, the cycle-grid model offers a frame for zooming in on contestations and identifying affected stakeholders' claims in relation to their degree of access to practices of validation. It is devised as a tool for 're-reading of events' thereby generating 'the data by which norm change is identified and evaluated'. It consists of two elements: a grid which is divided into nine ideal-typical sites where affected stakeholders engage in contestation in a conflict triggered by a norm, and a cycle which represents three potential practices of norm validation (formal, social, cultural). As a metaphor for the normative dimension of the model, the cycle 'hovers' over each site of the grid, indicating the potential power differential which comes with selective access to norm validation and, therefore, unequal input into 'normal contestation' pending on a stakeholder's position in the wider political opportunity structure. As such, the model enables the researcher to 'unearth' both 'normal' and 'deep' contestations (Wiener 2026, 39).

The cycle indicates three distinct practices of norm validation (that is, formal, social, cultural) which should ideally be accessible to all affected stakeholders. In real-life situations, however, access to norm validation is enabled or constrained by the normative political opportunity structure: it depends on the contestants' respective location in the context of the global order, as indicated by the nine sites. It is through this process of contestation that norms become validated, therefore the positionality of the contestants is of key importance here. Initially, formal validation occurs through negotiations involving committee members of international organisations, negotiating groups, ad hoc committees or similar bodies involving high-level representatives of states and/or governments. Formal validation therefore entails specific claims with regard to formal documents, treaties, conventions, or agreements. Habitual validation is practiced habitually through interactions within a social environment and therefore depends on the context of social groups. The higher the level of integration among the group, the more likely a norm becomes uncontested. This reflects a different process from formal validation, where validity claims are explicitly negotiated, with habitual validation reflecting mediated access to validity claims qua prior social interaction within a group. Finally, cultural validation is an expression of an individual expectation mediated by individually held background experience. Importantly, the qualifier 'cultural' is used to distinguish individual from group practices. It refers to background experience derived through everyday practice and as such carries a thin rather than a thick meaning of culture (Wiener 2014, 9). Norm clashes then indicate the sites for empirical research to study the sources of conflict by mapping meanings onto the normative grids as part of the cycle of contestation.

Mapping contestations about universal validity claims of a norm, such as for example the rule of law, in one of the nine sites takes account of the shared normative substance with regard to a selected fundamental or type 1 norm (Wiener 2018, 58–9). The approach enables norms researchers to determine which practices of norm validation are available to legitimate stakeholders at these sites. It therefore offers a novel perspective that allows for the exploration of the opportunities and constraints of agency in global governance. It also opens up important empirical questions including: what is the highest set of type 2 norms (i.e. organising principle) that is aggregated through cultural validation of type 3 norms (i.e. standardised procedures and regulations)? The arrow on the spinning cycle indicates the normative condition for the best-case scenario, namely that each of the three practices of norm validation become available for the stakeholders affected by a norm.

The practice of contestation can be either a deliberate or inadvertent process. Stimmer and Wisken (2019, 516–19) have argued that contestation should be understood as including 'any differences in the understanding of norms, no matter what the source'. Deliberate contestations reflect societal agents knowingly contesting different understandings of a norm's validity, which leads to a norm conflict. But agents can also have unknowingly adopted different interpretations of what a given norm means. Societal agents reflect a notion of a corporate actor: they are composed of many individuals, whether in a state, organisation or other agglomeration. Particularly as a given norm moves downwards through the meso and micro-levels, it will primarily be subject to contestations by societal agents within the state (or within large organisations). Specific implementation processes, during which formal legal and policy mechanisms are introduced in order to routinise compliance (see Betts and Orchard 2014, 22) will be particularly prone to these forms of contestation. They note: 'the implementation process itself can open up a new arena for interpretation and contestation of the norm by relevant actors, with the result that the adopted norm is understood differently across states and other international actors' (Betts and Orchard 2014, 3). This leads Stimmer and Wisken to suggest that we can differentiate between discursive contestations and 'contestation by means of action that affect implementation', which they refer to as behavioural contestation (Stimmer and Wisken 2019).

The key issue here is that this domestic implementation process (as it occurs across the micro-level sites) may incorporate both visible factors – such as formal constitutional functions – and invisible factors – including 'expectations of norms and the interpretation of their respective meanings derived from the historical and cultural contingency'. These constitutional functions are 'crucial for the interpretation of norms' (Wiener 2008, 7, 23) and yet may remain hidden or opaque to actors beyond the state.

Therefore, we can see three distinct types of norm contestation (Orchard and Wiener 2023; Orchard and Wiener 2024). Interpretative contestation reflects that any given agent may have interpretative variance on how they understand a given norm. Such variances may not be readily apparent without direct application of the norm and, in theory, can exist between any agent and any norm. Thus, interpretative contestations have a distinctly different character than other types; they may be inadvertent rather than deliberate and more likely to appear in the form of applicatory contestations rather than validity contestations as the agent believes their understanding of the norm is the same as others. This contrasts with two deliberate and distinct practices: reactive and proactive contestation (Wiener 2017b). As a reactive practice, contestation is indicated primarily as an objection to norms. By contrast, when conceptualised as a proactive practice, contestation is undertaken in order to engage with norms. Through these three practices of contestation, agents create both normality and normative effects.

Constitutive (behaviourally induced) generative practices focus primarily on norm content. Proactive contestations generally seek to improve the norm, while reactive contestations are generally about challenging the standards of behaviour indicated by a norm leading (at the extreme) to norm violation. Reactive contestations, however, can also have constructive effects by leading to norm improvements; hence, they too can be norm generative (Wiener 2020). Interpretative contestations may shade into both forms but will most likely take on the appearance of contested compliance by actors who feel that they are already following the norm's content. Constructive (normatively induced) generative practices focus instead on the legitimacy of a norm and its moral purposes. Proactive contestations more frequently focus on emergent norms, seeking to improve the norm's legitimacy. Reactive contestations will more frequently focus on challenging the legitimacy or moral principles of extant norms. Interpretative contestations focus on hidden understandings that an agent may have of the norm and implicit efforts to bring the wider understanding of the norm's precepts in line. It is therefore through the practice of contestation that we can see a legitimate and accepted understanding of the norm develop.

Which types of contestation are used does depend on the normative structure of the environment, which can most easily be observed from instances of norm conflict. It is through these conflictive encounters that we can shed light on stakeholder access to distinct practices of norm validation. These encounters therefore help localise empirically where and when *reactive* and *interpretative* contestation stands to be expected in the process of norm implementation. And it is through enhanced access to contestation that we can then see normative robustness emerge as it is based on a given norm's legitimacy in global society. The more access to practices of norm validation, the higher the robustness of a given norm in global society. Contestations, therefore, are critical for understanding the forms norms take, how they gain validity and whether they achieve widespread legitimacy. Sociological research on norms has generated manifold data to map distinct patterns of access to contestation on behalf of the variety of stakeholders. They can be distinguished with reference to type of actor (i.e., state vs non-state), role in the process of norm implementation (i.e., designated norm-setter or designated norm-follower) and socio-cultural background experience (i.e., individual background experience). While the former two have been thoroughly studied by social constructivists over the past two decades, the latter have been predominantly addressed by more recent pragmatist and Bourdieusian research (Adler-Nissen and Pouliot 2014; Kornprobst and Senn 2016; McCourt 2016; Sending 2016). In many cases stakeholder access will be uneven; power imbalances will exist tipped in favour of some agents and, consequently, there will be an inbuilt condition of injustice. Contestations can resolve this. Injustice increases the likelihood that some agents will not have a say in the norms that govern them, and this will generate gaps between what are viewed as legitimate and robust norms and the actual observed normative structure. This condition of injustice increases the likelihood that when these norms are engaged with, it will be either through reactive contestation as agents challenge and undermine the norm, or through interpretative contestations as agents become disconnected from the norm. Such challenges will undermine a norm's robustness. Reactive contestation can spiral out of control; it can lead to the undermining and violation of norms and even open political conflict. Interpretative contestation can also undermine the norm if not specifically targeted by political or policy means. Another pattern is possible. By enhancing access to practices of norm validation, by seeking to combat this inbuilt condition of injustice, norm ownership by all affected agents can increase and, with this, an increase in proactive contestation becomes possible. The empirical challenge therefore consists in both identifying *and* facilitating the institutional means for access to proactive contestation.

Contestations and the Russian Invasion

This specific norm conflict begins with Russia's invasion of Ukraine. This is a clear violation of established international norms, though which norms are being violated change over time. The initial focus is on the clear Article 2(4) violation, though rapidly the scale of the Russian military's willingness to engage in war crime becomes clear; these crimes are then clearly documented by the first report of the Independent International Commission of Inquiry (United Nations 2022, 11). This then gets extended as other actors also begin to argue that Russia's actions, given the widespread and systematic nature of their attacks against a civilian population, also constitute crimes against humanity (OSCE 2022, 8; Blinken 2023). There is also a growing focus on Russia's deliberately forcible transfers and deportations of the Ukrainian civilian population in occupied areas, including the deportation of children, leading to the ICC arrest warrants (Colvin and Orchard 2023).

Returning to the cycle-grid model above, the initial contestation occurs within site 3, reflecting the existing formal validation of these international norms and the high-level nature of the contestation within core UN bodies. While Russia is in clear violation of these norms and quickly uses its institutional power (Barnett and Duvall 2005) within the UN Security Council to block action there (reflecting behavioural contestations), in its rhetoric the government sought to engage in a mix of applicatory and reactive contestations seeking to justify the invasion based on supposed genocidal acts being undertaken by the Ukrainian government. In a televised address on the day of the invasion, President Vladimir Putin argued that the people of the breakaway Donetsk People's Republic and Lugansk People's Republic were facing genocide, and so Russia 'will seek to demilitarise and denazify Ukraine, as well as bring to trial those who perpetrated numerous bloody crimes against civilians . . . it is not our plan to occupy the Ukrainian territory' (Putin 2022). In vetoing the first UN Security Council resolution, Russian Permanent Representation Vassily Nebenzia made a similar argument, suggesting that 'neo-Nazis and militias continue to kill civilians' in Donetsk and Luhansk, and that Russia's actions 'would not target civilians'. While such claims continue to be made in the Russian press, a range of organisations have demonstrated that there is no evidence to support them. Alexander Hinton notes that 'in this case, Putin is misappropriating the term to justify invading Ukraine' (Hinton 2022). Ukraine responded by taking Russia to the International Court of

Justice, arguing this was a 'grotesque lie' (International Court of Justice 2022). This also is emblematic of a longer-term pattern of the use of such justifications by the Russian government in support of other military actions including in Crimea and to justify the Russo-Georgian War (Jose and Stefes 2018; Badescu and Weiss 2010).

While such claims may be easily disproven, the combination of Russia's behavioural and discursive contestations has meant that the UN Security Council has been unable to introduce sanctions. This has led to two separate forms of response at the state level which themselves reflect distinct types of contestation.

The first set of responses have been primarily dominated by Western states. They have engaged in significant coordinated sanctions against Russia, with then UK Foreign Minister Liz Truss noting in February 2022 that 'nothing is off the table' (Truss 2022). The goal of these actions was both to impose costs on Russia and also to seek to demonstrate that there remains a strong coalition of states which will take action to punish Russia in spite of the lack of Security Council action. As US President Joe Biden noted in a September 2022 speech, 'we will rally the international community to both denounce these moves and to hold Russia accountable' (The White House 2022). In this sense, their actions are a type of proactive contestation as they are trying to extend how sanctions are used to respond to certain types of norm violations. They are also proactive in another sense: that they are seeking to extend what can be incorporated under a sanctions umbrella, including through individual state use of autonomous and Magnitsky-style sanctions. Magnitsky Acts have been introduced by a number of states and are a form of autonomous sanctions designed to sanction individuals globally engaged in gross violations of internationally recognised human rights or corruption (Lilly and Arabi 2020, 164; Brosinsky and Orchard 2025). The United States and the EU have led the use of sanctions against individuals involved in Russia's invasion of Ukraine, including for human rights abuses, involvement in Russia's forced deportation campaign targeting Ukrainian civilians, and for supporting sham referendums in Russian-occupied Ukraine. The EU has also sanctioned a range of Russian government officials for human rights abuses under a separate 2014 regulation, including the head of Russia's Border Service for the involvement of bureaucrats under his command in 'systematic "filtration" operations and forced deportations of Ukrainians'. While these contestations are primarily focused on formal validation on both how sanctions are understood as a response to norm violation and widening how sanctions measures themselves are used, we can see aspects of both societal and cultural validation at play as well, based on views within these states that Russia's actions are wrong.

A second set of contestations is primarily from states in the Global South. As demonstrated across this volume, these contestations take on two broad forms. The first is focused on interpretative contestations. These contestations question whether sanctions which do not have the support of the UN Security Council are either legal or legitimate. Hofer notes that 'not all states have sanctioned Russia because not all states view unilateral sanctions as lawful' (Hofer, this volume). For her, this dispute reflects states negotiating the organising principles or metanorms 'that govern how states can bring breaches of international norms to an end'. Chauhan (this volume) adds that unilateral sanctions are frequently viewed as against international law 'as they give precedence to domestic law of the sanctioners, hinting that sanctions are being used as a tool to meddle in the affairs of other states'. Here, the contestation primarily occurs due to the failure of the Council to take action and a perceived ambiguity around the potential legality of sanctions mechanisms.

But such contestations also shade into reactive contestations, with some states using these justifications as a way of avoiding a requirement to take action. As Hellquist (this volume) finds, arguments that other international and regional organisations cannot legally apply sanctions neglects that both regional organisations and individual states have developed their own sanctions instruments and that the Security Council's growing involvement in sanctions regimes did not change the frequency with which these other organisations imposed sanctions. Belloni and Ramović (this volume) find that Serbia, while an EU candidate country, has not taken action because of its traditional political closeness to Moscow. Thus, while Serbia seeks to frame its behaviour as a 'principled stand', it is a reactive contestation seeking to block 'the adoption of sanctions while de facto endorsing Russia's foreign policy objectives'.

Conclusions and Outlook

The case of the Russian invasion represents a case of deep contestation because it cuts through to the very foundational elements of the UN Charter Order (UNCO) as well as the Liberal International Order (LIO). These elements are broadly rooted in liberal thought, and were codified into international law in the United Nations Charter, principally norms of national self-determination, non-intervention and the peaceful resolution of disputes. Following recent research on the significant rise of deep contestations around the world, we are currently 'witnessing a qualitative shift from "normal" to "deep" contestation as the foundations of both the LIO and elements of the UNCO are now being challenged' (Lake and Wiener 2026, 2). We argue that the Russian invasion needs to be analysed and its effects evaluated in this context where a growing number of cases of deep contestation are 'arising not only from countries that have long been outside or only partially integrated into the LIO. Significant political groups inside the core member states of the LIO are challenging the fundamental principles and norms of international order' (Lake and Wiener 2026, 1). This process is paired with growing contestations of the rule of law and the role of law as codified in the UN Charter (Nolte and Krieger 2019; Toope 2023). Even UN member states are contesting key norms of the UNCO. As Lake and Wiener point out,

> [W]e currently observe, therefore a dual dynamic of enhanced contestation of what were fundamental norms of order both in the domestic and in the international arenas. We identify this phenomenon as 'deep contestation' for it involves contestation of fundamental norms and procedures and it affects the LIO and the UNCO alike. The outcome of this deep contestation is unknowable, but worrisome for those who value order in general or who are still attached to liberal values. (Lake and Wiener 2026, 2)

While, as we noted in section one, practices of contestation are key for establishing legitimacy in international politics: the need for access to regular contestation – that is, the right to speak and participate in political decisions as a condition for achieving recognition and generating legitimacy for the norms of governance based on the *quod omnes tangit* principle (what touches all must be approved by all) (see Owen and Tully 2007; Wiener 2018). In the absence of access to regular contestation which enables both proactive and interpretative contestation as processes that facilitate the most adequate way of tackling issues in international politics, contestation can also be degenerative, moving political outcomes away from desired ends through ad hoc and perhaps inconsistent compromises. According to norms contestation research, the former type of contestation is facilitated by conditions that allow for proactive contestation (that is, based on regular access to engagement about norms and rules), whereas the latter type of contestation is more likely under restrictive political conditions that limit stakeholder access to reactive contestation (that is, objecting to a norm) only.

Following from section two, we conclude that future research on sanctions would therefore benefit from identifying both the norms that are violated and therefore require sanctions on behalf of the international community, and secondly, whether and if so which foundational elements of the entire relevant order – such as, in the case of the Russian invasion, the UNCO and the LIO – are *deeply* contested in order to then discuss the required measures, the opportunity to implement them as well as their desirable and possible effects.

References

Acharya, Amitav. 2004. 'How Ideas Spread: Whose Norms Matter? Norm Localization and Institutional Change in Asian Regionalism'. *International Organization* 58(2): 239–75.

Acharya, Amitav. 2013. 'The R2P and Norm Diffusion: Towards A Framework of Norm Circulation'. *Global Responsibility to Protect* 5(4): 466–79.

Adler-Nissen, Rebecca, and Vincent Pouliot. 2014. 'Power in Practice: Negotiating the International Intervention in Libya'. *European Journal of International Relations* 20(4): 889–911.

Badescu, Cristina G., and Thomas G. Weiss. 2010. 'Misrepresenting R2P and Advancing Norms: An Alternative Spiral?' *International Studies Perspectives* 11: 354–74.

Barnett, Michael, and Raymond Duvall. 2005. 'Power in Global Governance'. In *Power in Global Governance*, edited by Michael Barnett and Raymond Duvall. Cambridge University Press.

Betts, Alexander, and Phil Orchard. 2014. 'Introduction: The Normative Institutionalization-Implementation Gap'. In *Implementation and World Politics: How International Norms Change Practice*, edited by Andrew Betts and Phil Orchard. Oxford University Press.

Biersteker, Thomas J., and Zuzana Hudáková. 2021. 'UN Targeted Sanctions: Historical Development and Current Challenges'. In *Research Handbook on Economic Sanctions*, edited by Peter A. G. van Bergeijk. Edward Elgar.

Biersteker, Thomas J., Sue E. Eckert, Marcos Tourinho and Zuzana Hudáková. 2018. 'UN Targeted Sanctions Datasets (1991–2013)'. *Journal of Peace Research* 55, 404–12.

Blinken, Anthony J. 2023. 'Press Statement: Crimes Against Humanity in Ukraine'. Washington DC: US Department of State.

Brosinsky, Mareen, and Phil Orchard. 2025. 'Seeking International Accountability at Home: Australia's Use of the Magnitsky-Style Sanctions and Universal Jurisdiction in Response to International Crimes'. *Australian Journal of Human Rights* 30(2): 232–50.

Coleman, Katharina P. 2013. 'Locating Norm Diplomacy: Venue Change in International Norm Negotiations'. *European Journal of International Relations* 19(1): 163–86.

Colvin, Victoria, and Orchard, Phil. 2023. 'Forced Deportations and the Ukraine War: Russian Culpability in Atrocity Crimes'. *Violence: An International Journal* 3(2): 281–300.

Deitelhoff, Nicole, and Lisbeth Zimmermann. 2020. 'Things We Lost in the Fire: How Different Types of Contestation Affect the Robustness of International Norms'. *International Studies Review* 22(1): 51–76.

Doxey, Margaret. 1972. 'International Sanctions: A Framework for Analysis with Special Reference to the UN and Southern Africa'. *International Organization* 26(3): 527–50.

Draude, Anke, ed. 2019. *The Agency of the Governed in the Global South: Normative and Institutional Change*. Routledge.

Finnemore, Martha, and Kathryn Sikkink. 1998. 'International Norm Dynamics and Political Change'. *International Organization* 52: 887–917.

Giumelli, Francesco. 2011. *Coercing, Constraining and Signalling: Explaining UN and EU Sanctions After the Cold War*. ECPR Press.

Giumelli, Francesco. 2015. 'Understanding United Nations Targeted Sanctions: An Empirical Analysis'. *International Affairs* 91(6): 1351–68.

Hinton, Alexander. 2022. 'Putin's Claims That Ukraine Is Committing Genocide Are Baseless, but Not Unprecedented'. *The Conversation*, 26 February. https://theconversation.com/putins-claims-that-ukraine-is-committing-genocide-are-baseless-but-not-unprecedented-177511

International Court of Justice. 2022. 'Ukraine Institutes Proceedings against the Russian Federation and Requests the Court to Indicate Provisional Measures'. The Hague: International Court of Justice, 27 February. https://www.icj-cij.org/sites/default/files/case-related/182/182-20220227-PRE-01-00-EN.pdf

International Criminal Court. 2022. 'Statement of ICC Prosecutor, Karim A. A. Khan QC, on the Situation in Ukraine: "I Have Decided to Proceed with Opening an Investigation"'. The Hague: International Criminal Court, 28 February. https://www.icc-cpi.int/news/statement-icc-prosecutor-karim-aa-khan-qc-situation-ukraine-i-have-decided-proceed-opening

International Criminal Court. 2023. 'Situation in Ukraine: ICC Judges Issue Arrest Warrants against Vladimir Vladimirovich Putin and Maria Alekseyevna Lvova-Belova'. The Hague: International Criminal Court, 17 March. https://www.icc-cpi.int/news/situation-ukraine-icc-judges-issue-arrest-warrants-against-vladimir-vladimirovich-putin-and

Jose, Betcy, and Christoph Stefes. 2018. 'Russian Norm Entrepreneurship in Crimea: Serious Contestation or Cheap Talk?' *GIGA Working Papers, No. 311*. German Institute of Global and Area Studies (GIGA), Hamburg. https://www.econstor.eu/handle/10419/175431

Katzenstein, Peter. 1996. *The Culture of National Security: Norms and Identity in World Politics*. Columbia University Press.

Kornprobst, Markus, and Senn, M. 2016. 'Introduction: Background Ideas in International Relations'. *The British Journal of Politics and International Relations* 18(2): 273–81.

Krook, Monica L., and Jacqui True. 2012. 'Rethinking the Life Cycles of International Norms: The United Nations and the Global Promotion of Gender Equality'. *European Journal of International Relations* 18(1): 103–27.

Lake, David A., and Antje Wiener. 2026. 'Introduction: Deep Contestations of the Liberal International Order. In *Deep Contestations of the Liberal International Order*, edited by Antje Wiener, David A. Lake and Thomas Risse. Oxford University Press.

Lilly, Meredith, and Delaram Arabi. 2020. 'Symbolic Act, Real Consequences: Passing Canada's Magnitsky Law to Combat Human Rights Violations and Corruption'. *International Journal* 75(2): 163–78.

McCourt, David M. 2016. 'Practice Theory and Relationalism as the New Constructivism'. *International Studies Quarterly* 60(3): 475–85.

McKeown, Ryder. 2009. 'Norm Regress: US Revisionism and the Slow Death of the Torture Norm'. *International Relations* 23(1): 5–25.

Nolte, Georg, and Heike Krieger. 2019. 'The International Rule of Law: Rise or Decline? Approaching Current Foundational Challenges'. In The International Rule of Law: Rise or Decline? Foundational Challenges, edited by Heike Krieger, Georg Nolte and Andreas Zimmerman. Oxford University Press.

Orchard, Phil. 2020. 'Contestation, Norms and the Responsibility to Protect as a Regime'. In *Constructing the Responsibility to Protect: Contestation and Consolidation*, edited by Charles T. Hunt and Phil Orchard. Routledge.

Orchard, Phil, and Antje Wiener. 2023. 'Norms and Norm Contestation'. In *Routledge Handbook of Foreign Policy Analysis Methods*. Taylor & Francis.

Orchard, Phil, and Antje Wiener. 2024. 'Introduction: Norm Research in Theory and Practice'. In *Contesting the World: Norm Research in Theory and Practice*, edited by Phil Orchard and Antje Wiener. Cambridge University Press.

OSCE. 2022. 'Office for Democratic Institutions and Human Rights Mission of Experts Report on Violations of International Humanitarian and Human Rights Law, War Crimes and Crimes against Humanity, Committed in Ukraine (1 April–25 June 2022)'. Warsaw: Organization for Security and Co-Operation in Europe, 14 July. https://www.osce.org/odihr/522616

Owen, David, and James Tully. 2007. *Redistribution and Recognition: Two Approaches*. Cambridge University Press.

Panke, Diana, and Ulrich Petersohn. 2012. 'Why International Norms Disappear Sometimes'. *European Journal of International Relations* 18(4): 719–42.

Putin, Vladimir. 2022. 'Address by the President of the Russian Federation'. Office of the President of Russia, 24 February. http://en.kremlin.ru/events/president/news/67843

Risse, Thomas, and Kathryn Sikkink. 1999. 'The Socialization of International Human Rights Norms into Domestic Practice'. In *The Power of Human Rights: International Norms and Domestic Change*, edited by Thomas Risse, Stephen C. Ropp and Kathryn Sikkink. Cambridge University Press.

Sending, Ole Jacob. 2016. 'Agency, Order, and Heteronomy'. *European Review of International Studies* 3(3): 63–75.

Stimmer, Anette, and Lea Wisken. 2019. 'The Dynamics of Dissent: When Actions Are Louder Than Words'. *International Affairs* 95(3): 515–33.

Toope, Stephen J. 2023. *A Rule of Law for Our Age of Anxiety*. Cambridge University Press.

True, Jacqui, and Antje Wiener. 2019. 'Everyone Wants (a) Peace: The Dynamics of Rhetoric and Practice on "Women, Peace and Security"'. *International Affairs* 95(3): 553–74.

Truss, Liz. 2022. 'Nothing Is Off the Table in Our Response to Putin's Aggression towards Ukraine'. *The Times*, 23 February. https://www.gov.uk/government/speeches/nothing-is-off-the-table-in-our-response-to-putins-aggression-towards-ukraine-article-by-liz-truss

United Nations. 2022. 'Security Council Fails to Adopt Draft Resolution on Ending Ukraine Crisis, as Russian Federation Wields Veto'. New York: United Nations, 25 February. https://press.un.org/en/2022/sc14808.doc.htm

The White House. 2022. 'Statement from President Biden on Russia's Attempts to Annex Ukrainian Territory'. Washington DC: The White House, 30 September. https://www.whitehouse.gov/briefing-room/statements-releases/2022/09/30/statement-from-president-biden-on-russias-attempts-to-annex-ukrainian-territory/

Wiener, Antje. 2007. 'The Dual Quality of Norms and Governance beyond the State: Sociological and Normative Approaches to Interaction'. *Critical Review of International Social and Political Philosophy* 10(1): 47–69.

Wiener, Antje. 2008. *The Invisible Constitution of Politics: Contested Norms and International Encounters*. Cambridge University Press.

Wiener, Antje. 2009. 'Enacting Meaning-in-Use: Qualitative Research on Norms and International Relations'. *Review of International Studies* 35(1): 175–93.

Wiener, Antje. 2014. *A Theory of Contestation*. Springer.

Wiener, Antje. 2017a. 'Agency of the Governed in Global International Relations: Access to Norm Validation'. *Third World Thematics: A TWQ Journal* 2(5): 709–25.

Wiener, Antje. 2017b. 'Responsibility Contestations: A Challenge to the Moral Authority of the UN Security Council'. In *Moral Agency and the Politics of Responsibility*, edited by Cornelia Ulbert, Peter Finkenbusch, Elena Sondermann and Tobias Debiel. Routledge.

Wiener, Antje. 2018. *Contestation and Constitution of Norms in Global International Relations*. Cambridge University Press.

Wiener, Antje. 2020. 'Contestation of Norms – An Interview'. In *Yearbook on Practical Philosophy in a Global Perspective (YPPGP-JPPGP)*, edited by Michael Reder et al. 4th edition. Karl Alber Publishing.

Wiener, Antje. 2022. 'Societal Multiplicity for International Relations: Engaging Societal Interaction in Building Global Governance from Below'. *Cooperation and Conflict* 57(3): 348–66.

Wiener, Antje. 2023. 'Norm(ative) Change in International Relations: A Conceptual Framework'. In *Tracing Value Change in the International Legal Order: Perspectives from Legal and Political Science*, edited by Heike Krieger and Andrea Liese. Oxford University Press.

Wiener, Antje. 2026. 'Dealing with Sources, Substance and Effects of Deep Contestation: *Quod Omnes Tangit* as a Heuristic'. In *Deep Contestations of the Liberal International Order*, edited by Antje Wiener, David A. Lake and Thomas Risse. Oxford University Press.

2

The Delegitimation of International Sanctions

Stefano Palestini

Introduction

> A commitment to compliance requires that sanctions be perceived as just and contributing to peace and security [. . .] A regional consensus on the necessity and legitimacy of a sanctions regime can go long way towards ensuring that they are effectively implemented.
>
> Eugène-Richard Gasana, Permanent Representative of Rwanda to the UN

This volume is a collective attempt to address the question of why governments, as well as citizens and the private sector, interpret and challenge sanctions and their application (see the Introduction to this volume). In this chapter, I would like to address this question from the perspective of legitimacy. As expressed in Mr Gasana's speech, legitimacy is expected to facilitate compliance and effectiveness. In this logic, the contestation of sanctions and the 'lack of will' of state and non-state actors to align themselves with sanction regimes is connected to whether sanction regimes are considered legitimate.

The analysis of how agents in the international order perceive and evaluate the legitimacy of sanctions is a matter of empirical research (see for instance Hurd 2005; Hellquist 2020; Sejersen 2021; Palestini and Villarroel 2024). This chapter takes one step back and aims at providing an analytical grid that can help us to investigate the issue of the legitimacy of sanctions, as well as the related processes of legitimation and delegitimation of sanctions, in all its complexity. The extensive internation relations (IR) literature on international legitimacy gives us a starting point (for an overview see Tallberg et al. 2018; Zaum 2016). However, as I will argue, this literature has almost exclusively focused on the legitimacy of international organisations and global governance institutions. Instead, the legitimacy of international practices – such as sanctioning – has remained out of the radar of this specific literature. Similarly, while the IR literature on the contestation of norms provides crucial insights for understanding delegitimation processes, understood as the contestation of the validity of norms (see Orchard and Wiener in this volume), its application to the study of the delegitimation of sanctions is not direct. This is because to contest a norm is not equivalent to contesting the sanctioning of a norm violation. As an illustration, when African or Latin American states contest the unilateral sanctions against Russia (for instance, by not imposing sanctions) they are arguably contesting the practice of unilaterally sanctioning another state, and not necessarily the norms that Russia has violated (Palestini and Portela 2025).

By conceptualising international sanctions as a practice – the practice of *sanctioning* – and by distinguishing three legitimacy problems attached to this practice – the legitimacy of norms, the legitimacy of the enforcer and the legitimacy of the measures – I seek to contribute to a more nuanced study of the legitimacy of contemporary international sanctions. This is not a purely intellectual exercise. Its practical relevance lies in the realisation that a legitimate practice of sanctioning wrongdoings is a necessary condition for a legitimate global governance.

This chapter proceeds as follows. After providing some basic definitions of legitimacy, legitimation and delegitimation, it presents the three legitimacy problems entailed in the practice of sanctioning in the international order. Then, I will flesh out the analytical grid by identifying different delegitimation statements in resolutions of the UN General Assembly, in meetings of the UN Security Council and in joint declarations of China, India and Russia. These statements are not random or disconnected. There is a certain structure behind them that allows us to talk about a delegitimation discourse against international sanctions.

The (De)legitimation of International Sanctions

Let's start by defining the main concepts. In a state of the art of different conceptualisations of legitimacy in social and political theory, Zelditch (2001, 51) concluded that the concept has an 'astonishing breadth' referring to the acceptance of just about anything at all as 'right', and entailing consequences for the foundation and stability of any system of governance, from small groups and associations, passing by nations states up to international orders. Following Max Weber's early treatment of the topic, most scholars understand legitimacy as subjective (a belief) and socially constructed.[1] Legitimacy makes an agent or their actions appear as desirable, proper or appropriate within some socially constructed system of meaning (Hurd 1999; Reus-Smit 2007; Zaum 2013; Tallberg and Zürn 2019).

The concepts of legitimation and delegitimation, in turn, provide an entry to the issue of legitimacy from a process-oriented perspective. They bring attention to the role of agents, practices and strategies in the acquisition, maintenance, contestation and transformation of legitimacy (Beetham 2013; Bäckstrand and Söderbaum 2018). Legitimation is the active effort by agents to convince others about the legitimacy of actions and institutions, while delegitimation refers to the active effort by agents to contest and resist the legitimacy claims made by agents and institutions (Kelman 2001; Zaum 2016; Tallberg and Zürn 2019; Lenz and Söderbaum 2023). As they are concepts that mirror each other, I will refer to them together as (de)legitimation.

(De)legitimation in Contemporary IR Theory

While the concepts of legitimacy and (de)legitimation have been perennial in social and political theory, they entered the core of IR theory only at the end of the 1990s and closely related to the problem of the legitimacy gap of IOs in particular and global governance in general (see Zaum 2016). Ever since, IR scholars have been almost exclusively concerned with the legitimacy of organisations, whereas sociologists and social psychologists have focused on the legitimacy and (de)legitimation of practices (see Jost and Major 2001).

This restrictive focus of IR theory becomes apparent in the way in which IR scholars define their concepts. For instance, (de)legitimation is defined as processes of justification and contestation intended to shape the belief **on IOs' authority** (Zürn et al. 2012, 76; Tallberg and Zürn 2019, 583). In the same vein, Bäckstrand and Söderbaum (2018, 105) define the '(de)legitimation agent' as any actor who engages in delegitimation in relation to a particular **global governance institution**. In a recent work, Börzel and Zürn (2021) adopted an even more restricted use of delegitimation understood as contestation: 'discursive and behavioural practices that challenge the authority of international institutions, their liberal intrusiveness, or the Liberal International Order as a whole'. In this latter conception, delegitimation – or contestation,

[1] It has become common in the IR literature to distinguish between a normative and a sociological approach to legitimacy (see Agné 2018). This chapter adopts the sociological approach.

as the authors prefer – is not only to IOs but to liberal IOs and is associated to some sort of illiberal practice.

The IR literature on norms contestation has dealt with similar problems as the IR literature on the legitimacy of IOs, but from a different angle. Famously, Wiener (2004) opened the field by arguing that contestation processes are disputes over the meanings-in-use of norms. Contestation, in her view, is a norm-generative practice that has the potential of enhancing the legitimacy of norms (Wiener 2014), but not all forms of contestation lead to legitimation (see Orchard and Wiener in this volume). Some types of contestations can in fact amount to delegitimation. Deitelhoff and Zimmermann (2020) have introduced the distinction between applicatory contestation (the contestation of the ways in which norms are implemented) and validity contestation (the contestation of the norm itself). In my understanding, this latter form would be the equivalent of delegitimation.

In short, the IR literature on legitimacy has almost exclusively focused on the (de)legitimation of 'IOs', and the IR literature on contestation has almost exclusively focused on the delegitimation of 'norms' (Wiener 2004; 2007; 2014; Wiener and Orchard 2023; Welsh 2013; Deitelhoff and Zimmermann 2020; Zimmermann et al. 2023). This exclusive focus on IOs and norms becomes restrictive when we want to examine the (de)legitimation of sanctions.

International sanctions are closely related to both 'organisations' and 'norms'. International sanctions are not random or spontaneous reactions but are institutionalised reactions enacted by some sort of organisation, being a state, a regional organisation or an international one. Furthermore, they are reactions to 'norm violations', and therefore they are inherently connected to international norms (Doxey 1980; Nossal 1989; Kratochwil 2016; Hellquist 2015; Hofer 2017).[2] Yet, international sanctions are neither an organisation nor a norm.

Sanctions as Practices

If sanctions are neither organisations nor norms and, as a consequence, not adequately understood by the IR literature on IOs' legitimacy and norms'

[2] There is a split in the IR scholarship about sanctions regarding whether sanctions are necessarily connected to norms or not. For instance, influential works in the field define sanctions as a foreign policy tool oriented by political goals, such as changing targets' political behaviour (see Baldwin 1985; Lindsay 1986; Drezner 1999; Hufbauer et al. 2007; Farrall 2016); in this definition the connection between sanctions and norms is lost.

contestation, we must shift the conceptualisation to tackle the issue of the legitimacy of international sanctions, as well as the ensuing processes of (de)legitimation. In proposing to understand international sanctions as a practice – the practice of sanctioning – I follow Kratochwil (2016, 193–209) who argues that sanctioning is one practice – among others such as shaming and monitoring – oriented to securing social orders by deterring transgressions and inducing compliance. As such, sanctioning is constitutively related to notions of legitimacy, authority, harm, punishment and responsibility defining boundaries of what is right and wrong in the international order.

According to Kratochwil (2016, 208–9), most of the literature on sanctions has overlooked the distinction between the simple 'harm' connected with sanctions and the 'because of' reasons for which sanctions are imposed, and are part of the grammar of sanctions. It is precisely this 'because of' – or, in other words, the justification for sanctioning – that constitutively connects sanctions with legitimacy.

As with most practices, sanctioning can be studied from the perspective of the claim, the claimant and the action. Let me give an example from everyday life, the request of a favour. If Sofia does a favour to Anna, Sofia has the legitimate right – in keeping with the norm of reciprocity or the norm of friendship – to request a favour from Anna in return, and Anna has the obligation to reciprocate to the best of her ability. As a friend, Sofia has a right to make such a claim; Sofia is, therefore, the legitimate claimant. The claim is, however, an object of delegitimation if Sofia's request goes beyond what is expected in friendly relationships. In addition, the claimant can be an object of delegitimation, if Sofia has indeed not done a favour to Anna in the first place, or if she has not been a 'real friend' in the past. Finally, the actions taken by Sofia to make Anna comply with her request can be an object of delegitimation on their own, if they are 'out or proportion', as for instance threatening to accuse Anna to her parents (my adaptation of Kelman 2001, 56).

When a sanction is imposed, there is an implicit **claim** that an international norm has been violated, and that therefore there is the 'right to react'. Any such right to react (this is the legitimacy claim) has taken different forms throughout history, from the right to declare someone as *persona non grata* to the practice of feuds in medieval Europe (see Kratochwil 2016). In the modern international order – made up of sovereign nation states and regulated by international law – this right to react has taken two main forms: the claim to establish countermeasures and, more recently, the right to prosecute individual international responsibility. The former is the basis of the legitimacy of international sanctions against states and organisations, while the latter is the basis of the legitimacy of targeted sanctions against individuals (Giumelli 2015; 2023).

The **claimant**, in turn, is the agent that enforces the sanction, which in the jargon of the IR literature on sanctions is usually referred to as the sanction-sender. From the viewpoint of sanctioning as a practice, the sender is therefore not only the one enforcing the harm but it is also the claimant who makes the legitimacy claim of having the 'right to impose a sanction'.

Finally, there is the **action**, which is the application of one or a set of coercive measures whereby the harm is implemented on the norm violator (target, in the scholarly jargon). Most of the IR literature on sanctions has dealt with the 'action' part of sanctioning, identifying different goals (deterrence, punishment, signalling, and so on) and different types of coercive measures (from individual bans to fully-fledged economic embargoes), and trying to assess their effectiveness (Hufbauer et al. 2007; Biersteker et al. 2016; Giumelli 2011; Farrall 2016). However, from the point of view of a theory of legitimacy, the three parts are important since the legitimacy of all three – the claim, the claimant and the action – can be evaluated and therefore become differentiated objects of (de)legitimation (see Kelman 2001, 55).

The Legitimacy Problems of Sanctioning in the International Order

From the triple distinction between claim, claimant and action that makes up the practice of sanctioning in international relations it is possible to derive three legitimacy problems that oblige senders to engage in processes of legitimation (Palestini 2023). These are:

- Legitimacy of the violated norm: Has a norm been violated? Is there a right to react?
- Legitimacy of the enforcer: Who has the right to impose a harm?
- Legitimacy of the measure: Is the measure adopted the right action?

The Legitimacy of the Violated Norm

When imposing a sanction, an agent is making the claim that someone has violated an international norm, and therefore a reaction must follow. Most sanction regimes are based on the claim of violation of one or more norms ranging from international security to human rights or from the protection of democratic governance to anti-corruption. The validity of this claim can be challenged – and therefore can become an object of delegitimation – on two grounds: has a norm been violated in fact? If so, does the norm violated confers a right to react?

The first question points to whether the claim is true or not. Usually, the targets of an international sanction – individuals, organisations or governments – will argue that the claim is false and that no norm has been violated. This pushes senders to engage in legitimation strategies by proving evidence that a violation has indeed happened and that the reaction is not purely based on self-interests and/or realpolitik (see Palestini 2023). Any such legitimation process on the part of the claimant or sender is crucial to convince other potential senders to emulate them and align themselves with their sanctions, as well as to convince other non-state actors to comply and implement the sanctions. This attempt at legitimation is fundamental to make the practice of sanctioning appear as an appropriate instrument for global governance and not merely a foreign-policy tool linked to particular state interests (Ruggie 1992).

Even if the claimant can make the case that a violation has indeed occurred, a second challenge emerges on the way to legitimation: does the norm violation confers a right to react? This challenge is connected with the status or robustness of the violated norms vis-à-vis other norms. Norm theorists have proposed different ways to account for the status or robustness of norms (see Franck 1992; Wiener 2014; Zimmermann et al. 2023). From the viewpoint of an international lawyer, Franck (1992) proposes four indicators of norm robustness: pedigree, determinacy, coherence and adherence. Pedigree refers to the depth of the norm's historical roots; determinacy refers to the precision of its content; coherence and adherence refer to the internal consistency and connectedness with other norms. While coherence underlines the lateral connectedness with similar norms, adherence refers to the vertical connectedness in a normative hierarchy. What is important here is that, at the end of the day, audiences will evaluate the status of the norm violated vis-à-vis the status of other norms such as non-intervention and sovereignty in order to evaluate whether the sender has a 'right to react'. They may or may not do it through scholarly criteria such as those offered by Franck . . . but they will do it and they will come up with a judgement about the legitimacy of the claim.

There are two norms that senders can resort to in order to legitimise their 'right to react'. Most of the time senders do it in an implicit way. One is the right to establish counter-measures that can lend legitimacy to sanctions against states. Yet, this right is bounded. The main limitation is that counter-measures must be linked to breaches of international law. The second principle is that of individual international responsibility, according to which individuals that violate international norms are legally and, indeed, criminally responsible under international criminal law. As Giumelli has noted (2015, 2023) this principle is not only the basis for the establishment of war crime tribunals, but also the basis for the shift from comprehensive sanctions to targeted sanctions against individuals, today the most frequent type of international sanction. Yet, while the right to countermeasures has a long pedigree and high determination under international law and indeed in the history of international relations, to use Franck's (1992) criteria, the principle of international individual responsibility is an emergent principle and it is contested by many states including three permanent members of the UN Security Council: the United States,[3] China and Russia (Hurd 2019).

There are discursive tools to legitimate the 'right to react' in the contemporary international order, albeit these tools face important limitations. But even if the claim passes the test of legitimacy, what about the legitimacy of the claimant?

The Legitimacy of the Enforcer

Not only can the claim that a norm has been violated be an object of delegitimation, but so can the claimant. In particular, the question here is 'who' has the right to enforce a sanction. The object of delegitimation is, therefore, the enforcer or sender. In the contemporary international order, there are three classes of actors who engage in sanctioning: the United Nations Security Council (as the executive body of the UN), states (or coalitions of states) and international organisations (IOs). I have argued elsewhere that all three senders can be – and in fact have been – objects of delegitimation (Palestini 2023). Yet, the UNSC and IOs are theoretically in a better position to claim legitimacy based on the delegation of authority from member states enshrined in the UN Charter in the case of the former, and in constitutive treaties in the case of the latter. In contrast, states face serious problems to claim legitimacy for themselves as enforcers of unilateral sanctions.

The reasons are evident. In unilateral sanctioning, both the sender and the target are independent and formally equal sovereign states. Following the Hobbesian formula, the distinction between punishment and hostility is hard to sustain when a state unilaterally imposes a sanction on another. Since there is no contractual relationship between the sender and the target, it is harder for a state sanctioning another state to claim that its sanctions 'are appropriate' in accordance with a shared normative framework than it is for an IO sanctioning a member state.

Unilateral sanctions appear as intimately linked to the national interest of the sender and therefore unilateral senders become relatively easy objects of

[3] The US contest international individual responsibility in the context of the International Criminal Court, but not in the case of targeted sanctions.

delegitimation. The procedures that enable unilateral sanctions are only legally binding within the jurisdictions of the sender and are normally opaque for the target and audiences outside the sender's national boundaries. Furthermore, as Brzoska (2015) has pointed out, the relationship between the state that acts as sender (normally a global power) and the state that acts as target (normally a state in the Global South) is frequently characterised by a power asymmetry in favour of the former.

The Legitimacy of the Measure

The last component of the practice of sanctioning is the action, that is the enactment of a harm or deprivation through the application of concrete restrictive measures. Arguably this third component distinguishes sanctions from other closely related practices such as shaming. Like shaming, sanctioning works through the 'manipulation of the will' of the other (Kratochwil 2016, 208). However, unlike shaming, sanctioning has in addition a material component; coercive or restrictive measures are enacted with the intended effect of depriving the target from a benefit, harming the material capabilities of the target, imposing costs on the target, or all three together.

The measures imposed can also be an object of delegitimation on two main grounds. First, the proportionality of the measures can be challenged. Sanctions can vary a great deal in terms of the deprivation imposed, ranging from travel bans that affect the ability of specific individuals to move, to economic embargoes of core economic sectors, which compromise an entire national economy. Audiences and bystanders – as well as other potential senders – will evaluate whether the measure imposed is proportionate to the violation that it claims to address. Second, sanctions can have – and normally do have – serious unintended consequences that can pass the costs from those actors who are the intended targets to third parties, such as the population of the country or even third states and their populations.

The two issues of proportionality and negative externalities are entangled and normally manifest through (de)legitimation disputes about the level of comprehensiveness of the sanctions: do they affect an entire national economy or are they targeted enough to affect only those individuals or organisations who are directly responsible for the norm violation? While the negative effects of comprehensive sanctions affecting the entire economy and general population of a state are evident, targeted sanctions may also entail serious economic effects and potential humanitarian consequences, especially if they lead to over-compliance. Targeted sanctions are implemented mostly by private market actors who monitor lists of sanctioned individuals and organisations and, following cost–benefit calculations, will likely avoid commercial and financial operations in countries that figure too prominently in those lists (Giumelli and Onderco 2021; Moret 2021). Last but not least, measures entailed in targeted sanctions and listing can be delegitimised on procedural grounds as lacking adequate mechanisms of redress and/or failing short of standards of due process (Giumelli 2023).

The Delegitimation Discourse

Building on the previous theoretical discussion, this section will apply an analytical grid to analyse delegitimation statements pronounced by states against international sanctions. These statements are not disconnected from each other and, in fact, a certain structure is recognisable. For this reason, I refer to them as constituting a discourse. The statements analysed here are not exhaustive, but I believe are quite representative of this discourse. To make this reconstruction, I have analysed two UNGA resolutions, 'Human Rights and Unilateral Coercive Measures' and 'Economic Measures as a Means of Political and Economic Coercion against Developing Countries', which constitute the core of the delegitimation discourse as they are adopted by a majority of UN members (see Hofer 2017). The first resolution was adopted for the first time in 1996, and then annually submitted by the Non-Aligned Movement states coalition. In 1996, the resolution was endorsed by 57 states, while 45 states rejected it, and 59 abstained. By 2021, 131 states endorsed the Resolution and 54 rejected it, with no abstentions. As far as the second resolution is concerned, it was first adopted in 1997 and then introduced on a biannual basis on behalf of the Group of 77 and China. In 1997 it was endorsed by 109 states, with 50 abstentions and only the United States rejecting it. In 2021, it was endorsed by 126 states, with 6 rejections and 46 abstentions. I analysed the texts submitted and adopted in different years, as changes in the wording were introduced. I complemented this analysis with joint declarations made by China, India and Russia, as well as the Non-Aligned Movement.

Additionally, I analysed a session at the UNSC (S/PV8962) held on 7 February 2022, just before Russia's invasion of Ukraine. I added this document because, differently from the UNGA resolutions which deal with unilateral sanctions, this meeting concerned UN sanctions. It provides us, therefore, with a counterpoint to contrast the delegitimation of two different types of enforcers. I stopped the analysis before the Russian invasion since previous research has shown that this invasion marks a turning point in the delegitimation discourse against sanctions (see Palestini and Portela, 2025).

Table 2.1 contains the analytical grid. The first two columns, starting from the left, describe the three dimensions of sanctioning understood as a practice – the claim, the claimant and the action. Moving to the right, the third and fourth columns derive from those dimensions three possible objects of delegitimation – the norms, the enforcer or sender and the measures. The fifth column displays the main delegitimation statements identified in the various texts analysed. Finally, the last column at the right side singles out the international norms that are explicitly or implicitly linked to the delegitimation statements.

Delegitimation of the violated norms

In the texts analysed there is no statement that explicitly delegitimises the violated norm. This is not a surprise, as these statements are general and do not deal with specific sanction regimes. However, there are several statements that implicitly delegitimise the 'right to react' by arguing that any such right has a lower status than the norms of sovereignty, non-intervention and self-determination, which are presented as absolute.

> Calls upon the international community to condemn and reject the imposition of the use of such measures as a means of political and economic coercion against developing countries *with the purpose of exerting, directly or indirectly, coercion on the sovereign decisions of the countries subject to those measures* (UNGA 1991, emphasis added)

This resolution basically equates sanctions to unprovoked coercion, implicitly delegitimising any possible right to react to norms violations. The same statement is repeated in all the following UNGA resolutions entitled 'Economic Measures as a Means of Political and Economic Coercion against Developing Countries' (see UNGA 1991; 2011a; 2011b; 2013). These resolutions draw on the Charter of Economic Rights and Duties of States to delegitimise sanctions as coercive measures that violate sovereignty.

We find similar delegitimation statements that oppose sanctions imposed against a target that supposedly exercises the right to self-determination:

> in this context, the right of all peoples to self-determination, by virtue of which they freely determine their political status and freely pursue their economic, social and cultural development. (UNGA 2019)

And we find them again in recent joint declarations made by China and Russia, and by the Non-Aligned Movement. The first statement links sanctions to the (illegitimate) purpose of regime change.

Table 2.1 The analytical grid of (de)legitimation of international sanctions

Sanctioning as a practice		Delegitimation object		Delegitimation statements	Norms invoked
Claim	A norm has been violated; a reaction is legitimate	The violated norms	Has a norm been violated? If so, is there a right to react?	No norm has been violated. *If a norm has indeed been violated:* There is no right to react. The norm violated has lower status than fundamental principles of the UN Charter.	– Sovereignty – Non-intervention – Self-determination
Claimant	The agent who makes the claim	The enforcer (sender)	Who has the right to impose a harm?	Unilateral senders are unlawful. Unilateral senders undermine the UNSC. Unilateral senders engage in power politics. Unilateral senders violate the equality among states.	– Legality – Authority of the UNSC – Prohibition of the use of force – Multilateralism – Equality among states
Action	The action that follows the claim	The measures	Is the measure adopted the right action?	Measures violate the human rights of the targeted population or of the targeted individual. Measures have negative impact on international economic relations.	– Human Rights – Open markets (economic multilateralism)

> The People's Republic of China and the Russian Federation *fully support the principle of non-intervention in the internal or external affairs of States, and condemn as a violation of this principle any interference by States in the internal affairs of other States* with the aim of forging change of legitimate governments. (Declaration 2016, emphasis added)

> Non-Aligned countries agree to refrain from recognizing, adopting or implementing extra-territorial or unilateral coercive measures or laws, including unilateral economic sanctions, other intimidating measures, and arbitrary travel restrictions, that seek to exert pressure on Non-Aligned Countries – *threatening their sovereignty and independence, and their freedom of trade and investment – and prevent them from exercising their right to decide, by their own free will, their own political, economic and social systems* (Tehran Declaration 2012, emphasis added)

In short, the statements above show that unilateral sanctions are delegitimised on the grounds that they violate norms that are considered – by the contestants – as having a higher status: sovereignty, non-intervention and self-determination. The first two are core principles of the so-called Westphalian order (Lake et al. 2021), and the third is a constitutive norm of international law since the decolonisation process in the wake of Second World War (Getachew 2019).

Delegitimation of the Enforcer

The delegitimation of the enforcer is direct and explicit. The analysed statements make a sharp distinction between UNSC sanctions (which are deemed, from this point of view, as legitimate) and unilateral sanctions imposed by single states or coalitions of states. Here the main argument is that the unilateral character of the enforcer undermines the legitimacy of sanctions.

We can classify these delegitimation statements in three groups:

- Unilateral enforcers are unlawful.
- Unilateral enforcers engage in power politics.
- Unilateral enforcers violate the equality among states.

The first group of statements claim that unilateral sanctions are against international law and, particularly, the principles of the UN Charter (see UNGA 1997; 2019; 2015).

This position, which is strongly stated in the UNGA resolutions, is also reaffirmed in joint declarations:

> The Ministers agreed that the imposition of unilateral sanctions, which exceed the ones agreed by the United Nations Security Council, *is inconsistent with principles of international law, undermines the prerogatives of the United Nations Security Council as set forth in the UN Charter, reduces effectiveness of its sanctions regimes, disproportionally affects States against which they are imposed* [. . .] Good-faith implementation of principles of sovereign equality of States, non-intervention in the internal affairs of States and cooperation excludes imposition of unilateral coercive measures not based on international law (Joint Communiqué 2016, emphasis added)

A related argument is that unilateral enforcers undermine the authority of the UNSC as the legal enforcer of universal sanctions (Declaration 2016; UNSC 2022).

> The adoption of unilateral coercive measures by States in addition to measures adopted by the United Nations Security Council can defeat the objects and purposes of measures imposed by the Security Council, and undermine their integrity and effectiveness (Declaration 2016)

A second group of delegitimation statements claims unilateral enforcers engage in 'hegemonism and power politics' and are based on their national legislation instead of internationally shared norms (UNSC 2022).

> Sanctions should not be a tool for one country to use in pursuit of power politics. The domestic law of one country should not be the basis for sanctions against other States (UNSC 7323)

Finally, a third group of delegitimation statements argues that unilateral enforcers target a particular group of countries, developing countries or weaker states (UNSC 8992). Therefore, they are in violation of the equality of states. This claim is already present in the UNGA Resolution 58–198:

> Urges the international community to adopt urgent and effective measures to eliminate the use of *unilateral coercive economic measures against developing countries* that are not authorized by relevant organs of the United Nations or are inconsistent with the principles of international law (UNGA 2003, emphasis added)

Delegitimation of the Measures

Finally, we find delegitimation statements that have as their object the type of measures that are adopted to impose a harm on the target. Here we find two main claims: the measures violate the human rights of the targeted state's population or the targeted individuals, and the measures entail a negative impact for economic and trade international relations.

As regard the first group of statements, UNGA 1997 rejects unilateral coercive measures 'because of their negative effects on the realization of all the human rights of vast sectors of their populations, in particular children, women and the elderly'. An extended version of the same statement is found in UNGA 2004:

> Also urges all States to take steps to avoid and to refrain from adopting any unilateral measures not in accordance with international law and the Charter that impede the full achievement of economic and social development by the population of the affected countries, in particular children and women, that hinder their well-being and that create obstacles to the full enjoyment of their human rights, including the right of everyone to a standard of living adequate for their health and well-being and their right to food, medical care and the necessary social services, as well as to ensure that food and medicine are not used as tools for political pressure.

While the delegitimation statements contained in UNGA resolutions concern exclusively unilateral sanctions (known as unilateral coercive measures in the language of these resolutions), there are also a few statements concerning UNSC sanctions:

> United Nations sanctions can nevertheless have negative consequences for civilians and humanitarian operations (UNSC 2022)

The language of over-compliance is drawn from the scholarly and policy debates to justify the delegitimation of targeted sanctions, in the following intervention of the Under-Secretary for Humanitarian Affairs at a meeting of the UNSC:

> [C]ommercial operators that trade food, fuel and other necessities can also decide to err on the side of caution, or overcomply. That can lead to shortages and price rises. That is especially disastrous in fragile countries already heavily dependent on food imports and experiencing a humanitarian crisis (UNSC 2022)

Speaking on behalf of the African Union, the representative of Gabon claims:

> That is what led the African Union, at its thirty-third ordinary session, to urge all States to refrain from coercive and unilateral measures, which impede the full achievement of economic and social development and affect the full enjoyment of human rights (UNSC 2022)

A second group of statements emphasise the effects that sanctions can have on economic international relations:

> Gravely concerned that the use of unilateral coercive economic measures adversely affects the economy and development efforts of developing countries in particular and has a general negative impact on international economic cooperation and on worldwide efforts to move towards a non-discriminatory and open multilateral trading system (UNGA 2003)

> The Ministers agreed that [. . .] when applied extra-territorially, [unilateral coercive measures] have a negative impact upon third States and international trade and economic relations at large (Joint Communiqué 2016)

Conclusions

This chapter makes the case for addressing the issue of the contestation of international sanctions from the perspective of legitimacy. It offers an analytical grid that starts from the assumption that the practice of sanctioning in the international order faces three distinctive legitimacy problems: is there a right to react to norms violations, who has the right to impose a harm and are the measures adopted the right action? These three problems relate to three possible objects of delegitimation: first, the norms that have allegedly been violated and that would legitimise a reaction; second, the enforcer who claims the right to react; and third, the coercive measures that the enforcer enacts.

The main aim of this analytical grid is to provide a more nuanced and complex picture of the contestation of international sanctions. It provides clues to understand what exactly is being contested when a specific sanction regime is opposed. Any such understanding should come before we make judgements about the contestants and their possible motivations. It is possible that the contestation of sanctions is part of a wider contestation of the liberal script (Börzel and Zürn 2021) or an attempt at spoiling multilateralism as depicted in references to the lack of alignment of the Global South with Western sanctions against Russia, especially after the full-scale invasion of Ukraine. Yet, it could also be that there are good reasons to contest the validity of specific normative claims, enforcers and measures entailed in specific sanction regimes. These distinctions are only possible if we have a nuanced, differentiated and more complex picture of the delegitimation discourse of international sanctions.

The analytical grid also makes it apparent that the contestation of sanctions does not necessarily concern the three possible objects of delegitimation simultaneously: norms, enforcers and measures. In fact, the illustrative analysis of delegitimation statements in this chapter shows that most delegitimation statements cluster around the delegitimation of enforcers, especially when they act unilaterally. As such, UNSC sanctions remain largely outside the scope of the delegitimation discourse, although specific targeted measures enacted by the UNSC have been contested on the grounds of the consequences they may have for human rights and economic multilateralism.

This chapter does not want to make an apology of those who contest international sanctions. It does not argue that the delegitimation discourse against sanctions is fully coherent or immune to delegitimation of its own claims. It also does not exclude that the contestants might be using normative arguments with self-interested and strategic purposes in mind (see Palestini and Portela 2025). Instead, the chapter is an invitation to address the claims of those who contest sanctions from a more differentiated understanding. In this way, the chapter concurs with Ian Hurd's critique of what he calls the folk theory of legitimacy, prevalent in current IR scholarship on global governance and the contestation of the liberal script. This scholarship has assumed legitimacy as a good (related to and oftentimes conflated with stability and order) and delegitimation as a threat that must be dealt with through 'legitimation strategies'. In doing so, Hurd argues, IR scholars have privileged the viewpoint of 'the powerful' (those who need legitimacy to rule) over the viewpoint of those who contest and demand justification. Certainly, this chapter falls short of amending the folk theory of legitimacy in the lines of Hurd's critique as it has only focused on resolutions and declarations of states – and therefore political elites – as the main sources of the delegitimation discourse. Yet, nothing prevents its use to analyse the delegitimation discourse of other audiences, such as citizens and grass-roots organisations.

A variegated and more complex understanding of the view of those who contest sanctions matters, especially when we conceive of sanctioning wrongdoings as a central element of global governance. When we look at sanctions from this perspective – as a practice that constitutes global governance – we discover that what underlies most of the delegitimation discourse is in fact illustrative of the shortcomings and dysfunctionalities of our present international order.

References

Agné, Hans. 2018. 'Legitimacy in Global Governance Research: How Normative or Sociological Should It Be?' In *Legitimacy in Global Governance: Sources, Processes, and Consequences*, edited by Jonas Tallberg, Karin Bäckstrand and Jan Aart Scholte. Oxford University Press.

Bäckstrand, Karin, and Frederik Söderbaum. 2018. 'Legitimation and Delegitimation in Global Governance: Discursive, Institutional, Behavioral'. In *Legitimacy in Global Governance: Sources, Processes, and Consequences*, edited by Jonas Tallberg, Karin Bäckstrand and Jan Aart Scholte. Oxford University Press.

Baldwin, David A. 1985. *Economic Statecraft*. Princeton University Press.

Beetham, David. 2013. *The Legitimation of Power*. Palgrave.

Biersteker, Thomas J., Sue Eckert and Marcos Tourinho. 2016. *Targeted Sanctions: The Impacts and Effectiveness of United Nations Action*. Cambridge University Press.

Börzel, Tanja A., and Michael Zürn. 2021. 'Contestations of the Liberal International Order: From Liberal Multilateralism to Postnational Liberalism'. *International Organization* 75(2): 282–305.

Brzoska, Michael. 2015. 'International Sanctions Before and Beyond UN Sanctions'. *International Affairs* 91(6): 1339–49.

The Declaration of the People's Republic of China and the Russian Federation on the Promotion of International Law. 2016

Deitelhoff, Nicole, and Lisbeth Zimmermann. 2020. 'Things We Lost in the Fire: How Different Types of Contestation Affect the Robustness of International Norms'. *International Studies Review* 22(1): 51–76.

Doxey, Margaret P. 1980. *Economic Sanctions and International Enforcement*. Macmillan.

Drezner, Daniel W. 1999. *The Sanctions Paradox: Economic Statecraft and International Relations*. Cambridge University Press.

Farrall, Jeremy. 2016. 'Sanctions'. In *The Oxford Handbook of International Organizations*, edited by J. K. Cogan, I. Hurd and I. Johnstone. Oxford University Press.

Franck, Thomas M. 1992. 'The Emerging Right to Democratic Governance'. *American Journal of International Law* 86(1): 46–91.

Getachew, Adom. 2019. *Worldmaking after Empire: The Rise and Fall of Self-Determination*. Princeton University Press.

Giumelli, F. 2011. *Coercing, Constraining and Signalling: Explaining UN and EU Sanctions after the Cold War*. ECPR Press.

Giumelli, Francesco. 2015. 'Understanding United Nations Targeted Sanctions: An Empirical Analysis'. *International Affairs* 91(6): 1351–68.

Giumelli, Francesco. 2023. *Le sanzioni internazionali. Storia, obbiettivi ed efficacia.* Il Mulino.

Giumelli, Francesco, and Michal Onderco. 2021. 'States, Firms, and Security: How Private Actors Implement Sanctions, Lessons Learned from the Netherlands'. *European Journal of International Security* 6(2): 190–209.

Hellquist, Elin. 2015. 'Interpreting Sanctions in Africa and Southeast Asia'. *International Relations* 29(3): 319–33.

Hellquist, Elin. 2020. 'Regional Sanctions as Peer Review: The African Union against Egypt (2013) and Sudan (2019)'. *International Political Science Review* 42(4): 451–68.

Hofer, Alexandra. 2017. 'The Developed/Developing Divide on Unilateral Coercive Measures: Legitimate Enforcement or Illegitimate Intervention?' *Chinese Journal of International Law* 16(2): 175–214.

Hufbauer, Gary Clyde, Jeffrey J. Schott, Kimberly Ann Elliott and Barbara Oegg. 2007. *Economic Sanctions Reconsidered.* 3rd edition. Peterson Institute for International Economics.

Hurd, Ian. 1999. 'Legitimacy and Authority in International Politics'. *International Organization* 53(2): 379–408.

Hurd, Ian. 2005. 'The Strategic Use of Liberal Internationalism: Libya and the UN Sanctions, 1992–2003'. *International Organization* 59(3): 495–526.

Hurd, Ian. 2019. 'Legitimacy and Contestation in Global Governance: Revisiting the Folk Theory of International Institutions'. *Review of International Organizations* 14(4): 717–29.

Joint Communiqué of the 14th Meeting of the Foreign Ministers of the Russian Federation, the Republic of India and the People's Republic of China. 2016.

Jost, John T., and Brenda Major. 2001. *The Psychology of Legitimacy: Emerging Perspectives on Ideology, Justice, and Intergroup Relations.* Cambridge University Press.

Kelman, Herbert C. 2001. 'Reflections on Social and Psychological Processes of Legitimization and Delegitimization'. In *The Psychology of Legitimacy: Emerging Perspectives on Ideology, Justice, and Intergroup Relations*, edited by John T. Jost and Brenda Major. Cambridge University Press.

Kratochwil, Friedrich. 2016. *Praxis. On Acting and Knowing.* Cambridge University Press.

Lake, David A., Lisa L. Martin and Thomas Risse. 2021 'Challenges to the Liberal Order: Reflections on International Organization'. *International Organization* 75(2): 225–7.

Lenz, Tobias, and Frederik Söderbaum. 2023. 'The Origins of Legitimation Strategies in International Organizations: Agents, Audiences and Environments'. *International Affairs* 99(3): 899–920.

Lindsay, James M. 1986. 'Trade Sanctions as Policy Instruments: A Re-Examination'. *International Studies Quarterly* 30(2): 153–73.

Moret, Erica. 2021. 'Unilateral and Extraterritorial Sanctions in Crisis: Implications of Their Rising Use and Misuse in Contemporary World Politics'. In *Research Handbook on Unilateral and Extraterritorial Sanctions*, edited by Charlotte Beaucillon. Edward Elgar Publishing.

Nossal, Kim Richard. 1989. 'International Sanctions as International Punishment'. *International Organization* 43(2): 301.

Palestini, Stefano. 2023. 'The Politics of Legitimation in Combined Sanction Regimes: The Case of Venezuela'. *International Affairs* 99(3): 1087–107.

Palestini, Stefano, and Yancy Villarroel. 2024. '"What gives you the right?" Foreign Policymakers' Perceptions of the Legitimacy of Sanctions against Democratic Breakdown in Venezuela (2014–2019)'. *Cambridge Review of International Affairs* 37(5): 665–89.

Palestini, Stefano, and Clara Portela. 2025. 'The Global South and the Contestation of Unilateral Sanctions against Russia'. *Cooperation and Conflict*. Online first.

Reus-Smit, Chris. 2007. 'International Crises of Legitimacy'. *International Politics* 44(2–3): 157–74.

Ruggie, John G. 1992. 'Multilateralism: The Anatomy of an Institution'. *International Organization* 46(3): 561–98.

Sejersen, Mikkel. 2021. 'Winning Hearts and Minds with Economic Sanctions? Evidence from a Survey Experiment in Venezuela'. *Foreign Policy Analysis* 17(1): oraa008.

Tallberg, Jonas, and Michel Zürn. 2019. 'The Legitimacy and Legitimation of International Organizations: Introduction and Framework'. *Review of International Organizations* 14(4): 581–606.

Tallberg, Jonas, Karin Bäckstrand and Jan Aart Scholte, eds. 2018. *Legitimacy in Global Governance: Sources, Processes, and Consequences*. Oxford University Press.

Tehran Declaration. 'XVI Summit of Heads of State or Government of the Non-Aligned Movement'. 2012.

UNGA. 1991. Resolution 46/210. 'Economic Measures as a Means of Political and Economic Coercion against Developing Countries'.

UNGA. 1997. Resolution 51/103. 'Human Rights and Unilateral Coercive Measures'.

UNGA. 2003. Resolution 58/198. 'Human Rights and Unilateral Coercive Measures'.
UNGA. 2004. Resolution 59/188. 'Human Rights and Unilateral Coercive Measures'.
UNGA. 2011a. Resolution 65/217. 'Human Rights and Unilateral Coercive Measures'.
UNGA. 2011b. Resolution 66/186. 'Economic Measures as a Means of Political and Economic Coercion against Developing Countries'.
UNGA. 2013. Resolution 67/170. 'Human Rights and Unilateral Coercive Measures'.
UNGA. 2015. Resolution 69/180. 'Human Rights and Unilateral Coercive Measures'.
UNGA. 2019. Resolution 73/167. 'Human Rights and Unilateral Coercive Measures'.
UNSC. 2014. Security Council 7323rd meeting. 'General Issues Related to Sanctions'. 25 November 2014.
UNSC. 2022. Security Council. 8962nd meeting. 7 February 2022.
Welsh, Jennifer M. 2013. 'Norm Contestation and the Responsibility to Protect'. *Global Responsibility to Protect* 5: 365–96.
Wiener, Antje. 2004. 'Contested Compliance: Interventions on the Normative Structure of World Politics'. *European Journal of International Relations* 10(2): 189–234.
Wiener, Antje. 2007. 'The Dual Quality of Norms and Governance beyond the State: Sociological and Normative Approaches to "Interaction"'. *Critical Review of International Social and Political Philosophy* 10(1): 47–69.
Wiener, Antje. 2014. *A Theory of Contestation*. Springer.
Wiener, Antje, and Phil Orchard, eds. 2024. *Contesting the World: Norm Research in Theory and Practice*. Cambridge University Press.
Zaum, Dominik. eds. 2013. *Legitimating International Organizations*. Oxford University Press.
Zaum, Dominik. 2016. 'Legitimacy'. In *The Oxford Handbook of International Organizations*, edited by J. K. Cogan, I. Hurd and I. Johnstone. Oxford University Press.
Zelditch, Morris. 2001. 'Theories of Legitimacy'. In *The Psychology of Legitimacy*, edited by J. Jost and B. Major. Cambridge University Press.
Zimmermann, Lisbeth, Nicole Deitelhoff, Max Lesch, Antonio Arcudi and Anton Peez. 2023. *International Norms Disputes*. Oxford University Press.
Zürn, Michael, Martin Binder and Matthias Ecker-Ehrhardt. 2012. 'International Authority and Its Politicization'. *International Theory* 4(1): 69–106.

3

Sanctions and International Order: Contestation in UNGA Debates, 1946–2023

Elin Hellquist

Introduction

This chapter analyses how sanctions are discussed in the annual United Nations General Assembly (UNGA) debates between 1946 and 2023. Sanctions have undergone significant changes in this period. The measures subsumed under the label of sanctions have diversified beyond the classical comprehensive embargo, to comprise restrictions targeting individuals and entities held directly responsible for norm violations. Sanctions have also become more frequent, imposed by an expanding group of actors, and in reaction to a growing range of norm violations. Despite these far-reaching changes, sanctions retain essential traits over time. Sanctions characteristically combine some type of material punishment (infliction of harm, withdrawal of privilege) with a symbolic disapproval of the target's wrongdoing. This intricate combination of continuity and change allows us to observe how patterns of norm contestation evolve over time.

All sanctions refer to an alleged norm violation – a rupture with acceptable behaviour – but all norm violations do not result in sanctions. Much of the rebuilding of international order after two devastating world wars revolved around establishing red lines of intolerable behaviour, but disagreement has continued about the applied meaning of norms (Orchard and Wiener, this volume), the relationship between norms, and the authority and means to enforce norms (Palestini, this volume). According to Finnemore (2008, 221), '[f]ormulating a general policy would require us to specify a priori which among several conflicting norms we will privilege regardless of circumstance or consequence, yet the ethics of these interventions depends very much on both'. One need not believe in full anarchy to see that the international system lacks mechanisms for resolving norm conflicts or 'correct[ly] assessing circumstances' (Jackson 2000, 23). Thus, fully objective benchmarks for the imposition of sanctions are utopian. In addition, it is possible to disapprove of a norm violation without resorting to sanctions. These circumstances create a space for contestation.

Relying on Orchard and Wiener's typology of norm contestation (see Orchard and Wiener in this volume), the chapter applies the analytical lens of reactive, proactive and interpretative contestation to five particularly influential episodes: sanctions in the UN's first formative years, anti-apartheid sanctions, sanctions against Iraq, targeted sanctions and organised opposition to unilateral sanctions.

In the early post-war period, interpretative contestation unfolded over the role of sanctions in defining the UN's emerging identity. During the anti-apartheid struggle, widespread support for sanctions was accompanied by proactive calls to make them mandatory and more effectively enforced. The comprehensive embargoes on Iraq in the 1990s provoked both proactive demands for 'smarter' sanctions and reactive denunciations of their devastating humanitarian impact. The subsequent rise of targeted sanctions represents proactive attempts to reform the instrument, while persistent doubts about their precision echo reactive critiques. Finally, the organised opposition to unilateral sanctions in recent decades reflects strong reactive contestation of legitimacy and sovereignty, but also interpretative challenges that present alternative visions of international order. By situating these debates in terms of reactive, proactive and interpretative contestation, the chapter shows not only how sanctions have evolved as instruments but also how they serve as a prism through which competing visions of international order are articulated in the UNGA. Methodologically, the chapter draws on a systematic content analysis of UNGA General Debate speeches between 1946 and 2023, identifying references to sanctions and coding them in relation to their normative context.

The next section elaborates on the relationship between sanctions, norms and international order. Thereafter, the development of sanctions since the end of the Second World War is outlined. The second half of the chapter contains the empirical exploration of contestation over sanctions in UNGA debates.

Sanctions, Norms and International Order

As long as regularised interactions have existed between different entities in the world, there have been regularised interruptions to these interactions. These interruptions to normal exchanges amount to what we call 'sanctions'.

The logic of imposing a negative consequence on the one who breaks a norm exists at all levels of human society. The pupil who gets detention after breaking classroom rules, the speeder who gets fined, the sports(wo)man who is expelled from competing due to doping, the murderer who gets convicted to life in prison; they are all subject to sanctions. In all these situations, a symbolic disapproval with the norm breach is combined with a concrete, material, negative consequence.

In the international sphere, public ruptures with 'customary' or 'normal' interactions in reaction to an alleged wrongdoing (Hufbauer, Schott and Elliott 1990, 2; Baldwin 1985) were formalised after the First World War in the League of Nations (see Mulder 2022). In modifying the normal state of a relationship (economic or other), the sender of a sanction typically conveys that its 'limits of toleration' have been crossed (Rawls 1993). When senders publicly disapprove of the target's norm breach (Nossal 1989, 306), they also communicate their own adherence to the norm. As was pointed out by Lindsay (1986) and elaborated by Giumelli (e.g. 2011), this is a message not only for the target but also for different domestic and international audiences. If a critical mass of actors imposes sanctions in a given situation, their joint disapproval can be argued to represent a defence of the role of the violated norm in international order.

Since sanctions operate by altering normal terms of interaction, they also say something about the normal state of international relations (Hellquist 2024). Trade, political cooperation, diplomatic exchanges, investments and travel between state borders are all examples of regularised behaviours that can be manipulated through sanctions (see Baldwin 1999, 101).

Ceteris paribus, the more states interact, the more occasions they have to use sanctions. There is an intriguing twist here, however, since the expansion of sanctions will, step by step, modify the conception of the 'normal' (see Beaucillon 2021b). Organised sanctions at the international level have largely been a Western, liberal project (see Mulder 2022; Jones 2015). Yet, ultimately, the gradual expansion and consequential normalisation of punitive practices could end up counteracting liberal market globalism, and reinforce, rather than resolve, normative cleavages in the international system.

If sanctioning is about settling 'what actually holds international society together' (Adler-Nissen 2014, 144), the imposition of a stigma is only the first step. Without compliance, normative difference will be cemented rather than resolved. The prevailing dialectic of primary sanctions and counter-measures, which often have repercussions also for third countries, hardly indicates a 'shared sense of what is good or bad' (Adler-Nissen 2014, 149). The sprawling expansion of punitive measures suggests that we are far from reaching a normative equilibrium of acceptable behaviour in international relations. Rather, there is an ongoing battle about who has the authority to use sanctions and for what purposes.

The Post-war Evolution of Sanctions

As a central element in the launch of a new international order, the United Nations Security Council (UNSC) was vested with powers to impose sanctions against troublemakers (White and Abass 2006, 510).[1] Thanks to their explicit legality under international law, UN sanctions arguably still have a legitimacy advantage over sanctions from other actors (Jamnejad and Wood 2009, 369; see Hellquist 2024).

However, the UNSC has not lived up to early expectations that it would exercise consistent normative discipline in international relations. During the Cold War, the use and non-use of sanctions was shaped by superpower bipolarity. Chronic veto blockages at the UNSC hindered the UN from exercising its envisaged role as guarantor of international peace and security.

With superpower blockages largely eliminated at the end of the Cold War, the UNSC imposed sanctions on eleven occasions between 1990 and 1998 (Elliott and Hufbauer 1999). However, not only the UN but also regional organisations and individual states developed their sanctions instruments further after the end of the Cold War. Over the last decades, the number of non-UN-mandated sanctions regimes has reached new levels. With the formation of the common foreign and security policy in the Maastricht Treaty, the EU emerged as a highly active sender of sanctions outside of the UN framework. Such 'autonomous' measures follow from an understanding of the UNSC as a 'floor' rather than the 'ceiling' for action (see Biersteker and Moret 2015, 70). A separate category is the measures that regional organisations employ against their own members. These sometimes overlap with sanctions from the UN or unilateral senders, but they rely on a distinct in-group premise or treaty obligation (see Hellquist 2021 and 2022).

The portfolio of measures under the label of sanctions has also evolved. The humanitarian consequences of comprehensive embargoes employed during the 1990s against, among others, Iraq and Haiti profoundly delegitimised the instrument. Sanctions had imposed extensive harm on the societies, yet the expected political change did not materialise. This failure exposed the weakness of the long-theorised link between economic harm and political change. In reaction to this acute legitimacy crisis, three conferences gathering scholars

[1] The General Assembly can recommend sanctions.

and practitioners were held with the explicit aim to reinvent the instrument. The outcome of the Interlaken, Bonn–Berlin and Stockholm processes was the development of 'targeted' or 'smart' sanctions. The idea to place entire societies 'under siege' (Jones 2015) was, for the time being, abandoned. Targeted sanctions – particularly asset freezes and travel restrictions – were a part of a broader trend towards (allegedly) surgical security policy in post-Cold War international affairs (for example, drone warfare and targeted killings in the military domain). In contrast to traditional comprehensive sanctions which, by design, aimed to inflict broad harm, the new type of sanctions was envisaged as a precision instrument harming only those directly responsible for norm violations.

Today, sanctions refer to a plethora of measures, some of which deviate from the idea of precise targeting introduced at the end of the 1990s. Sanctions currently in force selectively or comprehensively sever trade with certain goods or services, cut relational privileges (for example, suspension/expulsion of membership), halt cultural exchanges, freeze assets, restrict travel or ban investments. Examples of recent sanctions approximating the old logic of collective punishment include those against crucial economic sectors in Iran, Syria and Russia. In parallel, attempts to use sanctions as a precision instrument continue and have further diversified.

Mirroring the expansion of concrete measures, the group of targets has also broadened. While most sanctions regimes are still described by country labels, specific targets can include companies or other legal entities, organisations or individuals. However, it has proved hard to define direct responsibility using conventional legal criteria. During the first years of targeting, the listing of people, organisations and entities was often justified with weak or little public evidence. When targets of EU sanctions began to challenge their listings at the European Court of Justice, they often won (Forwood et al. 2020, 26). Although efforts have been made to improve due process rights, sanctions remain essentially political tools that raise difficult legal questions. The requisite of direct responsibility for a wrongdoing has in practice been relaxed, as family members and other individuals associated with primary actors are sometimes included in sanctions lists. In its twelfth sanctions package against Russia, the European Union introduced a possibility to keep assets frozen after the death of designated individuals to prevent assets from being used for sanctioned purposes (Council of the European Union 2023).

In addition, the range of norm violations that sanctions seek to address has continuously grown. Relatedly, the emergence of transnational thematic sanctions – also called horizontal sanctions (see Portela 2021) – have relaxed the state-centrism of sanctions policies. Starting with UN measures against

Al-Qaida and the Taliban, so-called terrorist lists aim to constrain organisations, entities and individuals from access to financing for terrorist activities (UNSC 1999; UNSC 2001; US Department of State 2024; Council of the European Union 2001 [2024]). Another example of horizontal sanctions is the Magnitsky Act against human rights abuse and corruption as well as related regimes, such as the EU's Global Human Rights Sanctions Mechanism (Council of the European Union 2020 [2023]). According to analysis from the London Stock Exchange Group (LSEG), more than 60,000 persons were on sanctions lists in April 2023, more than a tripling since January 2017 (Meadon 2023).

Taken together, sanctions have become an increasingly defining feature of international relations. Most aspects of sanctions have multiplied and diversified: the senders, the targets, the measures and the norm violations. At first view, the spread of sanctions through the international system could be thought to indicate a higher degree of norm enforcement and thus a stronger international order. However, this only holds if there is sufficient acceptance of the norms, with a broad international coalition of senders willing and able to implement measures. The increasingly technical nature of many sanctions poses challenges to states as well as companies and individuals. The complex and encompassing web of sanctions invites implementation problems, including deliberate evasion (Early 2021), as well as the opposite tendency of over-compliance (Verdier 2022).

For sanctions to contribute to normative cohesion and stability, targets would need to comply. The dominant understanding among both policymakers and academics has long been that sanctions are effective when they bite. In this understanding of effectiveness as impact, the priority naturally becomes to maximise the harm that sanctions inflict on their targets. While scholarly estimations of sanctions effectiveness vary, it is clear that the experience of harm does not translate in any automatic way into political change (Jones 2015). Sometimes, the situation is further complicated by the norm violation being irreversible and the threshold for compliance unrealistic.

Sanctions are not an isolated affair between senders and targets but involve and shape international society as a whole and in its different parts. As sanctions have become the instrument of choice to ever more actors outside of the UN system, overt normative divisions in international order have become visible. Non-UN mandated ('unilateral', 'autonomous') measures have become a source of annoyance for a majority of the world's countries, not only the direct targets. The scope for neutrality has shrunk with extraterritorial application of sanctions and other strategies for involving bystanders (for a comprehensive discussion on extraterritoriality, see Beaucillon 2021a; on neighbourly alignment with Common Foreign and Security Policy sanctions, see Hellquist 2016). Targets likewise seek to gain the support of third countries by arguing that sanctions are illegitimate, illegal and have devastating effects.

The discontent with non-UN mandated sanctions has led to organised opposition within the UN system (see Hellquist 2024). Since 1997, the UNGA has approved, with vast majorities, yearly resolutions condemning what in this context are called 'unilateral coercive measures'. The critique voiced in these resolutions centres on sovereignty, human rights and the right to development. Negative effects for women, children and other vulnerable groups are given special attention (see, for example, United Nations General Assembly 1997, 2023). Since 2015, the UN has had a Special Rapporteur position specifically concerned with 'the negative impact of the unilateral coercive measures on the enjoyment of human rights' (OHCHR 2024). The human rights critique may appear flawed, since targets of sanctions often themselves have a problematic human rights record, even if another norm violation has provoked the action taken against them. Nonetheless, the organised opposition represents a widening gap in attitudes to norm enforcement, which warns of a crisis of international order.

Debating Sanctions at the UN General Assembly (UNGA)

The UNGA annual debates provide an observatory for grasping how senders, targets and bystanders argue about sanctions and their role in international order. The speeches have a fairly set format over time, thus facilitating comparative analysis. Furthermore, analysing general debates, rather than debates specifically devoted to sanctions, permits a better understanding of the role sanctions play in international relations at large.

The debates were downloaded from the dataset 'United Nations General Debate Corpus', in which each speech is an individual document named with nation and year (Jankin, Baturo and Dasandi 2017 [2023]). To facilitate a systematic overview of the vast material, the texts were uploaded to ATLAS.ti, a computer-based text analysis software. The corpus was thereafter delineated by filtering out the 2,520 (out of 10,760) UNGA speeches that contain a mention of the word sanction. The resulting material was scrutinised inductively at the paragraph level. The study does not aim at covering the complete universe of statements relating to the conceptual family of punitive measures, but a relevant sample defined by the presence of the central term 'sanctions'. Hence, the material does not capture all occurrences of words that are synonyms of or closely related to sanctions, such as embargo, blockade or ban. The term 'unilateral coercive measures' was likewise not used to delineate the material, since it is inherently negatively loaded and would have tilted the material accordingly. However, when any of these terms appear in conjunction with a paragraph in which the word sanction appears, they are included in the analysis.

Figure 3.1 displays how mentions of sanctions vary between years, in absolute numbers (grey) and share of all speeches (black). Notably, attention to sanctions in UNGA debate does not straightforwardly follow the number of ongoing cases. On the contrary, sanctions were most frequently mentioned in the mid-1980s, when there was a high degree of support for anti-apartheid sanctions specifically.

As depicted in Figure 3.2, leaders of some African states have been especially prone to raise the topic of sanctions in UNGA debates. This is partly because targets of sanctions are frequent speakers, whereas leading senders tend to keep a lower profile. Besides taking the occasion to raise opinions against their predicament at the UNGA, targets remain critically engaged in sanctions cases long after their own measures have been lifted. Sweden is the only Western country among the top ten most active speakers on sanctions.

Next, Figure 3.3 displays significant terms that are brought up in speeches that also mention sanctions (in black), as compared to speeches that do not mention sanctions (in light grey). Whereas there is negligible difference in how often 'sanctions speeches' and other speeches mention development (>90%), human rights (>60%), poverty (>50%) and democracy (>40%), the terms depicted below appear more often in speeches that mention sanctions. This gives a rough idea of the broader discursive context in which sanctions are discussed.

As the qualitative analysis will further illuminate, the meaning of sanctions in UNGA debates evolves over time. Figure 3.4 displays some of the prefixes given to sanctions, for instance demonstrating that the expression 'mandatory sanctions' is prevalent only in the era of anti-apartheid sanctions, whereas the attention to unilateral sanctions surfaces in the mid-1990s to further expand in recent years.

The remainder of this chapter zooms in on five key episodes in the contemporary history of sanctions: (1) the UN's first formative years; (2) anti-apartheid sanctions during the Cold War; (3) post-Cold War comprehensive sanctions, with a focus on Iraq; (4) the emergence of targeted sanctions; and finally (5) organised opposition to non-UN mandated sanctions in recent decades.

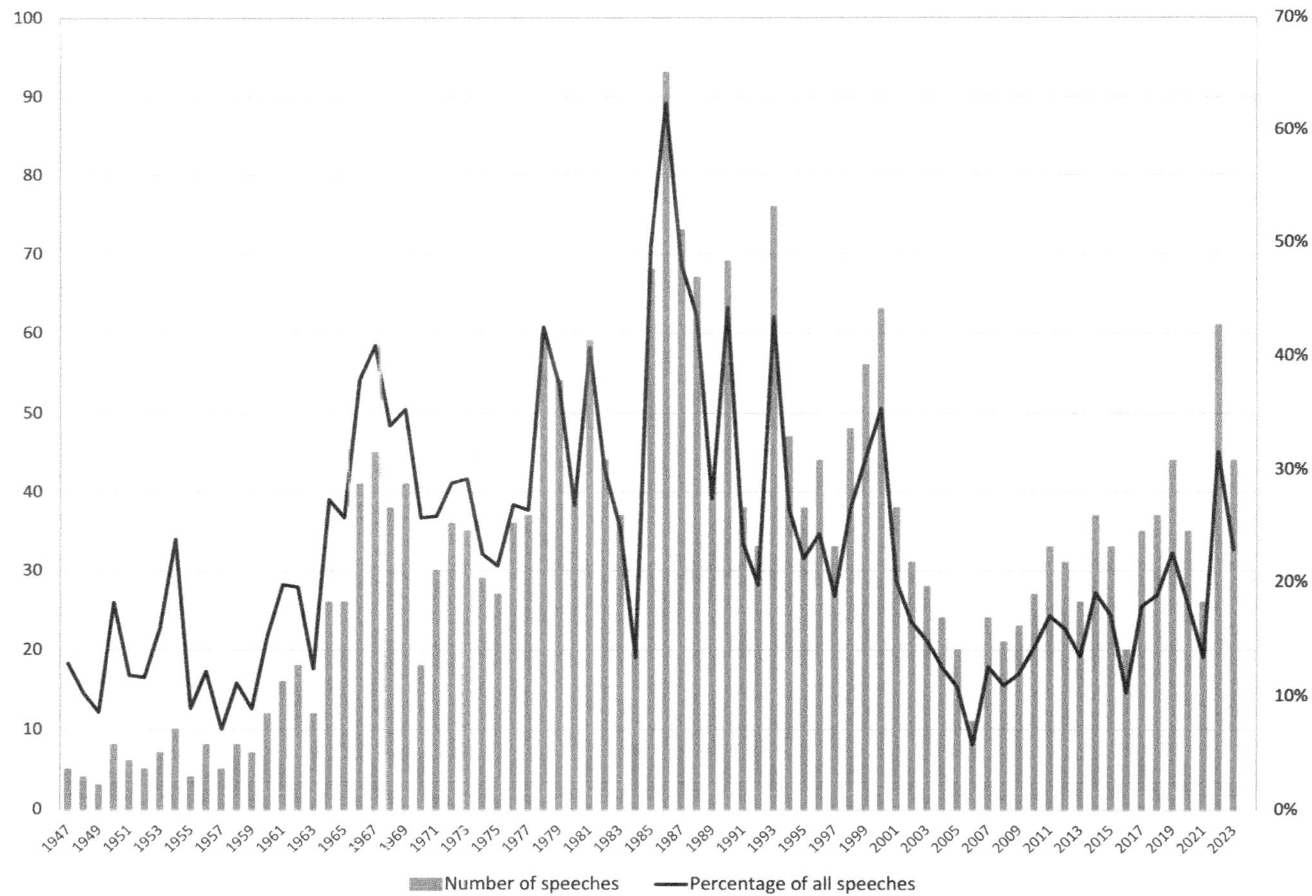

Figure 3.1 Speeches mentioning sanctions in UNGA debates, 1946–2023

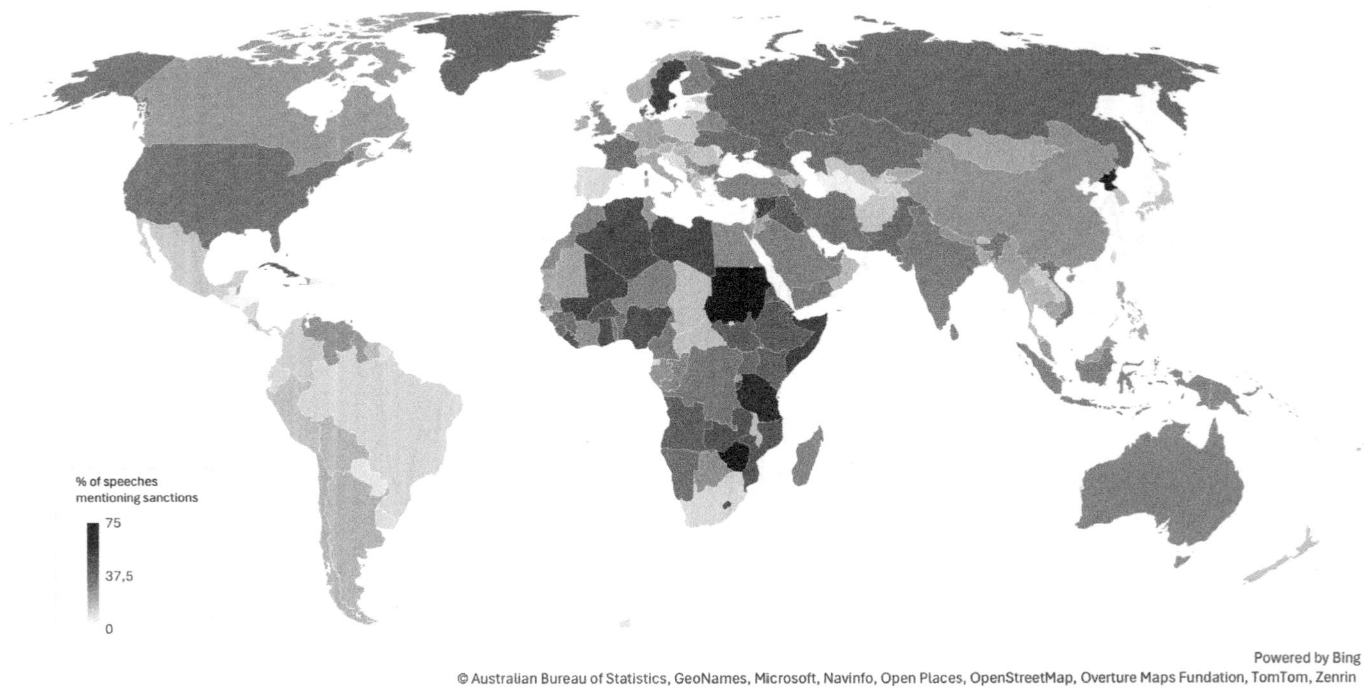

Figure 3.2 World distribution of UNGA speeches mentioning sanctions

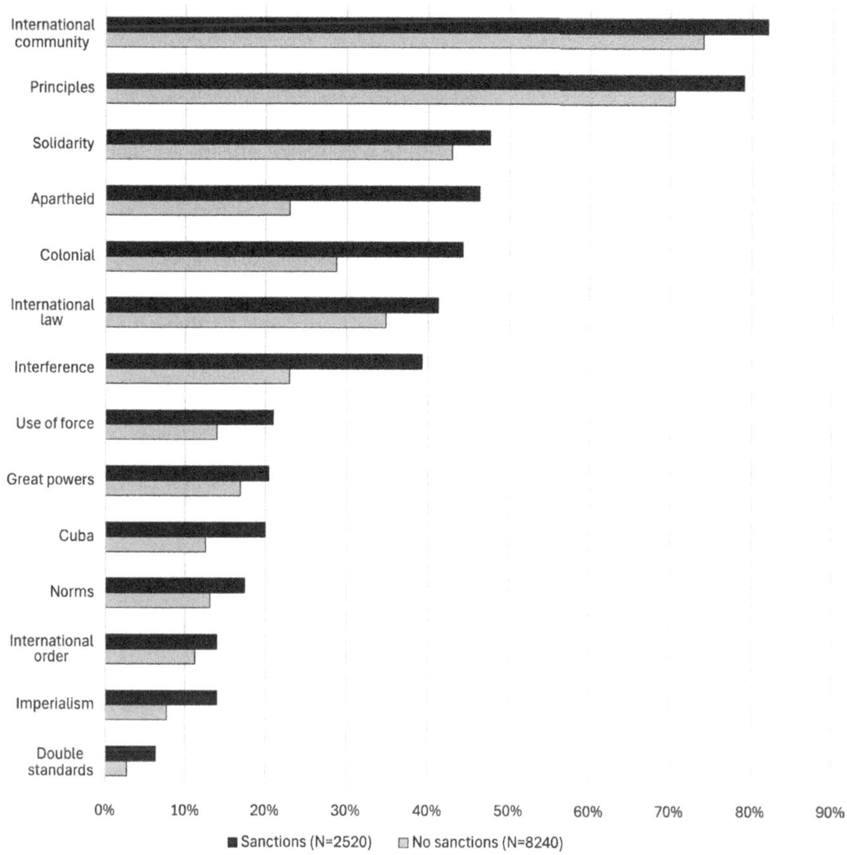

Figure 3.3 What (else) do they talk about?

Formative Years

In the early post-war period, sanctions surfaced in meta-discussions on how to organise international relations after the devastating world wars. In this period, the term 'sanction' was recurrently used in both its positive and negative sense: to endorse/reward and to penalise (see Baldwin 1971, 23). Both meanings help define the UN project in relation to other actors and different international norms, but here we focus on negative sanctions.

In these first years, statements on sanctions evoked expectations about the emerging identity of the UN, including the allocation of intra-organisational authority between the UNSC and UNGA. Hopes that sanctions would help the UN become a universally recognised safeguard of international peace and security resided alongside worries of great power interest contamination.

Sanctions were envisaged as a feature distinguishing the UN from its failed predecessor, the League of Nations. With the help of negative sanctions, the UN was to become a universal organisation capable of delivering collective security. Poland argued that the UN was 'in an infinitely better position' compared with the League of Nations, which was weak due to its 'lack of universality' and 'the absence of sanctions' (POL_02_1947). A few years later, China reasoned that '[i]f the League of Nations had applied effective sanction on the Axis powers [. . .] the Second World War might have been prevented' (CHN_09_1954). According to Panama (PAN_11_1956), the 'downfall' of the League was due to 'a lack of determination and courage' to agree on sanctions.

Iraq communicated the baseline function of sanctions in the post-war international order: '[a]n aggressor must be punished if aggression is not to be repeated' (IRQ_09_1954). In a world where 'very few matters [. . .] are still strictly and absolutely of national concern', those who 'try to ignore the rules of international co-operation' will meet the sanction of isolation (COL_09_1954).

At the time, sanctions were associated with the use of force, itself described as a 'military sanction' (AUS_02_1947). On the one hand, the US described the UN's purpose as 'making it unnecessary for the civilized world to resort again to the ultimate sanction of war against an aggressor' (USA_01_1946). On the other hand, to give the UN 'teeth, that is to say, its own military forces' was crucial for the organisation to play its envisaged role: 'there is no written law without sanction and no sanction without executory force' (EGY_01_1946; see SYR_02_1947; LBN_05_1950). In 1951, France deplored the absence of a permanent UN force 'capable of providing a minimum sanction to back its decisions' (FRA_06_1951). The USSR problematised how 'the whole so-called "community defence system" is based on the use of force, on the application of sanctions [. . .] against any State that may be declared an aggressor' (RUS_08_1953).

The UN's capacity to play a role in a major international crisis was put to the test with the outbreak of the Korea War in 1950 (PHL_05_1950). In June 1950, Soviet-backed North Korean forces broke through several points along latitude 38° N, since the end of the Second World War the official boundary between North and South Korea. At that time, the Soviet Union boycotted the Security Council,[2] which enabled the Council to swiftly issue resolutions UNSCR 82 and 83, condemning the invasion and urging all UN members to assist South Korea (United Nations Security Council 1950a, b). In its

[2] The boycott concerned China's representation at the UN, and lasted between January and August 1950.

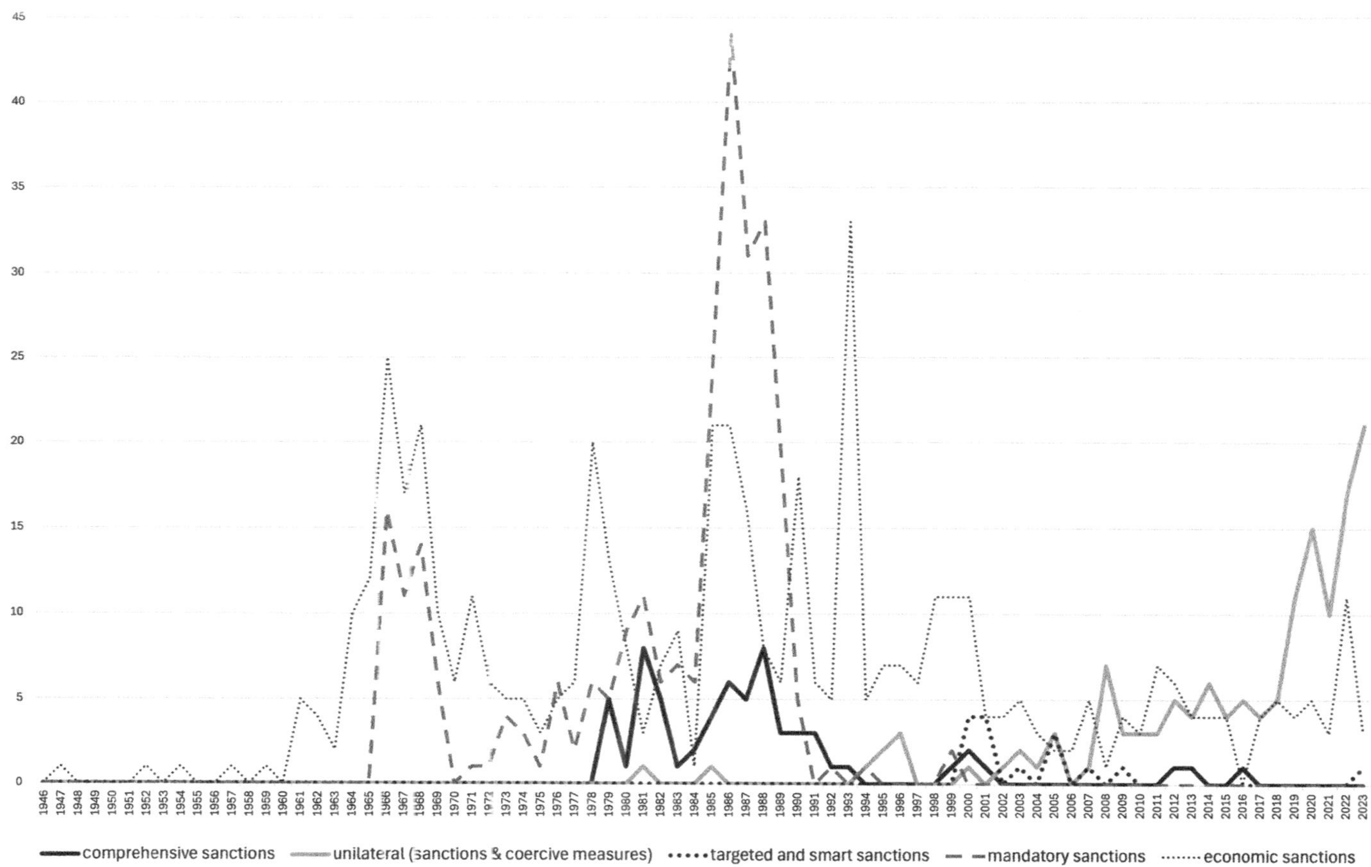

Figure 3.4 Sanctions vocabulary over time

subsequent resolution, UNSCR 84, the UNSC took the historic step of establishing a military force under UN flag: the United Nations Command (UNC) (United Nations Security Council 1950c). In 1954, the Philippines looked back at how the Security Council had been 'saved from total impotence only by the narrowest of accidents, that is, by the providential absence of the Soviet Union from the meeting which ordained military sanctions' (PHL_09_1954).

The UNC was lauded as a concrete incarnation of the UN's ambition to deliver collective security. The Philippines put forward that not only was '[t]he application of military sanctions in Korea [. . .] in itself an act of the greatest significance', but that member states increasingly wished that this improvised action would become regularised (PHL_05_1950). Greece (GRC_07_1952) interpreted the UN's handling of the Korea crisis as indicative of 'the resolution with which peoples have entered upon the path of collective security', concluding that 'the United Nations has become the supreme court of a new international order'.

Looking back at the UN's first years in 1961, New Zealand pointed out that the founders wished to create an international order where 'legal and moral sanctions of universal validity' take the place of 'physical power, based on brute strength and actuated by self-interest' (NZL_16_1961). However, geopolitical realities and institutional design together worked against the UN becoming a capable authority for collective security. The UN did not regulate the relationship between great, middle and small powers to everyone's satisfaction (see AUS_02_1947). Already in 1946, reservations were voiced at the UNGA about power politics – particularly the UNSC veto – corrupting the UN's potential to play its intended role. In a political landscape characterised by ideological polarisation, the idea of objectively identifying norm violations proved illusory. Instead, diverging positions on sanctions evoked different principled views about the substance of politics and limits of sovereignty in the context of superpower rivalry (e.g. RUS_08_1953; GRC_07_1952; FRA_11_1956). According to Lebanon (LBN_01_1946), power politics were 'the very negation of a healthy United Nations Organization', and only once this bias was corrected could sanctions – together with an international UN force – form 'a code of justice applicable to all'. The incapacitating consequences of power politics in international order remains a theme of concern throughout the period of study.

Sanctions against Apartheid

In the early confrontative stage of the Cold War, superpower rivalry impeded the UNSC from exercising the sanctioning powers vested in it after the end of the Second World War. The first cases of mandatory UNSC sanctions came in the détente of the 1960s and were directed at the racist regimes in Southern Rhodesia and South Africa. UNGA debates from then until the end of the Cold War mainly concerned these UN cases and paid less attention to the rather extensive use of unilateral sanctions at the time, especially by superpowers (see appendix 1A in Hufbauer et al. 2007, 20–9).

The fairly broad normative agreement among UNGA members against apartheid (see Klotz 1995) was reflected in an, in principle, favourable stance on sanctions. Apartheid was a threat to international peace (PAK_22_1967), a matter requiring 'a responsible attitude' from all UN members (BFA_27_1972). Sanctions were, thus, perceived as an instrument for building a (just) international order (e.g., PRY_25_1970), highlighting the UN's status as the world's designated sender of sanctions. In 1970, Sri Lanka discussed the role of sanctions in 'the preservation of international law and order', reasoning that 'in organized society, defiance of authority or any transgression of the law is punished with sanctions' and that '[r]espect for authority can be fostered' through public disapproval of misbehaving members (LKA_25_1970).

The main concern about the anti-apartheid sanctions was evasion, and the unwillingness of Western states – especially great powers – to pay the economic price of fully isolating South Africa (e.g. RWA_25_1970; SLE_25_1970; BEN_26_1971; BEN_20_1965). A recurrent worry was that the interests of individual (Western) members corrupted allegiance to UN authority and thereby undermined the rightful role of sanctions in the international system. Thus, for instance, Jamaica stated in 1980: 'Gross violations of international norms and conduct are punishable by sanctions. Some members of the international community appear to recognize this only when their immediate interests are directly threatened' (JAM_35_1980). The critique of interest contamination or double standards was often coupled with references to colonialism and imperialism (e.g. ALB_41_1986; AGO_35_1980; CUB_35_1980; HUN_35_1980; NGA_35_1980; BEN_26_1971). According to Ghana, evasion of sanctions against South Rhodesia risked undermining 'the whole idea of sanctions' (GHA_21_1966).

Thus, debates centred on strengthening sanctions and their implementation, to better meet their goals. In line with this understanding, during this era speakers continuously underlined that sanctions must be 'mandatory' (see Figure 3.4 above). In a logic of maximising harm – understood as the mechanism behind effectiveness – speakers called for 'total sanctions' (GHA_21_1966; KEN_40_1985; TZA_31_1976; LBR_20_1965; LBR_19_1964; KEN_33_1978). Congo even spoke of 'extreme' sanctions, arguing that any collaboration with the South African regime should be seen as 'a grave violation of human rights' (COG_33_1978).

Over the entire period of study, almost half of the speeches that mention sanctions mention 'apartheid' somewhere in the same speech. Thus, apartheid remained an important point of reference in UNGA debates, long after it was abolished.

Sanctions against Iraq

The fall of the Berlin Wall and the dissolution of the Soviet Union transformed international order and the role of sanctions within it. It permitted an end to the UNSC's Cold War paralysis and thus constituted an institutional window of opportunity for the UN to play a more proactive role as a sender of sanctions. The early post-Cold War years were also a time in which coherence around liberal values suddenly appeared within grasp. The liberal script appeared to have come out winning the ideological Cold War, offering a template of norms that needed to be collectively looked after by sanctioning wrongdoers.

Iraq's invasion of Kuwait in August 1990 was the last major international crisis on the UNSC's agenda during the USSR's existence. The two superpowers' handling of the crisis was a foretaste of the early post-Cold War dynamics, in which sanctions rose to prominence.

A blatant violation of the neighbour's sovereignty and territorial integrity, Iraq's invasion was an occasion for the reconstituting international community to unite. Beyond the urgency of the situation for Kuwait, the crisis demonstrated 'the inherent vulnerability of small States to assaults on their security, sovereignty and territorial integrity' and the importance of the UN protecting their interests (BRB_45_1990). International sanctions were a 'logical and imperative' reaction to Iraq's intolerable aggression (BLZ_45_1990), reflecting '[t]he common will of the States of the world' (BHR_45_1990). The issuing of sanctions represented 'collective action', 'solidarity' and 'determination' (FIN_45_1990). According to Iran, '[a] spectacular public international solidarity to corner the aggressor was painted in front of the unbelieving eyes of the world public' (IRN_45_1990).

At this point, support for and expectations on the UNSC were high. Belgium compared the situation to the one facing the League of Nations before the outbreak of the Second World War: '[f]ailure now would mean a particularly serious – possibly a fatal – loss of prestige' (BEL_45_1990). In this respect, sanctions were viewed as 'an important, a crucial, experiment' for the peaceful resolution of the conflict, with the potential to set 'an essential precedent for the future of the entire family of nations' (BEL_45_1990; AUS_45_1990).

Leaders commended the Council for the historic step it took in quickly agreeing to impose sanctions on the aggressor. In doing so, it 'proved that it is possible to apply the system of collective security in the post-cold war era'; this was what the United Nations was created for, Singapore professed, referring to the collective measures (SGP_45_1990). 'The United Nations has emerged from this test triumphant and stronger', as declared by Uruguay (URY_45_1990). China conveyed its dedication and loyalty to the UN and the UNSC, stating that the resolutions on sanctions gave 'full expression to the sense of principle inherent in China's foreign policy' (CHN_45_1990).

Next to the endorsements, some speakers argued that the Iraq crisis revealed the hypocrisy and double standards within the UNSC by the great powers (Western countries). Ghana and Cuba contrasted the handling of Iraq with the absence of sanctions against Israel, as well as Western powers' more reluctant stance to sanctions against South Africa (GHA_45_1990; CUB_45_1990). Unsurprisingly, Iraq criticised sanctions from the outset, contesting the wrongdoing it was accused of and lamenting the negative consequences of sanctions on their country. Sanctions deprived the Iraqi population, especially children, of basic supplies and thereby exposed them to 'famine and deadly epidemics' (IRQ_46_1991). In the target's narrative, a political agenda of dividing Iraq was behind the 'orchestrated vociferous campaign' that went as far as including 'an embargo even on toys for the children of Iraq' (IRQ_47_1992).

The broad initial backing for sanctions against Iraq declined when their humanitarian consequences became visible. The Iraqi situation came to be understood as a high impact–low effectiveness case of sanctions, shedding doubt on the fundamental assumption that economic harm would translate into political gain through target change. A summary of this perspective was articulated by Jordan in 1996: economic sanctions have 'punished [. . .] the brotherly people of Iraq [. . .] but have not affected their leaders' (JOR_51_1996). The theoretical linkage between harm and change did not appear to have worked in practice, since '[p]oorly nourished, isolated and sick people are hardly likely to rise up against a governing elite' (CZE_55_2000).

The trajectory of the Iraqi sanctions regime provoked contestation over UN authority and, by extension, the UN's role in international order. According to Iraq itself, the UNSC had misused the authorisation given to it by the international community to 'annihilate the people of Iraq', 'to kill the children of Iraq in their name' (IRQ_56_2001). For other countries 'the plight of children' in Iraq, 'many of whom do not survive beyond the age of five', were at the core of mounting criticism (MYS_56_2001). At the turn of the millennium, Morocco supported the lifting of sanctions against 'that fraternal country', feeling 'anxious' at the deterioration of the food and health situation in Iraq (MAR_55_2000). Criticism was vocal from fellow Arab countries (e.g. QAT_53_1998; MRT_54_1999; OMN_54_1999). Egypt warned against sanctions leading to 'the creation of angry generations who will continue to be embittered by their suffering, even after these actions are lifted' (EGY_55_2000).

Sanctions against Iraq started out as the international community's joint vehicle for condemning the invasion of Kuwait. It was considered a moral and legal necessity to stand up for the small neighbour that had been blatantly aggressed. Humanitarian suffering caused the moral economy of Iraqi sanctions to shift. After Kuwait regained its independence (through a UN-authorised military operation), sanctions lost their immediate connection to the initial norm violation. It was harder to generate international unity around a different norm violation, accusations that Iraq was developing nuclear weapons. Compliance became tied to regime change – Saddam Hussein's rule had to go for sanctions to be lifted – which meant that the incentive to comply was opaque. This combination of factors brought the belief in comprehensive sanctions that had formed through the experience of anti-apartheid sanctions (more harm = more effectiveness) to a halt, but it was not the end of sanctions.

Targeted Sanctions

Rather than delivering eternal peace, post-Cold War international politics brought new divisions and conflicts. As put by Qatar, '[t]he new international order to which we aspired did not materialize' (QAT_54_1999). Although the appetite for comprehensive sanctions dropped through the experiences of the 1990s, crises calling for an international response did not cease. In a changing threat environment, the assumptions underpinning state-centred comprehensive sanctions no longer appeared fit for purpose. The evolution of international terrorism, epitomised in the coordinated attacks on the New York World Trade Center and the Pentagon on 11 September 2001, strengthened the case for using sanctions as precision instruments.

To overcome the urgent effectiveness and legitimacy failure of 1990s embargoes, sanctions were to target those directly responsible for norm violations. Thus, the vocabulary of 'targeted' and 'smart' sanctions made its way into UNGA debates in the early 2000s.

Through 'smarter, more effective sanctions which apply pressure where it . . . will have maximum impact' (NZL_55_2000), collateral suffering was to be minimised and effectiveness maximised. A 'sound sanctions policy', Spain argued, needed to 'penalize' specific governments that threaten peace, but not the civilian population 'which in many cases is totally powerless to influence the decisions of its Government' (ESP_55_2000; also CZE_55_2000).

With regard to international order, the Netherlands saw targeted sanctions as 'elements in a more forceful multilateral system' (NLD_58_2003). According to the Czech Republic, the prospects for sanctions efficiency had changed through globalisation, thus making a case for 'smart sanctions targeted against leading representatives of a State' (CZE_55_2000). Canada also thought of 'building blocks for a new type of international system' influenced by globalisation. In its estimate, military force remained the last resort when (among other things) targeted sanctions 'do not work' (CAN_55_2000). Finally, Denmark identified targeted sanctions as crucial for the UNSC to enforce its decisions and thereby build credibility (DNK_60_2005; DNK_59_2004).

Already from the start, not everyone was convinced that 'smart' or targeted sanctions were genuinely different from their predecessors: '[e]ven so-called smart sanctions can have wide, unintended effects while leaving their objects largely unaffected', argued Papua New Guinea (PNG_55_2000). Burundi, which had recently been subject to sanctions from its neighbours, also put forward that targeted sanctions risk harming the population and should therefore only be imposed as measures of last resort (BDI_55_2000). Smart sanctions do not bring about political solutions, but harden attitudes of one community against the other, Fiji argued (FJI_55_2000; also FJI_62_2007).

Organised Opposition

In the past couple of decades, sanctions have become an umbrella term for highly diverse measures, with targeted and comprehensive measures existing in parallel. Critical voices, however, rarely distinguish between measures, but centre on the alleged lack of legitimacy and negative consequences of unilateral – or non-UN mandated – sanctions specifically. Economic interests and hidden agendas were earlier perceived to undermine anti-apartheid measures, and now feed into the broad critique of unilateral sanctions. A palette of negative adjectives has come to be attached to sanctions, such as unjust/unfair, illegal, suffocating, inhumane or even genocidal. Targets take the lead in disputing the existence of 'smart' sanctions, which despite this description are equally 'violent, pure and simple' (IRN_68_2013), 'nothing but tools for killing and collectively punishing the peoples who stand by their countries, their sovereignty and their armies' (SYR_77_2022). Rather than promoting good governance, 'these actions [. . .] described as smart sanctions' 'have had a debilitating impact on our struggles to revive, to recover and to reform' (FJI_62_2007).

Hence, critics consider sanctions a 'bullying doctrine' (ATG_75_2020), 'a manifestation of structural violence' that is 'intrinsically inhumane and against peace' (IRN_68_2013), 'serv[ing] only to oppress people' (ARG_75_2020). Even the term sanctions itself is regarded to be a euphemism, as indicated by the expression 'so-called sanctions' (VEN_73_2018; SYR_76_2021; VEN_78_2023). Through their alleged negative attributes, sanctions are understood to undermine an international order based on international law, cooperation, friendship and dialogue (e.g. VNM_75_2020; SYR_75_2020). Eritrea sees sanctions as part of a flawed 'global governance structure', having itself 'borne the brunt of this unfair international order through illicit sanctions'. Rather than stemming from a legitimate international authority, Saint Vincent and the Grenadines argue that 'faceless bureaucrats in imperial centres' are behind sanctions, 'without any regard for multilateral rulemaking or settled international law' (VCT_77_2022).

Russia's full-scale invasion of Ukraine in February 2022 has catalysed existing geopolitical divisions, leading observers to write the obituary of liberal world order. At the UNSC, Russia has vetoed resolutions on Ukraine since 2014 (SC/14808), despite 'in theory' –according to article 27(3) of the UN Charter – being obliged to abstain as a party to the conflict (Peters 2023; EU_78_2023). Russia has also constrained the UNSC's role as a sender of sanctions, vetoing the continuation of the sanctions regime in Mali, as well as the mandate renewal for the UN Panel of Experts on North Korea (United Nations 2023; United Nations 2024).[3]

Despite the devastating consequences of Russia's war against Ukraine for world politics and the global economy, sanctions against Russia were not in the focus of UNGA debates in 2022 or 2023. Certainly, the conflict draws attention, but disapproval with the norm violation does not consequentially lead to explicit support of sanctions. Only a few speakers (fellow targets) condemn sanctions against Russia (e.g. Belarus, Venezuela, Cuba). The main contention rather concerns whether sanctions have contributed to the global food and energy crisis. This is a rare occasion in which senders collectively defend their sanctions at the UNGA, dismissing claims (e.g. BLR_77_2002; BLR_78_2023; BRA_77_2022; RUS_78_2023) that their measures are to blame for rocketing prices and ensuing hunger (AUT_77_2022; LTU_78_2023; LVA_78_2023).

[3] Russia's blocking of further monitoring of the North Korean sanctions regime comes in the context of the latter sending both weapons and soldiers to support Russia's war (e.g. Hird, Shats and O'Neil 2024).

The most discussed sanctions in recent UNGA debates are those against Cuba and Venezuela, both developing countries under unilateral sanctions. These cases embody core messages in contemporary sanctions critique, arguably more so than sanctions against Russia. Characteristically, when it comes to Cuba and Venezuela, speakers argue that sanctions are unmotivated (that is, there is no norm violation), illegal (that is, senders lack legitimate authority) and have devastating consequences on local societies.

Sanctions Contestation in the UNGA

The five key episodes of sanctions debate at the UNGA illustrate the varied ways in which states have engaged in norm contestation. In the early post-war period, sanctions were important items in the deliberate redesigning of international order. Whereas sanctions were expected to help the UN to become the guarantor of international peace and security that the international community anticipated, interpretative contestation followed on the more precise meaning of both positive and negative sanctions. In particular, discussions on sanctions disclosed diverging interpretations of how to best allocate authority between different levels and groups of states in the international order, as well as within the UN system.

The anti-apartheid struggle exemplified proactive contestation: although there was broad normative agreement that apartheid violated the most fundamental principles of human dignity and international peace, the central debate revolved around how to strengthen the sanction regime and ensure its effectiveness. Calls for mandatory, total and even 'extreme' sanctions sought not to delegitimise the instrument but to improve it, making sanctions a more credible and forceful expression of international order. In this sense, anti-apartheid sanctions became a benchmark case in which the instrument was defended as legitimate and necessary, but also in need of reinforcement.

The case of Iraq in the 1990s reveals a more complex trajectory, marked by both proactive and reactive contestation. Initially, the sanctions imposed in response to Iraq's invasion of Kuwait were widely perceived as a crucial test of the UN's capacity to enforce collective security in the post-Cold War era. They were heralded as a proactive attempt to demonstrate unity and build a precedent for handling major norm violations. Yet as the humanitarian consequences of comprehensive sanctions became visible, contestation shifted toward reactive denunciations. Critics accused the Security Council of abusing its mandate, of collectively punishing the Iraqi population and of undermining the very legitimacy of international authority. The normative ground on which sanctions rested eroded, as the moral economy shifted from solidarity with Kuwait to outrage over the suffering of Iraqi civilians.

The emergence of targeted, or 'smart', sanctions in the early 2000s represented another wave of proactive contestation. This development was framed as a reform of the sanctioning instrument, designed to remedy the legitimacy and effectiveness crisis provoked by the Iraq experience. By concentrating coercive measures on leaders and entities held directly responsible for norm violations, targeted sanctions were meant to minimise collateral damage and enhance normative credibility. Supporters portrayed them as the building blocks of a new, more precise multilateral order. Still, doubts persisted, with some actors cautioning that even 'smart' sanctions could produce unintended harms, indicating that traces of reactive contestation lingered beneath the proactive thrust of reform.

In contrast, the organised opposition to unilateral sanctions in the late 1990s and beyond epitomises a combination of reactive and interpretative contestation. Here, critics not only rejected unilateral sanctions as unjust, illegal or inhumane, but also advanced alternative visions of international order. By describing sanctions as neo-colonial, a form of structural violence or the product of 'faceless bureaucrats in imperial centres', opponents framed the practice as an expression of Western hegemony rather than legitimate norm enforcement. This interpretative dimension was especially strong in the Global South, where the memory of colonial domination infused critiques of sanctions with broader claims about sovereignty, justice and the right to development.

Finally, the debates surrounding sanctions against Russia after its 2022 full-scale invasion of Ukraine reflect predominantly interpretative contestation, though reactive elements are also present. While Russia's aggression was widely condemned, opinions on sanctions vary. Some states have reinterpreted the meaning of sanctions by linking them to the global food and energy crisis, thereby casting doubt on their appropriateness as instruments of order. In this framing, sanctions are primarily understood not as measures to enforce the prohibition of aggression but as destabilising tools with adverse consequences for innocent bystanders. A small number of states, particularly those themselves subject to Western sanctions, have engaged in reactive contestation by rejecting outright the legitimacy of measures against Russia. However, the dominant dynamic in these debates lies in interpretative struggles over what sanctions signify for the international system and whose interests they serve.

Conclusions

This chapter has drawn a picture of how sanctions are discussed in nearly seven decades of UNGA debates. Through shifts in world politics, sanctions retain their core distinctiveness as normatively loaded instruments that inflict (warranted or illegitimate) harm between (non-contractual) parties on the international scene. Consequently, sanctions are consistently associated with central substantive and procedural norms in international relations. Arguments about sanctions characteristically distribute judgements of good and bad and assign who has legitimate authority to act. Meanwhile, the sanctions landscape evolves: what measures are used, by whom, against whom and in reaction to which norm violations. These factors (re)define which constellations of countries reject or endorse sanctions and which arguments they use in doing so.

The five episodes examined in this chapter illustrate the diversity of contestation practices across time. At first, there was an optimistic momentum for sanctions, which were seen as crucial enforcement tools enabling the UN to exercise its legitimate authority. However, in the context of Cold War bipolarity, interpretative contestation emerged over whose interests sanctions represent and promote. During the anti-apartheid struggle, broad normative consensus on the injustice of racial domination fuelled proactive contestation, as states called for mandatory and total sanctions to strengthen the legitimacy and effectiveness of the instrument. By contrast, the Iraq embargo in the 1990s followed a more complex trajectory: it began as a proactive demonstration of solidarity in defence of sovereignty and territorial integrity but gradually gave way to reactive denunciations as its devastating humanitarian impact undermined the moral economy of sanctions. The subsequent rise of targeted sanctions in the early 2000s reflected another moment of proactive contestation, as states sought to reform sanctions into 'smarter' tools that could address norm violations without inflicting disproportionate harm on civilian populations. Alongside this, the growing organised opposition to unilateral sanctions from the late 1990s onwards combined reactive and interpretative contestation, rejecting the legitimacy of non-UN measures while articulating alternative visions of international order rooted in post-colonial critiques of Western dominance. Finally, the debates over sanctions against Russia after 2022 highlight the salience of interpretative contestation, with many states acknowledging the gravity of aggression but disputing whether sanctions are an appropriate or effective response, often reframing them instead as destabilising instruments that deepen global inequalities.

Contestation over sanctions occurs in several layers: in the definition of norms that are worthy of protection; in different principled positions on how to handle violations of these norms; in judgements about who has the responsibility and authority to take action; in the identification of concrete norm violations; and in the assessment of likely consequences of sanctions, including considerations of how targets and bystanders may react. Critics of sanctions may insist that punishment has no place in an international order based on positive engagement and dialogue, and senders may in contrast appear to think that sanctions are the answer to any problem. However, contestation on sanctions reveals that there is room for multiple qualifications in both positive and negative views on sanctions. Sensibility to the context of each crisis is sometimes taken to signify hypocrisy, inconsistency and double standards, but it can also be seen as a necessary component to avoid misguided policy expectations and diminish unintended consequences.

The timeline of the study has revealed that contestation unfolds in waves, where paradigmatic turns in international politics modify applied perspectives on sanctions. From the formative debates about sanctions in the remaking of international order after the Second World War, to the proactive strengthening of anti-apartheid sanctions and the reactive rejection of Iraq's embargo, from the reformist logic of targeted sanctions to the broad interpretative opposition to unilateral measures, and finally to the ambivalent readings of sanctions against Russia, these episodes reflect how each moment in world politics shapes the role of sanctions in international order. With the rules-based liberal order under significant pressure, there is amplified uncertainty also regarding the future of sanctions. On the one hand, there is little sign that the inflation of unilateral sanctions will stop, or that the normative gap between the sender minority and targets and (most) bystanders will close. On the other hand, the spiralling politics of measures and counter-measures has begun to blur the distinction between senders and targets.

References

Adler-Nissen, Rebecca. 2014. 'Stigma Management in International Relations: Transgressive Identities, Norms and Order in International Society'. *International Organization* 68(1): 143–76.

Baldwin, David A. 1971. 'The Power of Positive Sanctions'. *World Politics* 24(1): 19–38.

Baldwin, David A. 1985. *Economic Statecraft*. Princeton University Press.

Baldwin, David A. 1999. 'The Sanctions Debate and the Logic of Choice'. *International Security* 24(3): 80–107.

Beaucillon, Charlotte, ed. 2021a. *Research Handbook on Unilateral and Extraterritorial Sanctions*. Edward Elgar Publishing.

Beaucillon, Charlotte. 2021b. 'An Introduction to Unilateral and Extraterritorial Sanctions: Definitions, State of Practice and Contemporary Challenges'. In *Research Handbook on Unilateral and Extraterritorial Sanctions*, edited by Charlotte Beaucillon. Edward Elgar Publishing.

Biersteker, Thomas J., and Erica S. Moret. 2015. 'Rising Powers and Reform of the Practices of International Security Institutions'. In *Rising Powers, Global Governance and Global Ethics*, edited by Jamie Gaskarth. Routledge.

Council of the European Union. 2001 [2024]. Council Common Position of 27 December 2001 on the application of specific measures to combat terrorism (2001/931/CFSP). Last amended by COUNCIL DECISION (CFSP) 2024/628 of 19 February 2024.

Council of the European Union. 2020 [2023]. COUNCIL DECISION (CFSP) 2020/1999 of 7 December 2020 concerning restrictive measures against serious human rights violations and abuses. Last amended by COUNCIL DECISION (CFSP) 2023/1716 of 8 September 2023.

Council of the European Union. 2023. COUNCIL DECISION (CFSP) 2023/2871 of 18 December 2023 amending Decision 2014/145/CFSP concerning restrictive measures in respect of actions undermining or threatening the territorial integrity, sovereignty and independence of Ukraine.

Early, Bryan R. 2021. 'Making Sanctions Work: Promoting Compliance, Punishing Violations, and Discouraging Sanctions Busting'. In *Research Handbook on Economic Sanctions*, edited by Peter A. G. van Bergeijk. Edward Elgar Publishing.

Elliott, Kimberly Ann, and Gary Clyde Hufbauer. 1999. 'Same Song, Same Refrain? Economic Sanctions in the 1990's'. *American Economic Review* 89(2): 403–8.

Finnemore, Martha. 2008. 'Paradoxes in Humanitarian Intervention'. In *Moral Limit and Possibility in World Politics*, edited by Richard Price. Cambridge University Press.

Forwood, Genevra, Sara Nordin, Matthias Vangenechten and Fabienne Vermeeren. 2020. 'EU Restrictive Measures'. In *The Guide to Sanctions*, edited by Rachel Barnes, Anna Bradshaw, Paul Feldberg, David Mortlock, Anahita Thoms and Nicholas Turner. Global Investigations Review.

Giumelli, Francesco. 2011. *Coercing, Constraining and Signalling: Explaining UN and EU Sanctions after the Cold War*. ECPR Press.

Hellquist, Elin. 2016. 'Either with Us or against Us? Third-Country Alignment with EU Sanctions against Russia/Ukraine'. *Cambridge Review of International Affairs* 29(3): 997–1021.

Hellquist, Elin. 2021. 'Regional Sanctions as Peer Review: The African Union against Egypt (2013) and Sudan (2019)'. *International Political Science Review* 42(4): 451–68.

Hellquist, Elin. 2022. 'The African Union in a World of Sanctions'. In *Multilateral Sanctions Revisited: Lessons Learned from Margaret Doxey*, edited by Andrea Charron and Clara Portela. McGill-Queen's University Press.

Hellquist, Elin. 2024. 'International Sanctions and Contested Normative Authority'. In *Punishment in International Society: Norms, Justice, and Punitive Practices*, edited by Wolfgang Wagner et al. Oxford University Press.

Hird, Karolina, Daniel Shats and Alison O'Neil. 2024. 'North Korea Joins Russia's War against Ukraine'. Institute for the Study of War. https://understandingwar.org/research/russia-ukraine/north-korea-joins-russias-war-against-ukraine/

Hufbauer, Gary Clyde, Jeffrey J. Schott and Kimberly Ann Elliott. 1990. *Economic Sanctions Reconsidered: History and Current Policy*. Peterson Institute.

Hufbauer, Gary Clyde, Jeffrey J. Schott, Kimberly Ann Elliott and Barbara Oegg. 2007. *Economic Sanctions Reconsidered*. 3rd edition. Peterson Institute for International Economics.

Jackson, Robert. 2000. *The Global Covenant: Human Conduct in a World of States*. Oxford University Press.

Jamnejad, Maziar, and Michael Wood. 2009. 'The Principle of Non-intervention'. *Leiden Journal of International Law* 22: 345–81.

Jankin, Slava, Alexander Baturo and Niheer Dasandi. 2017 [2023]. 'United Nations General Debate Corpus 1946–2023'. Harvard Dataverse, V12.

Jones, Lee. 2015. *Societies under Siege*. Oxford University Press.

Klotz, Audie. 1995. *Norms in International Relations: The Struggle against Apartheid*. Cornell University Press.

Lindsay, James M. 1986. 'Trade Sanctions as Policy Instruments: A Re-Examination'. *International Studies Quarterly* 30(2): 153.

Meadon, Michael. 2023. *The Global Sanctions Index (GSI): Unpacking Worldwide Sanctions*. 3rd edition. https://www.lseg.com/

Mulder, Nicholas. 2022. *The Economic Weapon: The Rise of Sanctions as a Tool of Modern War*. Yale University Press.

Nossal, Kim Richard. 1989. 'International Sanctions as International Punishment'. *International Organization* 43(2): 301–22.

OHCHR. 2024. 'Special Rapporteur on the Negative Impact of the Unilateral Coercive Measures on the Enjoyment of Human Rights'. http://www.ohchr.org/EN/Issues/UCM/Pages/SRCoerciveMeasures.aspx

Peters, Anne. 2023. 'The War in Ukraine and Legal Limitations on Russian Vetoes'. *Journal on the Use of Force and International Law* 10(2): 162–72.

Portela, Clara. 2021. 'Horizontal Sanctions Regimes: Targeted Sanctions Reconfigured?' In *Research Handbook on Unilateral and Extraterritorial Sanctions*, edited by Charlotte Beaucillon. Edward Elgar Publishing.

Rawls, John. 1993. 'The Law of Peoples'. *Critical Inquiry* 20(1): 36–68.

United Nations. 2023. 'Meetings Coverage Security Council SC/15399 30 August 2023'. https://press.un.org/en/2023/sc15399.doc.htm

United Nations. 2024. 'General Assembly Debates Russia's Veto of DPR Korea Sanctions Panel'. UN News, 11 April 2024. https://news.un.org/en/story/2024/04/1148431

United Nations General Assembly. 1997. Human Rights and Unilateral Coercive Measures. A/RES/51/103. 12 December 1996.

United Nations General Assembly. 2023. Human Rights and Unilateral Coercive Measures. A/RES/76/161. 19 December 2023.

United Nations Security Council. 1950a. Resolution 82 (1950) / [adopted by the Security Council at its 473rd meeting], of 25 June 1950.

United Nations Security Council. 1950b. Resolution 83 (1950) / [adopted by the Security Council at its 474th meeting], of 27 June 1950.

United Nations Security Council. 1950c. Resolution 84 (1950) / [adopted by the Security Council at its 476th meeting], of 7 July 1950.

United Nations Security Council. 1999. UN Security Council Resolution 1267 (1999). Adopted by the Security Council at its 4051st meeting on 15 October 1999.

United Nations Security Council. 2001. UN Security Council Resolution 1373 (2001). Adopted by the Security Council at its 4385th meeting, on 28 September 2001.

US Department of State. 2024. Terrorist Designations and State Sponsors of Terrorism. Available at: https://www.state.gov/terrorist-designations-and-state-sponsors-of-terrorism/

Verdier, Pierre-Hugues. 2022. 'Sanctions Overcompliance: What, Why, and Does It Matter?' *North Carolina Journal of International Law* 48: 471–98.

White, Nigel, and Ademola Abass. 2006. 'Countermeasures and Sanctions'. In *International Law*, edited by Malcolm D. Evans. 2nd edition. Oxford University Press.

4

Contesting Unilateral Sanctions through International Law

Alexandra Hofer

Introduction

Legal criticisms of unilateral sanctions – which are restrictions that are implemented by states on the basis of their own legislative or executive powers, or adopted by international organisations against non-member states – are not new. Through the UN General Assembly (UNGA), states have denounced 'economic coercion' and 'unilateral coercive measures' for decades (Hofer 2017a; Hellquist, this volume). For example, since 1992 members of the UNGA have found the US economic embargo on Cuba is contrary to the Charter of the United Nations, the principles of sovereign equality, non-intervention and non-interference, and the freedom of trade and navigation (A/RES/47/19 1993; A/RES/78/7 2023; see also Porotsky 1995). The Cuba sanctions regime is an outlier since the UNGA rarely condemns a specific sanction regime. Instead, it regularly adopts annual and biannual resolutions condemning the adoption of 'unilateral coercive measures' – which are generally understood to be measures that have not been approved by the UN Security Council (UNSC) or that are not adopted by an organisation against a member state (Dupont 2021, 371) – that are contrary to international law and that have a negative impact on human rights and economic development. The UNGA is not the only UN organ before which grievances against unilateral sanctions are expressed. States such as Iran and Qatar have had recourse to the International Court of Justice (ICJ) to challenge restrictions imposed upon them. Another example is Venezuela's complaint to the International Criminal Court claiming that the sanctions implemented by the United States of America (US) and other states constitute crimes against humanity (Venezuela, Referral to the ICC). Venezuela also disputed the legality of the European Union's (EU) restrictive measures against it before the European Court of Justice (ECJ), claiming that the sanctions violated, amongst others, the customary principle of non-intervention (*Venezuela* v. *Council*).

These examples illustrate that legal grievances are frequently expressed against unilateral sanctions, most often those adopted by the US and the EU. It is noteworthy that not only the target of sanctions but also third states condemn these measures. The latter, while not themselves directly affected, find unilateral sanctions are contrary to the basic tenets of the international system. Such protests can be understood as contestation, a practice through which states have recourse to norms to challenge the adoption and implementation of unilateral sanctions. It is important to understand that sanctions are a practice through which senders seek to enforce norms (see Palestini, this volume). Sanctions constitute the imposition of a restriction or the withdrawal of a benefit, often in response to wrongdoing. Active senders, such as the US and the EU, frequently justify the imposition of unilateral sanctions as a response to a normative transgression. It is for this reason that these measures are said to serve a signalling, or stigmatising, function (Giumelli 2016). States and groups that contest unilateral sanctions rarely object to the norm that the senders are seeking to enforce; rather they dispute the legality and legitimacy of unilateral sanctions as a means of enforcement (Hofer 2020; Palestini and Villarroel 2024). Whereas sanctions are a tool through which states seek to enforce international norms, for many states these measures are unlawful or a poor enforcement tool. For instance, the voting record for the UNGA resolution on 'Principles of the Charter of the United Nations underlying a Comprehensive, Just and Lasting Peace in Ukraine' demonstrates that the vast majority of UNGA member states find Russia has violated international law in invading Ukraine. However, a sizeable number caution that unilateral sanctions are ill-suited to resolve the conflict and call for negotiations and diplomacy (see the discussions during the 11th Emergency Special Session, held on 22 and 23 February 2023; UN Doc A/ES-11/PV.17 to 19). In other words, countries do not dispute the importance of the prohibition to use force,[1] but do not agree that unilateral sanctions are an appropriate response. Consequently, contestation against sanctions is an objection to these measures as practices to uphold international norms.

Targets and third states alike express their opposition to unilateral sanctions by invoking legal rules, which can be found in either customary international law or treaty provisions. Reference to international law should be understood

[1] Even Russia does not undermine the validity of the norm and has articulated a legal justification under the right to self-defence (see Corten and Koutroulis 2023).

as a means of resistance against unilateral sanctions, and at the very least as a means to push for policy change and improve how sanctions are adopted. In the former scenario, one could speak of 'interpretative contestation' (see Introduction and the chapter by Weiner and Orchard in this volume), as states are disputing the meta-norms or organising principles that lie at the basis of the international system. These are 'norms that create expectations and obligations of norm enforcement and regulate how actors legitimately punish norm violations' (Erickson 2020, 99). When states seek to improve how sanctions are adopted they refer to human rights obligations and the law on state jurisdiction to argue that unilateral sanctions should comply with these norms, thereby engaging in a form of 'proactive contestation'. It should be noted that there is not a neat distinction between the two. Invoking human rights obligations can also signal that unilateral sanctions are unlawful. Viewing unilateral sanctions as a practice, this chapter discusses how, through international law, states dispute not only the procedure for how sanctions are adopted and how they are implemented (proactive contestation), but also these policy tools' compatibility with the international system (interpretative contestation).

As we will see, legal norms have the potential to shape the way sanctions are put into practice, and when sanctioning states ignore legal grievances this can lead to long-term consequences affecting their ability to sanction. It should not be assumed that contestation is (solely) politically motivated and that legal grievances are not well-founded. Under international law there is no general regime that regulates unilateral sanctions' adoption (A/48/535 1993, para. 2(a); Akande et al. 2021, 501). While there are stark divisions over unilateral sanctions' legality, not only amongst states but also amongst scholars (discussed in Subedi 2021), there is nonetheless one overarching rule: a sanction is unlawful if it breaches an obligation the sender owes the target. In essence, whether a sanction is legally permissible needs to be assessed on a case-by-case basis as it depends on the legal commitments between the sender and the target, or even between the sender and third actors that are not targeted but nonetheless affected. Without a judicial decision, it is typically difficult to ascertain whether a sanction is lawful or not (see generally Ruys 2017). Because of the many disagreements over the legality of unilateral sanctions, it is frequently found that unilateral sanctions are in a legal 'grey area' (Bogdanova 2022, 309; White 2021) and it has been argued that sanctions are 'one of the least developed areas of international law' (White and Abass 2018, 524; see also Hovell 2019). This plethora of legal uncertainties provides plenty of opportunities for contestation.

This chapter focuses on legal contestation through four areas of international law. Beginning with 'interpretative contestation', it reviews unilateral sanctions' compatibility with the multilateral system and the principle of non-intervention. It then turns to forms of 'proactive contestation', reviewing human rights issues and exploring the issue of sanctions applied extraterritorially and their compatibility with the law of jurisdiction. As noted, these categorisations are not 'strict' divisions as the forms of contestation can overlap.

Areas of Contestation under International Law: The International System's Ordering Principles

International law is frequently characterised as a 'horizontal' system because there is no centralised authority that has the power to adjudicate and issue penalties. Though there are international courts and tribunals, these are consent based; they only have jurisdiction when states expressly accept their authority. While the UNSC has the power to adopt binding decisions, it is a political body that is tasked with overseeing international peace and security, not enforcing international law (though they are not mutually exclusive). Within this system, state relations should follow certain principles. This points to multilateralism, which 'centers on the collectively agreed norms, rules, and principles that guide and govern interstate behaviour' (Hampson and Heinbecker 2011, 300). In many ways, the precise content of multilateralism is subject to disagreement. As argued elsewhere, disputes over unilateral sanctions provide insight on the norms that states believe hold the international community together (Hofer 2017b). While sanctions are often justified as a means to enforce international law, whether such tools are an appropriate enforcement mechanism is hotly debated and not universally accepted among states. This is clearly illustrated by the debate over how best to respond to Russia's aggression against Ukraine. While the EU, the US and aligning states are coordinating to impose costs on Russia, a sizeable number have refrained from doing so. Most of these countries prefer to remain neutral and do not consider that unilateral sanctions are an appropriate method to respond to the conflict.

States often engage in 'interpretative contestation' when they challenge the legality of unilateral sanctions, as illustrated by the grievances expressed by the Group of 77 (G77) and the Non-Aligned Movement (NAM). Through these two alliances the so-called Global South has long condemned 'unilateral coercive measures' for contravening the principles that lie at the basis of multilateralism, such as sovereign equality between states, the peaceful settlement of disputes and especially the principle of non-intervention (this latter norm is discussed further below).

For example, both the G77 and NAM convened in Kampala, Uganda in January 2024. The NAM's statement following the meeting claims that unilateral coercive measures are one of the reasons why international peace and security have not been met (NAM, Kampala Final Outcome Document, para. 11), and that these measures also undermine multilateralism (para. 34.2) as well as countries' development goals (para. 133). It also asserts the collective agreement to not recognise, adopt or implement, inter alia, extraterritorial or unilateral coercive measures that aim to pressure NAM countries in a manner that threatens their sovereignty and independence (para. 32.4), thus pointing to the principle of non-intervention, which prohibits coercive interference in a state's internal affairs.

The statement explicitly condemns the sanctions imposed upon Zimbabwe (para. 608), Syria (para. 690) and Venezuela (paras 747–8). Whereas the sanctioning states justify their restrictions as a response to human rights violations, NAM condemns these tools as contrary to international law, often pointing to their impact on targeted states' societies. Similarly, the G77's 2024 statement (para. 60) reaffirms the coalition's opposition to 'coercive economic measures, including unilateral sanctions'. From their perspective, these measures are incompatible with the principles of the UN Charter and should be eliminated. Furthermore, the G77 and NAM frequently resort to the UNGA to contest unilateral sanctions, which they view as unlawful because of their negative impact on, amongst others, human rights and the right to development, as well as the fact that they run counter to fundamental principles of international law, such as the sovereign equality of states and the peaceful settlement of disputes (Hofer 2017a).

It should be noted that states that contest the adoption of unilateral coercive measures are not always consistent in their own practice. Whereas China is one of the more vocal critics of unilateral sanctions, it has taken to adopting its own restrictions and has become vastly more active over the years. In order to remain consistent with its 'anti-sanctions' rhetoric, it does not refer to its own sanctions as such but frames them as counter-measures adopted in response to harms from unlawful US and EU sanctions (see Yu, this volume).

While interpretative contestation of unilateral sanctions on the basis of international law's ordering principles has not changed the EU and the US's commitment, it reflects the disagreement among states over what these principles are and how they should be interpreted. This is further illustrated by the discussion over the principle of non-intervention.

Unilateral Sanctions as Unlawful Intervention: An Unresolved Grey Area

The principle of non-intervention bars a state from coercively intervening in the internal affairs of another state, thus aiming to protect state sovereignty

(Kriener 2023). The ICJ has defined a 'prohibited intervention' as 'one bearing on matters in which each State is permitted, by the principle of State sovereignty, to decide freely. [. . .] Intervention is wrongful when it uses methods of coercion in regard to such choices, which must remain free ones' (ICJ 1986, para. 205). As a corollary to sovereign equality, it is one of the international system's most important norms; it is also one of its most 'potent and elusive' (Lowe 2007, 104). This is because the interpretation of its two constitutive elements ('coercive interference' and the 'internal affairs of a state') is, once again, subject to debate. In the context of unilateral sanctions, the more contentious point is whether these measures are 'coercive enough' to amount to an unlawful intervention. It is often questionable whether sanctions interfere in a state's internal affairs, particularly when they aim to enforce international law. For example, to the extent that the US and the EU have sanctioned Russia for its aggression against Ukraine, these measures would not breach the principle of non-intervention because aggression does not fall within a state's internal affairs. As such conduct is prohibited, a state is not 'free' to engage in it. States' non-alignment with the Russia sanctions can be explained by the fact that many states do not believe unilateral sanctions are an appropriate means to solve disputes. In this author's view, when states invoke the principle of non-intervention to challenge the legality of unilateral sanctions, they are engaging in 'interpretative contestation'. They are expressing the view that unilateral sanctions are inconsistent with one of the founding principles of international law. From their perspective, such restrictions constitute an abuse of economic power whereby a minority of states are trying to impose their version of international norms (Hofer 2017a). The issue that these states encounter is that their interpretation of the principle of non-intervention is not compatible with the dominant understanding. Here, the ICJ played a crucial role.

In 1986, Nicaragua attempted to argue before the ICJ that the US's reduction of economic aid, its 90 per cent reduction of sugar imports and its total trade embargo breached the principle. Without providing much insight, the Court found that the US sanctions did not amount to coercion under the meaning of the prohibition of non-intervention, and therefore it did not violate this norm. The wording of the judgment suggests that the Court believes coercion should be limited to the use of force, thereby excluding sanctions which are typically defined as 'non-forcible' (ICJ 1986, paras 205 and 245). It follows that for coercion to constitute an unlawful intervention it needs to reach a certain threshold. This means that certain types of influence are permissible. In general, scholarship in Europe and North America tends to agree that economic coercion, or other types of unilateral sanctions, is not prohibited under customary international law (Akande et al. 2021; Tzanakopoulos 2015). That said, there are a series of UNGA resolutions that suggest that unilateral sanctions against a state's political and economic independence are prohibited (Subedi 2021, 29). Yet, these resolutions carry little legal weight (Carter 2009, para. 8), are ambiguous (Jamnejad and Wood 2009, 351–5) or are only applicable to a specific sanction regime (Subedi 2021, 30). Kriener summarises this debate succinctly: 'unilateral sanctions can amount to coercion. However, there is no consensus in the international community on when they reach this threshold' (Kriener 2023, para. 35). Additionally, for unilateral sanctions to violate the principle of non-intervention, they must intervene in a state's internal affairs, meaning areas where it is at liberty to decide freely and where it has no international obligations. Sanctions that aim to enforce compliance with international law would not fall within the principle's scope. Whereas it is obvious in the case of Russia's aggression against Ukraine, other cases are less clear-cut.

There have been instances where states that typically condemn unilateral sanctions have imposed restrictions. For instance, in the context of alleged Israeli genocide against the Palestinian people, Malaysia sanctioned Israeli vessels (Al-Jazeera 2023). Under these measures, ships with the Israeli flag or destined to Israel would be prohibited from docking in Malaysia. Such a move is rare for a Southeast Asian country which typically avoids adopting unilateral sanctions (Matteo Dian in this volume). This could showcase that unilateral coercive measures are, under certain exceptional circumstances, justified, such as in the context of allegations of genocide. The unilateral sanctions against South Africa in the 1980s were considered permissible because they were a response to the apartheid regime. The Palestinian cause has led Muslim and Arab countries to adopt sanctions, such as the Arab League's oil embargo in 1973. In both instances, South African and Israeli policies were considered matters that are regulated under international law, and thus not within the scope of state's internal affairs (Hellquist 2014).

Despite the legal challenges in invoking the prohibition of intervention, countries under sanctions consistently engage in interpretative contestation and frame economic sanctions as a form of unlawful intervention. However, they generally cannot bring these grievances before international courts and tribunals as these have limited jurisdiction. The prohibition to intervene coercively in another state's internal affairs is a rule of customary international law and because adjudication is consent based in the international system few adjudicatory bodies have jurisdiction over this principle. Nicaragua's case against the US was possible as at the time the US recognised the Court's jurisdiction over rules of customary international law.[2] In cases where sanctions have been disputed, the countries concerned could only invoke applicable treaties, and these rarely include the prohibition of intervention.

For example, in 2018 Qatar instituted proceedings before the ICJ against the embargo the United Arab Emirates had imposed on it. It described these measures as a means through which the UAE was 'unlawfully seeking to pressure Qatar to allow it to interfere in Qatari sovereignty over its affairs' (ICJ 2018, para. 2). Yet its legal arguments were limited to breaches under the Convention on the Elimination of Racial Discrimination, the treaty that gave Qatar access to the ICJ. Similarly, Qatar filed a complaint against Saudi Arabia's measures before the World Trade Organization's dispute settlement mechanism. There again the sanctions were framed as 'a scheme of coercive economic measures against Qatar' (WTO 2020, para. 2.18), but Qatar had to limit its legal arguments to the Trade-Related Aspects of Intellectual Property Rights.

An exceptional case is *Venezuela* v. *Council* before the ECJ. After the Grand Chamber of the ECJ accepted that Venezuela had an interest in bringing a complaint against the restrictive measures the EU had imposed on it, Venezuela asked the General Court to find, amongst other claims, that the EU's sanctions '[constitute] interference in the internal affairs of' Venezuela (*Venezuela* v. *Council*, paras 83 and 86). Unfortunately, the bench demonstrated a very poor understanding of public international law, erroneously conflating the principle of non-intervention with counter-measures and consequently failed to provide legal guidance on the matter (para. 92).

A shift may be occurring in how sanctions are understood. There is a growing body of literature that sheds light on the destructive capacity of sanctions and the far-reaching effects they can have on society. Due to their impact, these measures are being described as a form of warfare, as opposed to an alternative to war (Bajoghli et al. 2024; Mulder 2022; Davis and Ness 2022). This is especially the case when it comes to sectoral sanctions, which when imposed can have the impact of a comprehensive embargo (Moret 2015 and 2022). Such measures can amount to economic and structural violence (Hofer 2023), and the literature is steadily acknowledging that crippling a state's economy may constitute a use of force (Schmitt 2013, 52). Only time will tell if continued contestation will lead to a general acceptance that economic coercion falls under the principle of non-intervention. After all, the acknowledgement of comprehensive sanctions' humanitarian costs led to a shift in sanctions practice

[2] After the ICJ's judgment, the US withdrew its optional clause declaration recognising the Court's jurisdiction.

in the early 2000s. The next section considers the extent to which contestation under human rights law has changed how unilateral sanctions are adopted and implemented.

The Impact of Sanctions on Human Rights: Work in Progress?

The devasting humanitarian consequences of the UN sanctions regime against Iraq in the 1990s, which had severe ramifications on the country's infrastructure and heavily restricted the population's access to basic necessities (Popal 2000), led to concerted efforts to make comprehensive sanctions a less blunt instrument, and pressure mounted on the Council to reform how it adopted and implemented this tool (Cortright and Lopez 2002; Wallensteen and Staibano 2005). It was frequently maintained that the UNSC sanctions regime against Iraq violated human rights, most notably the right to life under the ICCPR, the right to health and an adequate standard of living under the ICESCR, and especially harmed children's rights under the Convention for the Rights of the Child (CESR 1996, 36–7). These measures were also found to be indiscriminate and disproportionate (CESR 1996, 38–9). Similar claims were made concerning the UNSC sanctions against Haiti in the early 1990s (Gibbons 1999). While there was legal discussion as to whether the UNSC actually has human rights obligations, it was argued that restrictions should be solely directed against those actors who are responsible for the behaviour the Security Council wishes to change, thus sparing the civilian population. In essence, sanctions should be targeted against specific individuals, which led to the creation of 'targeted', or 'smart', sanctions in the early 2000s. This new practice gave rise to new human rights issues and objections against unilateral sanctions. At the outset, one could question whether states are engaged in interpretative contestation (unilateral sanctions are unlawful because they breach human rights norms) or proactive contestation (they are permitted, but their adoption and implementation should not undermine human rights). How this form of contestation should be interpreted is dependent on the actor contesting the measures and whether they view unilateral sanctions as consistent with the international system.

The right to property and the freedom of movement are necessarily restricted by asset freezes and travel bans respectively. A listed individual's other human rights, such as right to family, right to private life, the right to reputation, due process rights, and so on, may all be affected by targeted sanctions as well. These rights are not absolute and can be restricted if there is a legitimate aim, the measure is necessary and proportionate, and it is provided by law. In the case of the UNSC, individuals found themselves listed, barred from travel and access to their assets, without being aware of the cause and without having a means of redress. This led to a number of criticisms, particularly under the right to due process. Following the *Kadi* v. *Council* decisions of the European Court of Justice, which found that the listed individual's right to due process had been violated, European states applied pressure on the Security Council and the Office of the Ombudsperson was established in 2009. Individuals listed by the EU have recourse to the ECJ, but it is generally those who are able to afford the proceedings who appeal before the Court. The latter typically limits its review to whether enough evidence has been provided to justify the limits imposed on the individual. As Moiseienko (2021, 415) writes, the ECJ very often 'finds interferences with fundamental rights to be justifiable and proportionate in view of the objectives pursued' and the question is generally whether the rights of defence and the right of effective review have been respected.

There is a growing debate whether the adoption of unilateral sectoral sanctions can violate human rights of a broader civilian society. It is rather paradoxical that 'the law demands safeguarding individual rights but largely fails to provide recourse against comprehensive sanctions that affect the lives of millions' (Moiseienko 2021, 405). Sectoral sanctions can especially undermine rights enshrined under the International Convention on Economic, Social and Cultural Rights, particularly when they impede access to food and medicine, undermine the right to work and the proper functioning of education and health infrastructures. States frequently argue that unilateral coercive measures breach economic and social rights and that they negatively affect countries' economic development, grievances that they express through UNGA resolutions. The latest resolution at the time of writing (A/RES/78/202) frames unilateral sanctions as an obstacle to the fulfilment of the Universal Declaration of Human Rights and as an impediment to the right to development. The resolution recalls 'the right of everyone to a standard of living adequate for his or her health and well-being and his or her right to food, medical care and education and the necessary social services', suggesting that unilateral sanctions may obstruct their realisation.

Unilateral sanctions' impact triggered some states to create the mandate of the Special Rapporteur on Unilateral Coercive Measures and Human Rights. In her preliminary report on the impact of unilateral sanctions against Syria, Special Rapporteur Alena Douhan noted the severe impact these measures have had on the country's economy, provoking a stark increase in prices and pushing many households into poverty (Special Rapporteur Syria Report 2022). They have affected Syria's agricultural and food security, healthcare services and education. In discussing the humanitarian consequences of sanctions, one broader issue is the 'causality conundrum' (Prezas 2021, 398–401), meaning that it is difficult to know what the precise impact of sanctions is. If these measures are adopted in the context of an armed conflict, such as in Syria, or a steep economic crisis, such as in Venezuela, to what extent are they responsible for the deterioration of a civilian population's living conditions? In the case of Syria, while the country obviously went through a lengthy civil war, according to the Special Rapporteur the restrictions have 'prevented the Government from having resources to maintain and improve key infrastructure and for rebuilding and developing projects vital to the population's needs' (Special Rapporteur Syria Report 2022, 4). Some may contest the legitimacy of Alena Douhan's reporting; however, scholarship has noted that the measures against Syria are far-reaching and suggest a return to comprehensive sanctions (Moret 2014, 2021 and 2022; Portela 2016) and the Special Rapporteur is not alone in voicing concern about sanctions' humanitarian costs. Speaking on the US sanctions against Venezuela, the UN High Commissioner for Human Rights, Volker Türk, noted that: 'While the roots of Venezuela's economic crisis predate the imposition of economic sanctions [. . .] it is clear that the sectorial sanctions imposed since August 2017 have exacerbated the economic crisis and hindered human rights' (OHCHR 2023). In their report on the sanctions against Venezuela, Mark Weisbrot and Jeffrey Sachs find that the measures 'have inflicted, and increasingly inflict, very serious harm to human life and health [. . .] and that these sanctions would fit the definition of collective punishment of the civilian population as described in both the Geneva and Hague international conventions' (Weisbrot and Sachs 2019, 1). Additionally, it has been acknowledged by sanctions' practitioners that when sanctions aspire to weaken a state's economy this will automatically affect its society as a whole (Demarais 2022, 53–66; Nephew 2018, 11–12).

Despite these human rights issues, and notwithstanding the UNGA resolutions, it is often argued that sanctions' senders do not have extraterritorial human rights obligations; they would only have such obligations within their own territory and when they are exercising 'effective control' over territory and persons abroad (for example, in the case of an occupation). In other words, the sanctioning country is not responsible for ensuring the human rights of a civilian population abroad under sanctions (Akande et al. 2021, 505; Prezas 2021, 391–2; Marks 1999). While the Human Rights Council and the UNGA seem to argue that human rights apply extraterritorially, this has been described as an 'innovative' and 'far-reaching' reading (Prezas 2021, 392), but others find this reading consistent with the ICESCR (Djourabi-Asadabadi 2024) and it is generally acknowledged that unilateral sanctions should not deprive a population of its basic means of subsistence or lead to starvation (Akande et al. 2021, 507–8).

Regardless of the debate over legal obligations, sanction senders appear to agree that their measures should not harm the civilian population. The EU, for example, continuously states that 'sanctions should always be targeted in such a way as to minimise any adverse humanitarian effects or unintended consequences for non-targeted persons' (European Commission 2022). They also adopt humanitarian exemptions and derogations to mitigate sanctions' humanitarian impact, but the extent to which these are effective and whether they are properly implemented is debated (Giumelli and Molesini 2023).

An important development took place in December 2022, when the UNSC adopted Resolution 2664 providing a global 'humanitarian carve-out' on the implementation of asset freezes, establishing that humanitarian organisations are allowed to carry out designated activities without violating UNSC asset freezes (Kapoor et al. 2023; Seatzu and Vargiu 2023). The resolution's application was limited in time, but it was subsequently extended through Resolution 2761 in December 2024. The latter applied the humanitarian carve-out to all UN sanctions regimes indefinitely but limited its application to the ISIL/Al-Qaida regime to two years. While such resolutions are a welcome development and have inspired the EU, the US and United Kingdom to adopt similar exemptions (McGowan and Debarre 2024), they are limited to allowing humanitarian aid. It does not mean that sanctions senders will withhold from imposing far-reaching unilateral sectoral sanctions which, as discussed above, can impact a society as a whole (Seatzu and Vargiu 2023, 8; McGowan and Debarre 2024). One may caution that not addressing the humanitarian consequences of sanctions (regardless of whether there is a legal obligation to do so) would come at a cost for senders, who frequently justify these tools as a means to protect and promote human rights. If they do not take the consequences of their actions on the promotion and protection of human rights seriously, then their own measures appear unfair and illegitimate, fuelling contestation.

The Extraterritorial Application of Sanctions: From Contestation to Reconciliation?

In comparison to multilateral sanctions that are adopted by an international organisation and implemented by and against its member states, the reach of unilateral sanctions is limited. The issue for sanction senders is that targeted states will compensate for the restrictions imposed on them by turning to third countries, thus rendering the 'pain' imposed by the sanctions ineffective. To improve their restrictions' reach and ensure the target still suffers the costs, the US often imposes sanctions on third countries that engage in trade with a state that it has targeted by applying secondary sanctions. In doing so, it essentially 'limit[s] third states' sovereignty to freely conduct their external economic relations with other states' (Ruys and Ryngaert 2020, 4 and 7; see also Kerbrat 2021, 166–8). Ruys and Ryngaert argue that:

> The incentive to impose secondary sanctions arises where primary sanctions fail to effect the envisaged behavioural change in the target state. If third states are allowed to maintain their economic relations with the target state, and economic operators from the sanctioning state are not, the former could supplant the presence of the latter [. . .], thereby undermining primary sanctions (Ruys and Ryngaert 2020, 8)

One of the means through which the US ensures its sanctions cannot be circumvented is by utilising its 'exorbitant privilege' as the global currency holder. It does so by denying targets access to the dollar, which is essential for financial transactions and trade, and enables the US to impose far-reaching costs unilaterally (Zoffer 2019). The US has also applied its restrictions extraterritorially and imposed stringent fines on breaches. In some instances, it has gone as far as issuing arrest warrants against, and even arresting, persons engaging in transactions outside of US jurisdiction. These measures are extremely controversial, and their legality has been hotly contested, particularly under the customary rules of jurisdiction. In such cases, US secondary sanctions target 'the conduct of third state actors occurring on third states' territory where that conduct is lawful' (Terry 2022, 371), thereby leading to claims of unlawful extraterritorial sanctions. Here again, contestation can be understood as either 'interpretative' or 'proactive'. The EU often challenges such measures' legality, seeking to improve the way in which unilateral sanctions are adopted. To the extent that the argument is that the extraterritorial application of sanctions is incompatible with present international law, this could be seen as 'interpretative contestation'.

In Ruys and Ryngaert's view, as long as secondary sanctions remain limited to US jurisdiction, they do not pose an issue under the laws of jurisdiction. This would be the case of access restrictions, which 'create obligations for US persons, and regulate activities that occur in the US and involve US persons as counterparties' (Ruys and Ryngaert 2020, 12; see also Schmidt 2022, 67). If non-US persons are affected, such measures constitute the denial of privileges, which is legally permissible (Ruys and Ryngaert 2020, 12; for a contrary view see Rodriguez Silvestre 2024). However, the imposition of fines, which is the application of a state's 'prescriptive jurisdiction', and the arrest of third parties are more controversial, as these 'are more onerous and intrusive enforcement measures that go beyond a denial of access and may result in a forfeiture of assets and even imprisonment' (Ruys and Ryngaert 2020, 17). For prescriptive jurisdiction to be exercised there needs to be a personal or territorial link to the US and the conduct it wishes to regulate (Kerbrat 2021, 167; Terry 2022, 372). The issue here is that the connection is generally too weak for the US to justify the exercise of its prescriptive jurisdiction. In other words, these restrictions are contested because they apply to individuals or companies that fall outside of the US's jurisdiction (Terry 2022, 371–3).

States' universal condemnation of US extraterritorial application of sanctions demonstrates that these measures are not permitted under customary international law (Terry 2022, 374–5; Schmidt 2022, 56). The EU was historically a rather vocal objector to this US practice. In the 1980s, in response to the USSR's intervention in Poland, the US attempted to prevent the construction of a gas pipeline from Siberia to western Europe through the imposition of sanctions on foreign companies owned or controlled by US nationals or residents, which in the US's view was subject to its jurisdiction (Kerbrat 2021, 170). This resulted in European subsidiaries of US companies having to suspend their participation in the pipeline's construction, which led the European Community member states to protest vehemently (Kerbrat 2021, 170). Whereas US sanctions apply to its nationals, this does not include foreign subsidiaries of national companies. The US backed off, but another dispute between the US and the EU arose in the context of the Helms Burton Act, also known as the LIBERTAD Act. In response, the EU adopted a 'Blocking Statute' to protect European economic operators from being subjected to US sanctions when they engage in international trade or financial exchanges with a state that is under US sanctions, and threatened to take Washington before the WTO. This could be illustrative of 'interpretative contestation' against the extraterritorial application of sanctions, and 'proactive contestation' to improve how unilateral sanctions are implemented. The US acquiesced and agreed to provide a waiver for European companies, but the issue returned with a vengeance when the US sought to reimpose restrictions on Iran in 2018 (Kerbrat 2021; Schmidt 2022). In reaction, the EU's Blocking Statute was updated in 2018 and revised again in 2021. However, the European Union has failed to provide a solution as in practice it places European firms between a 'rock and a hard place', making them choose between complying with US sanctions or with the EU law (Ruys and Ryngaert 2020, 86). As Terry writes, the problem with the Blocking Statute is that 'instead of [. . .] directly confronting the United States' unlawful conduct, the burden of taking on the United States is shifted to the EU persons concerned' (Terry 2022, 376). When President Trump imposed 'maximum pressure' against Iran, the EU adopted a Special Purpose Vehicle, which was a means through which the EU wanted to ensure trade with Iran. However, this tool was ineffective (Terry 2022, 377–8). In December 2023, the EU Commission adopted the 'anti-coercion instrument' (Regulation (EU) 2023/2675), which is intended to protect the EU from coercive policies, including the US's extraterritorial application of sanctions (Ruys and Rodriguez Silvestre 2023, 662; Portela 2021, 4).

The EU's contestation was initially successful as it caused the US to recalibrate its sanctioning approach; however, it seems to have progressively given in. Whereas European states were outspoken in the 1980s, its reaction throughout the 2010s has been rather tepid. Portela (2021, 4) finds that: 'Overall, European responses are manifestly insufficient, both in terms of their efficacy in mitigating the extraterritorial effects of US bans and the message of EU cohesion they convey to third actors' (see also Terry 2022, 378). Kerbrat suggests that the EU's measured response is because its own legislation is steadily stretching the limits of jurisdiction and it does not want to be accused of breaching its own standards (Kerbrat 2021, 174–5 and 183). This is especially perceptible in the context of its restrictive measures against Russia, where the EU has gradually engaged in adopting its own extraterritorial sanctions, albeit not acknowledging this explicitly (Rhades 2023).

Failing to be mindful of states' legal grievances may come at a high price for the US (Demarais 2022), which the EU should be wary of lest it suffers the same consequences. For example, there have been reports of states attempting to step away from the US dollar as they engage in international trade, and we are gradually witnessing a 'multipolarity of currencies' (Giustra 2023). In 2021, Portela wrote that: 'Ironically, unilateral US sanctions have already enhanced the popularity of the euro as a currency for energy trade as companies in countries under sanctions have moved to denominate their export contracts in euro to de-link their business from the US-centred financial system' (Portela 2021). With the EU engaging in its own extraterritorial sanctions its currency may become less attractive. It appears BRICS is seeking to propose an alternative world order, notably by providing an alternative currency to challenge the US dollar's hegemony. This development has gone hand in hand with the use of aggressive financial sanctions, as countries such as Russia and Iran are also keen to step away from the dollar. It was reported that Russia's partial exclusion from SWIFT in 2022 set off alarm bells, incentivising countries to look for alternatives where financial transactions are not dependent on the US dollar (Tan 2023). At the BRICS summit in Russia in October 2024, Vladimir Putin took the opportunity to announce a new BRICS payment system, BRICS Pay (Corbin 2024). During a press conference, he raised the unfairness of the current global financial system, expressing grievance against the US and EU's abuse of 'their exclusive positions in global finance, in terms of both the dollar and the euro' (President of Russia 2024). Though not explicitly mentioned, the extraterritorial application of sanctions could fit within these grievances. While the US and the EU have sought to estrange Russia through far-reaching restrictions, the BRICS summit demonstrates that many other countries are not interested in taking part. The attempt to increase pressure on third countries through the extraterritorial application of unilateral sanctions may come at a heavy cost for the senders, undermining their ability to impose restrictions altogether as states become motivated to pursue de-dollarisation (McDowell 2023).

The discussion on the extraterritorial application of sanctions demonstrates that persistence pays off. Whereas there is widespread agreement that US claims of extraterritorial application of its unilateral sanctions are unlawful, successive US administrations have stayed the course and gradually wore down EU opposition, with the EU eventually caving in and adopting its own extensive measures. That said, they are still considered unlawful and if contestation is not taken seriously this could lead to outcomes that go beyond challenging their legality. States are progressively trying to restructure their economic and financial relations so as to escape the long arm of US sanctions. Although this may be a slow process, if it is successful, it will undercut a prominent US foreign policy tool. As acknowledged by the former Secretary of the US Treasury, Janet Yellen: 'There is a risk, when we use financial sanctions that are linked to the role of the dollar, that, over time, it could undermine the hegemony of the dollar' (Fareed 2023).

Conclusion

This chapter has demonstrated that states invoke international law to contest unilateral sanctions, employing legal norms for interpretative and proactive contestation. If we consider the most invoked norms against unilateral sanctions, law appears to have had the most impact on sanctions' human rights consequences, but even there, legal norms have their limits. In general, there appears to be a stalemate: either uncertainty remains, or senders remain committed to these instruments even when they breach legal principles. Law is not entirely powerless as it has had an influence in some cases, but overall one is tempted to conclude that in the area of unilateral sanctions, 'might makes right'.

Sanctioners should nonetheless be wary. The overzealous imposition of restrictions may encourage third states to rearrange their financial and trade relations in a manner that enables them to shield themselves from sanction effects, which would have long-standing consequences for senders. It also encourages states to engage in their own economic statecraft.

References

A/48/535. 1993. Note by the UN Secretary General, Economic Measures as a Means of Political and Economic Coercion against Developing Countries.

A/RES/47/19. 1993. 'Necessity of Ending the Economic, Commercial and Financial Embargo Imposed by the United States of America against Cuba'. Adopted by the UNGA, 17 March.

A/RES/78/7. 2023. 'Necessity of Ending the Economic, Commercial and Financial Embargo Imposed by the United States of America against Cuba'. Adopted by the UNGA, 2 November, by 185 votes, to 2 against (US, Israel) and 2 abstentions (Brazil, Ukraine). https://news.un.org/en/story/2023/11/1143112

A/RES/78/202. 2023. 'Human Rights and Unilateral Coercive Measures', adopted by the General Assembly on 19 December.

Akande, Dapo, Payam Akhavan and Eirik Bjorge. 2021. 'Economic Sanctions, International Law, and Crimes Against Humanity: Venezuela's ICC Referral'. *American Journal of International Law* 115(3): 493–512.

Al-Jazeera. 2023. 'Malaysia Bans Israel-Flagged Ships from Its Ports in Response to Gaza War'. 20 December. https://www.aljazeera.com/news/2023/12/20/malaysia-bans-israeli-affiliated-and-israel-bound-ships-from-its-ports

Bajoghli, Narges, Vali Nasr, Djavad Salehi-Isfahani and Ali Vaez. 2024. *How Sanctions Work: Iran and the Impact of Economic Warfare*. Stanford University Press.

Bogdanova, Irina. 2022. *Unilateral Sanctions in International Law and the Enforcement of Human Rights: The Impact of the Principle of Common Concern of Humankind*. Brill Nijhoff.

Carter, Barry E. 2009. 'Economic Coercion'. *Max Planck Encyclopedia of Public International Law*. https://opil.ouplaw.com/display/10.1093/law:epil/9780199231690/law-9780199231690-e1518

CESR (Center for Economic and Social Rights). 1996. 'Unsanctioned Suffering: A Human Rights Assessment of United Nations Sanctions on Iraq'. https://www.cesr.org/sites/default/files/Unsanctioned%20Suffering%201996.pdf

Corbin, Michael. 2024. 'BRICS Signals Shift from US Dominated Financial System'. *Responsible Statecraft*, 23 October. https://responsiblestatecraft.org/brics-new-world-order/

Corten, Olivier and Vaios Koutroulis. 2023. 'The 2022 Russian Intervention in Ukraine: What Is Its Impact on the Interpretation of *Jus Contra Bellum*?' *Leiden Journal of International Law* 36(4): 997–1022.

Cortright, David, and George Lopez, eds. 2002. *Smart Sanctions*. Rowman and Littlefield.

Davis, Stuart, and Immanuel Ness, eds. 2022. *Sanctions as War: Anti- Imperialist Perspectives on American Geo-Economic Strategy*. Brill Nijhoff.

Demarais, Agathe. 2022. *Backfire: How Sanctions Reshape the World Against U.S. Interests*. Columbia University Press.

Djourabi-Asadabadi, Tabasom. 2024. 'Unilateral Sanctions and Extraterritorial Obligations in the Area of Economic, Social and Cultural Rights'. In *International Sanctions in Practice: An Interdisciplinary Perspective*, edited by Antonio Bultrini, Francesco Giumelli, Clara Portela and Mirko Sossai. Routledge.

Dupont, Pierre-Emmanuel. 2021. 'Unilateral Sanctions as Unilateral Coercive Measures: Discussing Coercion at the UN Level'. In *Research Handbook on Unilateral and Extraterritorial Sanctions*, edited by Charlotte Beaucillon. Edward Elgar Publishing.

Erickson, Jennifer L. 2020. 'Punishing the Violators? Arms Embargoes and Economic Sanctions as Tools of Norm Enforcement'. *Review of International Studies* 46(1): 96–120.

European Commission. 2022. 'Frequently Asked Questions Restrictive Measures (Sanctions)', 26 February. https://ec.europa.eu/commission/presscorner/detail/en/qanda_22_1401

Fareed, Zakaria. 2023. 'Zakaria Fareed Interview with US Treasury Secretary Janet Yellen'. *CNN*, 16 April. https://www.youtube.com/watch?v=bwgHwzhfoXo&t=246s

G77. 2014. Declaration of the Summit of Heads of State and Government of the Group of 77, 'For a New World Order for Living Well', Annex to UN Doc A/68/948, July 7.

G77. 2024. 'Third Summit Outcome Document'. Kampala, Uganda, 21–2 January. https://www.g77.org/doc/3southsummit_outcome.htm

Gibbons, Elizabeth D. 1999. *Sanctions in Haiti: Human Rights and Democracy under Assault*. Praeger.

Giumelli, Francesco. 2016. 'The Purposes of Targeted Sanctions'. In *Targeted Sanctions: The Impacts and Effectiveness of United Nations Action*, edited by Thomas J. Biersteker, Sue E. Eckhart and Marcos Tourinho. Cambridge University Press.

Giumelli, Francesco, and Aurora Molesini. 2023. 'Paper: Forging the Chain of European Humanitarian Action: A Study on the Implementation of Humanitarian Exceptions to Sanctions in the European Union'. Presented at the 7th World Conference on Humanitarian Studies (IHSA), 5–7 November 2023 in Dhaka, Bangladesh.

Giustra, Frank. 2023. 'De-dollarization: Not a Matter of If, but When'. *Responsible Statecraft*, 3 May. https://responsiblestatecraft.org/2023/05/03/de-dollarization-not-a-matter-of-if-but-when/?highlight=BRICS

Hampson, Fen Osler, and Paul Heinbecker. 2011. 'The 'New' Multilateralism of the Twenty-First Century'. *Global Governance* 17: 299–310.

Hellquist, Elin. 2014. 'Regional Organizations and Sanctions against Members Explaining the Different Trajectories of the African Union, the League of Arab States, and the Association of Southeast Asian Nations'. KFG Working Paper Series, No. 59, Kolleg Forschergruppe (KFG), The Transformative Power of Europe, Freie Universität Berlin.

Hofer, Alexandra. 2017a. 'The Developed/Developing Divide on Unilateral Coercive Measures: Legitimate Enforcement or Illegitimate Intervention?' *Chinese Journal of International Law* 16(2): 175–214.

Hofer, Alexandra. 2017b. 'Negotiating International Public Policy through the Adoption and Contestation of Sanctions'. *Revue Belge de Droit International* 2: 440–73.

Hofer, Alexandra. 2020. 'Creating and Contesting Hierarchy: The Punitive Effect of Sanctions in a Horizontal System'. *Revista CIDOB d'Afers Internacionals* 125: 15–37.

Hofer, Alexandra. 2023. 'Violence at a Distance: Correcting International Law's Short-Sighted Vision of Economic Coercion'. In *Routledge Handbook on the Political Economy of Sanctions*, edited by Knesia Kirkham. Routledge.

Hovell, Devika. 2019. 'Unfinished Business of International Law: The Questionable Legality of Autonomous Sanctions'. *AJIL Unbound* 113: 140–6.

ICJ. 1986. *Military and Paramilitary Activities in and against Nicaragua (Nicaragua v. United States of America)*, Merits, Judgment.

ICJ. 2018. *Application of the International Convention on the Elimination of All Forms of Racial Discrimination (Qatar v. United Arab Emirates)*, Application Instituting Proceedings, 11 June.

International Law Commission. 2001. 'Articles on State Responsibility for International Wrongful Acts', see Annex to UN General Assembly Resolution 56/83 'Responsibility of States for Internationally Wrongful Acts' (28 January 2002).

Jamnejad, Maziar, and Michael Wood. 2009. 'The Principle of Non-Intervention'. *Leiden Journal of International Law* 22: 345–81.

Kapoor, Radhika, Dustin A. Lewis and Naz A. Modirzadeh. 2023. 'An Interpretative Note for UN Member States on Security Council Resolution 2664'. Published online: https://pilac.law.harvard.edu

Kerbrat, Yann. 2021. 'Unilateral/Extraterritorial Sanctions as a Challenge to the Theory of Jurisdiction'. In *Research Handbook on Unilateral and*

Extraterritorial Sanctions, edited by Charlotte Beaucillon. Edward Elgar Publishing.

Kriener, Florien. 2023. 'Intervention, Prohibition of'. *Max Planck Encyclopedia of Public International Law*. https://opil.ouplaw.com/home/MPIL

Lowe, Vaughan. 2007. *International Law*. Oxford University Press.

McDowell, Daniel. 2023. *Bucking the Buck: US Financial Sanctions and the International Backlash against the Dollar*. Oxford University Press.

McGowan, Lauren, and Alice Debarre. 2024. 'An Indefinite Humanitarian Carve-out for the ISIL/al-Qaida UN Sanctions Regime: What it Means and What Comes Next' *The Global Observatory*, 17 December. https://theglobalobservatory.org/2024/12/resolution2761-indefinite-humanitarian-carveout-un-sanctions-regime/

Marks, Stephen R. 1999. 'Economic Sanctions as Human Rights Violations: Reconciling Political and Public Health Imperatives'. *American Journal of Public Health* 89(10): 1509–13.

Moiseienko, Anton. 2021. 'Due Process and Unilateral Targeted Sanctions'. In *Research Handbook on Unilateral and Extraterritorial Sanctions*, edited by Charlotte Beaucillon. Edward Elgar Publishing.

Moret, Erica. 2014. 'Humanitarian Impacts of Economic Sanctions on Iran and Syria'. *European Security* 24(1): 120–40.

Moret, Erica. 2021. 'A Lifeline under Threat? Syrian Household Remittances in Light of Sanctions, Financial Sector De-risking, COVID-19, and Regional Developments'. Economic and Social Commission for Western Asia. https://nafs.unescwa.org/index.php/resource/publications/lifeline-under-threat-syrian-household-remittances-light-sanctions-financial

Moret, Erica. 2022. 'More Civilian Pain Than Political Gain (Again?). The Demise of Targeted Sanctions and Associated Humanitarian Impacts'. In *Multilateral Sanctions Revisited: Lessons Learned from Margaret Doxey*, edited by Andrea Charron and Clara Portela. McGill Queen's University Press.

Mulder, Nicolas. 2022. *The Economic Weapon: The Rise of Sanctions as a Tool of Modern War*. Yale University Press.

NAM. 2024. Kampala Final Outcome Document. Available online: https://nam.go.ug/sites/default/files/2024-02/Kampala%20Final%20Outcome%20Document.pdf

NAM. 2024. Kampala Declaration. Available online: https://nam.go.ug/sites/default/files/2024-02/Kampala%20Declaration.pdf

Nephew, Richard. 2018. *The Art of Sanctions: A View from the Field*. Columbia University Press.

OHCHR. 2023. Statements and Speeches: 'UN High Commissioner for Human Rights Volker Türk Concludes Official Mission to Venezuela'.

https://www.ohchr.org/en/statements-and-speeches/2023/01/un-high-commissioner-human-rights-volker-turk-concludes-official

Palestini, Stefano, and Yancy Villarroel. 2024. '"What gives you the right?' Foreign Policymakers' Perceptions of the Legitimacy of Sanctions against Democratic Breakdown in Venezuela (2014–2019)'. *Cambridge Review of International Affairs* 37(5): 665–89.

Popal, G. R. 2000. 'Impact of Sanctions on the Population of Iraq'. *Eastern Mediterranean Health Journal* 6(4): 791–5.

Porotsky, Richard D. 1995. 'Economic Coercion and the General Assembly: A Post-Cold War Assessment of the Legality and Utility of the Thirty-Five-Year-Old Embargo against Cuba'. *Vanderbilt Journal of Transnational Law* 28: 901–58.

Portela, Clara. 2016. 'Are European Union Sanctions "Targeted"?' *Cambridge Review of International Affairs* 29(3): 912–29.

Portela, Clara. 2021. 'Countering the Extraterritorial Effects of US Sanctions'. European Union Institute for Security Studies, Brief 22.

President of Russia. 2024. 'News Conference following 16th BRICS Summit'. Official website of the Kremlin, 24 October. http://www.en.kremlin.ru/events/president/news/75385

Prezas, Ioannis. 2021. 'From Targeted States to Affected Populations: Exploring Accountability for the Negative Impact of Comprehensive Unilateral Sanctions on Human Rights'. In *Research Handbook on Unilateral and Extraterritorial Sanctions*, edited by Charlotte Beaucillon. Edward Elgar Publishing.

Regulation (EU) 2023/2675 of the European Parliament and of the Council of 22 November 2023 on the Protection of the Union and Its Member States from Economic Coercion by Third Countries.

Rhades, Moritz. 2023. 'Extraordinary, Extraterritorially A New Category of EU-Sanctions Against Russia?' *Voelkerrechts*, 13 December. https://voelkerrechtsblog.org/extraordinary-extraterritorially/

Rodriguez Silvestre, Felipe. 2024. 'The Jurisdictional Intricacies of Secondary Sanctions Consisting of Access Restrictions'. In *International Sanctions in Practice: An Interdisciplinary Perspective*, edited by Antonio Bultrini, Francesco Giumelli, Clara Portela and Mirko Sossai. Routledge.

Ruys, Tom. 2017. 'Sanctions, Retorsions and Countermeasures: Concepts and International Legal Framework'. In *Research Handbook on UN Sanctions and International Law*, edited by Larissa van den Herik. Edward Elgar Publishing.

Ruys, Tom, and Cedric Ryngaert. 2020. 'Secondary Sanctions: A Weapon out of Control? The International Legality of, and European Responses to, US Secondary Sanctions'. *British Yearbook of International Law*: 1–116.

Ruys, Toms, and Rodriguez Silvestre, Felipe. 2023. 'Economic Statecraft: A Closer Look Inside the European Union's Expanding Toolbox'. *Georgia Journal of International and Comparative Law* 51(3): 647–70.

Schmidt, Julia. 2022. 'The Legality of Unilateral Extra-territorial Sanctions under International Law'. *Journal of Conflict and Security Law* 27(1): 53–81.

Schmitt, Michael N. 2013. *Tallinn Manual on the International Law Applicable to Cyber Warfare: Prepared by the International Group of Experts at the Invitation of the NATO Cooperative Cyber Defence Centre of Excellence*. Cambridge University Press.

Seatzu, Francesco, and Paolo Vargiu. 2023. 'Is the UNSC Resolution No. 2664 (2022) on Humanitarian Exemption a Paradigm Shift for Sanction Regimes?' *Peace & Security – Paix et Sécurité Internationales* 11: 1–22.

Special Rapporteur Syria Report. 2022. 'Lift "Suffocating" Unilateral Sanctions against Syrians, Urges UN Human Rights Expert'. UN News, 10 November. https://news.un.org/en/story/2022/11/1130427

Subedi, Surya P. 2021. 'The Status of Unilateral Sanctions under International Law'. In *Unilateral Sanctions in International Law*, edited by Surya Subedi. Hart Publishing.

Tan, Huileng. 2023. '3 reasons countries around the world want to break up with the dollar'. *Business Insider*, 27 December. https://markets.businessinsider.com/news/commodities/de-dollarization-reasons-why-countries-move-away-us-dollar-2023-7

Terry, Patrick C. R. 2022. 'Secondary Sanctions: Why the US Approach Is Unlawful and the EU's Response Is Ineffective'. *Global Trade and Customs Journal* 17(9): 370–80.

Tzanakopoulos, Antonios. 2015. 'The Right to Be Free from Economic Coercion'. *Cambridge International Law Journal* 4(3): 616–33.

UN Doc A/ES-11/PV.17. General Assembly official records, 11th emergency special session: 17th plenary meeting, Wednesday, 22 February 2023, New York.

UN Doc A/ES-11/PV.18. General Assembly official records, 11th emergency special session: 18th plenary meeting, Wednesday, 23 February 2023, New York.

UN Doc A/ES-11/PV.19. General Assembly official records, 11th emergency special session: 19th plenary meeting, Wednesday, 23 February 2023, New York.

Venezuela, Referral to the ICC, 12 February 2020. Available online (in Spanish): https://www.icc-cpi.int/sites/default/files/itemsDocuments/200212-venezuela-referral.pdf

Venezuela v. *Council of the European Union*. 2023. Judgment of the General Court, 13 September. Case n: T-65/18 RENV.

Wallensteen, Peter, and Carina Staibano, eds. 2005 *International Sanctions: Between War and Words in the International System*. Routledge.

Weisbrot, Mark, and Jeffrey Sachs. 2019. 'Economic Sanctions as Collective Punishment: The Case of Venezuela'. Centre for Economic and Policy Research, April. https://cepr.net/images/stories/reports/venezuela-sanctions-2019-04.pdf

White, Nigel D. 2021. 'Shades of Grey: Autonomous Sanctions in the International Legal Order'. In *Unilateral Sanctions in International Law*, edited by Surya P. Subedi. Hart Publishing.

White, Nigel, and Ademola Abass. 2018. 'Countermeasures and Sanctions'. In *International Law*, edited by Malcolm D. Evans. 5th edition. Oxford University Press.

WTO, 2020. 'Saudi Arabia, Measures Concerning the Protection of Intellectual Property Rights'. Report of the Panel, 16 June.

Zoffer, Joshua P. 2019. 'The Dollar and the United States' Exorbitant Power to Sanction'. *AJIL Unbound* 113: 152–6.

5

Blowing Hot against Sanctions: How African Leaders Seek to Redefine International Politics

John Agbonifo

Introduction

On 2 March 2022, the UN General Assembly voted on the Resolution A/RES/ES-11/1, titled 'Aggression against Ukraine', to condemn Russia's invasion of Ukraine. Although the resolution received widespread support, African countries were divided in their votes. Out of the fifty-four African countries represented, just twenty-eight voted in favour of the resolution, or just over 51 per cent vote for the resolution as against 81.29 per cent of non-African votes in favour of the resolution. Again, seventeen out of the thirty-five countries that voted to abstain were African countries, including Algeria, Angola and South Africa. Eight African countries did not vote, and one, Eritrea, voted against the resolution. Africa's divided vote on the UN resolution is the most recent episode in the tapestry of sanctions norms contestation by African leaders. The resolution was prepared by the European Union, Ukraine and other countries, and deplored in very strong terms Russia's aggression against Ukraine in violation of the Charter of the UN. The text was approved by 141 countries. Only five UN member states voted against it: Russia, Belarus, DPRK (North Korea), Eritrea and Syria.

Africa's divided vote and its rationalisations echo not only deliberate contestation of sanctions norms but an alternative understanding of sanctions here described as the 'communitarian' approach to sanctions. South African President Cyril Ramaphosa explained that the failure to achieve united African support for the resolution was because the resolution 'did not foreground the call for meaningful engagement' between the parties, and that it 'does not provide the encouragement and international backing that the parties need to continue with their efforts' (White and Holz 2022). Senegalese President

Macky Sall emphasised that Africans 'do not want to be aligned on this conflict, very clearly, we want peace. Even though we condemn the invasion, we're working for a de-escalation, we're working for a ceasefire, for dialogue . . . that is the African position' (Dettmer 2022). Similarly, Zimbabwe held that the resolution 'poured more fuel to the fire, thus further complicating the situation' (ibid.). The leaders underline features of, and express preference for, communitarian sanctions, with elements of 'meaningful engagement', 'de-escalation' and peace, dialogue and on-going international encouragement for peaceful resolution. This underscores fundamental contestation over the primary purpose of sanctions, and how and when to use them.

The African communitarian approach rests on the logic that an individual's violation of group norms does not deny the violator their inherent connectedness to the group. It reflects inherent connectedness, inclusion, dialogue and reconciliation, which bode well with the African Union (AU)'s emphasis on peace and security as the primary purpose of its sanctions policy. Emphasising connectedness and reconciliation, the concept of communitarian sanctions dovetails with the logic of the African parable: 'flog an erring child with the right hand, and with the left hand draw the child closer'. A related parable observes that 'you do not flog a child and, at the same time, forbid the child from crying'. This worldview recognises that a sanctioned party would 'cry' or react to the pains of sanctions. The comforting and healing process is initiated when the 'left' hand draws the sanctioned party closer for collective resolution of the situation that instigated the sanctions. Thus, there is a need to unpack what happens in the 'sick room', as sanctions might isolate or engage with the 'sick' in the 'sick room' (Hellquist 2020). Western sanctions are perceived as isolating and humiliating in their effect. Placed under sanctions, or in the 'sick room', the 'sick' is expected to heal itself, renounce its sanctioned behaviour or risk the tightening of the sanctions.

> AU sanctions build on a special chemistry combining punishment and reconciliation. Sanctions are sharp but friendly interventions carried out by the community in its constituency. Truly resolution-oriented, AU sanctions prioritise a return to normality over full compliance (Hellquist 2020, 464)

Yet, the literature has given scant attention to whether there is anything unique about how African leaders understand sanctions. Some have described the coexistence of UN, regional and unilateral sanctions as indicative of collaboration, legitimacy and usefulness of sanctions as foreign policy measure (Charron and Portela 2015; Charron and Portela 2016, 101). Ignoring possibilities of differences or competition in the use of sanctions, Charron and Portela

(2015) conclude that only a small number of sanctions imposed on African targets are unilateral (see Hellquist 2020). Yet, that small number of unilateral sanctions underscores differences, rather than cooperation or collaboration, and provides the rationale for evolving pattern of contestation of sanctions' norms. Contestation of sanctions norms subject the latter to processes of interpretation, appropriation, resistance and change (Introduction, this volume). Contestations of Western sanctions can undermine sanctions norms, lead to violation of sanctions norms and potentially result in political conflict (Orchard and Wiener, this volume). The outcome imperils the capacity of the UNSC to achieve a united and decisive international response to threats to international peace and security (Palestini, this volume).

This chapter investigates African leaders' contestation of Western sanctions, outlining an African approach to sanctions that may be described as communitarian. By Western sanctions, we refer to sanctions initiated and implemented by the US, UK or EU member states without the support of the AU or authorisation of the UNSC. Unilateral sanctions are sanctions imposed, usually, by the US and/or UK and France on non-European states without UN authorisation, to coerce a change in the behaviour of the target. African states consistently support UN resolutions condemning unilateral coercive measures (UNGA 2018) and emphasise the non-negotiability of 'African unity and solidarity' in the context of externally induced, or its own, sanctions. The rest of the chapter is divided into six sections. The following section briefly reviews the theory on sanctions norms' legitimacy and contestation. The second section examines the literature on why African leaders contest unilateral sanctions after which we outline in section three Africa's communitarian approach to sanctions. Section four gives credence to the communitarian approach through examination of two cases of AU sanctions. Section five briefly reflects on sanctions on Russia, while section six is the conclusion.

Sanctions and Contestations

Contestation may be seen as 'any differences in the understanding of norms, no matter what the source' (Stimmer and Wisken 2019, 3). The implementation of norms can create a space for interpretation and contestation of the norm by stakeholders, resulting in different understanding of the norm (Betts and Orchard 2014). Orchard and Wiener (this volume) elaborate three distinct types of contestations. First, reactive contestations, wherein certain actors object to or violate norms. Second, proactive contestations, which occur when actors engage with norms in order to improve them. Third, interpretative contestations where actors push different understandings of global norms, which becomes visible in the direct application of the norm. They are more likely to manifest as applicatory contestations rather than validity contestations. The authors argue that the consideration of sanctions centralises two sets of norms, sanctions as a form of international response to a situation of norm violation, and whether the application of sanctions by actors other than the UN Security Council is appropriate.

Orchard and Wiener (this volume) further argue that 'Constitutive (behaviourally induced) generative practices' focus primarily on norm content. And so, proactive contestations seek to improve the norm, while reactive contestations challenge the standards of behaviour represented by a norm, leading at worst to norm violation. Interpretative contestation may manifest as contested compliance. Constructive (normatively induced) generative practices engage with the legitimacy of a norm and its moral purposes. Proactive contestations focus on emergent norms, seeking to improve the norm's legitimacy. Reactive contestations focus on challenging the legitimacy or moral principles of extant norms. Interpretative contestations focus on hidden understandings that an actor may have of the norm and efforts to shape the wider understanding of the norm accordingly.

Access to regular contestation, or the right to participate in political decisions, is a condition for achieving recognition and legitimacy for norms. Usually, stakeholder access is uneven due to power imbalance, and by implication an 'inbuilt condition of injustice' (Orchard and Wiener, this volume). Injustice increases the likelihood that some actors are excluded from having a say in the norms that govern them. Against the condition of injustice, there is the likelihood that when the norms are engaged with, 'it will either be through reactive contestation as agents challenge and undermine the norm, or through interpretative contestations as agents become disconnected from the norm'.

Palestini (this volume) argues that 'the contestation of sanctions and the "lack of will" of state and non-state actors to align themselves with sanctions regimes is connected to whether sanction regimes are considered legitimate'. The author identifies three legitimacy problems associated with the practice of sanctioning: legitimacy of norms, legitimacy of enforcer and legitimacy of the measures. Imposition of sanctions is a claim that an actor has violated an international norm, demanding a reaction. The validity of the claim can be disputed. Where the claimant successfully shows norm violation, they are faced with the additional burden of showing that the violation legitimises a right to react. Here, the consideration is the status of the norm violated vis-à-vis the status of other norms such as non-intervention and territorial integrity. Similarly, the claimant can be an object of delegitimation on the basis of the question of who has the right to enforce a sanction. The measures imposed in reaction to norms violation is subject to delegitimation also. Are the measures proportional to the violation that they claim to address? Sanctions, even targeted sanctions, often have unintended consequences on innocent citizens, opening a ground for contestation.

Contestations of Western Sanctions

The literature gives scant attention to how sanctions may be deployed to achieve aims at variance with the stated objectives of sanctions. The usage of sanctions for outcomes at variance with their stated goal delegitimises sanctions as a credible and safe tool for achieving international peace and security. Generally, sanctions work by coercing, constraining and signalling. However, sanctions are often made to work by inducing instability and regime change. If African leaders have little assurance that, in the hands of Western senders, sanctions will give rise to or be used to achieve aims other than those stated, a legitimacy crisis is created. For instance, US sanctions often entrench divisions or reinforce tensions with targets 'in a way that is difficult to reverse even when the circumstances underlying the sanctions have changed' (ICG 2023, 24). Such use of sanctions is at variance with the communitarian approach symbolised by the trope of flogging a child with the right hand and drawing them closer with the left. If the instrument is lacking in legitimacy, it is almost inevitable that African leaders will engage with it reactively and interpretatively.

Sanctions are often vigorously deployed with the aim of demonising and isolating targets (ICG 2023). This results in entrenched distrust, becoming 'a factor in locking in the perception among US policymakers and the public that peaceful relations with the target are impossible' (ICG 2023, 24). Actors can manipulate or leverage sanctions for political capital in the context of destabilising rivalries and political instability (ibid). The EU/US sanctions on Zimbabwe aimed at removing Mugabe and the ruling party from power, an outcome which favoured the opposition party Movement for Democratic Change (MDC). Prime Minister of the United Kingdom, Tony Blair, in June 2004 claimed that his government was working closely with the MDC on strategies to adopt with respect to Zimbabwe, 'because there is no salvation for the people of Zimbabwe until that regime is changed' (UK Parliament 2004). Sanctions for regime change deepen domestic instability, undermine peaceful resolution of conflict and negate the African communitarian objective of sanctions. The EU approach articulates little with the AU norm of peaceful resolution of conflict, and reflects the illegitimate use of sanctions for the purpose of regime change (see Palestini in this volume). The EU sanctions and the declared aim of regime change ran counter to the AU's principles of non-intervention and sovereignty. As a result, African leaders engaged with it reactively by undermining it, and interpretatively by describing it as needless. Below, we examine other points of delegitimation and contestation of Western sanctions.

Contesting Breach of State Sovereignty and Territorial Integrity

The logic and norms of unilateral sanctions stand in conflict with the norms of non-intervention and respect for the territorial integrity of a sovereign state (Palestini, in this volume). While the process authorising unilateral sanctions has force within the sending country, its application against African targets negates the norms upon which African leaders challenge unilateral sanctions. Thus, there is a norms conflict between unilateral sanctions senders and the principles of the AU. As argued above, different interpretations of the Westphalian state system, and related principles of non-interference in the domestic affairs of sovereign states, including unilateral measures in the international system, raise issues of legitimacy and legality. For instance, the principle of non-interference has been the OAU/AU's guiding principle since its formation in 1963. Unilateral coercive measures are frequently imposed by the United States, Canada, Australia, the European Union member states and other states (Bogdanova 2022). To African leaders, the status of unilateral sanctions pales in comparison with the weightier norms of sovereignty and non-intervention.

The illegitimacy of unilateral sanctions elicits African leaders' reactive and interpretative contestations. African leaders have consistently denounced unilateral sanctions even as the latter's illegality is enshrined in the resolutions of various United Nations bodies (Tehran Declaration 2012; AU Assembly 2023). The United Nations General Assembly adopted several resolutions declaring that developed countries should desist from threat of use and actual use of economic sanctions against developing countries as a means of coercion incompatible with the Charter of the United Nations (UNGA 2003; UNGA 2004). In that context, continuing use of unilateral sanctions suffers delegitimation being perceived as inconsistent with the principles of international law, and a continuation of Western imperialism with impunity. Being adversarial to AU's principles of non-interference, territorial integrity and state sovereignty, African leaders reactively engage with unilateral sanctions to undermine or violate it.

The promise of targeted sanctions remains doubtful as it is unclear how it can completely avoid damaging the larger population (Tostensen and Bull 2002). This is the case because it seems practically difficult to design sanctions whose impact affects the targets only (Draca et al. 2023). UNGA declarations (2004; 1997) reject unilateral sanctions because of their negative impacts on civilians and the economy. African leaders delegitimise unilateral sanctions as not being entirely targeted, both in application and impact. The EU and US sanctions on Zimbabwe were claimed to be targeted, but they coincided with, if not caused, Zimbabwe's economic meltdown (Dendere 2022). It was widely believed that while the sanctions were targeted, its impacts were not (Dendere 2022). Having prioritised peace and security, African leaders are wary about the destabilising impacts of unilateral sanctions given the possibility of their use for regime change, as was the intent in the case of Zimbabwe, and their potential to instigate domestic political crisis. African leaders interpretatively contest such sanctions as being adversarial to norms of sovereignty and non-intervention as well as the AU's communitarian approach to sanctions, which privileges peaceful resolution of conflicts. Similarly, interpretative contestation of unilateral sanctions is articulated in the argument that unilateral sanctions exclude African voices from actions that affect Africa. The injustice of the exclusion of African voices in the imposition of sanctions provokes reactive contestation.

Contesting Double Standards of Sanctions Senders

The selective application of sanctions by Western countries suggests that unilateral sanctions are not motivated by deep commitment to international norms, but rather by geopolitical and economic interests. The failure to impose sanctions on oil-rich Saudi Arabia or the United Arab Emirates in the face of grave human rights violations, and support for Israel's invasion of Gaza while imposing sanctions on Cuba, Iran, North Korea and Russia reflect duplicity in commitment to international norms (see Rodriguez 2024). It reflects power asymmetries in international relations where the rich and powerful West can act with impunity against the poor and less powerful Global South countries (UNGA 2003). Unilateral enforcers target weaker states or states in the Global South, which violates the principle of sovereign equality of states and non-intervention. Such sanctions are often tied to the national interest of the senders, becoming an object of delegitimation by African leaders. The duplicity that characterises the use of sanctions foregrounds the view among African leaders that Western senders deploy sanctions in furtherance of Western imperialism. African leaders engage reactively with Western sanctions that reflect double standards.

In early 2022, the US and EU swiftly imposed massive and unprecedented sanctions on Russia following the latter's invasion of Ukraine in what was viewed in the Global South as a display of double standards in the use of sanctions. Whereas African leaders acknowledged that Russia breached international norms, it was not the first time such violations would occur. The US and EU are notorious for their support for foreign interventions in countries such as Libya and Iraq. More recently, the US supported the Israeli invasion of Gaza and has consistently vetoed efforts to bring the war to an end (Fassihi 2024). Similarly, the US and EU have failed to sanction their ally Saudi Arabia despite grave human rights violations in that country (ECDHR 2024). Thus, US and EU foreign policy is laced with clear examples of double standards. The question that agitates the mind is why Western countries condemned and imposed sanctions on Russia over the invasion of Ukraine when they equally breached international law when they invaded and destroyed Libya (2011), Iraq (2003) and Syria (2014). With Ukraine, Western countries have suddenly realised that the invasion of Ukraine is a breach of international law, unimaginable and unprecedented, and must attract consequences (see Traore 2022).

Double standards delegitimise Western sanctions and enforcers, and the deficit induces reactive and interpretative contestations that make it difficult for African leaders to support sanctions. The standard of behaviour represented by Western sanctions on Russia was subject to Western whims and caprices eliciting reactive contestation from African leaders. Reactive contestation challenged the legitimacy or moral weight of sanctions that reflect double standards. Relatedly, African leaders engage with the sanctions interpretatively, emphasising that sanctions for breach of international norms cannot be used only when the offender is non-Western or non-ally. African leaders hold the view that sanctions should be applied to violations of the norms of sovereignty and territorial integrity regardless of the status of the violator. The African communitarian approach supports the fair and objective use of multilateral sanctions for international peace and security. Deploying sanctions in pursuit of the Western agenda and against perceived enemies imperils international peace and defeats the purpose of sanctions. The use of sanctions is not an occasion for isolating and weakening targets but for promoting communication, dialogue and encouraging sanctioned parties to yield to sanctions demand. Western sanctions on Russia create little opportunity for dialogue and negotiation, which are necessary for bringing the war to an end. Thus, African leaders engage with the sanctions reactively.

Contesting Who Uses Sanctions: Sanctions Senders Are Former Colonial Masters

Colonialism involved the projection of military violence and aggression by European colonial states against less powerful states. Western sanctions undermine African states' right to equality and sovereignty, exacerbate the imbalance of power between them 'and thus become an instrument of neo-colonialism' (Philpot and Dubois 2023, 1). France and the US utilised sanctions as an instrument of war across the nineteenth century (Karuka 2022). As decolonisation accelerated, sanctions were targeted at states that questioned the colonial 'right to commerce' by undertaking reforms that altered inherited colonial economic structures (ibid). In contemporary times, former colonial states deploy sanctions against weak post-colonial states, and not vice versa, shaping the perception of sanctions as an instrument of the strong (West) against the weak (non-West) and, therefore, a tool of domination. The use of unilateral and multilateral sanctions, or interventions without UN authorisation, has further strengthened the view of sanctions as a tool of domination to advance Western interests.

Unilateral sanctions by the US, UK, France and other Western powers evoke colonial domination, motivating African leaders' contestation. The dilemma for African countries, given their founding principles of sovereignty and non-interference, is that as post-colonial states they have not advanced anti-colonial claims as a result of the Russian invasion of Ukraine. This framing is problematic because some African leaders have expressed disagreement with Russia over its violation of the territorial integrity of Ukraine. What they failed to do was endorse sanctions imposed on Russia. Africa's cautionary temper reflects the view among African leaders that the war is a proxy war between NATO and Russia. Endorsement of Western sanctions would have reduced African countries to pawns in the hands of the West. The refusal to endorse Western sanctions against Russia thus reflects proactive contestation, indicating that sanctions should not be an occasion for a rehash of Cold War rivalry and polarisation.

Western sanctions senders often seek to use sanctions for ends that undermine the principles of non-interference and sovereignty. Moreover, senders often do not provide for dialogue and negotiations, a basic requirement of the communitarian approach. As a result, legitimacy problems attend unilateral sanctions senders.

Contesting the Confrontational Logic of Sanctions

Humiliating the weak, the impoverished and the non-powerful has been erected as a paradigmatic trait of international politics (Traore 2022). Far from being an alternative to war, sanctions actually are just another form of deadly aggression (Philpot and Dubois 2023). Sanctions are imperialist measures designed to isolate targets. Sanctions operate similarly to military force since both aim at the 'political disintegration of the enemy so that he gives up the pursuit of his goals' (Galtung 1967, 386). Both comprehensive and targeted sanctions operate through value deprivation, including undermining financial and economic stability (Portela 2014). With targeted sanctions, however, the harm produced by sanctions is focused on the responsible leadership and supporters, but the method remains value deprivation. Thus, targeted sanctions transpose the logic of the naive theory to the individual or elite level (Portela 2014). The measures imposed in reaction to norms violation is subject to delegitimation. Sanctions, even targeted sanctions, often do have unintended consequences on innocent citizens, opening a ground for contestation.

Thus, the confrontational logic of Western sanctions provides a basis for the latter's contestation by African leaders. Regarding Zimbabwe, while South Africa mediated a power-sharing arrangement, the EU labelled Mugabe and the ZANU-PF as illegitimate and insisted on their removal from power (Portela 2014). Using sanctions to foment political disintegration and instability is antithetical to the AU's principle of non-intervention and understanding of sanctions as a tool for supporting compliance with sanctions demands rather than instigating domestic crisis. The EU and US measures sought to oust Mugabe, becoming a subject of delegitimation to African leaders who prioritised non-intervention, peaceful resolution of conflict, sovereignty and stability over regime change or instability. The attempt to remove Mugabe from power through sanctions negated the African communitarian approach that regarded sanctions as a means to signal the unacceptability of sanctioned behaviour and to help the target to comply with sanctions demand with a view to reinstating the status quo ante. Thus, the action elicited reactive and interpretative contestations.

Contesting Disrespect for African Voices

Africa's inability, and the international community's failure, to effectively deal with violent conflicts in the 1990s, particularly with regard to the Rwanda genocide and collapse of Somalia, led to the resolve among African leaders to develop indigenous solutions to emerging problems in the continent (Potgieter 2021). Thus, concern about the challenges Africa faces and the failure of the international community to give adequate attention to conflict management in Africa contributed towards the mantra 'African solutions to African problems . . . to show that Africa has both the capability and determination to solve problems' (Lobakeng 2017, 1). It was against that backdrop that the Heads of State and Government of the Organisation of African Unity meeting at the 36th Ordinary Session in July 2000 adopted the Lome Declaration, which established a framework for responding to unconstitutional changes of government. Nevertheless, the leaders resolved to make the year 2000, a year of peace, intensifying actions for peace, and peaceful settlement of conflicts in Africa, through strengthening of the OAU Mechanism for Conflict Prevention, Management and Resolution, and of African capacities for conflict management and the maintenance of peace and security.

African leaders have articulated strategies for peaceful resolution of conflicts in the continent, including the use of sanctions against unconstitutional changes of government. The African leaders' approach, or communitarian sanctions, aims at de-escalation, and peaceful management and resolution of conflicts. Taken in context, the communitarian approach represented an African indigenous solution to the violent conflicts of the 1990s, offering a peaceful pathway to achieving the goal of making 2000 a year of peace. African leaders evolved conflict-management capacities based on informed understanding of internal African dynamics, and against a backdrop where Africans were left to resolve their own problems. Former Under Secretary-General of the United Nations and Special Adviser on Africa, Professor Ibrahim Gambari (2012), emphasised that African leaders have a better grasp of political developments in the continent and, as such, they are bound to resist 'top-down decisions' or decisions taken without inputs from them. If the international community continues to disregard the views or sensibilities of African leaders, it could lead African regional organisations to resist or limit their engagement with the UN. Western sanctions are 'top-down decisions' that disregard the informed understanding of African leaders, and their commitment to peaceful resolution of conflict through the communitarian framework enunciated in the Lome Declaration. Contestation of such sanctions disputes the use of unilateral sanctions to enforce international norms.

The process of imposing sanctions on African targets often ignores the views of African leaders, eliciting contestation. A case in point is the unilateral imposition of sanctions on Zimbabwe by the EU in 2002, and the subsequent tabling of a resolution for sanctions on Zimbabwe at the UN Security Council by the US and EU despite opposition from African leaders. The UN Security Council failed to impose sanctions on Zimbabwe's leadership only because two permanent members, China and Russia, vetoed the resolution (UNSC 2008). In this instance, African leaders were denied the right to participate in a decision that affected Africa. The perceived injustice of the case could have shaped Africa's contestation of the EU sanctions. African leaders did not object to the claim that a norm had been breached requiring a reaction, but they made the claimants (EU and US) objects of delegitimation. The representative of Zimbabwe described the action of both the UK and US as an 'expression of imperialist conquest'. Also questioned was the status of the norm violated vis-à-vis the status of other norms such as non-intervention and 'African solutions to African problems'. The South Africa representative argued 'the African Union did not see the need for sanctions' (UNSC 2008). Here, African leaders questioned the use of sanctions in a situation where they envisaged other conflict resolution measures as more appropriate. Thus, the sanctions met with reactive and interpretative contestation being considered unnecessary.

African Communitarian Sanctions

The literature on sanctions emphasises the interactions between sanctions and other foreign policy instruments as a key determinant of sanctions effectiveness. Biersteker and van Bergeijk (2015, 18) emphasise the importance of implementing sanctions along with other foreign and security instruments, including 'Active negotiations, peace mediation efforts, threats of force, use of force, peacekeeping operations, and/or covert operations.' The argument aligns with Security Council reliance on the use of sanctions committees in supervising the implementation and monitoring of imposed sanctions across the world (Vines 2007). Sanctions committees are required to report regularly to the Council on suspected and/or reported embargo-bursting activities (Wallensteen and Staibano 2005). Apart from sanctions committees, the Council makes use of peacekeepers, sanctions monitoring groups and panels of experts as other means of monitoring its embargoes.

Three internal documents are relevant to EU's restrictive measures policy, including the 'Basic Principles on the Use of Restrictive Measures (Sanctions)', the 'Guidelines on Implementation and Evaluation of Restrictive Measures (Sanctions) in the Framework of the EU Common Foreign and Security Policy' and 'The EU Best Practices for the Effective Implementation of Restrictive Measures'. None of these documents accord recognition to peaceful resolution of conflict or termination of sanctions through informal pressures, and negotiations or dialogue towards quick termination of sanctions (see Giumelli 2013). Sanctions are considered part of a more comprehensive policy 'including political dialogue, incentives, conditionality, and could even involve, as a last resort, the use of coercive measures' (Council of the European Union 2004, 2). This section of the 'Basic Principles' is honoured more in the breach. The imposition of sanctions on Russia did not foreground, and appears to have foreclosed, the possibility for dialogue, negotiation and use of incentives. As happened to Zimbabwe under sanctions, Russia has been abandoned in the sick room and is expected to retrace her steps as a condition for sanctions termination.

Elements of the Communitarian Approach

The OAU was formed on 25 May 1963 with the aim to 'safeguard African interest by promoting the unity and solidarity' of African nations (Omorogbe 2021, 125). It adopted non-interference as its guiding principle, which barred any form of intervention in the domestic affairs of member states. Regimes that acquired power violently were, thus, not punished. At its 36th Ordinary Session, however, the body moved against unconstitutional changes of government, defining coups as a threat to peace and security (OAU 2000). Article 4 of the Constitutive Act, a founding treaty of the AU, prescribes the right of the AU to intervene in a member state in the event of unconstitutional change of government (AU 2002), marking a clear departure from the traditional policy of non-interference. Article 30 of the Act provides that the 'Governments which shall come to power through unconstitutional means shall not be allowed to participate in the activities of the Union' (AU 2000, 17).

The Lome Declaration states that in the event of unconstitutional change of government, the Chairman and Secretary-General should publicly denounce the change, urge a speedy return to constitutional order and issue a stern warning to the perpetrators that their illegal action was intolerable and unacceptable (OAU 2000). The Peace and Security Council (PSC) of the African Union (AU), which inherited and continued these rules, shall thereafter deploy a three-pronged strategy: first, impose sanctions on perpetrators of the unconstitutional change, and set a six months deadline to restore constitutional order; second, require the Secretary-General to 'gather facts relevant to the unconstitutional change of Government and establish appropriate contacts with the perpetrators with a view to ascertaining their intentions regarding the restoration of constitutional order in the country' (OAU 2000); third, he shall 'seek the contribution of African leaders and personalities in the form of discreet moral pressure on the perpetrators of the unconstitutional change in order to get them to cooperate with the OAU and facilitate the restoration of constitutional order in the Member State concerned' (Ikome 2007, 32).

The Lome Declaration fleshes out in one policy document the features of the African communitarian approach to sanctions. The following major elements can be distilled from the declaration: impose sanctions on targets involved in unacceptable behaviour; determine a deadline for the restoration of constitutional order; establish appropriate contact with the targets in order to understand better their intention regarding the set deadline for restoring constitutional order; and use informal pressure, deploying African leaders and personalities, in order to get targets to cooperate with the AU to restore constitutional order. The African approach to sanctions comprises an integrated or coherent set of activities, which are not only interrelated and interdependent, but undertaken methodically. Unconstitutional change of government has to be denounced in order to impose sanctions. Having imposed sanctions, there is a need to determine a deadline for restoring constitutional order. Sanctions could not be contemplated without the accompanying informal contact and communication with a view to pressuring the target to cooperate with the AU.

While the communitarian approach prioritises using informal pressure to get the target to cooperate with sanctions senders, Western sanctions emphasise efficient sanctions implementation, giving limited attention to less adversarial policy instruments (see Kreutz 2005). As the EU's 'Basic Principles' indicates, unilateral sanctions make little provision for informal mechanisms of communication and pressure with a view to securing the target's cooperation. Western sanctions simply isolate the 'sick' in the 'sick room', as the cases of Russia, Libya and Zimbabwe exemplify. To the contrary, the communitarian approach rests robustly on active and sustained negotiation and peace mediation with sanctions targets in consonance with the stipulations of the Lome Declaration.

Communitarian Sanctions: The Cases of Mauritania and Guinea

Africa's regional sanctions display 'resolution-orientation' (Hellquist 2020). Thus, regional sanctions episodes in place between 2002 and 2016 were on average resolved in approximately eighteen months, whereas EU sanctions as of 17 January 2017 had on average been in force for over eleven years. According to Hellquist (2020, 456), 'the brevity of AU sanctions reflects an eagerness to return to normality'. Hellquist's overall observations about the brevity of African regional sanctions and the hurry to return to normality dovetails with the communitarian approach. It is not evident that the goal of normality was achieved at the expense of a regional norm. There is no African target that has returned to 'perfect democracy' as a result of Western sanctions. Two sanctions regimes discussed below demonstrate the African communitarian approach to sanctions.

Mauritania

Following a military coup, President Maaouya Ould Sid'Ahmed Taya of the Islamic Republic of Mauritania was deposed on 3 August 2005. The next day, in line with the Lome Declaration, the AU's PSC condemned the coup, and suspended Mauritania's participation in AU activities until the restoration of constitutional order (Omorogbe 2021). Also, the PSC decided to send a delegation of ministers to Mauritania to reiterate to the coup makers the position of the AU and commit them to the swift return to constitutional order. This was in keeping with the principles enunciated in the Lome Declaration that indicate that sanctions were not meant to isolate the target, but to signal unacceptability of a behaviour and initiate a dialogue with the target with a view to helping the latter yield to sanctions demand. Following presidential elections held in March 2007, Sidi Mohamed Ould Cheikh Abdallahi became Mauritania's first democratically elected president. Following the elections, Mauritania`s membership to the AU was restored.

On 6 August 2008, the Presidential Guard staged a coup against the government. President Sidi Mohamed Ould Cheikh Abdallahi, the Prime Minister and the Minister of the Interior were arrested on grounds of corruption. The coup followed removal of four key military generals from office through a presidential decree (Omorogbe 2021). In keeping with the Lome Declaration, the PSC immediately condemned the military coup, demanding the release of those who had been arrested, as well as restoration of constitutional order and of the institutions democratically chosen by the population in 2006–7 (Omorogbe 2021). Negotiations and informal pressure led to the release of Ould Abdallahi in December, but the military junta failed to reinstate civilian rule. Accordingly, the AU activated the terms of the Lome Declaration in February 2009, imposing sanctions on Mauritania.

Additionally, and in compliance with the Lome Declaration's stipulation for use of informal contacts and support, a delegation of ministers, under the leadership of Oluyemi Adeniji, Nigeria's Foreign Affairs Minister acting on behalf of the Chair of the AU, and comprising C. Ngakula, Minister of Safety and Security of South Africa acting on behalf of the PSC Chairman, and Mathieu Kinouani, Analyst in the Peace and Security Department of the AU Commission, was dispatched to Nouakchott on 9 August 2005. On arrival, the delegation was received by the Chairman of the Military Council for Justice and Democracy (CMJD), Colonel Ely Ould Mohamed Vall. Thereafter, the delegation met successively with the representatives of different interest groups in the country. During a two-hour meeting with the CMJD Chairman, Minister Adeniji emphasised that their mission was not punitive but to establish dialogue in order to agree with them on the modalities for the restoration of constitutional order as soon as possible.

The conversation and negotiation that followed underscored the equality of member states of the AU, and the clear understanding that the visit represented the left hand of the AU reaching out to bring the country back to the family fold. In other words, the AU sanctions were not meant to punish or isolate the target. The AU Head of Delegation pointed out that the particularity of the AU was its willingness to take the initiative of engaging and supporting the Mauritanian authorities in a process leading to the return of the country to the AU. On his part, the CMJD Chairman expressed the junta's plan towards restoration of the democratic institutions. He specified that it would be in two stages, which together would span a period of twenty-four months. In his response, Minister Adeniji stressed the need to shorten the period, arguing that the longer the transition lasted, the more difficulties would accumulate that could disenchant stakeholders. Under sanctions and discreet moral pressure, the junta organised a new round of elections in July 2009, which was won by the coup leader, Ould Abdel Aziz.

Guinea

Following the death of President Conte of Guinea in December 2008, the military took over and formed a new government under the leadership of Moussa Dadis Camara (Arieff and Cook 2010). In reaction, following the procedure laid down in the Lome Declaration, the AU's Peace and Security Council (PSC) condemned the coup as an unconstitutional change of government (Arieff and Cook 2010). On 29 December 2008, the PSC imposed diplomatic sanctions on the military junta and suspended Guinea from the AU. Following the AU's lead, the Economic Community of West African States (ECOWAS) on 10 January 2009 condemned the military coup, suspended Guinea's membership of ECOWAS and called on the military regime to respect democratic processes. To that end, ECOWAS heads of state established a consultative forum consisting of all components of civil society in Guinea to serve as a basis for dialogue, and to support the completion of the transition process through the organisation of free and fair elections in 2009. Also, as demanded by the Lome Declaration, ECOWAS spearheaded the formation of the International Contact Group on Guinea (ICG-G) composed of representatives of international organisations within and outside Africa (ACCORD 2017). The ICG-G was to monitor progress towards restoration of constitutional rule, and engage in direct talks with the coup leaders and other political stakeholders.

When the military junta appeared to renege on its promises, the AU threatened to impose tougher sanctions on the regime. Following the massacre in Conakry Stadium on 28 September 2009, the PSC imposed a new round of sanctions against the military regime of Camara (Global Centre for the Responsibility to Protect 2010). ECOWAS condemned the killings and called for an International Committee of Inquiry that would identify the people responsible for the barbaric act. Rather than isolating Guinea, ECOWAS appointed the President of Burkina Faso, Blaise Compaoré, as a mediator 'who would have direct consultations' with the coup leaders (ACCORD 2017). Compaoré was to re-establish talks among Guinea's political actors with the aim of ensuring a short and peaceful transition to constitutional order through credible, free and fair elections (ACCORD 2017). Constitutional rule was restored on 15 November 2010 after Alpha Condé won 53 per cent of the votes in a run-off election. Beyond sanctions, African leaders engaged with the junta to restore the constitutional order. When the need arose, sanctions were ratcheted upward, but the leaders kept the channels of communication open. Despite sanctions, which suspended Guinea from the ECOWAS and the AU, sanctions senders sustained dialogue with the target. This practice is in keeping with the Lome Declaration of 2009 and has remained a standard practice in the implementation of African sanctions (see Agbonifo 2017).

African Perspectives on the Russia Sanctions

The Russian invasion of Ukraine failed to resonate with Africa's experience of colonialism simply because it is not an attempt to colonise. History is replete with cases of Western invasions that were not described as colonialism. Such violations of territorial integrity include France's invasion of Haiti, and the invasions of Afghanistan (2001), Syria (2014), Libya (2011) and Iraq (2003) by the US and its 'Coalition of the Willing'. In some of these instances, African leaders sued for peace, drawing attention to the global norm of sovereignty and territorial integrity, as they did with regard to the Russian invasion of Ukraine. African leaders would be guilty of the charge of double standards, a charge which they levy against Western senders, if they had taken further actions against Russia. Moreover, the AU does not have a history of imposing sanctions on non-members states.

While African leaders are irrevocably committed to the principle of non-interference and respect for the territorial integrity of a sovereign state, they failed to endorse Western sanctions or provide unified support for UN resolutions condemning Russia's invasion of Ukraine. African leaders' dilemma arises from caution against being used by the West to fight Russia for what is seen as a conflict involving Western geopolitical interests. African leaders perceive the war in Ukraine as a proxy war between the two rival world powers. Moreover, the reaction of the West to Russia's invasion of Ukraine reflects double standards and hypocrisy. If indeed the sanctions were motivated by concern for international law, and the norms of territorial integrity and national sovereignty, Western countries would not have spearheaded or supported external interventions in Libya and Iraq.

Western sanctions against a world power appears as an attempt to create a unipolar world system. Even if Russia capitulates, the sanctions have divided the world, entrenched distrust, and the repercussions of these will remain for a long time. Anger and distrust do not make for international peace and security. This explains why the African communitarian approach to sanctions emphasises getting targets to cooperate with sanctions senders without alienating them. The legitimacy problems associated with sanctions and their senders, together with examples of reactive, proactive and interpretative contestation, ensure that there could be no united front against Russia's violation of international norms. Will the West sustain sanctions against Russia despite contestations of Western sanctions? And for how long? While the stalemate remains, the UNSC might find it impossible to deal with lesser or greater security issues that might arise. This paints a bleak future for international relations. However, the West could bend over backwards and in good faith suspend all sanctions on the proviso that Russia would end the war, respect international norms and contribute to rebuilding Ukraine. Such a line of action would likely receive the acceptance of African leaders and help apply concerted pressure on Russia to respect international norms.

Conclusion

This chapter articulates an African communitarian approach to sanctions. The OAU at its 36th Ordinary Session distilled elements of its understanding and approach to sanctions. Activation of the elements gives rise to the 'communitarian' approach, which reflects inclusion, dialogue and reconciliation. Emphasising connectedness and reconciliation, the concept of communitarian sanctions dovetails with the logic of the African parable: 'flog an erring child with the right hand, and with the left hand draw the child closer'. This understanding diverges from the logic and practice of Western sanctions, giving rise to contestations of the latter by African leaders.

There are three broad types of norms contestation by African leaders: reactive, interpretative and proactive contestations. Whereas reactive contestations engage with norms with a view to object or undermine them, interpretative contestations reflect divergent understanding of norms, while proactive contestations engage with norms with a view to improving on them. Reactive factors that shape African contestations of sanctions include opposition to the unilateral imposition of sanctions, Western double standards, the confrontational logic of sanctions and disrespect for African voices or views in the application of sanctions. Interpretative contestations arise from African leaders' understanding that sanctions should not be a basis for undermining the fundamental norms of non-interference and respect for the territorial integrity of a sovereign state. Unilateral sanctions affront the AU's commitment to sovereigntist principles, giving substance to the perception that Western sanctions are a continuation of neo-colonial domination. Deployment of communitarian sanctions by African regional senders signals a proactive engagement with sanctions norms as the sanctions present an alternative model to conventional uses, especially unilateral sanctions. There is, however, a thin line between reactive, interpretative and proactive contestations. Reactive contestation of Western sanctions by African leaders is both interpretative and proactive at the same time.

African leaders' contestations have also been premised on the legitimacy of sanctions and sanctions senders. To African leaders, unilateral sanctions are not only at variance with the principles of international law; senders employ double standards in their use of sanctions, supporting the view that unilateral sanctions are employed to promote Western strategic interests rather than upholding international norms. For the foregoing reasons, Western sanctions bear a legitimation problem. Sanctions have been used for ends, such as regime change, at variance with the stated objectives for their application, and undermining the principles of sovereignty and non-intervention. Moreover, Western senders are accused of double standards in their application of sanctions. Thus, the ways Western sanctions' senders use and implement sanctions introduces a legitimation problem. These legitimation issues, together with African reactive, interpretative or proactive engagement with sanctions norms, explain Africa's divided vote on the UN resolution condemning Russia's invasion of Ukraine. African leaders' contestation of sanctions norms need not create a crisis for the international system. The extent to which Western sanctions senders listen to African voices and engage with the African communitarian approach to sanctions could go a long way in determining the impact of African leaders' contestation of sanctions norms.

References

ACCORD. 2017. Regional Organisations' Support to National Dialogue Processes. Conflict Trends 2017/3, 12 October. https://www.accord.org.za/conflict-trends/regional-organisations-support-national-dialogue-processes/

Agbonifo, John. 2017. 'Sanctions, Conflict Prevention and Peacebuilding: Coercing Non-State Armed Actors in Africa'. *Journal of Peacebuilding and Development* 12(1): 65–78.

Arieff, Alexis, and Nicholas Cook. 2010. 'Guinea: Background and Relations with the United States'. http://fpc.state.gov/documents/organization/141629.pdf

AU (African Union). 2000. Constitutive Act of the African Union. Adopted by the Assembly of Heads of State and Government at the 36th Ordinary Session, 11 July, Lomé, Togo.

AU Assembly. 2023. Resolution on the Impact of Sanctions and Unilateral Coercive Measures, A/RES/39/210, Thirty-Sixth ordinary session, 18–19 February 2023, Addis Ababa, Ethiopia.

Betts, Alexander, and Phil Orchard. 2014. 'Introduction: The Normative Institutionalization Implementation Gap'. In *Implementation of World Politics: How International Norms Change Practice*, edited by Alexander Betts and Phil Orchard. Oxford University Press.

Biersteker, T., and Peter A. G. van Bergeijk. 2015. 'How and When Do Sanctions Work? The Evidence'. In *On Target? EU Sanctions as Security Policy Tools*, edited by Lana Dreyer and José Luengo-Cabrera. ISSUE (September) Report No. 25.

Bogdanova, Iryna. 2022. 'The Legality of Unilateral Economic Sanctions under Public International Law'. In *Unilateral Sanctions in International Law and the Enforcement of Human Rights*, edited by Iryna Bogdanova. Brill.

Charron, Andrea, and Clara Portela. 2015. 'The UN, Regional Sanctions and Africa'. *International Affairs* 91(6): 1369–85.

Charron, Andrea, and Clara Portela. 2016. 'The Relationship between United Nations Sanctions Regimes'. In *Targeted Sanctions: The Impacts and Effectiveness of United Nations Action*, edited by T. J. Biersteker, S. E. Eckert and M. Tourinho. Cambridge University Press.

Council of the European Union. 2004. 'Basic Principles on the Use of Restrictive Measures (Sanctions)'. 10198/04.

Dendere, Chipo. 2022. 'Zimbabwe: The Long Shadow of Sanctions'. In *The Southern Mirror: Reflections on Europe from the Global South*, edited by Rosa Balfour, Lizza Bomassi and Marta Martinelli. Carnegie Endowment for International Peace.

Dettmer, Jamie. 2022. 'Why African States Are Reluctant to Pick Sides on Ukraine'. *Politico*, 3 June. https://www.politico.eu/article/africa-reluctant-to-pick-sides-on-ukraine-russia-war-food-shortage-crises/

Draca, Mirko, Jason Garred, Leanne Stickland and Nele Warrinnier. 2023. 'On Target? Sanctions and the Economic Interests of Elite Policymakers in Iran'. *The Economic Journal* 133(649): 159–200.

ECDHR 2024. 'Unfulfilled Resolutions and Saudi Arabia's Poor Human Rights Record'. European Centre for Democracy and Human Rights.

Eriksson, Mikael. 2007. 'Targeting the Leadership of Zimbabwe: A Path to Democracy and Normalisation?' Department of Peace and Conflict Research, Uppsala University.

Fassihi, Farnaz. 2024. 'US Vetoes Gaza Cease-fire Resolution at UN Security Council'. *The New York Times*, 20 November.

Galtung, J. 1967. 'On the Effects of International Economic Sanctions: With Examples from the Case of Rhodesia'. *World Politics* 19(3): 378–416.

Gambari, Ibrahim A. 2012. 'The Role of Africa in the United Nations. African Security Briefing'. *American Foreign Policy Interests* 34: 178–81.

Giumelli, Francesco. 2013. 'How EU Sanctions Work: A New Narrative'. Chaillot Papers (May), EU Institute for Security Studies.

Global Centre for the Responsibility to Protect. 2010. 'The International Response to 28 September 2009 Massacre in Guinea and the Responsibility to Protect. Policy Brief'. 11 January. https://www.globalr2p.org/wp-content/uploads/2021/07/the-international-response-to-28-september-2009-massacre-in-guinea-and-the-responsibility-to-protect.pdf

Hellquist, Elin. 2020. 'Regional Sanctions as Peer Review: The African Union against Egypt (2013) and Sudan (2019)'. *International Political Science Review* 42(4): 451–68.

ICG. 2023. 'Sanctions, Peacemaking and Reform: Recommendations for U.S. Policymakers'. *International Crisis Group*, 28 August.

Ikome, Francis Nguendi. 2007. 'Good Coups, Bad Coups'. Institute for Global Dialogue Occasional Paper no. 55: 28–33.

Karuka, M. 2022. *Hunger Politics: Sanctions as Siege Warfare*. In *Sanctions as War*, edited by Stuart Davis and Immanuel Ness. Brill.

Kreutz, Joakim. 2005. 'Hard Measures by a Soft Power? Sanctions Policy of the European Union 1981–2004'. Bonn International Centre for Conversion (BICC) Paper 45.

Lobakeng R. 2017. 'African Solutions to African Problems: A Viable Solution towards a United, Prosperous and Peaceful Africa?' Institute for Global Dialogue (IGD) Occasional Paper 71 (October). https://media.africaportal.org/documents/Occassional_paper_by_Remofiloe.pdf

OAU (Organization of African Unity). 2000. Lomé Declaration on the framework for an OAU response to unconstitutional change of government. Adopted at the 36th Ordinary Session of the Assembly of Heads of State and Government, 10–12 July, Lomé, Togo.

Omorogbe, Eki Y. 2021. 'A Club of Incumbents? The African Union and Coups d'Etat'. *Vanderbilt Law Review* 44(1): 123–54.

Philpot, John, and Karine Konan Dubois. 2023. 'Unilateral Coercive Measures (Sanctions) and the African Continental Free Trade Area (ACFTA)'. African Bar Association Annual Conference, Pretoria, South Africa.

Portela, Clara. 2011. 'Impact of Sanctions and Isolation Measurement with North Korea, Burma/Myanmar, Iran and Zimbabwe as Case Studies'. Research Collection School of Social Sciences, Paper 1685.

Portela, Clara. 2014. 'The EU's Use of "Targeted" Sanctions Evaluating Effectiveness'. CEPS Working Document No. 391 / March.

Potgieter, Thean. 2021. 'Exploring African Solutions to African Problems'. *African Journal of Public Sector Development and Governance* 4(1): 5–25.

Rodriguez, Francisco. 2024. 'The Human Consequences of Economic Sanctions'. *Journal of Economic Studies* 51(4): 942–63.

Stimmer, Anette, and Lea Wisken. 2019. 'The Dynamics of Dissent: When Actions Are Louder Than Words'. *International Affairs* 95(3): 515–33.

Tehran Declaration. 2012. 'XVI Summit of Heads of State or Government of the Non-Aligned Movement'. Issued on 30–31 August.

Tostensen, A., and B. Bull. 2002. 'Are Smart Sanctions Feasible?' *World Politics* 54(3): 373–403.

Traore, Sa Benjamin. 2022. 'Making Sense of Africa's Massive Abstentions during the Adoption of the UNGA Resolution on the Aggression against Ukraine'. *AfricLaw*, 21 April.

UK Parliament. 2004. 14 June, Column 523. http://www.publications.parliament.uk/pa/cm200304/cmhansrd/vo040614/debtext/40614-06.htm#40614-06_spmin0

UN Security Council. 1998. Resolution 1192.

UNGA. 2003. Resolution 58/198. Human Rights and Unilateral Coercive Measures.

UNGA. 2004. Resolution 59/188. Human Rights and Unilateral Coercive Measures.

UNGA. 2023. 'Unilateral Economic Measures as a Means of Political and Economic Coercion against Developing Countries'. Report of the Secretary-General, A/78/506, 4 October.

UNSC. 2008. 'Security Council fails to adopt Sanctions against Zimbabwe Leadership as Two Permanent Members cast Negative Votes'. Security Council SC/9396, 11 July.

Vines, Alex. 2007. 'Can UN Arms Embargoes in Africa be Effective?' *International Affairs* 83(6): 1107–21.

White, Abraham, and Leo Holz. 2022. 'Figure of the Week: African Countries' Votes on the UN Resolution Condemning Russia's Invasion of Ukraine'. *Brookings*, 9 March.

Wallensteen, Peter and Carina Staibano, eds. 2005. *International Sanctions: Between Words and Wars in the Global System*. Frank Cass.

6

Investigating the Grounds for Iran's Narrative Contestation of International Sanctions

Fariba Alikarami and Nasser Hadian Jazy

Introduction

Following the end of the Cold War, the use of coercive sanctions by a government or a coalition of governments to exert pressure on a target country in order to achieve a desired goal gained momentum in the international arena and in states' foreign policies (Drury 2000, 627; Drezner 2003, 643). However, there are concerns about the effectiveness and efficiency of sanctions, which have been revived particularly after the sanctions against Iraq in the 1990s and Russia since 2022. The conventional wisdom is that economic sanctions often fail. If so, why do countries apply them? Daniel Drezner, in *The Sanctions Paradox*, argues that existing literature has not fully explained sanctions (Drezner 1999). Possibly, this inability is partly explained by the fact that the literature has focused almost exclusively on the perspective of a few countries while ignoring others, particularly those who have been targeted by sanctions.

While senders view sanctions as a legitimate tool to uphold international norms, targeted countries often see them as illegitimate, serving Western interests and potentially leading to wars, such as in the case of Iraq. This differing perception of sanctions has resulted in states either contesting the international sanctions narrative or showing indifference to them, which can be seen today with those countries that have not joined sanctions against Russia. This chapter investigates how Iran views sanctions, as one of the countries that has been targeted by sanctions in recent decades.

Opinions on sanctions and their effectiveness may vary among different groups in Iran, including opposition factions. However, this study focuses on the prevailing perspective in Iran, as reflected in statements from official entities and the writings of the country's academic elite. This dominant view is particularly significant because it shapes Iran's responses and behaviour regarding sanctions.

Iran's perception of sanctions is defined by legal and identity-political lenses. Iran sees sanctions as a tool of the Western/American system to silence different voices from the global system, which is actually a tool to pursue its hegemonic interests. Sanctions fit well with America's self-image as a benevolent hegemon that maintains international order as non-violently as possible, although history has shown that the use of sanctions does not mean ignoring military tools (Alikarami 2019, 5). Especially the recent Israeli and American strikes only reinforced the long-held belief among Iranian leaders that the world demands their surrender – and leaves them alone, at constant risk of betrayal and invasion (Khatami 2025). This chapter is composed of five sections: the first discusses Iran's historical experience with sanctions; the second identifies major areas of contestation; the third examines Iran's grounds for contestation, concluding by exploring Iran's view on the delegitimisation of sanctions, drawing insights from both the Palestini and the Orchard and Wiener chapters in this volume. The fourth section assesses Iranian society's view of sanctions; and the final section concludes the analysis.

Iran's History of Sanctions

As an ancient civilisation rich in oil and gas resources (Energy Information Administration 2022), Iran occupies a strategic position in the Persian Gulf, with the Strait of Hormuz in the south serving as a critical waterway for crude oil transportation. For over forty years, Iranian individuals, entities and key sectors such as energy, banking, finance and transportation have been subjected to sanctions by the United Nations, the United States and the European Union. These sanctions constitute one of the most expansive and long-lasting regimes in history.

One of the earliest sanctions against Iran was the 1950s oil embargo imposed by the UK on the Mossadegh government (Sajjadpour 1997, 7). However, the majority of sanctions were implemented following the 1979 Islamic Revolution. In response to the hostage crisis and the seizure of the US embassy, President Jimmy Carter issued Executive Order No. 12170 on 14 November 1979. This action, based on the International Emergency Economic Powers Act (IEEPA) and the National Emergencies Act (NEA), blocked Iranian government assets.

By designating Iran as a State Sponsor of Terrorism (SSOT) in January 1984, the United States imposed a new round of trade sanctions on Iran under

US law (Congressional Research Service 2023). On 5 August 1996, President Bill Clinton signed the Iran and Libya Sanctions Act (ILSA). ILSA did not directly mandate companies to divest from existing investments in Iran or Libya. Instead, it imposed sanctions on foreign companies making new investments of $20 million or more in the energy sectors of Iran or Libya (Iran and Libya Sanctions Act 1996).

In the 2000s, as Iran developed its nuclear programme, Tehran faced a new and broader array of sanctions. These included measures by the United Nations Security Council (UNSC), the European Union (EU) and the United States (Islami and Naghdi 2016, 16). Between 2006 and 2012, the Security Council adopted seven sanctions resolutions – UNSCRs 1696, 1737, 1747, 1803, 1835, 1929 and 1984 – targeting Iran's nuclear programme. Resolution 1737, approved by the UNSC on 23 December 2006, placed Iran under Chapter 7, Article 41 of the United Nations Charter. It warned that if Iran failed to comply and halt its nuclear activities within the stipulated timeframe, tougher sanctions would follow (Security Council 2006).

The Council of the European Union also passed several independent resolutions sanctioning Iran's nuclear programme (Zachary 2015). Nevertheless, the UK, France and Germany pursued diplomatic dialogues alongside these sanctions. However, escalating pressure from the White House and the presidency of Mahmoud Ahmadinejad in Iran led Europe to distance itself from negotiations with Tehran (Moradi 2019, 149). By 2010, the EU had aligned more closely with US actions, significantly strengthening its sanctions regime. It blocked European financial institutions from transacting with Iranian banks, including the Central Bank, and restricted trade with Iran's energy and transportation sectors.

Brussels' efforts to isolate Iran peaked in 2012 with a ban on oil and petrochemical imports and the suspension of shipping insurance. This occurred when the EU was Iran's largest oil importer, averaging 600,000 barrels per day (Zachary 2015).

US sanctions after 2010, implemented primarily through executive orders and Congressional acts, restricted US market access for foreign companies engaging with Iran's banking, energy and shipping sectors (Congressional Research Service 2023, 16). Notably, the Comprehensive Iran Sanctions, Accountability, and Divestment Act (CISADA) of 2010 imposed severe restrictions on companies investing in Iran's oil and gas sectors, curtailing their access to US financial systems (US Congress 2010). This act played a pivotal role in deepening Iran's economic isolation and limiting opportunities for global economic cooperation and investment.

After extensive preliminary meetings, the Joint Comprehensive Plan of Action (JCPOA) between Iran and the P5+1 was finalised in July 2015 and implemented in January 2016 (Islami and Naghdi 2016, 39). This agreement marked a significant diplomatic achievement for Iran. However, despite initial hopes for resolving the nuclear issue in exchange for sanctions relief, the sanctions on Iran were not fully lifted. Following the United States' withdrawal from the JCPOA in 2018, the US imposed a new wave of sanctions under its 'maximum pressure' strategy. Executive Order 13846 reinstated all prior US sanctions and rescinded the concessions granted under the JCPOA, including sanctions on the Central Bank of Iran (Executive Order 13846, 2018). Additionally, in March and April 2023, the European Union imposed further sanctions on high-ranking Iranian individuals and entities, citing human rights violations and arms cooperation between Iran and Russia (Council of the European Union 2023).

Sanctions as an Essentially Contested Concept – Legitimate or Illegitimate?

Sanctions are subject to contestation on a variety of principles and levels, ranging from the doctrine of non-intervention in the internal affairs of sovereign states to the humanitarian consequences they often entail as well as historical legacies between states. These principles reflect differing interpretations of the international order, which is largely shaped by Western liberal democratic ideals, and the purposes sanctions are intended to serve. Reactions to sanctions can be reactive, proactive or interpretative, depending on how nations perceive these guiding principles. Iran's narrative originates from these global discussions. While this section outlines the foundational principles underlying debates over sanctions, the section that follows will explore Iran's distinct perspective, shedding light on its unique framing of sanctions and their implications.

The Principles of Non-intervention and Equality of Sovereignty

Although the principle of non-intervention is not explicitly mentioned in the United Nations Charter, it can be inferred from the Charter (United Nations 1945, Article 2, Paragraph 7). States critical of sanctions argue that sanctions violate this principle, constituting interference in a country's internal and external affairs (Shafi'i and Akhavan 2019, 44–5). However, contradictions in the UN Charter and the potential justification for intervention under Chapter 7 complicate this contention, especially when the behaviour of the target country is considered a global threat and disrupts international security.

The Rights of Individuals and the Rights of Governments

By examining the international standards of human rights in the United Nations Charter (1945), the Universal Declaration of Human Rights (1948), the Convention on the Rights of the Child (1989) and related documents that account for internationally accepted principles, it can be argued that if economic sanctions lead to rights deprivation and human suffering, these sanctions are not justified from the point of view of international law. The shift from comprehensive to targeted sanctions attempts to mitigate adverse humanitarian effects, yet concerns persist regarding potential conflicts with individual rights (Ziyai and Mohammadi Mutlaq 2014, 57).[1]

The Shadow of Colonialism in Global Arrangements

Most sanctioning countries today are former great powers that played significant roles in colonising other nations over the past two centuries. As a result, differing perceptions of the international order – and the relationship between the current Western/American order and the colonial order of the past – have shaped contrasting views on sanctions. For some, sanctions are seen as a tool to uphold a just international system, while others view them as a modern instrument serving colonialist agendas. In this context, many governments did not interpret Russia's invasion of Ukraine as an act of re-colonisation. Instead, they refrained from condemning Russia's actions, perceiving it as a demonstration of opposition to the West. This stance is often informed by the principle that 'the enemy of my enemy is my friend'.

Prioritising the Interests of Countries over Global Interests

While some argue that sanctions can be legitimate, others contest this view, asserting that Paragraph 4 of Article 2 of the United Nations Charter – regarding the obligation of member states to refrain from the use of force – applies not only to military force but also to political and economic coercion. Sanctions

[1] One result of legally establishing targeted sanctions is the formation of a new concept in international law known as 'Sanctions of Natural Persons'. In this type of embargo, the embargo of 'government officials' replaces the embargo of the 'responsible government', in order to reduce the risk of citizens' vulnerability. In this framework, instead of affecting governments as a whole, sanctions target some individuals identified as those responsible for international violations (Ziyai and Mohammadi Mutlaq 2014, 157).

may be justified under the collective actions of the Security Council pursuant to Chapter 7 of the UN Charter. However, because UN-imposed and unilateral sanctions are primarily economic restrictions, they naturally fall within the domain of major economic powers, such as the United States. Consequently, the adoption and implementation of sanctions often serve to protect the interests of these great powers rather than advancing international and public order (Takhshid and Alikarami 2021, 672).

States can have different commitments to these principles and, consequently, the legitimacy of sanctions can be questioned. The point of contention is not only about how they are used, but also about the motivations that lead to their adoption, as discussed in Palestini's chapter earlier in this volume. When sanctions are not perceived as legitimate, states can engage in various forms of contestation, and the next section shows how Iran's contestation can be categorised as a combination of interpretative and reactive contestations.

Iran's Narrative of Sanctions

Although Iran's narrative of sanctions focuses on US unilateral sanctions, its view of sanctions has been shaped by various periods, including Khatami's presidency in the early 2000s, when Iran tried to align with international norms. Recently, perceptions of Western violations of the JCPOA and the imposition of maximum pressure have reinforced Iran's sense of unfairness regarding combined international sanctions. Iran's narrative is informed by two perspectives – legal and historical-political – based on ideas from the previous section, the Islamic Revolution and interactions with the West.

Legal Perspective (Principle of Non-intervention, Equality of States and Human Rights)

Iran proposes that the imposition of unilateral sanctions by Europe and the United States on the grounds of human rights violations, non-proliferation of weapons of mass destruction or international terrorism is not within the jurisdiction of these countries; therefore Iran engages in reactive contestation as it attempts to challenge the legitimacy of the sender. Resorting to economic sanctions can be legitimate only through the United Nations Security Council, and any unilateral economic sanctions are viewed as a violation of the UN Charter (Momtaz 1981, 220). Referring to UNSC Resolution 2625, the Iranian legal community articulates the principle prohibiting countries from interfering in each other's affairs. Hence, the US unilateral sanctions against Iran are a violation of international obligations (Rahmani and Jafari 2019, 70).

In its legal narrative, Iran adheres to the principle of sovereign equality as outlined in Article 2, Paragraph 1 of the United Nations Charter. This principle supports the stability of the post-World War II world order and the solidarity of the UN, requiring member states to cooperate across political, economic and social differences to maintain international peace, security and economic stability (Shafi'i and Akhavan 2019, 55). One of the sanctions being criticised the most in this regard is the Iran and Libya Sanctions Act (US Congress 1995–6), on the basis that it is in clear violation of Paragraph 3 of Article 1 of the United Nations Charter regarding international cooperation in solving international problems that have economic, social, cultural or humanitarian aspects (United Nations 1945).

Regarding the JCPOA, Tehran considers the US withdrawal from the JCPOA on 8 May 2018 and the reinstatement of all economic sanctions that were suspended or stopped by the JCPOA as a violation of international law, including United Nations Security Council Resolution 2231.[2]

Iran's reference to the violation of citizens' rights and human rights is another difference between Iran's legal approach and that of sanctioning countries. It has been discussed more with the expansion of the scope of sanctions, including targeted sanctions against Iran and its extension to individuals. Iran considers the sanctioning of individuals in government positions as a violation of diplomatic and consular immunity, state asset immunity and the obligations of the host government. In addition, the sanctioning of these individuals when their official service ends, as well as the sanctioning of nuclear scientists who do not have a government position, conflicts with human rights obligations, including the right to freedom of movement, the right to private property and the right to access justice (Ziyai and Mohammadi Mutlaq 2014, 169).

Legal studies in Iran have denounced the impacts of sanctions on the lives of ordinary people and their basic rights (Rahmani and Jafari 2019). The dramatic devaluation of Iran's currency has deepened poverty for the middle and lower classes. Sanctions have also significantly harmed civilian life, particularly in the health sector, a situation worsened during the COVID-19 pandemic. While Executive waivers were granted for COVID-19-related assistance,

[2] On 16 July 2018, Iran filed a lawsuit against the US in the International Court of Justice, claiming that the reinstatement of nuclear sanctions violated the 1955 Treaty of Amity. Iran requested a temporary order to halt sanctions, including extraterritorial ones, and prevent further sanctions. The court later issued a temporary order requiring the US to remove obstacles to the export of medication, medical equipment, food, agricultural items and equipment related to the safety of passenger flights to Iran (International Court of Justice 2021, 11).

delineating crucial exemptions such as medical gowns, ophthalmic shields, protective glasses, surgical gloves and face shields by the US Treasury Department (OFAC 2023, 3), Iran encountered practical hurdles due to imposed sanctions, particularly the closure of the Society for Worldwide Interbank Financial Transfers (SWIFT). These restrictions notably affected the import of essential equipment embedded with advanced technology, encompassing vital tools like real-time PCR and X-ray machines, along with specific hospital gear indispensable for Intensive Care Unit (ICU)/ Coronary Care Unit (CCU) beds. Moreover, during the COVID-19 pandemic in Iran, impediments persisted in accessing advanced testing and hospital equipment (Pormasoumi et al. 2022).

Consequently, Iran claims that the rights of its citizens have been threatened and violated as a result of international sanctions, since accessing medications and medical and therapeutic equipment requires more time and a much higher cost with a higher risk. Rather than importing food and medication from major producing countries, they are purchased from intermediate and third-producing countries. Even after the JCPOA, when the interactions between European and Iranian banks were permitted in the scope of trading humanitarian goods including food, medication and agriculture, concerns about the potential reintroduction of restrictive conditions from the US led Western banks to pursue a cautious strategy of de-risking and they generally avoided cooperation with Iranian banks (Islami and Naghdi 2016, 51).

Another example is air pollution, which is a particular concern in Iran, reportedly causing high levels of respiratory and other diseases that lead to 4,000 premature deaths per year in Tehran and 40,000 premature deaths annually in all of Iran. The sanctions make it impossible for Iran to obtain equipment and technology to reduce vehicle emissions (OHCHR 2022a). As Alena Douhan, the United Nations High Commissioner for Human Rights Special Rapporteur on the negative impacts of unilateral coercive measures, stated during her visit to Iran in May 2022, economic sanctions have increased inflation and poverty and aggravated the humanitarian situation (OHCHR 2022b).

Historical-Identity Lens

Iran's political identity and historical memory of confronting great powers (particularly Europe and the US) have shaped influential ideas that significantly affect Iran's perception of the international order, including its views on international sanctions. This dynamic reflects a form of interpretative contestation, as Iran's historical experiences influence its understanding and interpretation of global power structures and the legitimacy of external pressures like sanctions.

Iran's Historical Memory: Falling from an Ancient Empire to a Semi-colonised Country in the Nineteenth Century

Iran is a country with a long history of civilisation, and in this regard, it rightly prides itself on being one of the oldest cultures in the world (Jordet 2002, 13–14). Ancient Iran during the Achaemenids and the Sasanians, with stunning wealth and power, was a reality in political affairs and the manifestation of people who were able to rule half of the world with very effective and admirable methods (Eslami 2014, 130).

However, Iran has historically faced conflicts with great powers like Ancient Greece, the Roman Empire and the Ottoman Empire, contributing to a sense of insecurity (Jordet 2002, 12). This vulnerability continued in its relations with European powers, such as Britain and Portugal, whose colonial expansion led to Western interference in Iran. The Portuguese occupied parts of southern Iran, and British influence led to the separation of Herat and parts of Khorasan (Moradi 2019, 138). During World War II, Iran was occupied by the Allies after Germany attacked the Soviet Union (Eslami 2014, 126). A key moment in Iran's historical memory of Western intervention is the 1953 coup against Dr Mossadegh, a respected nationalist who advocated for non-alignment in foreign policy (Abrahamian 2021, 76). This event marked the beginning of a period of foreign presence in Iran that shaped the understanding of the current elite towards existing power structure of the international system led by the US and its Western allies.

Iran's Political Identity

After the Islamic Revolution, a strong anti-colonial and anti-imperialist tendency became institutionalised in Iran. In fact, Iran's ancient glory, its historical memory of confronting the West and its feelings of insecurity and mistrust towards great powers – combined with religious teachings – shaped a new identity for the country. This identity has three dimensions: revolutionary, Islamic and third-world. From this perspective, Iran has pursued a just order that rejects colonial and hegemonic policies (Moshirzadeh and Jafari 2012, 57). Additionally, the concept of self-reliant development emerged, emphasising the minimisation of reliance on external aid, fostering local industries, and advancing economic and social initiatives driven by internal resources and capacities.

In this context, the Western approach to engaging with the Islamic Republic of Iran has also played a role in intensifying Iran's political identity and behaviour. A significant portion of Western reactions stems from mistrust of Iran and perceptions of it as a threat (Jordet 2002, 23). Since the establishment of the Islamic Republic, the West has adhered to a 'status quo challenger' stance. Despite President Rafsanjani's efforts to reduce tensions and diminish

Iran's revolutionary identity, relations with Europe remained strained (Moradi 2019, 140), and US hostility escalated following the hostage crisis. The West continues to view Iran's nuclear and missile programmes as threats to regional and European stability. Concerns about Iran's nuclear ambitions have been amplified by perceptions of the country's potential threat to the Middle East and Europe, including its missile programme (Rasouli Sani Abadi 2010, 2). These apprehensions were further heightened during the Ahmadinejad administration through the securitisation of Iran's nuclear programme and, in recent years, by the West's aggressive sanctions policies.

At present, given Iran's political-historical identity, resistance to the colonial order and the belief that hegemonic powers prioritise their own interests over global well-being, these factors prominently shape Iran's perception of the international system, including its response to international sanctions.

Anti-colonial and Anti-imperialist Views

Iran perceives sanctions as a tool used to restrain and punish any country that diverges from the liberal democratic order of the West. Consequently, it engages in an interpretative contestation over the meaning of international sanctions. From Iran's perspective, sanctions are not an instrument of global governance but rather a means for the United States to distinguish between allies and adversaries. The US, as the leader of this order, adopts a distinct identity and a global mission for itself, shaping its own identity and defining others as either friends or enemies (Moshirzadeh and Salavati 2013, 77).

One aspect of Iran's understanding of the international system is its strategic loneliness in the context of the unfairness of the order and regional threats, which deepened during the eight-year war with Iraq. The war with Iraq institutionalised the belief in Iran not only that one cannot trust international rules and order (Hadian and Hormozi 2010, 187), but also that this war was a 'systemic war', in the sense that a wide range of global and regional powers kept silent against Saddam Hussein's aggression and his illegitimate use of chemical weapons to contain Iran, which is defined as a state outside of the liberal order (Mesbahi 2011, 16). This interpretation, along with the perception of regional threats, led Iran to develop its nuclear programme (Hadian and Hormozi 2010, 188), and to perceive the behaviour of the West, with its economic and political punitive sanctions, in the context of a reluctance to engage Iran and potentially befriend it (Mesbahi 2011, 17).

Iran points out that even with strict hardliners in power and an atmosphere full of anger and mistrust from the international order in the early days of Iran's Islamic revolution (1979–80), it continued to adhere to its commitments to the Treaty on the Non-Proliferation of Nuclear Weapons (NPT). However, the international community did not recognise Iran's security challenges and adopted a double standard, imposing sanctions on Iran but not on other countries such as Israel.

Iran also argues that, although US, EU and UN sanctions contributed to its decision to enter negotiations leading to the JCPOA (Congressional Research Service 2023), the achievements of these sanctions were not as beneficial for the West as often portrayed. This is because developments within the region, the US withdrawal from the JCPOA, the expansion of Western demands and the focus on Iran's ballistic missile programme demonstrated that sanctions were not solely a response to Iran's nuclear programme. Instead, they served as a tool of the Western international system to address broader grievances with Iran, including its very existence.

Since the inception of the nuclear agreement and the phased relaxation of UN sanctions, the West and its regional allies, deeply mistrustful of Iran, have expressed concerns about Iran's growing influence. This mistrust, which has overshadowed interactions between Iran and the West, remains pervasive today (Heffron 2015, 7; Katzman, McInnis and Clayton 2020). In November 2022, European Commission President Ursula von der Leyen emphasised that 'in addition to preventing the development of Iran's nuclear weapons, we must also focus on other forms of weapon proliferation, from drones to ballistic missiles. It is a security risk [. . .] for us all' (Immenkamp and Claustre 2023). The West's dual standards and contradictory behaviour, especially considering the recent developments in Gaza and Israel's attacks on Iran in 2024 and 2025, have intensified Iran's distrust towards the West – on the one hand, saying that we don't want to see escalation; on the other hand, providing the Israelis with every piece of equipment, every bomb, every piece of intelligence that allows them to escalate, then offering them protection against any Iranian retaliation, which in turn reduces the cost of escalation for the Israelis. This approach effectively lowers the cost of aggressive actions for Israel' (Parsi 2024) – while deeply reinforcing Iran's sense of isolation and vulnerability.

From the standpoint of the authorities of the Islamic Republic of Iran, the issue of sanctions should be considered as part of the pattern of limiting Iran's power in international politics (Clawson 2012, 16). Sanctions have isolated Iran from the international system and pushed it closer to powers like China and Russia. In this context, Iran perceives Western sanctions against Russia as an effort by the liberal democratic order to silence dissenting voices, whether revolutionary Islam or illiberal.[3]

The Interests of the International System against the Interests of Countries

The intensification of US unilateral and secondary sanctions against Iran is seen as an example of great powers prioritising their interests over international norms, including the non-compliance with Article 6 of the NPT on nuclear disarmament (Keyvan Hosseini and Eshrati 2014, 50). This view is rooted in historical events, such as Britain bringing the 1951 oil dispute with Iran to the Security Council as a threat to international peace (Marsh 1951).[4]

In the years following the 1979 revolution, the US designated Iran as a 'State Sponsor of Terrorism (SSOT)' during the Reagan administration, while the George W. Bush administration called Iran a part of 'the axis of evil' (Congressional Research Service 2023, 16). This was despite the fact that the Rafsanjani and Khatami governments took great steps to improve Iran's relationship with the international system.

However, the US withdrawal from the JCPOA under Donald Trump was a strong confirmation for those in Iran who do not trust the West and it marginalised centrists and moderationists who welcomed negotiations with the West. The fundamentalists believe the sanction regime is basically a punitive tool, in line with the interests of the West, since Iran's interaction and cooperation with the West did not reduce or eliminate the sanctions. In fact, the

[3] At the G7 summit, member states (Canada, France, Germany, Italy, Japan, the UK and the US) claimed that Russia–Iran arms cooperation in Ukraine violates the UN missile embargo under Security Council Resolution 2231 (Immenkamp and Claustre 2023). Iran's sanctions programme is significant not only for Iran but for the entire international legal system. The G7's actions towards sanctions can be seen as institutionalising them against a country. The US and some Western countries' efforts to reimpose UN sanctions under the JCPOA's snap-back procedure mark a turning point that could widen divisions within the international system and the UN.

[4] Britain occupied Iran in World War II to protect a supply route to its ally, the Soviet Union, and to prevent the oil from falling into the hands of the Nazis. It retained control over Iran's oil after the war through the Anglo-Iranian Oil Company (New York Times 2000). Also, Iran's historical memory remembers, in the issue of the struggle over the nationalisation of Iranian oil, the serious concern of the United States and other Western powers as well as Great Britain was due to the fact that differences with Iran might throw that strategically placed country into the arms of Moscow (Marsh 1951).

policy of maximum pressure against Iran is indicative of purely punitive sanctions against Tehran to weaken its internal and regional power and to gain more objectives beyond Iran's nuclear programme (Takhshid and Alikarami 2021, 685). This does not imply that Iran is rigid or unwilling to negotiate. Yet, its starting point is not trust but prudence. Over the years, this prudence has only intensified, particularly as the West frequently resorts to what it terms 'alternatives' to diplomatic efforts. History always comes before any conversation. And for Iran, history repeatedly delivers the same warning: you are isolated, so act accordingly (Khatami 2025).

Based on the four principles of sanction legitimacy discussed earlier, Iran views any international mechanism linked to sanctions as serving Western/American interests. Consequently, as outlined in Orchard and Wiener's chapter, Iran's contestation of sanctions converges into a blend of interpretative and reactive contestation.

Reactive contestation is evident in Iran's efforts to delegitimise both the basis of the sanctions and the entities imposing them. Interpretative contestation reflects differing understandings of the underlying norms of the sanctions regime. Iran's objection to sanctions is partly rooted in anti-colonial principles, which shape its interpretation of sanctions as instruments aligned with the interests of former colonial powers.

Despite this ideological stance, Iran has displayed measured responses to sanctions over time. While contesting the legitimacy of sanctions, it has exercised restraint by refraining from immediate counter-measures. Instead, Iran strategically channels its criticisms through established international frameworks, such as the United Nations General Assembly and diplomatic consultations. This approach reflects a commitment to diplomatic engagement while challenging conflicting principles.

Conversely, during periods of intensified sanctions, Iran has often adopted a more reactive stance. This is exemplified by the implementation of counter-measures, colloquially referred to as the 'counter-measure plan', which has garnered domestic support. Notable examples include discussions surrounding potential withdrawal from the Nuclear Non-Proliferation Treaty (NPT) and the expulsion of inspectors, illustrating Iran's more assertive reactions to heightened sanctions.

Iran's narrative about sanctions can also be described in terms of a delegitimisation of sanctions, drawing on Palestini's chapter in this volume. He categorises the delegitimisation of sanctions based on claim, claimant and action (or contestation of the norm, the sender and the measure), in which the countries opposing sanctions challenge their legitimacy by resorting to one or a combination of these aspects.

Iran's critical discourse primarily focuses on two aspects: the claim and the claimant. Regarding the claim, Iran asserts that it has not violated any international norms. This assertion has been strongly supported by Iran's political and legal circles, which challenge the allegations of norm violation. With reference to its nuclear programme, Iran always maintains that it is not seeking nuclear weapons and not threatening international peace, and considers its nuclear programme a fundamental right of its people. In addition, Iran expresses the belief that even if a norm has been violated, it does not guarantee the violation of the principles of sovereign equality and non-interference in the internal affairs of countries. Citing United Nations Security Council Resolution 2625, Iran argues that the sanctions violate these principles and are inherently illegitimate.

Since most sanctions against Iran come from the United States, Iran's narrative of sanctions is shaped by its understanding of US sanctions. Iran's discourse on delegitimisation focuses on the claimant (sender of sanctions). Palestini examines this perspective by discussing the right to respond to norm violations, emphasising principles like sovereign equality, UNSC authority and prohibitions against force. Iran rejects the authority of Europe and the US to unilaterally impose sanctions, considering them legitimate only if sanctioned by the UN Security Council. Additionally, Iran challenges the legitimacy of sanctioning bodies based on the principles of international cooperation and stability outlined in the UN Charter and the 1970 Declaration of Friendly Relations.

Iranian Society's Understanding of Sanctions

There are different views of sanctions outside of the dominant political elite that challenge the legitimacy of sanctions.[5] Different views among Iranians outside the political elites are focused on the economic effects of the sanctions such as the fall in the value of the Iranian currency and increasing inflation,

[5] It is not possible to provide a detailed study of the opinions of all Iranian groups regarding sanctions, because it requires a quantitative study, taking into account time variables (such as the coincidence with the economic demands of the people from the government or the occurrence of a national incident and the emergence of nationalist sentiments, etc.) and spatial variables (different cultural and economic conditions of Iran's regions), and such studies have not been done yet. While it is necessary to mention this point, there are also different spectrums among the groups opposed to the Iranian government, which do not all equally support the severity of the sanctions against Iran. In this regard, their views on sanctions should be discussed in a different political context, which is beyond the purpose of this study.

as well as their historical memory of Iran's civilisation. Even among groups opposed to the Islamic Republic, there is a view that Western sanctions, though seen as necessary, have harmed the Iranian people's economic life more than they have weakened the government's power. The impact of these sanctions has reinforced the Iranian government's belief that sanctions are part of an international effort aimed at regime change through social unrest.

The economic life of the Iranian people has been weakened drastically since the application of US 'maximum pressure' sanctions in 2018. For the working class and low-income people, the new sanctions and renewed isolation have meant fewer jobs, less security and more poverty. For the middle class and people in large cities, renewed sanctions – especially alongside the talk of war – present an existential threat to the meagre well-being they worked so hard to cobble together (Arian and Bouzari 2018).

For this reason, the society in general considers sanctions as a cruel and unjust tool applied to their country, their lives and their children's future. Those who are in favour of reaching a nuclear agreement became very hopeful about their future interaction with the world, the potential for tension-free relations, and even celebrated the achievement of the JCPOA. However, with the escalation of mutual tensions and the US government's tightening of sanctions after 2018, this group also distrusted the West and the goals of the sanctions. The mentalities and perceptions of people are involved in interpreting the consequences of sanctions (Rasoulinezhad and Sung 2021).

Since summer 2014, the Centre for International and Security Studies at Maryland (CISSM) has surveyed Iranian public opinion on nuclear policy, regional security, economics and domestic issues. Three surveys in 2019 showed a notable decline in Iranian confidence regarding the nuclear deal and the commitment of involved nations, with initial trust in other countries being higher than in the US (CISSM 2019). Confidence in the other P5+1 countries remained stable until April 2018 but then steadily declined, especially in 2019. By May 2019, only 41 per cent trusted these countries to fulfil their obligations and scepticism grew, dropping to 30 per cent by August, with 67 per cent expressing doubt (CISSM 2019, 8).

Other findings from the report highlight a significant shift in the economic concerns of Iranians, with a pronounced move from worries about unemployment to inflation. When asked about the negative effect of sanctions on the lives of ordinary citizens, 57 per cent described it as 'great', with 26 per cent acknowledging some negative impact. Interestingly, those who perceived a significant negative impact from sanctions were just as resistant to concessions on enrichment as the overall surveyed population (CISSM 2019, 28).

The reimposition of US sanctions altered the attribution of Iran's economic challenges. Although a majority still attribute the economy's woes to domestic mismanagement and corruption, there is a growing percentage placing blame on sanctions (CISSM 2019).

Conclusion

Iran is a country that has been under sanctions for a long period of time. Sanctions originated with US unilateral sanctions imposed on Iran after the Islamic Revolution in 1979. Between 2006 and 2010, Iran's nuclear programme was securitised, first by the UN and later by the European Union. These sanctions cumulatively developed into a nearly comprehensive regime of sanctions, including restrictions on banking, finance, commerce, energy, transportation and individual sanctions on both institutions and individuals. Although Iran's narrative of sanctions is mostly a response to the unilateral sanctions of the United States, particularly since 2018, this view has also spread to the sanctions of the international community by the United Nations and the European Union.

The understanding of Iran's narrative of sanctions is deeply rooted in its identity as a revolutionary Islamic country and its experience interacting with the West. Especially, the colonial legacies and the role of the UK and the US in the fall of Mossadegh government in 1953 are particularly relevant. This historical-identity lens has led to two important concepts in understanding Iran's contestation of sanctions. Firstly, Iran sees the liberal system as a continuation of the nineteenth-century imperialist system and sanctions as a purely punitive tool used against all countries that are different from or challenge the liberal system. Iran's revolutionary identity endangers the liberal world order. The belief that sanctions are a legitimate tool in the service of world peace traps Iran in a situation of strategic loneliness and regional threats. The West has not accepted the identity and existence of the Islamic Republic of Iran and has constructed it as a permanent threat. This issue gained even more resonance following the 2025 war between Israel and Iran. Iran perceives this war as a real threat to its existence, accompanied by the silence and support of the West. This situation not only highlights the West's double standards, especially in parallel with developments in Gaza, but also rekindles the sense of strategic loneliness and security concerns for Iran's survival – concerns that had deepened during the eight-year war with Iraq.

Secondly, sanctions not only did not lead to Iran's integration in the international system but, because sanctions serve the interests of the hegemon's foreign policy more than global interests, they forced Iran to move further away from the international system and join forces with countries that challenge the system, namely China and Russia.

The legal lens is the second framework that informs Iran's narrative of sanctions. Referring to legal principles such as the principle of non-intervention, sovereign equality, the rights of individuals, and human rights, Iran considers unilateral sanctions as an intervention in the country and a threat to its sovereignty. Furthermore, based on the negative effects of international sanctions, especially since 2018, such as the increase in poverty and limitations of access to medicine and food, Iran has called sanctions an illegitimate and unfair tool.

Influenced by dual lenses of its historical identity and legal framework, Iran has concluded that any international mechanism or organisation associated with sanctions is under the influence of Western/American interests. Consequently, the observed contestation in Iran's behaviour during periods of sanctions tends to manifest itself more as a combination of interpretative and reactive contestation, rather than a proactive one. The coexistence of interpretative contestation and its proponents within Iran introduces a unique dimension also to its reactive contestation. Unlike some other nations, such as Russia and North Korea, Iran's reactive contestation does not unilaterally dominate its response to Western sanctions. In essence, Iran's reactive contestation manifests itself within the realm of diplomatic and strategic threats, coupled with the escalation of relations with countries perceived as challenging the international order. At the same time, it refrains from outright violations of international commitments, such as withdrawing from the NPT or abandoning the JCPOA.

Iran's reaction to Russia's attack on Ukraine and subsequent Western sanctions offers insight into its historical and political understanding of sanctions. While Iran condemned the attack on another country's territory, it also highlighted the West's efforts to deploy NATO near Russia and Russia's security concerns as factors contributing to the conflict. The stance, as characterised by the Atlantic Council, is attributed to Iran's strategic partnership with Russia and the strained relations between Iran and the United States (Grajewski 2022). However, Iran refrained from unilaterally defending Russia. Iranian Foreign Minister Amir Abdollahian emphasised Iran's commitment to avoiding war and called for a diplomatic resolution. Additionally, Iran's abstention during the United Nations General Assembly vote on 2 March (Grajewski 2022) further underscored its cautious approach and unwillingness to fully endorse Russia's aggressive actions. Regarding the Western sanctions against Russia, Iran deemed them illegitimate, arguing that they served to protect Western interests rather than promote global stability. Iran's decision not to participate in these sanctions underscores its alignment with Russia in opposing Western narratives on sanctions.

Overall, Iran's response reflects a complex interplay of geopolitical considerations, emphasising the need for diplomatic solutions while maintaining a critical stance on Western interventions and sanctions policies.

References

Abrahamian, Ervand. 1982. *Iran between Two Revolutions*. Princeton University Press.

Alikarami, Fariba. 2019. 'American Economic Sanctions, Substitute for Military Tools or a Platform for War'. *International Conference on World Economy and Sanctions* [in Persian].

Arian, Amir, and Rahman Bouzari. 2018. 'What Sanctions Mean to Iranians'. *New York Times*, 10 May.

CISSM. 2019. 'Iranian Public Opinion under "Maximum Pressure"'. The Centre for International and Security Studies at Maryland, 16 October.

Congressional Research Service. 2023. 'Iran: Background and U.S. Policy Updated'. 23 March.

Council of the European Union. 2023. 'Iran: EU Restrictive Measures'. 5 June.

Clawson, Patrick. 2012. 'Sanctions Are Only a Stop-Gap'. *Foreign Affairs*, 9 May.

Drezner, Daniel. 1999. *The Sanctions Paradox: Economic Statecraft and International Relations*. Cambridge University Press.

Drezner, Daniel W. 2003. 'The Hidden Hand of Economic Coercion'. *International Organization* 57(3): 643–59.

Drury, A. Cooper. 2000. 'U.S. Presidents and the Use of Economic Sanctions'. *Presidential Studies Quarterly* 30(4): 623–42.

Energy Information Administration (EIA). 2022a. 'Country Analysis Executive Summary: Iran', 17 November.

Energy Information Administration (EIA). 2022b. 'Executive Order 13846 – Reimposing Certain Sanctions with Respect to Iran', 6 August.

Eslami, Rouhollah. 2014. 'Iran's Foreign Policy between the Two Revolutions'. *Iranian Review of Foreign Affairs* 5(1): 121–54.

Grajewski, Nicole. 2022. 'As the World Shuns Russia over Its Invasion of Ukraine, Iran Strengthens Its Ties with Moscow'. *Atlantic Council*, 7 March.

Hadian, Nasser, and Shani Hormozi. 2010. 'Iran's Nuclear Program: Lawful Capability'. *Research Letter of Political Science* 5(3): 179–214 [in Persian].

Heffron, Daniel. 2015. 'How the Iran Deal Will Re-shape the Balance of Power in the Middle East: A Look at Saudi Arabia and Iran'. *Centre for Geopolitics & Security in Realism Studies*, 12 August.

International Court of Justice. 2021. 'Alleged Violations of the 1955 Treaty of Amity, Economic Relations, and Consular Rights (Iran v. U.S.)'. 3 February.

Immenkamp, Beatrix and Julie Claustre. 2023. 'EU Relations with Iran'. *European Parliamentary Research (EPRS).*

Islami, Mohsen, and Farzaneh Naghdi. 2016. 'Sanction Tool and US Government's Foreign Policy towards Iran'. *Foreign Relations Quarterly* 8(4): 3–71 [in Persian].

Jordet, Nils. 2002. 'Explaining the Long-term Hostility between the United States and Iran: A Historical, Theoretical and Methodological Framework'. PhD diss., The Fletcher School of Law and Diplomacy, Tufts University.

Katzman, Kenneth, Kathleen McInnis and Thomas Clayton. 2020. 'U.S.–Iran Conflict and Implications for U.S. Policy'. *Congressional Research Service*, 8 May.

Keyvan Hosseini, Asghar, and Fahimeh Eshrati. 2014. 'A Conceptual Structural Approach to the Evolution and Intensification of the US Sanctions Policy on Iran (1980–2012)'. *Policy Research Quarterly* 2(8) [in Persian].

Khatami, Emad. 2025 'What the West Misunderstands about Iran'. *Responsible Statecraft*, 21 July.

Marsh, Michael. 1951. 'Oil Nationalization'. *CQ Press*, 30 October.

Mesbahi, Mohiaddin. 2011. 'Free and Confined: Iran and the International System'. *Iranian Review of Foreign Affairs* 2(5): 9–34.

Momtaz, Jamshid. 1981. 'Economic Sanctions and Public International Law'. *Journal of Faculty of Law and Political Science* 22: 215–26 [in Persian].

Moradi, Massoud. 2019. 'Interaction and Confrontation in the Foreign Relations of Iran and the European Union'. *Journal of Historical Researches of Iran and Islam* 1(25): 136–54 [in Persian].

Moshirzadeh, Homeira, and Fatemeh Salavati. 2013. 'Islamic World/the Fundamentalist Other and the Myth of the American Ideal in America's Foreign Policy'. *Foreign Relations Quarterly* 5(1): 73–105 [in Persian].

Moshirzadeh, Homeira, and Hormoz Jafari. 2012. 'Hegemon Power and Revolutionary Governments: A Case Study of America and the Islamic Republic of Iran'. *Foreign Relations* 4(1): 47–77 [in Persian].

New York Times. 2000. 'Secrets of History: The CIA in Iran'. *New York Times*. Available at https://archive.nytimes.com/www.nytimes.com/library/world/mideast/041600iran-cia-chapter1.html (accessed on 4 October 2025).

OFAC. 2023. 'Fact Sheet: Provision of Humanitarian Assistance and Trade to Combat COVID-19 Date'. The Office of Foreign Assets Control, Department of the Treasury, 14 June.

OHCHR 2022a. 'US Sanctions Violate Iranian People's Rights to Clean Environment, Health and Life: UN Experts'. The Office of the United Nations High Commissioner for Human Rights, 20 December.

OHCHR. 2022b. 'Iran: Unilateral Sanctions and Overcompliance Constitute Serious Threat to Human Rights and Dignity: UN Expert'. The Office of the United Nations High Commissioner for Human Rights, 19 May.

Parsi, Trita. 2024. 'We Are in an Escalatory Cycle'. *Democracy Now*, 28 October.

Pormasoumi, Hosein, Daryoush Rostami, Khosro Jamebozorgi, Hosein Mirshekarpour and Jalal Heshmatnia. 2022. 'COVID-19 Management in Iran and International Sanctions'. *European Journal of Translational Myology* 32(4).

Rahmani, Shahram, and Afshin Jafari. 2019. 'Confrontation of Unilateralism and the Rule of Law in International Law; Case Study: US Sanctions against Iran'. *Political Studies of the Islamic World* 9(4): 53–71 [in Persian].

Rasoulinezhad, Ehsan, and Jinsok Sung. 2021. 'Determinants of the Intention of Iranian People to Accept the Changes of Social Welfare under the Imposed Sanctions'. *Journal of World Sociopolitical Studies* 5(1): 133–56.

Rasouli Sani Abadi, Elham. 2010. 'Maintaining Ontological Security and Irreconcilability of the Islamic Republic of Iran in Nuclear Policy'. *Political Sciences* 11(51) [in Persian].

Sajjadpour, Mohammad Kazem. 1997. 'Evaluation of Dual Deterrence: Four Different Views'. *Foreign Policy* 11(1): 7–16 [in Persian].

Security Council. 2006. Resolution 1737. 23 December.

Shafi'i, Mahmoud, and Bahar Akhavan. 2019. 'Sanctions of Iran and the United States of America against the Islamic Republic of Iran from the Perspective of International Law'. *Journal of Human Rights Research* 1(15): 41–60 [in Persian].

Takhshid, Mohammad Reza, and Fariba Alikarami. 2021. 'Economic Sanctions and War in US Foreign Policy in the Post-Cold War Era'. *Politics Quarterly* 51(3): 669–91 [in Persian].

United Nations. 1945. *Charter of the United Nations*. 26 June.

United Nations. 1967. 'International Covenant on Civil and Political Rights'. Available from https://treaties.un.org/doc/treaties/1976/03/19760323%2006-17%20am/ch_iv_04.pdf

US Congress. 1995–6. 'Iran and Libya Sanctions Act of 1996'. 104th Congress H.R.3107.

US Congress. 2010. 'Comprehensive Iran Sanctions, Accountability, and Divestment Act of 2010'. Public Law 111–195 111th Congress, 1 July.

Zachary, Laub. 2015 'International Sanctions on Iran'. *Foreign Council Relation*, 15 July.

Ziyai, Yaser, and Alireza Mohammadi Mutlaq. 2014. 'Sanctions of Natural Persons from the Perspective of International Law with an Emphasis on the Sanctions of Some Iranian Nationals'. *Judicial Law Journal* 78(88): 146–78.

7

Unilateral Sanctions: China's Contestations and (De)legitimation Orientations

*Wenjie Yu**

Introduction

For the purpose of explaining why governments challenge sanctions and their application, the second part of this volume brings together a collection of reflections on how sanctions have been experienced and understood in different national and regional contexts. This chapter provides a nuanced exploration of China's stance on international sanctions, in particular the unilateral ones, and reveals a subtle interplay between rhetoric and action.

As a traditional target of sanctions, China has gradually grown into a dual role of target and source country in the use of sanctions. On the one hand, being perceived as a 'strategic, near-peer, global competitor' (United States Congress 2021) and 'a systemic rival promoting alternative models of governance' (European Commission 2019), China remains targeted by a constant and dramatic number of sanctions. On the other, China's own use of sanctions, much 'more assertive' (Reilly 2012; Friedberg 2018) since 2010 and 'not merely for retaliation but as an affirmative tool of policy and to advance a wide range of national interests' (Nephew 2019, 2), has been 'observed' and discussed repeatedly since 2012 (Hufbauer and Jung 2020; Wisniewski 2021; Ghiretti 2023).

In contrast to this pivotal inflection in action, China has maintained long-standing rhetorical opposition to the use of unilateral sanctions, though

* This research is supported by National Social Science Fund (21BFX146). This chapter is a follow-up to an earlier article, *China's Emerging Unilateral Sanctions: Heading towards the Rule of Law?* This chapter has greatly benefited from the comments of Professor Thomas Biersteker.

some fine-tuning has been made in its rhetoric. Until very recently, the Foreign Ministry spokespersons were long reiterating in a series of regular Ministry of Foreign Affairs (MFA) press conferences that China firmly opposes 'unilateral sanctions that have no basis in international law or authorization of the UN Security Council' or 'illegal unilateral sanctions' (MFA 2024f; MFA 2024g). This has resulted in a widespread perception among scholars and analysts that China has landed in a paradox where, despite contesting unilateral sanctions as interference in internal affairs, China strategically employs them as tools in political diplomacy and economic statecraft when safeguarding its national interests, which in turn makes China's sanction behaviour seemingly puzzling.

The majority of the existing international relations literature and international law literature, with their emphasis on whether and/or how sanctions are effective in achieving policy outcomes, and on whether and/or how sanctions are/can be legal or legitimate, has neglected this important element of sanctions rhetoric and, more importantly, the sophisticated interplay between rhetoric and action, and consequently has provided little information for deciphering this puzzle.

One valuable endeavour in this regard is the norm contestation theory (Orchard and Wiener, this volume), which defines contestation in international relations as 'the range of social practices which discursively express disapproval of norms' (Wiener 2014, 1) and articulates a set of tools for analysing a nation state's stance on international sanctions. Norm contestation theory, with its focus on how international norms are formulated and/or reformulated, is broadly similar to the approach employed by the international law discipline. Although it views norms as processes, 'as works-in-progress, rather than as finished products' (Krook and True 2012, 105), which seemingly deviates from the general understanding of international norms as result of norm-making processes in the international law discipline, the norm contestation theory actually corresponds with the international law discipline in identifying the fundamental characteristic of international norms, that is 'while stable over particular periods, they always remain flexible by definition' (Wiener 2007, 49). With its three distinct types of norm contestations (Orchard and Wiener 2023), as *interpretative, proactive and reactive* contestations, norm contestation theory provides exactly for analysing the variance between rhetoric and the actual application of measures such as sanctions.

The further development of contestation theory on international sanctions, adding the analytical grid of (de)legitimation of international sanctions, is also helpful (see the Introduction to this volume). Viewing international sanctions as a practice, the grid describes the three dimensions of sanctioning understood as a practice – the claim, the claimant and the action – to better analyse (de)legitimation statements pronounced by states against international sanctions as delegitimation of the violated norms, delegitimation of the enforcers and delegitimation of the measures (Palestini, this volume).

This chapter, with its comprehensive review of China's change of rhetoric and practice of unilateral sanctions in the second and third sections respectively, focuses on applying norm contestation theory on international sanctions, to analyse whether China's perspective on sanctions constitutes a reactive, proactive or interpretative contestation of different international norms, and based upon such analysis, further reveals whether the Chinese contestation is focused on the norms themselves, criticism of the self-appointed enforcers of norms or the use of sanctions as a policy tool to enforce norms. In conclusion, China's current position on the international sanctions imposed on Russia is addressed in response to the initial questions that triggered this volume, which is why most states have decided not to adopt sanctions and how they explain and justify their 'lack of will' among the wave of sanctions against the Russian Federation.

China's Rhetorical Contestations of Unilateral Sanctions

China's rhetorical contestations of unilateral sanctions originate from its endeavour in countering the sanctions of Western states since its founding in 1949. It has been reiterated in the rhetoric of Chinese spokespersons/delegations on numerous occasions, particularly since 1971 when the People's Republic of China secured a permanent seat at the UN. In an early 2024 statement, the Foreign Ministry spokesperson reiterated China's stance against unilateral sanctions in a comment on the export controls on semiconductors imposed by the US against Chinese companies (MFA 2024g).

In a 2015 statement, the Chinese delegation argued that unilateral coercive measures obstruct developing states' efforts to protect human rights. It called on states to cease imposing measures inconsistent with the UN Charter, international law and international humanitarian law, and urged the international community to oppose the use or threatened use of unilateral sanctions and to mitigate their negative effects.

The Foreign Ministry spokespersons of China have regularly reiterated its oppositions against unilateral sanctions, in particular the 'illegal' or 'illicit' ones, when making comments on a variety of events involving sanctions. No matter in 'the comments on the imposition of unilateral sanctions against Iran by the US (MFA 2011; MFA 2019b) and the EU (China Daily 2010) over its refusal to halt its uranium enrichment programme, against North Korea by Japan (People 2017) over its nuclear and ballistic missile programmes, or against China by US (Global Times 2018) over its alleged infringement on national security' (Yu 2021, 361–2), China has repeatedly stressed:

> China remains consistent in its opposition to the US imposition of unilateral sanctions and so-called 'long-arm jurisdiction' on other countries invoking its domestic law, which is in violation of International Law and fundamental principles of international relations. (Central People's Government 2020)

A full review of the Foreign Ministry spokesperson's remarks at regular press conferences held in 2020–4, as recorded on the MFA website from 25 August 2020 to 3 December 2024, reveals that out of the total 997 regular press conferences, 192 referred to unilateral sanctions. Of these 192 conferences, 188 expressed clear opposition or reiterated opposition against unilateral sanctions, of which 94 referred specifically to unilateral sanction with the qualifier 'unlawful', 'illicit', 'in violation of international law' and so on, and the other 94 referred to unilateral sanction in general. Although the total number of references with qualifiers is comparable to the number of references in general, it is clear from Figure 7.1 that the use of qualifiers to refer specifically to illegal unilateral sanctions, namely to raise contestations on the 'illegal' unilateral sanctions specifically in these statements, has increased significantly in recent years.

Almost all of these contestations fall right into the scope of interpretative contestation, as they clearly challenge the legality or the legitimacy of the unilateral sanctions on the ground that unilateral sanctions invoking domestic law are in violation of international law and fundamental principles of international relations. Such contestations reflect China's perception of legitimate international sanctions as only those under the authorisation of the UN Security Council, as the only authoritative body in the international community, and/or international laws.

Such contestations are also a type of proactive contestation as they try to clarify the definition of the 'unilateral' sanctions, as imposed under one state's sole competence, no matter invoking international law or domestic law, for the purpose of its political interest or as retaliations, other than those imposed by one state under its international obligation to implement the UN sanctions decisions.

Some of the statements are a type of proactive contestation as well, as they attempt to refine the conditions for the use of sanctions. It's worth noting that

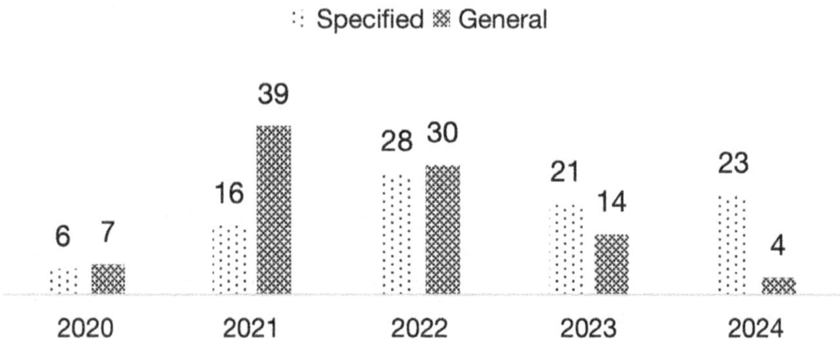

Figure 7.1 Comparison between specific and general reference in regular press conferences (2020–4), as recorded on the MFA website from 25 August 2020 to 3 December 2024

for UN sanctions, which include sanctions imposed by member states individually for the purpose of implementation, China sets the precondition that all peaceful means should have been exhausted before sanctions be imposed (Permanent Mission 2005).

One consistent pattern throughout these official statements is the emphasis on the (de)legitimation of unilateral sanctions. In terms of delegitimation of the violated norms, China remains discreet and alert to the political instrumentalisation of unilateral sanctions, especially those imposed to intervene into other state's national affairs, or impede the right of targeted countries to economic and social development, even with the 'legitimate' unilateral sanctions. In this sense, Chinese contestation is focused on the norms themselves, implicitly delegitimising unilateral sanctions as coercive measures that constitute external intervention on internal affairs and violation of state sovereignty.

The delegitimation of the enforcer is prominent in statements by China that draw a clear line between the UN sanctions as legitimate as opposed to unilateral sanctions imposed by states invoking domestic laws. From China's perspective, only those under the authorisation of UN or international law are recognised as legal unilateral sanctions. Though sanctions under the authorisation of UN Security Council are sometimes mis-categorised as unilateral, China has all along only opposed those invoking domestic laws, and those sneaking beyond the authorisation of multilateral decisions, as illegal ones. The expressions in Foreign Ministry spokespersons' regular press conferences are mostly identical as 'China firmly opposes any country citing its domestic laws to impose unilateral sanctions' (MFA 2020d; MFA 2020b). On one hand, unilateral sanctions imposed under the authorisation of UN are legal because they serve for authorised multilateral regulatory purpose. On the other hand, unilateral sanctions imposed by source countries as a counter-measure against a target country's illegal action are also justified under international law, just as those imposed by China.

Furthermore, the delegitimation of the enforcer that engages in power politics and violates the equality among states is also reflected in the statement of China that 'the abuse of unilateral sanctions stems from power politics and the law of the jungle. It gravely violates the purposes and principles of the UN Charter, the basic principle in international law of sovereign equality, and the basic norm governing international relations of non-interference in internal affairs' (MFA 2023b).

There is also delegitimation of the measures in the statements of China that 'object the type of measures that are adopted to impose a harm on the target' (Palestini, this volume). Such delegitimation statements are easy to find. For example, when commenting on the US's wantonly imposing illegal unilateral sanctions and 'long-arm jurisdiction' over Chinese companies, China claims that 'such practices gravely disrupt the international economic and trade order, destabilize global industrial and supply chains and harm the interests of all countries' (MFA 2024g). On the illegal sanctions imposed on Chinese companies by the US invoking the so-called US 'Uyghur Forced Labor Prevention Act', China objects that it

> does not protect human rights, but undermines the right to subsistence, employment and development of people in Xinjiang in the name of human rights. The act might as well be called the most notorious and egregious law against human rights in the 21st century. This act not only imposes illegal sanctions on Chinese companies, but also forces companies around the world to join in the US attempt to contain and suppress China in the name of 'compliance' and tries to create a coalition for economic coercion. This is a deliberate US action to serve its selfish agenda at the expense of international economic and trade rules and industrial and supply chains. (MFA 2024a)

China's Behavioural Contestations on Unilateral Sanctions

China's behavioural contestations on unilateral sanctions can be observed from two perspectives.

China's Unilateral Sanctions Practice as Behavioural Contestations

One is embedded in its own practice of adopting unilateral sanctions as a counter-measure against external intervention or infringement of China's right as a sovereign state. By chronological order, together with the frequency of adoption of sanctions, China's practice in this regard can be observed in three stages: stage I (1949–2009) when China seldomly imposed unilateral sanctions; stage II (2010–19) when China became active in adopting unilateral sanctions; and stage III (2020–) when China became even more assertive in the use of unilateral sanctions.

In terms of frequency, in contrast with China's unilateral sanctions practice before 2009, the decade of 2010–19 that is referred to as China's 'decade of sanctions'[1] witnessed twelve observed unilateral sanctions episodes imposed by China, as documented in Table 7.1, while only seven occurred throughout the sixty years between 1949 and 2009 (Yu 2021, 363). It is this 'decade of sanctions' rather than the pre-2009 period that has drawn attention from foreign observers and led to the suspicion that though China's stance against unilateral sanctions appears to be implacable, its practice speaks otherwise (Yu 2021, 363). Examination of the variables of the observed sanctions reveals three distinctive features of China's unilateral sanctions practice in its own 'decade of sanctions' (Yu 2021, 363, 366–7).

The first and foremost feature is 'act without words'. As in some cases, where throughout the entire unilateral sanctions episodes there were hardly any official words (Hufbauer et al. 2007),[2] the majority of China's unilateral sanctions episodes wrapped up in silence. Of twenty-one observed/alleged unilateral sanctions, only seven episodes were initiated via government press announcement, four of which related to US arms sales to Taiwan (CCTV 2010; People 2015; MFA 2019a; MFA 2020c), two related to China Central Government's exertion of sovereignty in Hong Kong Special Administrative Region (MFA 2019c) and Xinjiang Uygur Autonomous Region (MFA 2020a), and one related to the US imposing additional tariffs on Chinese goods (MFA 2018). For the remaining fourteen sanctions, no official declaration

[1] 'Decade of sanctions' has been used widely in the literature to describe the booming period of sanctions practice of US throughout the 1990s. See for example Cortright and Lopez 2000; Chan and Drury 2000; Haass 1997.

[2] As in the US sanctions against the United Kingdom over withdrawing troops from Suez in 1956, US and Dutch sanctions against Indonesia over conflict and human rights violations in East Timor between 1991 and 1997.

can be found and there only exist chronological connections that aligned the sanctions together with the corresponding triggers.

The second feature is 'triggered rather than initiated'. For each documented unilateral sanction, there is a perceived infringement of China's right as a sovereign state, and the unilateral sanctions that followed immediately after are considered from China's perspective 'retaliations' in accordance with international law. The main type of trigger that provoked China's imposition of unilateral sanctions against other states lies in challenge or infringement to its state sovereignty, which in particular includes those related to its territorial claims, the domestic political system or national security. For example, China adopted a series of sanction measures in 2002 (Fang 2020) and 2016 (Harrell et al. 2018, 47) against Mongolia for hosting the Dalai Lama, an identified separatist by China. Japan in 2010–12 (Harrell et al. 2018, 42) and the Philippines in 2012–16 (Harrell et al. 2018, 43–4) became recipients of unilateral sanctions imposed by China for incidents relating to territorial claims over disputed island and maritime areas.

The third feature is 'more expressive than instrumental'. David Baldwin divides economic sanctions into instrumental economic sanctions that aim at coercing the target country to obey and change, and expressive economic sanctions that respond to the need of domestic interest or deter the target country (Baldwin 1985). China used the unilateral sanctions or the threat of sanctions as an instrument of statecraft, 'to signal its frustration – a warning that if a country does not reverse a certain action, stronger repercussions will come' (Reilly 2012, 123). Hence, other than formal measures, the measures adopted in sanctions are more like gestures rather than actual goal-oriented instruments and mainly confined to 'vague threats, variation in leadership visits, selective purchases (or non-purchases), and other informal measures' (Reilly 2012, 123). For instance, over the THAAD deployment in South Korea in 2016–17, China adopted measures including curbing tourism, cutting imports of cultural products and taking regulatory measures against auto companies and Korean-owned Lotte Mart Stores in China (Harrell et al. 2018, 46–7). Also, in 2017 over Australia's legislation to control foreign influence, China issued warnings to Chinese students to maintain vigilance and nationalist newspapers campaigns (Harrell et al. 2018, 48–9). These measures were taken not to make the target country reverse their decision/action but rather as a signal or expression of China's frustration and a gesture of retaliation.

Two of the three distinctive features, as 'triggered' and 'expressive', of China's unilateral sanctions practice in 2010–20 remain all the way through to 2024, when China's unilateral sanctions behaviour started booming. Compared with the twelve alleged sanctions in the 'decade of sanctions', there were twenty-one sanctions imposed in just five years (2020–4). This is only half a decade. Nine of them came in a single year, 2024 (documented in Table 7.2). An outstanding change of practice is that sanctions are more imposed officially via the MFA press announcements at the beginning, and then the government orders, such as MFA orders.

In terms of contestation, the documented sanctions are in general a type of interpretative and proactive contestation as they are imposed as counter-measures justified under international law against certain types of norm violations, which in particular include the illegal unilateral sanctions that do not have the endorsement of the UN or international law. In this sense, they correspond with the consistent rhetorical contestations of China.

The observed unilateral sanctions imposed and provided for in China's sanctions law are claimed to be counter-measures whose wrongfulness is precluded under the Draft Articles on Responsibility of States for Internationally Wrongful Acts (Draft Articles on Responsibility 2001),[3] adopted by the International Law Commission in 2001, if they constitute responses of an injured state to a prior wrongful act of another state in accordance with Chapter II of Part Three of the Draft. Accordingly, for China's unilateral sanctions to be legal and legitimate, the substantive and procedural elements set out in the Draft should be complied with. For example, substantively, counter-measures shall not affect the obligation to refrain from the threat or use of force as embodied in the UN Charter, obligations for the protection of fundamental human rights, obligations of a humanitarian character prohibiting reprisals and other obligations under peremptory norms of general international law.[4] And procedurally, before taking counter-measures, an injured state shall call upon the responsible state, in accordance with Article 43, to fulfil its obligations under Part Two, and notify the responsible state of any decision to take counter-measures and offer to negotiate with that state.[5]

However, the Draft Articles on Responsibility 2001 is not a binding treaty *per se*. The rules stipulated in it are generally recognised and often applied as customary international law, which always involves interpretation in such application and forever evolves. As 'customary international law is the generalization

[3] International Law Commission, Draft Articles on Responsibility of States for Internationally Wrongful Acts, 53rd Sess., U.N. Doc. A/CN.4/SER.A/2001/Add.1 (2001), adopted on 23 April 2001, Geneva.

[4] Article 50, Obligations not affected by countermeasures, Draft Articles on Responsibility 2001.

[5] Article 52, Conditions relating to resort to countermeasures, Draft Articles on Responsibility 2001. See also Article 43, Notice of claim by an injured State.

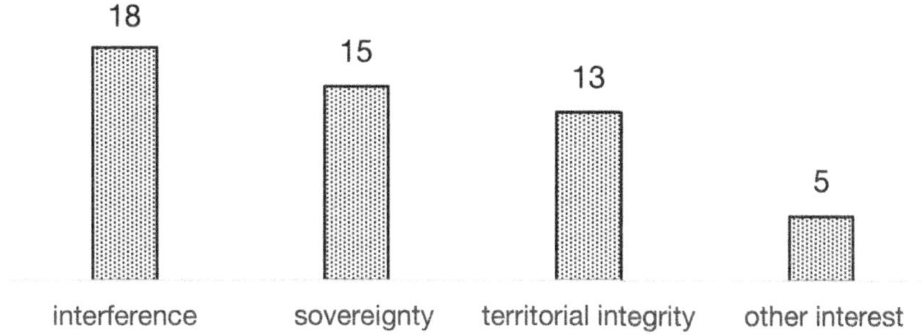

Figure 7.2 Grounds invoked in the sanctions imposed in 2020–4, as recorded on the MFA website from 13 July 2020 to 3 December 2024

of the practice of States',[6] by adopting the tool of unilateral sanctions and invoking the relevant articles on counter-measure under the Draft Articles on Responsibility 2001, China actually contributes to such 'practice of states', which will in turn lead to the effect of reformulating customary international law on counter-measures and unilateral sanctions.

China's behavioural contestations are also proactive in the way that they are constraining the trigger of sanction within the scope of limited types of norm violations. As observed by Poh, up until 2018, there had been no signs of formal Chinese unilateral sanctions, and any 'informal sanctions' appeared to be fairly limited in scope (Poh 2021, 16). China has been self-constrained in the use of sanctions against only severe violations of fundamental norms, including interference in internal affairs, violation of sovereignty, undermining territorial integrity and undermining China's interest, which further includes security interest, legitimate and lawful interests of Chinese companies, entities and individuals (MFA 2024c). To take the sanctions imposed in 2020–4 as an example, eighteen out of the twenty-one sanctions are imposed against the interference of China's internal affairs, fifteen against violation of state sovereignty and thirteen against violation of territorial integrity (as shown in Figure 7.2).

China's Building of Unilateral Sanctions Regime as Behavioural Contestations

What's more noteworthy is that China's building of unilateral sanctions regime also constitutes a type of proactive contestation in the sense that it is trying to (re)form the state practice in the unilateral sanctions regime which consequently

[6] Fisheries (*UK* v. *Norway*), ICJ Reports 1951, pp. 116, 191 (Judge Read).

(re)forms, or in terms of contestation theory, 'engages with' (Orchard and Wiener, this volume), the international norms. As revealed above, China's stance on unilateral sanctions has always grounded on (de)legitimation of unilateral sanctions. Such (de)legitimation has two layers, as (de)legitimation in international law and domestic law respectively, which interact with each other.

Although there remain controversies over the potential legitimacy of unilateral sanctions mechanisms, there is little ambiguity around the applicability of unilateral sanctions in general, though the tests for determining the legality of a specific unilateral sanction to some extent can be ambivalent. As observed by many scholars, 'states have been using unilateral sanctions for all sorts of political and economic purposes for a long time . . . there is neither clarity in the law on unilateral sanctions nor a compulsory legal mechanism to settle disputes associated with such sanctions' (Subedi 2021, 8), and 'unilateral extra-territorial sanctions are neither lawful nor unlawful under international law *per se* in the absence of the development of international customary law to the contrary' (Schmidt 2022, 80). It is safe to conclude that international law, in particular the UN Charter, does not prohibit unilateral sanctions in general and hence it is within the discretion of a state to take such actions unless they are in violation of its obligations under the international law or other applicable international laws.

Therefore, for the purpose of legitimatising its own use of unilateral sanctions, China has been building a rule of law-oriented unilateral sanctions regime since 2008 when the rule for extraterritorial application of domestic law was incorporated in the Anti-monopoly Law. In 2016, a specific rule authorising sanctions/counter-measures when necessary was incorporated in the Foreign Trade Law 2016, which was followed by the Securities Law 2019.

The year 2020 serves as a pivotal division point for better dissecting China's legislative practice, because this is the year when domestically China began to fast forward its construction of an anti-sanction mechanism, or unilateral sanctions regime, to target firms that damage the interests of Chinese companies. In essence, Beijing aimed at responding to the US Entity List, which names foreign individuals, companies and organisations deemed by Washington as a national security concern, by promulgating a series of fundamental legislations. The Provisions on Unreliable Entity List 2020 and Export Control Law 2020 were followed by Rules on Counteracting Unjustified Extra-Territorial Application of Foreign Legislation and Other Measures 2021, Anti-Foreign Sanctions Law 2021 and, at last, the very programmatic Law on Foreign Relations 2023, which is the first basic foreign-related law since the founding of P.R. China that focuses on China's general policy, principles, positions and institutional regime for foreign-related issues.

Such consistent legislative actions of China serve not only for legitimation of its own unilateral sanctions under its domestic law, but also for its promotion of rule of law at both the international and domestic levels. By promulgating and later applying these legislations, China is also contributing to the 'practice of states' regarding the legitimacy of sanctions in the international order, including exactly whether there is a right to react when what kind of norm is violated, who has the right to impose a harm and what kind of measure adopted is the right action. This will no doubt form/reform the relevant international norms, which is exactly what China wishes for, as its goals and mission of conducting foreign relations is to 'uphold the international system with the United Nations at its core, the international order underpinned by international law, and the fundamental norms governing international relations based on the purposes and principles of the Charter of the United Nations' and to 'participate in the development of international rules, promotes democracy in international relations'.[7]

China, in this regard, is not alone. Many states have been taking legislative actions to counter or block foreign sanctions. For example, Japan adopted the Act on Special Measures concerning the Recovery of Damage Resulting from the United States Anti-Dumping Act of 1916 (Act No. 162 of 2004). The Russian Federation adopted the Federal Law on Corrective Actions (Counteraction) on Unfriendly Actions of the United States of America and Other Foreign States (No. 127-FZ, 4 June 2018), authorising the Russian government to adopt restrictions and prohibitions on the import and export of goods and services against 'unfriendly countries', such as the United States. The European Union, as one of the major sources of unilateral sanctions, also has adopted the Council Regulation Protecting against the Effects of the Extraterritorial Application of Legislation Adopted by a Third Country and Actions Based Thereon or Resulting Therefrom (No. 2271/96, 22 Nov. 1996) and, more significantly, the Treaty on the Functioning of the European Union 2009, where its over three-decades-long extraterritorial sanctions practice is provided for in a constitutional treaty.

Such legislative actions among states all together produce behavioural regularities to which 'international law often grants legal significance' and 'became codified in international law doctrine, most notably in the customary international law's basis in general practice (requiring an empirical assessment of how states behave) and *opinio juris* (requiring a subjective assessment of why they behave that way)' (Cohen and Meyer 2021, 2–3).

[7] The Law on Foreign Relations of the People's Republic of China 2023 Article 19.

Table 7.1 Chronological summary of 'alleged' Chinese unilateral sanctions (1978–2019)

No.	Active Years	Target Country	Triggers	Measures
1	1978–85	Albania	Anti-Chinese rhetoric	Halt economic and military assistance, withdraw experts
2	1978–91	Vietnam	Border dispute and Kampuchea issue	Restrictions on cross-border trade
3	1992–4	France	Arms sales to Taiwan	Withdraw from proposed cooperation projects
4	2002	Mongolia	Dalai Lama visit	Halt the train passage for two days
5	2006–16	Iran	Nuclear weapons programme	Lower the oil imports over 20%, reduce investment in energy sector and SOEs delay or pull-out projects
6	2006–	North Korea	Missile and nuclear tests	Shut off oil exports and coal imports
7	2009	France	Dalai Lama visit	Cancel the order for 150 aircrafts from Airbus
8	2010	United States	Arms sales to Taiwan	Sanctions against US arms manufacturers involved
9	2010–12	Japan	Confrontation in Diaoyu Island dispute	Halt the rare earths export
10	2010–16	Norway	Awarding of 2010 Nobel Peace Prize	Sanitary and regulatory measures on salmon imports
11	2012–16	Philippines	Scarborough Shoal incident and the South China Sea arbitration	Sanitary controls on Filipino banana imports; restriction on Chinese tourists to the Philippines
12	2015	United States	Arms sales to Taiwan	Sanctions against US arms manufacturers involved
13	2016	Mongolia	Dalai Lama visit	Raise fees on mining products, backups at border crossing, suspend bilateral interactions and cut off talks regarding a major loan
14	2016–17	South Korea	THAAD deployment	Curb tourism, cut imports of cultural products and take regulatory measures against auto companies and Korean-owned Lotte Mart Stores in China

Table 7.1 (*contd*)

No.	Active Years	Target Country	Triggers	Measures
15	2017	Australia	Legislation to control foreign influence	Issue warnings to Chinese students to maintain vigilance and nationalist newspapers campaigns
16	2018	United States	Additional tariffs on Chinese goods	Additional tariffs on US goods
17	2019–	Canada	Detainment of Huawei CFO MENG Wanzhou	Revoke two canola company's licences and halt the canola import
18	2019–	United States	Arms sales to Taiwan (July–August)	Sanctions against US arms manufacturers involved
19	2019–	United States	Hong Kong Human Rights and Democracy Act	Sanctions against US NGOs involved in Hong Kong's ordinance amendment issue

Conclusion: China's Dual Role in the Hail of Sanctions against Russia

To apply the norm contestation theory on international sanctions to diagnose China's sanction rhetoric and actions, there are both the interpretative contestations and proactive contestations. Although with some subtle changes, China's sanction contestations remain grounded on the (de)legitimation of unilateral sanctions. When imposing its own unilateral sanctions, China claims that the international norms of state sovereignty and non-intervention have been violated and therefore a legitimate reaction, often in the form of counter-measures under international law, must follow.

China is positioned in a dual role by the Western states in the hail of sanctions against Russia for the Ukraine crisis. From the official outbreak of the Russia–Ukraine conflict on 24 February 2022, Chinese companies and entities have become the target of a variety of sanctions imposed by the US, EU, UK and others on 'Russia-related' grounds. On 22 February 2024, the UK announced more than fifty sanctions on Russia. The new targets included three electronics companies based in China (UK Government 2024a). On 23 February 2024, the US Commerce Department's Bureau of Industry and Security (BIS) added ninety-three entities under ninety-five entries to the Entity List on 'Russia-related' grounds, eight of which are based in China (BIS 2024); the Office of Foreign Assets Control (OFAC) of the US Department

Table 7.2 China's unilateral sanctions (2020–4), as recorded on the MFA website from 1 January 2020 to 31 December 2024

No.	Date	Order	Target Country	Triggers	Sanctions
1	2020	MFA Press Announcement	United States	Sanction Chinese government officials over treatment of Uygurs in Xinjiang	Sanctions against the US arms manufacturer and individuals involved
2		MFA Press Announcement	United States	Arms sales to Taiwan	Sanctions against Lockheed Martin, Boeing Defense and Raytheon, and the individuals involved
1	2021	MFA Press Announcement	United States	Interfere in China's internal affairs, undermine China's interests	Sanctions on individuals and their immediate family members including Pompeo
2		MFA Press Announcement	European Union	Sanction Chinese individuals and entity over human rights issues in Xinjiang	Sanctions on individuals and entities concerned on the EU side
3		MFA Press Announcement	United Kingdom	Sanction Chinese individuals and entity over human rights issues in Xinjiang	Sanctions on individuals and entities concerned on the UK side
4		MFA Press Announcement	United States and Canada	Sanction individuals and entity in Xinjiang	Sanctions against individuals and one entity concerned on the US and Canada side
5		MFA Press Announcement	United States	'Hong Kong Business Advisory', sanction deputy directors of the Liaison Office of the Central People's Government in HKSAR	Sanctions on US individuals and one entity

1	2022	MFA Press Announcement	United States	Visit Taiwan	Sanctions on Pelosi and her immediate family members
2		MFA Press Announcement	Vaiciukevičiūtė	Visit Taiwan	Sanctions on Vaiciukevičiūtė and Ministry of Transport and Communications of Lithuania
3		MFA Order (No. 4)	United States	Sanction Chinese officials over human rights issues in Tibet	Counter-measures against Miles Maochun Yu and Todd Stein
1	2023	MFA Order (No. 1)	United States	Provide facilities for separatist activities in the US	Counter-measures against US Hudson Institute, the Ronald Reagan Presidential Library and the relevant people in charge
2		MFA Order (No. –)	United States	Interfere in China's internal affairs and undermine China's sovereignty and territorial integrity; visit Taiwan	Counter-measure against US Congressman Michael McCaul
1	2024	MFA Order (No. 5)	United States	Arms sales to Taiwan	Counter-measure against US General Atomics Aeronautical Systems, General Dynamics Land Systems and senior executives
2		MFA Order (No. 6)	United States	Interfere in China's internal affairs and undermine China's sovereignty and territorial integrity	Counter-measures against former US Congressman Mike Gallagher
3		MFA Order (No. 7)	United States	Sanction 'Russia-related' Chinese entities; arms sales to Taiwan	Counter-measures against relevant US military companies and senior executives
4		MFA Order (No. 8)	United States	Arms sales to Taiwan	Counter-measures against Lockheed Martin and senior executives

Table 7.2 *(contd)*

No.	Date	Order	Target Country	Triggers	Sanctions
5		MFA Order (No. 10)	United States	Arms sales to Taiwan	Counter-measures against relevant US military companies and senior executives
6		MFA Order (No. 11)	United States	Interfere in China's internal affairs and undermine China's sovereignty and territorial integrity	Counter-measures against Mike Gallagher
7		MFA Order (No. 12)	United States	Arms sales to Taiwan	Counter-measures against relevant military companies of the US
8		MFA Order (No. 13)	United States	Arms sales to Taiwan	Counter-measures against relevant US military companies and senior executives
9		MFA Order (No. 14)	United States	Arms sales to Taiwan	Counter-measures against relevant US military companies and senior executives

of the Treasury announcing that OFAC was sanctioning almost three hundred individuals and entities on 'Russia-related' grounds, six of which were technology suppliers based in China (US Department of the Treasury 2024). On the same day, the EU adopted its thirteenth package of restrictive measures against Putin's regime, which added twenty-seven new entities to the list of those allegedly 'directly supporting Russia's military and industrial complex in its war of aggression against Ukraine', including four entities located in China (Council of the European Union 2024). On 7 November 2024, the UK announced fifty-six new sanctions in its largest sanctions package against Russia since May 2023, and ten China-based entities were included (UK Government 2024b).

To respond to such relentless unilateral sanctions, in rhetoric, the Ministry of Foreign Affairs made clear in *China's Position on the Political Settlement of the Ukraine Crisis* that

> unilateral sanctions and maximum pressure cannot solve the issue; they only create new problems. China opposes unilateral sanctions unauthorized by the UN Security Council. Relevant countries should stop abusing unilateral sanctions and 'long-arm jurisdiction' against other countries, so as to do their share in deescalating the Ukraine crisis and create conditions for developing countries to grow their economies and better the lives of their people. (MFA 2023a)

In fact, as recorded on its website from 24 February 2022 to 3 December 2024, the MFA held 647 regular press conferences, of which 55 commented on the sanctions against Russia. Of these 55 comments, 28 are on sanctions imposed against Chinese companies by other states on Russia-related grounds, seven on other states' deterrence or stigmatisation of China on Russia-related grounds, and 20 are mere comments on the unilateral sanctions imposed against Russia.

The majority of comments by China on the Russia-related unilateral sanctions focuses on the delegitimation of unilateral sanctions as they are imposed without either the authorisation of the UN Security Council or basis in international law. These statements show that unilateral sanctions are delegitimised on the grounds that they violate some of the core principles, or the fundamental norms of state sovereignty, territorial integrity and/or national security.

The delegitimation of the enforcer, in particular those that engage in power politics, is manifest in the statements of China, such as 'overstretching the concept of national security and abusing state power' (MFA 2023c), 'wantonly resorting to unilateral sanctions or threat of sanctions . . . constitutes power politics and hegemonic bullying, which gains no support and is increasingly rejected' (MFA 2021).

There is also delegitimation of the Russia-related measures in the statements of China as they 'have created victims all over the world, severely undermined other countries' sovereignty and security, caused humanitarian tragedies and disrupted industrial and supply chains' (MFA 2024d) and 'disrupt international trade and investment' (MFA 2024e).

Targeted by so many Russia-related sanctions, China has so far only taken one counter-measure in return. It has imposed unilateral sanctions only once as counter-measure, for the reason that

> for some time now, the United States has ignored China's objective and impartial position and constructive role in the Ukrainian crisis and, on the basis of the so-called Russia-related factors, has imposed unlawful and unilateral sanctions indiscriminately on a number of Chinese entities, engaging in unilateral bullying and economic coercion, and seriously infringing on the legitimate and lawful rights and interests of Chinese enterprises, institutions and individuals. (MFA 2024b)

All the above rhetoric and behavioural contestations show that China's current position on the international sanctions imposed on Russia mirrors its long-term stance on the use of unilateral sanctions. This explains its resistance to the wave of sanctions against Russia.

The application of unilateral sanctions is a delicate issue domain, where not only different disciplines of international relations and international law but also different principles of international law come across each other. Being a major player in the world economy and politics, China has been promoting the rule of law at the international level, which it considers a shared responsibility of all countries, and confining the meaning of rule of law at international level as to safeguard the purposes and principles of the UN Charter that establish the basic norms governing international relations and form the cornerstone of modern international law (Chinese Mission to the United Nations 2023). China will no doubt keep upgrading its unilateral sanctions regime in a way that fits with its overall implementation of the rule of law at the international level, but it 'cannot be considered to have moved closer to the norm within the Western world' (Poh 2021, 269) because of the discrepancies in the understanding of 'rule of law' at both international and domestic levels.

References

Baldwin, David. A. 1985. *Economic Statecraft*. Princeton University Press.

BIS (US Commerce Department, Bureau of Industry and Security). 2024. 'Commerce Stands Strong with Ukraine, Takes Further Action against Ongoing Russian Aggression'. 23 February. https://www.bis.doc.gov/index.php/documents/about-bis/newsroom/press-releases/3452-2024-02-23-bis-press-release-russia-two-year-actions/file

CCTV. 2010. 'China to Halt Military Exchanges, Punish U.S. Companies for Arms Sales to Taiwan'. 31 January. http://english.cctv.com/20100131/100960.shtml

Central People's Government of the People's Republic of China. 2020. 'Ministry of Foreign Affairs: Firmly Oppose to the US Unilateral Sanctions and the So-called "Long-arm Jurisdiction" against Other Countries'. 21 July. http://www.gov.cn/xinwen/2020-07/21/content_5528487.htm

Chan, Steve, and A. Cooper Drury. 2000. *Sanctions as Economic Statecraft: Theory and Practice*. Macmillan Press.

China Daily. 2010. 'China Opposes EU Sanctions on Iran: Spokeswoman'. 30 July. http://www.chinadaily.com.cn/china/2010-07/30/content_11075047.htm

Chinese Mission to the United Nations. 2023. 'Remarks by China's Permanent Representative to UN Ambassador Zhang Jun at the UN Security Council Open Debate on the Promotion and Strengthening of the Rule of Law in the Maintenance of International Peace and Security'. 12 January. https://www.fmprc.gov.cn/eng/xw/zwbd/202405/t20240530_11365381.html

Cohen, Harlan Grant, and Timothy Meyer. eds. 2021. *International Law as Behavior*. Cambridge University Press.

Cortright, David, and George H. Lopez. 2000. *The Sanctions Decade: Assessing UN Strategies*. Lynne Rienner.

Council of the European Union. 2024. 'Russia: Two Years after the Full-Scale Invasion and War of Aggression against Ukraine, EU Adopts 13th Package of Individual and Economic Sanctions'. 23 February. https://www.consilium.europa.eu/en/press/press-releases/2024/02/23/russia-two-years-after-the-full-scale-invasion-and-war-of-aggression-against-ukraine-eu-adopts-13th-package-of-individual-and-economic-sanctions/

European Commission. 2019. 'Joint Communication to the European Parliament, the European Council and the Council EU-China – A Strategic Outlook'. 12 March. https://eur-lex.europa.eu/legal-content/EN/TXT/?uri=CELEX:52019JC0005

Fang Jiongsheng. 2020. 'Restricted Fightback: Chinese Economic Sanctions since 2010'. *Foreign Affairs Review* 37(1): 65–87. https://doi.org/10.13569/j.cnki.far.2020.01.065

Friedberg, Aron. L. 2018. 'Globalisation and Chinese Grand Strategy'. *Survival* 60(1): 7–40. https://doi.org/10.1080/00396338.2018.1427362

Ghiretti, Francesca. 2023. 'How China Imposes Sanctions: A Guide to the Evolution of Beijing's New Policy Tool'. *MERICS.* https://merics.org/en/report/how-china-imposes-sanctions

Global Times. 2018. 'China Opposes U.S. Unilateral Sanctions against Chinese Firm', 31 October. http://www.globaltimes.cn/content/1125247.shtml

Haass, Richard N. 1997. 'Sanctioning Madness'. *Foreign Affairs* 76(6): 74–85. https://doi.org/10.2307/20048277

Harrell, Peter, Elizabeth Rosenberg and Edoardo Saravalle. 2018. 'China's Use of Coercive Economic Measures'. Center for a New American Security. https://www.cnas.org/publications/reports/chinas-use-of-coercive-economic-measures

Hufbauer, Gary, and Euijin Jung. 2020. 'What's New in Economic Sanctions?' *European Economic Review* 130. https://doi.org/10.1016/j.euroecorev.2020.103572

Hufbauer, Gary Clyde, Jeffrey J. Schott, Kimberly Ann Elliott and Barbara Oegg. 2007. *Economic Sanctions Reconsidered.* 3rd edition. Peterson Institute for International Economics.

Krook, Mona Lena, and Jacqui True. 2012. 'Rethinking the Life Cycles of International Norms: The United Nations and the Global Promotion of Gender Equality'. *European Journal of International Relations* 18(1): 103–27. https://doi.org/10.1177/1354066110380963

MFA. 2011. 'Foreign Ministry Spokesperson Hong Lei's Regular Press Conference on December 6, 2011'. *Ministry of Foreign Affairs of the People's Republic of China*, 6 December. http://www.chinanews.com/gn/2011/12-06/3512766.shtml

MFA. 2018. 'Foreign Ministry Spokesperson Lu Kang's Remarks on USTR's Proposed Tariff List on Chinese Products Pursuant to Section 301 Investigation'. *Ministry of Foreign Affairs of the People's Republic of China*, 4 April. https://www.fmprc.gov.cn/mfa_eng/xwfw_665399/s2510_665401/2535_665405/t1547901.shtml

MFA. 2019a. 'Foreign Ministry Spokesperson Geng Shuang's Remarks on Chinese Government's Sanctions on US Enterprises Involved in Arms Sale to Taiwan'. *Ministry of Foreign Affairs of the People's Republic of China*, 12 July. https://www.fmprc.gov.cn/web/wjdt_674879/fyrbt_674889/t1680700.shtml

MFA. 2019b. 'Foreign Ministry Spokesperson Geng Shuang's Regular Press Conference on July 19, 2019'. *Ministry of Foreign Affairs of the People's Republic of China*, 19 July. https://www.fmprc.gov.cn/mfa_eng/xwfw_665399/s2510_665401/2511_665403/t1682201.shtml

MFA. 2019c. 'Foreign Ministry Spokesperson Hua Chunying's Regular Press Conference on December 2, 2019'. *Ministry of Foreign Affairs of the People's Republic of China*, 2 December. https://www.fmprc.gov.cn/mfa_eng/xwfw_665399/s2510_665401/2511_665403/t1720852.shtml

MFA. 2020a. 'Foreign Ministry Spokesperson Hua Chunying's Regular Press Conference on July 13, 2020'. *Ministry of Foreign Affairs of the People's Republic of China*, 13 July. https://www.fmprc.gov.cn/mfa_eng/xwfw_665399/s2510_665401/2511_665403/t1797455.shtml

MFA. 2020b. 'Foreign Ministry Spokesperson Wang Wenbin's Regular Press Conference on July 20, 2020'. *Ministry of Foreign Affairs of the People's Republic of China*, 20 July. https://www.fmprc.gov.cn/mfa_eng/xwfw_665399/s2510_665401/2511_665403/t1799096.shtml

MFA. 2020c. 'Foreign Ministry Spokesperson Zhao Lijian's Regular Press Conference on October 26, 2020'. *Ministry of Foreign Affairs of the People's Republic of China*, 26 October. https://www.fmprc.gov.cn/mfa_eng/xwfw_665399/s2510_665401/2511_665403/t1826657.shtml

MFA. 2020d. 'Foreign Ministry Spokesperson Zhao Lijian's Regular Press Conference on December 9, 2020'. *Ministry of Foreign Affairs of the People's Republic of China*, 9 December. https://www.fmprc.gov.cn/mfa_eng/xwfw_665399/s2510_665401/2511_665403/t1838915.shtml

MFA. 2021. 'Foreign Ministry Spokesperson Wang Wenbin's Regular Press Conference on April 26, 2021'. *Ministry of Foreign Affairs of the People's Republic of China*, 26 April. https://www.fmprc.gov.cn/eng/xw/fyrbt/lxjzh/202405/t20240530_11347031.html

MFA. 2023a. 'China's Position on the Political Settlement of the Ukraine Crisis'. *Ministry of Foreign Affairs of the People's Republic of China*, 24 February. https://www.fmprc.gov.cn/eng/xw/zyxw/202405/t20240530_11331711.html

MFA. 2023b. 'Foreign Ministry Spokesperson Wang Wenbin's Regular Press Conference on March 20, 2023'. *Ministry of Foreign Affairs of the People's Republic of China*, 20 March. https://www.fmprc.gov.cn/eng/xw/fyrbt/lxjzh/202405/t20240530_11347486.html

MFA. 2023c. 'Foreign Ministry Spokesperson Wang Wenbin's Regular Press Conference on November 3, 2023'. *Ministry of Foreign Affairs of the People's Republic of China*, 3 November. https://www.fmprc.gov.cn/eng/xw/fyrbt/lxjzh/202405/t20240530_11347628.html

MFA. 2024a. 'Foreign Ministry Spokesperson Wang Wenbin's Regular Press Conference on May 21, 2024'. *Ministry of Foreign Affairs of the People's Republic of China*, 21 May. https://www.fmprc.gov.cn/eng/xw/fyrbt/lxjzh/202405/t20240530_11347760.html

MFA. 2024b. 'Decision on Countermeasures against United States Military Industrial Enterprises and Senior Executives, Order No. 7 of Ministry of Foreign Affairs of the People's Republic of China'. *Ministry of Foreign Affairs of the People's Republic of China*, 22 May. https://www.mfa.gov.cn/web/wjb_673085/zfxxgk_674865/gknrlb/fzcqdcs/202405/t20240522_11309756.shtml

MFA. 2024c. 'Foreign Ministry Spokesperson Announces Sanctions on Pompeo and Others'. *Ministry of Foreign Affairs of the People's Republic of China*, 30 May. https://www.fmprc.gov.cn/eng/xw/fyrbt/fyrbt/202405/t20240530_11349683.html

MFA. 2024d. 'Foreign Ministry Spokesperson Lin Jian's Regular Press Conference on June 13, 2024'. *Ministry of Foreign Affairs of the People's Republic of China*, 13 June. https://www.fmprc.gov.cn/eng/xw/fyrbt/lxjzh/202407/t20240730_11463238.html

MFA. 2024e. 'Foreign Ministry Spokesperson Lin Jian's Regular Press Conference on September 24, 2024'. *Ministry of Foreign Affairs of the People's Republic of China*, 24 September. https://www.fmprc.gov.cn/eng/xw/fyrbt/lxjzh/202412/t20241217_11495572.html

MFA. 2024f. 'Foreign Ministry Spokesperson Mao Ning's Regular Press Conference on November 26, 2024'. *Ministry of Foreign Affairs of the People's Republic of China*, 26 November. https://www.fmprc.gov.cn/eng/xw/fyrbt/lxjzh/202411/t20241126_11533442.html

MFA. 2024g. 'Foreign Ministry Spokesperson Lin Jian's Regular Press Conference on December 3, 2024'. *Ministry of Foreign Affairs of the People's Republic of China*, 3 December. https://www.fmprc.gov.cn/eng/xw/fyrbt/lxjzh/202412/t20241203_11537550.html

Nephew, Richard. 2019. 'China and Economic Sanctions: Where Does Washington Have Leverage?' The Brookings Institution. https://www.brookings.edu/research/china-and-economic-sanctions-where-does-washington-have-leverage/

Orchard, Paul, and Antje Wiener. 2023. 'Norms and Norm Contestation'. In *Routledge Handbook of Foreign Policy Analysis*, edited by Patrick A. Mello and Falk Ostermann. Routledge.

People. 2015. 'China Will Sanction U.S. Arms Sales to Taiwan'. 17 December. https://world.people.com.cn/n1/2015/1217/c157278-27942428.html

People. 2017. 'China Opposes Japan's Unilateral Sanctions', 25 August. http://en.people.cn/n3/2017/0825/c90883-9260461.html

Permanent Mission. 2005. 'Position Paper of the People's Republic of China on the United Nations Reforms'. Permanent Mission of the People's Republic of China, 7 June. http://www.fmprc.gov.cn/ce/ceun/eng/zt/gaige/t199101.htm

Permanent Mission. 2015. 'Statement of China at the Biennial Session on the Unilateral Coercive Measures at the 30th Regular Session of the Human Rights Council'. Permanent Mission of the People's Republic of China to the United Nations Office at Geneva and Other International Organizations in Switzerland, 17 September. http://www.china-un.ch/chn/hyyfy/t1305283.html

Poh, Angela. 2021. *Sanctions with Chinese Characteristics: Rhetoric and Restraint in China's Diplomacy*. Amsterdam University Press.

Reilly, James. 2012. 'China's Unilateral Sanctions'. *The Washington Quarterly* 35(4): 121–33. https://doi.org/10.1080/0163660X.2012.726428

Schmidt, Julia. 2022. 'The Legality of Unilateral Extra-territorial Sanctions under International Law'. *Journal of Conflict and Security Law* 27(1): 53–81. https://doi.org/10.1093/jcsl/krac005

Subedi, Surya P., ed. 2021. *Unilateral Sanctions in International Law*. Hart Publishing.

UK Government. 2024a. 'New UK Sanctions Mark Two Years since Russia's Illegal Invasion of Ukraine'. 22 February. https://www.gov.uk/government/news/new-uk-sanctions-mark-two-years-since-russias-illegal-invasion-of-ukraine

UK Government. 2024b. 'UK Strikes at Heart of Putin's War Machine'. 7 November. https://www.gov.uk/government/news/uk-strikes-at-heart-of-putins-war-machine

United States Congress. 2021. 'S.1169 – Strategic Competition Act of 2021', 10 May. https://www.congress.gov/bill/117th-congress/senate-bill/1169

US Department of the Treasury. 2024. 'On Second Anniversary of Russia's Further Invasion of Ukraine and Following the Death of Aleksey Navalny, Treasury Sanctions Hundreds of Targets in Russia and Globally'. 23 February. https://home.treasury.gov/news/press-releases/jy2117

Wiener, Antje. 2007. 'The Dual Quality of Norms and Governance beyond the State: Sociological and Normative Approaches to "Interaction"'. *Critical Review of International Social and Political Philosophy* 10(1): 47–69. https://doi.org/10.1080/13698230601122412

Wiener, Antje. 2014. *A Theory of Contestation*. Springer.

Wisniewski, Rafal. 2021. 'Economic Sanctions as a Tool of China's Hybrid Strategies'. *Polish Political Science Yearbook* 50(3): 91–103. https://doi.org/10.15804/ppsy202133

Yu Wenjie. 2021. 'China's Emerging Unilateral Sanctions: Heading towards the Rule of Law?' *The Chinese Journal of Comparative Law* 9(3): 359–86. https://doi.org/10.1093/cjcl/cxac005

8

BRICS Stand on Sanctions: An Evident Contestation

Rishika Chauhan

Introduction

In January 2024 the intergovernmental organisation BRICS admitted four new members and expanded from a group of five to that of nine states. The enlargement, which is the second expansion after South Africa's addition in 2010, comes at a crucial time and brings important partners onboard. Previously comprising Brazil, Russia, India, China and South Africa as members, BRICS has welcomed Egypt, Ethiopia, Iran and the United Arab Emirates within its fold. While each new member has their own motivations for joining the group, from gaining economic leverage to acquiring political capital, enhancing cooperation with the member states is an evident intention among the new members. Their collaboration is particularly significant at this juncture, as it comes at a time when Russia, a prominent BRICS member, is dealing with extensive Western sanctions following its invasion of Ukraine in 2022. Moreover, each new member brings along its contentious history with the West, fraught with conflict and distrust as a consequence of their colonial past, Western interference or economic control, along with a dislike for sanctions –a feature already discernible in the BRICS discourse. In conformity with the volume's attempt to explore why and how are sanctions understood and challenged by different actors, this chapter examines BRICS' perspective on sanctions.

BRICS' discomfort with, as well as disregard for, unilateral sanctions is understandable given that its own member states and their partners have faced primary or secondary sanctions on multiple occasions. However, the group has couched its objections to sanctions in general terms, as grievances that all members share and are affected by, rather than focusing on a particular state's experience with sanctions. These objections can be termed as contestations, and traces of reactive, proactive and interpretative contestations are evident in the BRICS discourse. Reactive contestation is most obvious as BRICS has challenged unilateral sanctions and advanced arguments to justify their disregard for the measures. Firstly, as a form of reactive contestation, the group has argued that unilateral sanctions are against international law as they give precedence to domestic law of the sanctioning states. BRICS supports sanctions imposed by the United Nations Security Council (UNSC) but is against sanctions imposed unilaterally.

Secondly, BRICS has attempted to forward an 'us vs them' narrative. Sanctions are understood as impediments to free trade as well as growth of the Global South, where most of the sanctioned states are based. Thirdly, the group has followed a hyper-realist agenda and justified their economic cooperation with sanctioned states, stressing that their decision to not support sanctions is made in the pursuit of their 'national interest'. Finally, they have also attempted to impede sanctions by taking steps that could weaken Western sanctions and offset them, such as building institutions like BRICS bank (New Development Bank) and Reserve Fund, as well as focusing on processes like de-dollarisation. While reactive contestation remains prevalent, BRICS has also adopted proactive contestation, for instance it has encouraged sanctions seminars on specific issues[1] when initiated by its own member states. Interpretative contestation is also observable, as many BRICS members have understood sanctions as an instrument used by the former colonisers to interfere in the affairs of other states, an understanding rooted in their anti-Western outlook.

While both economists and political scientists have engaged with issues concerning the BRICS, the group has more often been the subject of short policy reports rather than academic studies. The literature on BRICS has dealt with several topics, including economic cooperation among members, the successes and failures of group initiatives (Greene 2023), its status and the challenge it poses to the Western-led world order (Stuenkel 2014), the diverse perspectives of member states (Han and Papa 2022), as well as the different leadership styles within the group (Han and Papa 2024). However, the question that has predominantly occupied scholars is the survival or 'impending demise' of the group (Pant 2013). With members engaged in long-term conflicts, competing ambitions and internal challenges – such as the diminishing influence of South Africa and Brazil within BRICS as stronger economies take

[1] As discussed later in the chapter, sanctions against terrorist organisations and financing have particularly garnered support from BRICS members.

the lead – it is understandable why the organisation's survival is frequently questioned. Nevertheless, the research on BRICS is gradually increasing, and granular details of the group's policies as well as future orientation are being explored. This chapter is one such attempt, as it aims to understand BRICS' opposition to sanctions and how it contests the measures.

Understanding the BRICS view on sanctions is important. BRICS represents states that collectively occupy about 30 per cent of the world's surface area and over 41 per cent of its population, a figure that has increased to around 45 per cent after BRICS' latest expansion (UN 2020). In addition, based on purchasing power parity, the BRICS economies are larger than the developed G7 economies (O'Neill 2023). With both China and India, the second and fifth largest economies in the world, as members, BRICS' view is crucial not only for the number of voices it represents but also for the economic might that backs the organisation.

The context in which BRICS has experienced sanctions needs elucidation to fully appreciate the various contestation practices. This chapter delves into how BRICS has collectively reacted when sanctions have been imposed on its own member states, as well as on its partners. The study focuses on BRICS discourse before its expansion, as the organisation's first summit after expansion had not taken place at the time of writing this chapter. This chapter is divided into three sections. The first part discusses the formation of BRICS, its alternative worldview and its stated position on sanctions. The second section discusses the reaction of BRICS to sanctions imposed against Russia and Iran as a partner state. Finally, the last section examines how BRICS has contested sanctions, and concludes by assessing specific features of the group's position on sanctions, discussing rhetoric versus action as well conflicting interests and internal competition among members.

BRICS and an Alternative Worldview

The acronym 'BRIC' was devised by a Goldman Sachs analyst in 2001 in a report titled, 'Building Better Global Economic BRICs'. The report, however, did not recommend that the states form a group, but identified the cluster as a potential investment portfolio. The report argued that by 2050, BRIC economies would become bigger than the leading economies of the day (O'Neill 2001). However, it is generally accepted that the reason for 'continued cooperation' was not economic, but political (Salzman 2019, 23). BRICS members were provided a political context to form a committed group long before the organisation came into existence. The need to present a united front, express a common viewpoint of the Global South and gain visibility are ideas rooted in

BRICS' origin (Miller 2021). In the late 1990s and early 2000s, the aspiration of states in the Global South to influence global governance became apparent, as groups of emerging states began to coalesce. For them, a change in global governance did not only entail changing the dominant institutions but also the norms that drive the agenda. BRICS' intent was to not merely be a 'rule taker' but a 'rule maker' (Duggun 2015, 17). In 1998 during his visit to India, Russian Prime Minister Yevgeny Primakov shared his idea of forming a trilateral with India and China (Mohan 2002). The goal was realised in 2001 when the foreign affairs ministers of Russia, China and India – Igor Ivanov, Tang Jiaxuan and Yashwant Sinha – met in New York on the sidelines of the United Nations (UN) General Assembly.

At the time, the objective of addressing and amplifying issues concerning prominent emerging powers drew these states closer. Finally, in September 2006 the foreign ministers of Brazil, Russia, India and China (BRIC) met on the sidelines of the UN General Assembly in New York, to discuss the prospect of forming a group. The idea was executed in 2009, as the first BRIC summit was held in Yekaterinburg, Russia on 16 June 2009. South Africa joined in 2010, making the group BRICS. At the time the issues that the group collectively sought to highlight at international forums were those concerning the developing world, like food and energy security, climate change and infrastructure development (Duggun 2015, 20).

As developing economies, BRICS member states share similar concerns, which often differ from those of developed Western states. Moreover, while dealing with similar problems, they present an alternative perspective on global economic and political issues. At the first BRIC summit the members called for reform of the 'financial and economic architecture' (BRIC 2009), with the group's concerns encompassing both 'institutional and ideational' issues (Salzman 2019, 30). Institutional issues included reform of the International Monetary Fund (IMF) and the UN Security Council (UNSC), with the group demanding an increase in their quota shares and thus voting power in the former organisation, and an expansion of the latter, through the inclusion of India, Brazil and South Africa as permanent members. Ideationally, BRICS sought to oppose the West's domination in global governance, observable at international institutions, specifically US hegemony over the international order. Questioning the West's violations of international law, in particular its disregard for national sovereignty, the BRICS states have sought a 'world order that allows for a multiplicity of values and domestic orders rather than the perceived imposition of a single set of norms and standards' (Salzman 2019, 30).

BRICS aims to bring about a change in global governance by working from within and outside international institutions: internally, by advancing their agenda within existing international organisations, and externally, by creating new institutions to address issues affecting both themselves and developing states, thereby driving change (Duggun 2015, 21). While their attempts to influence the world order were discernible in the statements of the first few summits, it was only at the fourth BRICS summit in New Delhi in 2012 that the idea of a development bank was proposed. However, BRICS did not suggest treading on the toes of existing multilateral and regional financial institutions, but only to 'supplement the existing efforts' with an aim to promote 'global growth and development' (BRICS 2012). At the fifth BRICS summit in Durban in 2013, the group decided to establish the New Development Bank, as well as a Contingent Reserve with the objective of helping BRICS members to 'forestall short-term liquidity pressures, provide mutual support and further strengthen financial stability' (BRICS 2013). At the sixth BRICS Summit in Fortaleza, the agreement for establishing the New Development Bank was signed and the signing of the Treaty for the establishment of the BRICS Contingent Reserve Arrangement was announced (BRICS 2014). To make the new institution representative, responsibilities as well as duties were dispensed among all members.

Though BRICS clarified that the new institutions were only a 'supplement' to the existing international organisations (BRICS 2012), the New Development Bank as well as the Contingent Reserve Arrangement were viewed as alternatives and even as competition to established Western institutions like the World Bank and IMF. Moreover, the institutions were also seen as a proof of South-South cooperation and a part of efforts adopted to wean the developing world off its dependence on the dollar. Other endeavours include interbank cooperation mechanisms, like BRICS Export Credit and Guarantees Agencies initiated in 2014 to 'improve the support environment for increasing trade opportunities among members' (BRICS 2014). New areas of economic cooperation, such as common BRICS currency and alternative payment mechanisms, continue to be proposed, while existing institutions are being better adapted, in accordance with the geopolitics and the needs of members.

BRICS states' development trajectories are not alike, but their interests often align. Their position in the international system, along with their contentious historical relationship with the West, has brought them together, while the group provides members a platform to unite, support common causes and to contest sanctions in similar ways. BRICS has become a forum for its members to inform the world of their view, support each other and form alliances to advance their interests at regional and global level. The group offers opportunities to emerging states in the Global South to improve cooperation among themselves, as well as strengthen their bargaining power on the international stage. Although the group provides certain advantages, the persistent risk of a few dominant powers shaping and projecting their worldview through the organisation remains apparent. Influencing the economically weaker members to toe their line is also possible on a range of issues, including sanctions. While each member state has its own policy, and at times different understanding of the measures, evidence suggests that over time the dominant members' perspective has prevailed, and the relatively reticent states have articulated their policy on sanctions in a similar way. China and Russia have particularly influenced BRICS stance on sanctions, since they have dealt with contemporary sanctions against themselves more often than other states. Understandably, at BRICS summits and other meetings, representatives from Russia and China have engaged with the subject of sanctions and strategies to circumvent the measures, like de-dollarisation, more actively.[2] States like India, Brazil and South Africa have articulated the same position as their national stand, especially on sanctions against Russia.

BRICS and Sanctions

In 2013, four years after the formation of BRICS, sanctions emerged as a significant topic of discussion within the group. Shortly after that, Russia became the primary target of several sanctions regimes, while Chinese and Indian companies increasingly came under the purview of secondary sanctions initiated by the West. BRICS states decided to express their stand on sanctions collectively. Though the first four BRICS summit declarations did not mention sanctions, the fifth, sixth, seventh, eighth and ninth did. Starting in 2013 at the fifth summit, the BRICS declarations criticised Western sanctions. At the fifth BRICS summit held in Durban in March 2013, the summit declaration stated: 'We are concerned about threats of military action as well as unilateral sanctions' (BRICS 2013). The 2017 declaration of the ninth BRICS summit held in Xiamen further explained, 'We condemn economic sanctions and arbitrary use of unilateral coercive measures. We emphasize that no country should enhance its security at the expense of the security of others' (BRICS 2017).

In 2018, 2019 and 2020 there was no mention of sanctions in the joint statement or declaration. However, in 2021 at the thirteenth BRICS summit held in New Delhi, sanctions were again mentioned in the official documents

[2] Exploring the statements is beyond the scope of this chapter. However, while researching on the topic the author discovered that the discourse was particularly advanced by Russia and China.

of the group, with the declaration emphasising that the UN Security Council was the 'sole authority' for imposing sanctions and states should refrain 'from any coercive measures not based on international law, in particular the UN Charter' (BRICS 2021). Furthermore, the declaration called for 'consolidation and strengthening of the working methods of the UN Security Council Sanctions Committees', underscoring that BRICS sought to continue 'engagement' with the topic (BRICS 2021).

The BRICS statements have reflected the geopolitics of the years they were formulated in and the convictions of the member state hosting the annual summit. Between 2013 and 2017, sanctions, especially unilateral measures, were used by Western states against BRICS members and their allies.[3] Therefore, the group felt the need to explain its stance. Moved by the intention of advancing and supporting their own interests and perspectives, BRICS members sought to articulate in their statements the inconvenience and distress that they were experiencing. Moreover, it represented BRICS' effort to present a unified front against the sanctioning states while signalling intra-member cooperation aimed at weakening the impact of sanctions. Thus far, the members have criticised and condemned unilateral sanctions, and emphasised an alternative – multilateral sanctions imposed by the UN.

In 2021, when sanctions were mentioned in BRICS' annual statements, secondary sanctions were still a concern for India, the host of that year's summit. The summit statement reiterated that the UN was the 'sole authority to impose sanctions' (BRICS 2021), signalling the members' aversion to unilateral sanctions. However, the 2022 BRICS statement marked a shift. While BRICS continued to recognise the UN as the only authority to impose sanctions, it also commended China, the host country, for 'hosting a seminar on targeted sanctions' (BRICS 2022).

In 2022, the scope of sanctions against Russia was significantly expanded, making the members' rejection of unilateral sanctions predictable. Previous BRICS statements had questioned the utility of such measures, with members consistently critiquing and even 'condemning' their use. Therefore, the commendation of China's hosting of a seminar on sanctions was unexpected. Although the seminar focused on targeted sanctions against terrorist organisations and their financing – a topic supported by all member states – it also illustrated how a single state could pursue its interests through an international organisation of which it was a member.

In 2021, China passed the Anti-Foreign Sanctions Law (AFSL), which included provisions for imposing unilateral sanctions (Simmons &

[3] Primary on states like Russia and secondary on India and China.

Simmons 2021). The law, enacted in response to the growing number of sanctions targeting Chinese companies and individuals, built on earlier sanctions legislation adopted by Beijing (Chauhan and Tzinieris 2014). The AFSL did not directly address multilateral sanctions but granted the Chinese government authority to impose unilateral sanctions or 'counter-measures' if other states sanctioned Chinese entities. Furthermore, the law imposed legal liabilities on organisations and individuals that failed to implement these counter-measures (Hung 2022).

Yet, BRICS official statements should not be taken at face value. Often the discussions among member state representatives on the sidelines of summits are more revealing of individual positions than the bloc's joint statements and declarations. Media interactions with these representatives also offer insights into the internal proceedings. While joint statements are neither fully representative of all members' views nor immune to influence by the host country, they still provide a general sense of the organisation's discourse on sanctions. Undoubtedly, BRICS has developed an anti-unilateral sanctions discourse over time. However, these official statements reflect the image the group wishes to project collectively, without accounting for the adjustments individual states make to sanctions regimes to serve their own interests. Subtle changes in wording further suggest that BRICS' stance on sanctions is not fixed but open to change.

Sanctions against BRICS Member States and Partners

The BRICS has defended its members and trade partners under sanctions. It has criticised Western sanctions against them at annual summits and at times articulated the group's disregard for sanctions in joint statements. Generally, BRICS has taken a stand against the imposition and extension of unilateral sanctions, calling for resolution through dialogue and not sanctions. The group's stance on sanctions is markedly tougher when directed at its members than when similar measures target its partners.

Sanctions against Member States: Russia

Sanctions against Russia have been a recurring concern for BRICS, eliciting strong reactions from its members. Following Russia's annexation of Crimea in 2014, several states and international organisations imposed sanctions, which were significantly expanded in 2022 in response to the invasion of Ukraine. Led by the US and the EU, many other states adopted harsh measures targeting Russia's financial, energy and defence sectors, aiming to coerce Moscow into changing its policies and behaviour. Despite these measures, Russia has remained defiant, employing strategies to circumvent them, including deepening cooperation with non-Western states (Tran 2024). Throughout this period, all BRICS members have refused to support the sanctions and have voiced their disapproval of such unilateral measures in official statements, signalling the bloc's intention to cooperate and counter efforts to isolate Russia.

Speaking to the media on the sidelines of the 2014 BRICS summit, Russian Foreign Minister Sergei Lavrov emphasised BRICS' stand against unilateral sanctions. Stressing that the BRICS bloc 'stood against one-sided economic and political measures by third countries', he insisted that the member states were not 'seeking confrontation' against the West but were choosing a common approach to resolve global issues (Reuters 2014a). Moreover, ahead of that year's summit, Russian President Vladimir Putin made his strategy clear as he implied that he would ask the member states to understand the sanctions against Russia as 'attacks' and 'harassment' as well as reactions to policies that the Western states did not agree with. He urged BRICS to collectively consider 'a system of measures' that could 'prevent the harassment' of countries that did not conform to decisions made by the US and its allies (Reuters 2014b). It was following these sanctions that BRICS accelerated its efforts to reduce its members' dependence on Western institutions, and gradually move away from the US dollar, thus initiating a process called de-dollarisation. As mentioned above, an agreement for the creation of the New Development Bank and Contingency Reserve Fund was signed at the sixth BRICS Summit in Fortaleza in 2014. While sanctions on Russia were initiated between February and March 2014, the BRICS, at their July summit, signed an agreement to establish a BRICS bank and fund – measures that could help mitigate the sanctions' impact on Russia.

In 2022, when stronger sanctions were imposed against Russia, none of the BRICS members supported the measures. Intending to target significant sectors of the Russian economy, the sanctions focused on trade, finance and energy industries, barred major Russian banks from the SWIFT financial messaging system and froze Russia's central bank assets (Greene 2022). Speaking ahead of the 2022 Beijing BRICS summit, Chinese leader Xi Jinping stressed that Western sanctions were a 'double-edged sword' that led to the weaponisation of the global economy (CNN 2022). Citing their own economic and energy interests, both India and China increased their crude oil imports from Russia. To fill the void created by the absence of demand from Western states, Russia offered the oil at a discounted price to emerging states (Indian Express 2022).

Western sanctions against Russia were a major topic at the 2022 BRICS summit. Speaking virtually at the BRICS Business Forum, Russian President

Vladimir Putin condemned the sanctions as politically motivated and contrary to 'common sense and basic economic logic' (DW 2022). Moreover, Putin hinted at his plan to limit the negative impact of sanctions by redirecting exports meant for the EU to BRICS states, explaining that Russian trade with the members was growing, and emphasising that India and China had substantially increased their oil imports (Russian Briefing 2022). Although BRICS members have remained cooperative and supportive of Russia, it cannot be assumed that they are unaware of the broader political and economic consequences of the sanctions. Anticipating the Russian economy's plunge, the New Development Bank has placed new transactions in Russia 'on hold', citing 'unfolding uncertainties and restrictions' (New Development Bank 2022).

In 2023, Putin once again called for solidarity among BRICS members and proposed the formation of a trading bloc representing the 'global majority', emphasising cooperation based on 'principles of equality, mutual support, and respect for each other's interests' (Guardian 2023). Addressing the fifteenth BRICS summit in Johannesburg through a recorded video, the Russian president reiterated his disapproval of sanctions, blaming the measures for 'volatility in global markets for food and other commodities,' and urged BRICS to take action to address the situation (Guardian 2023). Sanctions were also referenced in the joint statement of BRICS, which echoed Putin's stance by condemning 'trade-restrictive measures . . . including unilateral illegal measures such as sanctions' that could affect 'agricultural trade' (BRICS 2023a). However, divisions and differing perspectives among member states regarding sanctions on Russia became evident. Speaking ahead of the 2023 summit, South African President Cyril Ramaphosa, the host, expressed his intention to advocate for the resumption of the Black Sea Grain Initiative, which had facilitated the export of Ukrainian grain before Russia withdrew from the agreement in July 2023 (Guardian 2023).

Sanctions against Trade Partners: Iran

BRICS has also taken a strong stand against sanctions imposed on allies and partners of member states. Iran, previously a trade partner now a BRICS member, is an important case as it maintains trade relations with most BRICS members. Since Iran's membership of BRICS commenced only recently, in January 2024, the analysis focuses on the time before Iran's acceptance into BRICS. Beginning in early 2000s, the US, EU and other Western powers imposed several sanctions on Iran to pressure Tehran into halting its nuclear weapons programme. BRICS members were concerned about the constraints that sanctions were placing on trading with Iran. US secondary sanctions also posed a significant challenge, as many businesses and individuals in BRICS countries faced penalties under US law for trading with Iranian entities. Following the signing of the Joint Comprehensive Plan of Action (JCPOA) in 2016, the issue seemed resolved. However, dissatisfied with the agreement, then-US president Donald Trump withdrew from the agreement and reinstated sanctions in 2018. Under US President Joseph Biden, no major changes were made to US policy on Iran (Reuters 2021), although the administration sought to re-join the JCPOA.

Speaking to the media at the 2012 BRICS summit in New Delhi, Chinese and Indian representatives expressed their disregard for US unilateral sanctions on Iran. Clarifying his state's position, then Chinese trade minister Chen Deming said, 'China wants to develop normal trade relationship with all countries including Iran'. Subsequently, his Indian counterpart, Anand Sharma, added, 'Iran has been and continues to be one of our key energy suppliers' (Mishra and Roche 2012). While both the Asian states registered their opposition to new US sanctions, that year the subject did not find a mention in the joint statement issued by the five BRICS states, but the statement expressed concern for the potential escalation of the Iran–US conflict. Although the fourth BRICS summit's Delhi Declaration highlighted Iran's nuclear issue, stressing that the situation should not be 'allowed to escalate into conflict', it also warned that failure to address the matter could have 'disastrous consequences'. The statement noted that BRICS supported resolving the issue, 'in accordance with the provisions of the relevant UN Security Council Resolutions' (BRICS 2012), thereby discouraging unilateral sanctions.

In the following years, unilateral sanctions were criticised and their extension was particularly opposed by BRICS. While Iran was not always directly mentioned in BRICS statements, a diplomatic resolution of the issue was emphasised, implying the BRICS stand against sanctions (Shargh Daily 2022). Meanwhile, seeking to mitigate the impact of Western sanctions and proactively explore alternative markets, Iran applied for BRICS membership in 2022. In August 2023, it was admitted alongside Argentina, Egypt, Ethiopia and the United Arab Emirates. Beyond Iran, BRICS members have also united in support of other trade partners. For instance, regarding sanctions on North Korea, the group consistently condemned unilateral measures and advocated for resolving the stalemate through diplomacy (Reuters 2017).

Narratives of BRICS Contestation

The BRICS has contested unilateral sanctions by challenging norms, senders' intentions, as well as measures. However, the group's objection to the 'measure' is most noticeable. BRICS has questioned the 'legitimacy of the measures', an approach of contestation also discussed by Stefano Palestini (Chapter 2 in this volume). The group is uncomfortable with sanctions, and often questions if their adoption is the 'right action' or reaction to an international problem. There are three arguments that can be understood as evidence of reactive contestation. Firstly, BRICS has frequently implied that sanctions are a form of intervention and has elucidated how the tool is detrimental to common goods like international law (BRICS 2021). It has argued that sanctions, especially unilateral sanctions with extra-territorial application, are against international law as they give precedence to the domestic law of the sanctioning state, hinting that sanctions are being used as a tool to meddle in the affairs of other states. The BRICS was formed to support and promote the development of the Global South. Hence, the group's stance is in line with the bloc's attempts to support a perspective on sanctions that is different to the West – the BRICS members understand sanctions as a means of restricting and interfering in the affairs of the non-Western world. BRICS has emphasised that it supports sanctions imposed by the UNSC but is against sanctions imposed unilaterally by states. It has not elaborated on its stand on sanctions imposed by organisations like the EU or the African Union, but since it argues that UN is the 'sole authority to impose sanctions' (BRICS 2021), it can be presumed that the group stands against sanctions imposed by other multilateral organisations.

Secondly, BRICS maintains that sanctions impede the development of the Global South by restricting trade and consequently the global economy suffers. Reproof of the sender has remained a corollary of the members' arguments. This is evident in the cases of sanctions against Russia, China and Iran. In the case of sanctions against Russia, Chinese President Xi Jinping stressed that Western sanctions are a 'double-edged sword' that was weaponising the global economy and bringing 'harm to the people of the world'. He also called for unity among the emerging states to face the financial challenges that emerge as a consequence of unilateral sanctions (CNN 2022). Moreover, BRICS members contested reactively by disregarding sanctions. In the absence of Western demand, Russia turned to BRICS members and offered oil to them at a discounted price (Indian Express 2022). To support their energy requirements, both India and China, as well as other members, overlooked sanctions and increased their crude oil imports from Russia (Indian Express 2022). In 2023, Putin also blamed the Western sanctions for increasing food prices (Guardian 2023), thus using the BRICS as a forum to criticise sanctions, stressing that they hinder trade and cause scarcity.

In the case of sanctions against Iran, preserving trade relations with the sanctioned state became a reason for BRICS members to contest sanctions.

In 2012, speaking to the media at the BRICS summit in New Delhi, Chinese trade minister Chen Deming shared his country's intention to continue to trade with Iran (Mishra and Roche 2012). His Indian counterpart, Anand Sharma, echoed the same sentiment for his country (Mishra and Roche 2012). Moreover, BRICS has contested unilateral sanctions explicitly in its annual statements, asserting that 'economic sanctions and arbitrary use of unilateral coercive measures' should be condemned (BRICS 2013–17).

Thirdly, BRICS members have invoked the concept of national interest to justify their stance against sanctions, emphasising that their economic engagement with sanctioned states is guided by their own national priorities. Highlighting that sanctions harm their countries' interests, they have criticised the sanctioning states, arguing that such policies are misguided and that other nations should not be coerced into supporting sanctions, particularly unilateral ones. As discussed above, in the case of Russia and Iran, BRICS members increased or continued to trade with the sanctioned states after sanctions were imposed.[4] Moreover, BRICS leaders have occasionally pointed out that their countries' needs differ from those of the developed world, and that they cannot support global norms or sanction regimes that come at the expense of their populations' interests (Reuters 2019).

Finally, BRICS also attempted to reduce the effect of Western sanctions by attempting to diminish their own dependence on Western currency. De-dollarisation is an important initiative in this regard. Attempts have been made by various BRICS members to use their own currencies for global transactions, to circumvent or reduce the impact of sanctions (Demarais 2022, 123–39). For instance, to continue importing oil from Iran, India used rupees for its oil payments (Reuters 2019). There is also evidence suggesting that, following the 2022 sanctions on Russia, India is considering conducting trade with Russia in rupees as well (Bloomberg 2022). According to a report published by the Carnegie Endowment for International Peace, due to rising geopolitical tensions and dollar shortages, 'new financial channels built upon BRICS local currencies are increasing' (Greene 2023, 5). China's renminbi use was particularly observable between 2016 and 2022, as cross-border transactions in the Chinese currency increased from about 20 per cent to 50 per cent (Greene 2023, 7). Formation of the New Development Bank and Contingency Reserve Fund in 2015 is also a step in the direction of diminishing dependence on financial institutions led by the West.

BRICS has adopted proactive contestation, by applauding its member China for conducting a seminar on sanctions. As mentioned earlier in the

[4] Though in the case of Iran, its trade with many BRICS members eventually dropped.

chapter, at the fourteenth BRICS summit in Beijing in 2022, the group declaration lauded a member state for hosting a seminar on sanctions, while acknowledging the UNSC as the 'sole authority' to sanction (BRICS 2022). The statement implied that sanctions imposed by a BRICS member would be regarded differently – suggesting a proactive contestation. In 2023 at the fifteenth BRICS summit, the Joint Statement by BRICS Deputy Foreign Ministers and Special Envoys on the Middle East and North Africa (MENA) mentioned sanctions in a positive light as well, as it called for 'further consolidation and strengthening of the working methods' of the UNSC Sanctions Committees to ensure their 'effectiveness, responsiveness and transparency' (BRICS 2023a). Another instance of the BRICS members working to change the nature of sanctions and contesting them proactively is that of sanctions imposed by some of the BRICS members, often termed by them as 'counter-sanctions'. China and Russia do so to emphasise that their measures are distinct from Western sanctions, and stress that they do not impose sanctions but merely 'counter' them. However, the fifteenth BRICS summit declaration was again critical of unilateral sanctions and declared that the BRICS members were concerned about 'trade restrictive measures which are inconsistent with WTO rules, including unilateral illegal measures such as sanctions, that affect agricultural trade' (BRICS 2023b). This suggests that reactive contestation is still most prevalent within BRICS.

Interpretative contestation is observable in the case of BRICS. Several BRICS members have implied in their rhetoric that sanctions are not unlike the tools of statecraft used by former colonisers on weaker states (Chauhan 2022). Given BRICS states' experience of subjugation, interference or loss of sovereignty as former colonies of Western states, it is not surprising that they are often sceptical of Western policies as well as instruments of statecraft. Taking into account the historical interactions of members, the BRICS' distrust of sanctions imposed by states in the West can be better understood. Moreover, in interpretative contestation, often the norm that a sanction regime seeks to promote is also criticised. China, for instance, has frequently argued that sanctions serve as a tool for the West to interfere in the 'internal affairs of developing countries in the name of "democracy" and "human rights"' (Wang 2023). Brazil has remained sceptical of unilateral sanctions, especially their use in its own region (Chivvis and Geaghan-Breiner 2023), given that such measures have often been used to support or oppose certain governments. Similarly, Indian leaders described sanctions imposed on New Delhi in 1998, following its nuclear tests, as 'hypocritical', a label that appears justified since Western counterparts faced no consequences for comparable actions (Vajpayee 1998).

In the case of Russia, its officials have linked national sovereignty to economic sovereignty and denounced sanctions for endangering its economic development (Connolly 2018, 70). For South Africa, its resistance to unilateral sanctions is explained by its belief that the West has attempted to change 'regime' in states like Iraq or Libya through sanctions. Durban has found this action of the West 'problematic' as well as a 'violation of state sovereignty' (Sidiropoulos 2022). Thus, each member has resisted sanctions through interpretative contestation.

Conclusion

BRICS countries exhibit diverse and often conflicting approaches to sanctions, shaped by their individual interests and shifting geopolitical priorities. Although the group consistently promotes discourse opposing unilateral sanctions, not all members adhere to this stance in practice. Despite publicly condemning unilateral sanctions, India and China have partially complied with US sanction regimes to avoid secondary penalties and secure incentives such as waivers (Chauhan 2022). The New Development Bank's decision to freeze transactions with Russia and exclude it from the BRICS reserve fund following sanctions (OMFIF 2022) further demonstrates how member states prioritise pragmatic economic concerns over solidarity.

BRICS' actions also reveal contradictions. The group lauded China for hosting a seminar on targeted sanctions (BRICS 2022), even as China and Russia developed their own counter-sanctions regimes, challenging their own notion that sanctions are solely Western tools (Mohan 2023). This shift indicates that BRICS members recognise the utility of sanctions for their statecraft. Hypocrisy is also evident in their muted anti-colonial critique of Russia following its invasion of Ukraine, highlighting selective application of anti-sanctions rhetoric based on political alignment.

Internal divisions further weaken BRICS' collective stance. China and Russia rhetorically support UNSC reforms but refrain from explicitly endorsing expansion to include India, Brazil or South Africa (Salzman 2019). Economic dominance by stronger members raises concerns about the bloc's democratic balance. As Jim O'Neill and C. Raja Mohan argue, the group's influence remains limited and far from overturning the global order (O'Neill 2023; Mohan 2023).

It comes as no surprise that we can find examples of reactive, proactive and interpretative forms of contestations to sanctions. The BRICS countries' strongest objection is against unilateral sanctions, which they argue violate international law by prioritising domestic law over global norms. BRICS prefers sanctions imposed by the UNSC and views unilateral sanctions as tools for Western interference, particularly in the Global South. The group criticises sanctions for impeding economic growth and trade, citing cases like sanctions on Russia and Iran, where BRICS members increased trade despite restrictions, prioritising national interests. To counter sanctions, BRICS promotes de-dollarisation and develops alternative financial systems, such as the New Development Bank. China and Russia have introduced 'counter-sanctions' to differentiate from Western practices. Proactive efforts include hosting discussions on sanctions, highlighting UNSC's sole authority and improving sanctions' transparency. BRICS also contests the legitimacy of the norms underlying sanctions, viewing them as remnants of colonial control. Members express scepticism about the West's use of sanctions for democracy and human rights promotion, equating them with interference in sovereignty. Historical experiences, like India's reaction to nuclear sanctions in 1998, reinforce their stance. Russia ties economic sovereignty to national sovereignty, while South Africa opposes regime-change tactics linked to sanctions. BRICS' contestation reflects its collective stance against Western dominance in international governance.

In sum, BRICS should not be regarded as a bloc uniformly opposed to sanctions, as its member states evidently acknowledge and, at times, leverage the strategic utility of sanctions as an instrument of statecraft. It is discernible that the members' perspective on the issue is also changing, much like their economies. The BRICS stand is emergent and not set in stone. While there are conflicting interests that can unravel BRICS, the utility of forming a collective group is not lost of any of the members. To quote a former Indian diplomat, BRICS seem to represent 'fluid multilateralism', which brings states together when they want to pursue common interests, even though not all their views are aligned (Sidhu 2015). The anti-sanctions stand of member states has brought the group together at various points; however, it might not be enough to hold them together in the future.

References

Bloomberg. 2022. 'India Is Said to Consider Rupee Payments for Trade with Russia'. 11 March. https://www.bloomberg.com/news/articles/2022-03-11/india-is-said-to-consider-rupee-payments-for-trade-with-russia

BRIC. 2009. 'Joint Statement of the BRIC Countries' Leaders'. Yekaterinburg, Russia, 16 June. www.brics-ysf.org/sites/default /files/ 2nd_ Summit.pdf

BRICS. 2012. 'Summit: Delhi Declaration'. New Delhi, India, 29 March. https://www.brics.unipr.it/wedit/uploads/contenuti/95/fourth-brics-summit-delhi-declaration_action-plan.pdf

BRICS. 2013. 'Summit: Ethekwini Declaration'. Durban, South Africa, 27 March. http://www.brics.utoronto.ca/docs/130327-statement.html

BRICS. 2014. 'Summit: Fortaleza Declaration'. Fortaleza, Brazil, 15 July. http://www.brics.utoronto.ca/docs/140715-leaders.html

BRICS. 2017. 'Summit: Xiamen Declaration'. Xiamen, China, 4 September. http://english.scio.gov.cn/topnews/2017-09/05/content_41531768.htm

BRICS. 2021. 'Summit: New Delhi Declaration'. New Delhi, India. https://brics2021.gov.in /brics/public/uploads/docpdf/getdocu-51.pdf

BRICS. 2022. 'Summit: Beijing Declaration'. Beijing, China. https://www.fmprc.gov.cn/eng/wjdt_665385/2649_665393/202206/t20220623_10709037.html

BRICS. 2023a. 'Joint Statement by BRICS Deputy Foreign Ministers and Special Envoys on the Middle East and North Africa (MENA)'. Cape Town, South Africa, 26 April. https://brics2023.gov.za/wp-content/uploads/2023/07/Joint-Statement-BRICS-MENA-26-April_2023.pdf

BRICS. 2023b. 'Summit Johannesburg II Declaration BRICS and Africa: Partnership for Mutually Accelerated Growth, Sustainable Development and Inclusive Multilateralism'. Sandton, South Africa, 23 August. https://brics2023.gov.za/wp-content/uploads/2023/08/Jhb-II-Declaration-24-August-2023-1.pdf

Chauhan, Rishika. 2022. 'Why India and China Won't Sanction Russia'. *The National Interest*, 11 May.

Chauhan, Rishika, and Sarah Tzinieris. 2024. 'Deciphering China's Uncomfortable Sanctions Discourses'. *E-International Relations*, 7 April. https://www.e-ir.info/2024/04/07/opinion-deciphering-chinas-uncomfortable-sanctions-discourses/

Chivvis, Christopher S., and Beatrix Geaghan-Breiner. 2023. 'Brazil in the Emerging World Order'. *Carnegie Endowment for International Peace*, 18 December.

CNN. 2022. 'Western Sanctions Are "Weaponizing" World Economy, China's Xi Jinping Says ahead of BRICS Summit'. *CNN*, 23 June.

Connolly, Richard. 2018. *Russia's Response to Sanctions: How Western Economic Statecraft Is Reshaping Political Economy in Russia*. Cambridge University Press.

Demarais, Agathe. 2022. *Backfire: How Sanctions Reshape the World against U.S. Interests*. Columbia University Press.

Duggun, Niall. 2015. 'BRICS and the Evolution of a New Agenda within Global Governance'. In *The European Union and the BRICS Complex Relations in the Era of Global Governance*, edited by Marek Rewizorski. Springer.

DW. 2022. 'Putin Vows to Reroute Russian Exports to BRICS Nations'. *Deutsche Welle*, 22 June.

Greene, Robert, 2022. 'How Sanctions on Russia Will Alter Global Payments Flows'. *Carnegie Endowment for International Peace.*

Greene, Robert, 2023. 'The Difficult Realities of the BRICS' De-dollarization Efforts – and the Renminbi's Role'. *Carnegie Endowment for International Peace.*

Guardian. 2023. 'Putin says Brics Should Become Trading Bloc Representing "Global Majority"'. *The Guardian*, 22 August.

Han Zhen and Mihaela Papa. 2022. 'Brazilian Alliance Perspectives: Towards a BRICS Development–Security Alliance?' *Third World Quarterly* 43(5): 1115–36.

Han Zhen and Mihaela Papa. 2024. 'Leadership and Performance in Informal Institutions: The Internal Dynamics of BRICS'. *Contemporary Politics* 30(1): 87–107.

Hung, Ho Ting. 2022. 'China Should Not Over-Rely on Its Anti-Foreign Sanctions Law'. *Oxford Political Review*, 30 August.

Indian Express. 2022. 'National Interest First, Buying Discounted Russian Crude: FM Nirmala Sitharaman'. *The Indian Express*, 2 April.

Miller, Manjari Chatterjee. 2021. 'Why BRICS Still Matters'. *Foreign Policy*, 27 September.

Mishra, Ranjan, and Elizabeth Roche. 2012. 'BRICS Say Will Follow UN, Not US Sanctions against Iran'. *The Mint*, 29 March.

Mohan, Raja. C. 2002. 'Strategic Triangle in Focus During Putin's Visit'. *The Hindu*, 3 December.

Mohan, Raja. C. 2023. 'BRICS Expansion Is No Triumph for China'. *Foreign Policy*, 29 August.

New Development Bank. 2022. 'Statement by New Development Bank'. 3 March.

O'Neill, Jim. 2001. 'Building Better Global Economic BRICs. 2001'. Goldman Sachs, Global Economics Paper 66.

O'Neill. Jim. 2023, 'Does an Expanded BRICS Mean Anything?' *Chatham House*, 27 August.

OMFIF. 2022. 'Russia Frozen Out of Brics Countries' Reserve-Sharing'. The Official Monetary and Financial Institutions Forum.

Pant, Harsh V. 2013. 'The BRICS Fallacy'. *The Washington Quarterly* 36(3): 91–105.

Reuters. 2014a. 'BRICS Stand against Western Sanctions – Russian Foreign Minister'. *Reuters*, 15 July.

Reuters. 2014b. 'Putin Seeks BRICS Moves to Protect against US "sanction attacks"'. *Reuters*, 14 July.

Reuters. 2017. 'BRICS Foreign Ministers Call for Diplomacy to Tackle Korean Tensions'. *Reuters*, 19 June.

Reuters. 2019. 'India Cannot Sacrifice Economic Strength to Comply with U.S. Sanctions – Finance Minister'. *Reuters*, 16 October.

Reuters. 2021. 'Iran Says It Will End Snap IAEA Inspections if Nuclear Deal Terms Not Met'. *Reuters*, 15 February.

Russian Briefing. 2022. 'Russia Relocating Trade from EU To BRICS'. Russian Briefing, 26 June.

Salzman, Rachel S. 2019. *Russia, BRICS, and the Disruption of Global Order*. Georgetown University Press.

Shargh Daily. 2022. 'BRICS Emphasizes Diplomatic Solution to Iran's Nuclear Issue'. *Shargh Daily*, 24 June.

Sidhu, W. P. S. 2015. 'Brics: Shaping a New World Order, Finally'. *Brookings*, 7 July.

Sidiropoulos, Elizabeth. 2022. 'How Do Global South Politics of Non-alignment and Solidarity Explain South Africa's Position on Ukraine?' *Brookings*, 2 August.

Simmons & Simmons. 2021. 'What You Need to Know about the Chinese Anti-Foreign Sanctions Law'. *Simmons & Simmons*, 11 August.

Stuenkel, Oliver. 2014, 'Emerging Powers and Status: The Case of the First BRICs Summit'. *Asian Perspective* 38(1): 89–109.

Tran, Hung. 2024. 'The Underestimated Implications of the BRICS Summit in Russia'. *The Atlantic*, 1 November.

UN. 2020. 'World Population Prospects 2019'. Population Division, Department of Economic and Social Affairs.

Vajpayee, Atal Bihari. 1998, 'We Live in a World Where India Is Surrounded by Nuclear Weaponry: Atal Bihari Vajpayee'. *India Today*, 25 May.

Wang Wenbin. 2023. 'Foreign Ministry Spokesperson Wang Wenbin's Regular Press Conference'. *Ministry of Foreign Affairs*, 14 June.

9

Contesting Sanctions: Mexican Foreign Policy in American Shadow

María-Cristina Rosas

Introduction

Mexico has traditionally insisted that diplomacy and political concertation should prevail over coercive measures such as sanctions. This approach has resulted in a modest and low-profile presence of Mexico on the world stage, despite being the second-largest economy in Latin America and the fifteenth largest economy in the world. This isolationist stance has also aimed at preventing international involvement in Mexico's own domestic affairs. Mexico is concerned about its proximity to the United States, a country with which it has a complex relationship and a border of more than 3,000 kilometres. Additionally, this perspective is rooted in a narrative that began in the mid-nineteenth century and was consolidated during the Mexican Revolution at the beginning of the twentieth century, when the tradition of defending national sovereignty and self-determination served as a tool for national unity and identity (Familiar Ávalos 2018; Pellicer 2023). Thus, nationalism is a key component of Mexican foreign policy, which occasionally prevents the country from engaging on the world stage, shapes its relations with the United States and even undermines interactions with different international organisations, regions and countries (Patrick 2016).

This inward orientation is reflected in the lack of a domestic legislation adequate to implement international commitments, and is discussed in the first section of this chapter. The second section addresses Mexico's views vis-à-vis UN sanctions, which, even though they are considered as legitimate, are frequently contested. Generally speaking, the UN has been seen as a body legitimised to adopt and apply sanctions, but at times it is perceived as being manipulated by major powers – for instance, when the United States (US) declared war against

Iraq in March 2003 based on questionable assumptions. Third, the chapter discusses Mexico's problematic relationship with its powerful neighbour – the US – while the fourth section explains its contestation of the sanctions imposed against Russia as a result of its invasion of Ukraine in February 2022. As a whole, Mexico has adopted both a reactive strategy, for example with regard to sanctions against Latin American states and Russia, and an interpretative approach – in particular criticising the negative human rights implications of individual sanctions.

Sanctions and the Domestic Legislation Problem

As explained in the Introduction of this volume, and further explored in Chapter 1 by Orchard and Wiener, although states perceive multilateral UN sanctions as legitimate, problems emerge in the process of their adoption and enforcement (Charron and Portela 2022). As the case of Mexico confirms, the lack of appropriate internal legislation makes it very difficult to comply with sanctions. A comparison between the United States and Mexico clarifies the situation.

Despite the strong economic interdependence between Mexico and the United States, the two countries have enormous differences in their understanding of sanctions. The North American Free Trade Agreement (NAFTA), which came into force on 1 January 1994, and its successor, the United States-Mexico-Canada Agreement (USMCA), which replaced NAFTA on 1 July 2020, did not enable the three states to better coordinate on foreign policy matters. This is due, at least in part, to domestic institutional constraints: whereas in the US the Executive branch has clear competences in conducting foreign policy and, in the case of sanctions, in enforcing legislation through, for instance, the International Emergency Economic Powers Act, the United Nations Participation Act (UNPA) and the Office of Foreign Assets Control, the Mexican Executive faces a number of difficulties in coordinating actions of administrative bodies and ensuring their compliance with the sanctions adopted by the UN Security Council.

Contrary to the UNPA, which was adopted when the United States joined the United Nations, Mexico does not have a similar law enabling the enactment of UN Security Council resolutions, including those related to sanctions (Congressional Research Service 2023). Despite this, the Mexican government regularly publishes UN resolutions, or relevant parts of them, in the Federal Official Gazette, where legal ordinances are announced to society once they become law.

Since the nineteenth century, in the US many international treaties have been translated into federal laws (Council on Foreign Relations 2007).

By contrast, in Mexico it was only as recently as 2011 that the Supreme Court clarified the process through which international legislation can become domestic law. Pursuant to Article 133 of the Mexican Constitution, international treaties become domestic laws based on the following procedure. First, the president signs a treaty, which is then ratified by the Congress; second, the international treaty must not contradict the Mexican Constitution; finally, the related national legislation comes into force (Peña Haller and Sánchez Contreras 2017). Sanctions-related international treaties endorsed by Mexico include the Palermo Convention of 2000, the Inter-American Convention Against Corruption of 1996, the Forty Recommendations of the Financial Action Task Force of 1990 (Garay Garzón 2019) and free trade agreements with the European Union and with Canada and the US (USMCA), where provisions on democracy and the fight against corruption are included.

When the UN Security Council adopts a resolution on sanctions, Mexican authorities inform the public through circular notes that, as a rule, do not allow for the correct implementation of the restrictive measures by the relevant authorities and regulators, such as the Mexican Foreign Ministry, the Financial Intelligence Unit of the Ministry of Revenue and the Attorney General. An additional challenge in the implementation of sanctions involves the need to comply with legal due process, particularly because sanctions increasingly tend to be both more focused/targeted and more invasive, potentially conflicting with international humanitarian law norms (Schaar 2021). Yet, the lack of legislation on the implementation of sanctions may increase the risks of human rights violations against individuals residing in Mexico and, more generally, contrasts with the constitutional provisions stating that all persons should be granted the widest possible human rights protection within the country (Peña Haller and Sánchez Contreras 2017). As suggested before, in these cases Mexico adopts an interpretative approach to sanctions.

In sum, the domestic legislation issue is not simply a technical problem but reflects Mexico's half-hearted commitment to both international and unilateral sanctions – as explained below further.

Mexico and UN Security Council Sanctions

Mexico has been a non-permanent UN Security Council member only five times since 1945 (in 1946, 1980–1, 2002–3, 2009–10 and 2021–2) and thus, as opposed to other elected members such as Brazil and Japan who have sat on the Security Council twelve times, Mexico is less experienced in dealing with UN activities and much less eager to get involved in sanctions regimes. That said, Mexico has voted in favour of UN Security Council sanctions during its mandates as an elected member both during the Cold War and in the post-Cold War period. For instance, in October 2022 the UN Security Council approved unanimously – with Mexico's vote included – Resolution 2653 to sanction Haiti. In addition, despite its criticism over sanctions against individuals associated with the Taliban due to their collateral effects on innocent civilians, Mexico expressed its humanitarian concerns but did not contest the adoption of the resolution (United Nations 2022).

The UN Security Council is the key multilateral body tasked with adopting sanctions with the goal of maintaining and restoring international peace and stability (Scherz and Zysset 2020). However, its competences are occasionally challenged by Mexico on procedural standards. Since sanctions are increasingly targeted, there are no proper mechanisms to guarantee due process to review their impacts, or to correct mistakes in applying them to individuals and companies. Part of the problem is that the purpose of the UN Security Council, in particular since the end of the Cold War, has evolved significantly. Besides maintaining and restoring international peace and stability, the Council has increasingly acted to protect individual human rights. As Scherz and Zysset (2020, 374) put it, 'the political power of an institution understood as rule-setting and applying competences have to be justified to those subjected to its rules in order to be legitimate'.

In general terms, when contesting UN sanctions Mexico tends to adopt both a reactive and an interpretative posture. During the Cold War, when sanctions were less frequently endorsed by the Security Council, Mexico applied them. Even though at that time Mexico perceived sanctions as potentially conflicting with its national interest, it nonetheless endorsed them. Notably, Mexico refrained from establishing diplomatic relations or any other political contact with the South African apartheid regime in pursuance of sanctions agreed upon by the UNSC in October 1993, once apartheid started to come to an end (Fajer Flores 2021).

While Mexico considers UN economic and trade sanctions as generally legitimate, it interprets other kinds of multilateral measures as less so. During the Cold War, the possible participation of South Africa in the Mexico City 1968 Olympics put Mexico in a difficult situation, since many countries and athletes from Asia, Africa, the Caribbean and even African Americans indicated that they would not participate. Their proposed boycott was not against Mexico but was due to the decision of the International Olympic Committee (IOC) to extend an invitation to apartheid South Africa to participate. The application of sanctions against South Africa due to the political interests of some powerful IOC members may have damaged Mexico's efforts to host a successful Olympics. In response, Mexico developed a diplomatic strategy to work with African countries, the Soviet Union and the IOC to address the situation. As a result, the IOC withdrew the invitation to South Africa by arguing the international political environment was not appropriate and that the safety of South African athletes could be at risk (Rodríguez Kuri 2015). This experience shows how Mexico could be harmed by multilateral sanctions applied to third parties and supported the determination of Mexican authorities to react and contest them.

After the end of the Cold War multilateral sanctions are increasingly targeted against elites including, for example, influential businesspeople, army officers and senior government officials. Since they are supposedly less likely to harm innocent civilians, they seem to be less of a concern to Mexico. At the same time, this situation has paved the way to novel challenges. While during the Cold War sanctions were directed against states, after that period they have a much wider scope, targeting non-state and individual actors. Even though no UN Security Council resolution has so far targeted Mexico, the potential of being punished due to corruption, drug trafficking and other illicit activities has increased significantly. Mexico has reacted to this possibility. Most notably, the Legal Adviser Office of the Mexican Ministry for Foreign Affairs periodically analyses UN sanctions resolutions and evaluates the need to adapt or update the Mexican legal system to implement, or better contest, these resolutions.

In the meantime, Mexico has also adopted an interpretative approach. Mexico contests multilateral sanctions on the basis of potential violations of the human rights of targeted persons residing permanently or temporarily in the country, as this may contradict either domestic legislation or constitutional provisions. Mexico suggests that because the UN Security Council has failed to grant targeted persons and companies due process – despite the adoption of Resolutions 1730 (2006) and 1904 (2009), which created a focal point and an ombudsman for targeted individuals and companies – it is necessary to create domestic legislation regulating the application of UN sanctions within the country. Furthermore, it claims both the focal point and the ombudsman lack transparency and accountability. This is why Mexico believes that creating domestic legislation on sanctions that guarantees due process and upholds human rights granted by the Mexican Constitution is essential (Peña Haller and Sánchez Contreras 2017).

While engaging in this kind of interpretative contestation, Mexico often faces pressure from Washington to apply UN sanctions. This pressure has constrained Mexican multinational corporations as well, which have frequently withdrawn their operations from countries targeted by sanctions, like Cuba, due to fears of being punished under the United States' Helms-Burton legislative provisions, which prescribe that any non-US company that deals economically with Cuba can be subjected to legal action. In response, Mexico enacted legislation to protect national companies from foreign laws but limited impact on trade with Cuba. Because many Mexican private companies also have important investments and commercial interests in the United States and did not want to be exposed to secondary sanctions, they decided to quit their operations in Cuba.

During the Peña Nieto Administration (2012–18), tensions between the two countries were particularly high, especially during the first Donald Trump presidency (2017–21), which targeted Mexico because of undocumented migrants flowing from its territory into the US. At that time, Trump insisted that NAFTA was the worst trade pact ever negotiated and threatened Mexico and Canada with denouncing it. Later he decided to support the negotiation of a new trade pact but, in the meantime, relations deteriorated to the point that Mexico, in order to restore an acceptable rapport with Washington, agreed to follow the United States on UN sanctions against North Korea. The 'North Korea affair' showed how Mexico is vulnerable to heavy American pressure that, at particular times, may lead the country to adopt sanctions regardless of its assessment of the appropriateness of the measures endorsed.

Diplomatic relations between Mexico and North Korea were established in 1980. Since 1993 Pyongyang has had an embassy in Mexico City while Mexico managed its relations with North Korea through its embassy in Seoul. During the Cold War, through the 'good offices' of the Soviet Union, North Korea became a supporter of Mexican guerrillas. This led to a crisis in Mexico–Soviet relations. The issue was resolved by establishing a direct line of communication between Mexican and Soviet authorities. However, for Mexico diplomatic relations with Pyongyang were and still are a way of monitoring suspicious activities of subversive groups that may be supported by North Korea (Rosas 2017). Considering this background, the decision of the Mexican government to expel the North Korean ambassador, Kim Hyong Gil, on 7 September 2017, because of US pressure was an unexpected response to the North Korean nuclear programme, which had been ongoing since 2006 and continues to this today. While the UN Security Council sanctioned North Korea because of its nuclear weapons programme (Council on Foreign Relations 2022), Mexico reduced its relations with North Korea not because of UN requirements, but rather due to the pressure coming from Washington. Pressures coming from the US prevailed over existing national security concerns about North Korea's activities in Mexico.

Throughout 2017 US Vice President Mike Pence toured several Latin American countries that maintained diplomatic relations with North Korea. In Santiago de Chile, Pence suggested that Mexico, Chile, Peru and Brazil should have stopped their economic and political relations with North Korea, implying the US may have sanctioned any of these countries if American demands were not met. As a result, Mexico decided it was time to support the US in punishing North Korea (Rinna 2020). Mexican President Peña Nieto wanted to avoid more tensions and controversies with Washington and thus declared the North Korean ambassador persona non grata. The ambassador left the country, and bilateral relations between Mexico and North Korea dropped to their lowest level ever (Brown Solá, 2017).

The declaration of persona non grata against the North Korean ambassador in 2017 proceeded very expeditiously, in sharp contrast with the Mu Du Bong confiscation case a few years earlier. Indeed, in 2014, a ship named *Mu Du Bong* owned by North Korea was detained in the port of Tuxpan, Veracruz, Mexico, following the UN Sanctions Committee Resolution 1718 that condemned the nuclear weapons programme of the country. The ship, arriving from Cuba, destroyed 3,600 square metres of coral reefs, but it was not detained over environmental concerns. During 2014 and 2015, the Mexican Foreign Ministry liaised with the UN Sanctions Committee 1718 in order to clarify whether the owner of the ship was deliberately avoiding sanctions (Peña Haller and Sánchez Contreras 2017). The UN Sanctions Committee 1718 provided information to the Mexican government which finally led to the detention of the ship despite coordination problems between the Mexican institutions involved, including the Ministry for Foreign Affairs, the Ministry of the Interior, the Ministry of the Treasury, the Ministry of Economy, the Attorney General's Office, the Financial Intelligence Unit of the Ministry of the Treasury and the Center for Research and National Security (the then Mexican intelligence services) (Plaza 2015). The process took two years and faced some ups and downs due to the lack of experience in dealing with the implementation of UN multilateral sanctions. By contrast, in 2017, pressure coming from Washington was much more persuasive. Even though the *Mu Du Bong* affair was a multilateral issue involving the UN and thus measures to deal with it were perceived as legitimate, Mexican authorities acted less expeditiously. They appeared to be willing to comply with the UN Security Council resolution, but without a fixed timeline to be met (Brandoli 2015). In sum, in assessing the pros and cons of international sanctions, Mexico not only considers the legitimacy of the sender and/or the content of the measures, but also has to take into account the views of its powerful northern neighbour.

Mexico and US Unilateral Sanctions

The asymmetrical relationship between Mexico and the United States, combined with such a complex bilateral agenda, determines whether or not the

Mexican government contests US sanctions. Mexico was a Security Council elected member when the George Bush administration decided to attack Iraq. At that time, the Mexican government was led by Vicente Fox (2000–6), representing the first democratic administration after almost seventy years of rule by the Institutional Revolutionary Party (PRI). Under President Fox, who had a cordial personal relationship with President Bush, Mexico was able to escape the pressures from Washington to vote for a proposed UN resolution, drafted by the Americans and authorising the war against Iraq on questionable grounds (Wilkinson and O'Sullivan 2004). Mexico favoured the search for deadlines and fixed goals that could be met in the process of disarming Iraq, always keeping in mind the need to comply with requests arriving from a multilateral framework (Montaner Peralta 2020). When the US realised it would not have the authorisation of the UN Security Council, it proceeded with the war plans supported by a few of its close allies, especially the UK and Spain.

That decision by the US created the perception in Mexico – and arguably in several other countries – that the noble purposes of the Security Council could be undermined by major powers pursuing their specific national interests. In other words: the US tried to get the 'OK' from the Security Council to start the war against Iraq, and when this was not possible, it went to war anyway, thus abandoning a legitimate process to embark on an illegal behaviour. In this example, the legitimacy of the norm – maintaining and restoring international peace and security – was under scrutiny since the US was not able to demonstrate the existence of nuclear weapons in Iraq, nor the imminence of a war that presumably would be initiated by the Iraqi government against the US and its allies. In the eyes of Mexico, the enforcer – the US – transformed itself from a legitimate international actor to an illegal warrior. This episode represented a key event for Mexico in undermining its belief that the UN is the main body at a multilateral level in charge of enacting sanctions.

The Peña Nieto government (2012–18) decided it was in the country's best interest to cooperate with Washington for both economic and political reasons, particularly after Donald Trump's inauguration. Thus, as suggested above, UN multilateral sanctions against North Korea were implemented within the scope of the bilateral relationship between Mexico and the United States, while the 2014 *Mu Du Bong* affair proceeded less expeditiously since the Obama administration did not push Mexico hard on the issue. Upon the inauguration of López Obrador (December 2018), despite the suggested empathy between him and Trump, trade and migration issues became critical in the bilateral relationship, and Mexico was threatened with sanctions unless it controlled undocumented migration heading north of the common border.

During the first Donald Trump administration, Mexico faced the threat of US sanctions and quickly acted to pre-empt the possibility of being targeted by Washington. Besides the UN resolutions on North Korea that led to the declaration of persona non grata to the ambassador of that country in Mexico, another example is the threat of trade sanctions announced by President Trump to force Mexico to stop the flow of undocumented migrants into the US. In response, Mexico complied with American requests despite the lack of any economic support and turned itself into a 'third-safe country' by stopping migrants at the southern border with Guatemala and Belize. Mexico detained thousands of undocumented migrants and processed their applications for asylum and refugee status on Mexican territory (Brice 2019).

In addition, the sanctions against Nicolás Maduro's regime in Venezuela, adopted by the Trump administration, also indirectly involved Mexico. Sanctions against Venezuela, intended to promote a democratic transition in the South American country, were endorsed by both the US government and the Organization of American States (OAS). Even though the OAS has long been perceived as a regional body dominated by the United States, its involvement in the sanctions against Venezuela initially provided some legitimacy. However, the OAS efforts were not successful. Thus, Mexico, together with the members of the Lima Group – a coalition of thirteen Latin American countries plus Canada – participated as a facilitator for a peaceful political dialogue and transition between the opposition and the Nicolás Maduro administration (Bernstein 2020).

The Venezuela case is interesting because it showed through the formation of the Lima Group (2017) that a collective Latin American response to the authoritarian government of Nicolás Maduro and its threat to democracy was possible. The fact that Mexico and the Lima Group perceived the Maduro regime as a threat to the region eroded the principle of non-intervention. However, at the time many of the Latin American countries involved in the Lima Group had governments either located at the centre or centre-right of the political spectrum. Currently, however, most of the Latin American governments – including Mexico's – are on the centre-left or left of the political spectrum, and thus are less critical of the Nicolás Maduro administration. Besides that, Palestini (2023) suggests the legitimacy of sanctions against Venezuela suffered due to the confrontational language adopted by both the US and the OAS. For instance, the OAS Secretary General referred to the Maduro regime as a 'tyrannical dictatorship', whereas the Trump administration invoked the Monroe Doctrine to justify sanctions, thus putting the Lima Group countries – including Mexico – on the defensive. The way the OAS and the Trump administration referred to the Venezuela regime led Nicolás

Maduro to exploit the situation, taking advantage of the divisions emerging among Latin American countries which undermined the possibility to address sanctions collectively. The legitimacy of sanctions in this context was badly harmed.

That said, it is common for sanctioned entities to look for ways to evade restrictions imposed by the US and other actors (such as the European Union). The Venezuelan government was able to elude some of them through Mexican and Colombian companies that sold Venezuelan state oil on world markets, something forbidden under the US sanctions regime against Caracas (Sutherland 2020). The US Department of the Treasury targeted Libre Abordo, a company based in Mexico City, for providing financial and technological support for PDVSA – Venezuela's state company and the fifth largest oil company in the world. In 2017, the Mexican government quickly reacted to prevent Libre Abordo from reselling Venezuelan oil. In May 2020, Libre Abordo filed for bankruptcy but the US Department of the Treasury discovered it was still reselling around 30 million barrels a day of Venezuelan crude oil (PBS 2020). In 2021, it rejected an offer from a 'ghost' Venezuelan company to do business with PEMEX, the Mexican state-owned oil company.

At the beginning of his administration in December 2018, President López Obrador bet on closer links with Latin American countries. Mexico held the rotating presidency of the Latin American and Caribbean States Community (CELAC) and hosted the Sixth CELAC Summit on 18 September 2021, in Mexico City with the participation of the presidents of Cuba, Miguel Díaz-Canel, and Venezuela, Nicolás Maduro. This created tensions in the CELAC meeting but showed Mexico invoking a nationalist narrative for domestic consumption, which also carried an implicit message to Washington: Mexico, as a sovereign country, was capable of chairing a summit with the participation of all countries, including those that Washington tends to exclude due to human rights and democracy concerns. By the end of 2021, US President Biden hosted a virtual summit on democracy to which Cuba, Nicaragua, Guatemala, Russia, China, Iran and North Korea were not invited. Mexico was invited to the meeting, but López Obrador criticised the exclusion of these countries. When President Biden hosted the Ninth Summit of the Americas in Los Angeles in June 2022 and did not invite Cuba, Nicaragua and Venezuela, López Obrador announced he would not attend because exclusion was contrary to the spirit of an 'Americas' summit (Long and Verza 2023). Other leaders – such as those of Saint Vincent and the Grenadines, Peru, Bolivia, El Salvador, Honduras and Guatemala – also did not attend, showing the Biden administration's diminished convening power in a region once considered its 'backyard'.

López Obrador also flirted with the idea of restoring diplomatic relations with North Korea and, in June 2021, a formal announcement was made to this effect (Stillman 2021). A high-level political North Korean delegation was present at López Obrador's inauguration on 1 December 2018. Evo Morales, then president of Bolivia, was also in attendance. Some months later, Evo Morales was offered political asylum in Mexico after he was ousted from government over fraud and corruption charges in Bolivia between 10 and 20 November 2019.

By 2021, relations between Mexico and the US were quickly evolving, in particular following the arrival of the Biden administration in Washington. Perceived by President López Obrador as a character weaker than Trump (Camhaji 2023), the Mexican president initially cooperated with President Biden to face the SARS-CoV-2 pandemic. Once the health emergency decreased, however, López Obrador turned increasingly critical of US foreign policy, challenging it on nationalist and sovereign grounds, and became more and more reluctant to comply with the US sanctions regimes against countries like Cuba, Russia, Nicaragua and Venezuela. The narrative of President López Obrador was closely linked to denouncing unilateral sanctions as illegitimate.

Cuba is one of the leading topics in the contestation of sanctions by Mexico under López Obrador and his successor Claudia Sheinbaum. From the beginning of his term, López Obrador insisted on the importance of putting an end to the US embargo and even invited Cuban President Díaz-Canel to Mexico. Significantly, on 16 September 2021, Miguel Díaz-Canel was the guest of honour during the Mexican independence anniversary and parade. López Obrador was a guest of honour in Havana too. In addition, Mexico contracted the services of Cuban doctors during the COVID-19 pandemic, despite criticism by Mexican health personnel who lamented Cubans' better salaries and labour conditions. Mexico also purchased the COVID-19 Cuban vaccine Abdala, despite it not being authorised by the World Health Organization (Mexico News Daily 2022).

In a similar mood, López Obrador called for an end to US sanctions against Venezuela. He insisted that sanctions force Venezuelans, Cubans, Nicaraguans and other nationals to emigrate from their countries. He made that statement at the very same time his Foreign and Economy Ministers, Alicia Bárcena and Raquel Buenrostro, were in Washington addressing Secretary of State Blinken and other prominent members of the Biden administration to foster agreements and cooperation initiatives between the two countries (PBS 2023).

Overall, during his mandate President López Obrador sided more and more with countries considered threats or concerns to the United States. By doing so, he underlined Mexican independence and showed Mexico's political distance with respect to its powerful northern neighbour. His successor, Claudia Sheinbaum, has been more cautious under the second Trump administration, possibly fearing more tensions in Mexico–US Relations. Thus, it has sent humanitarian assistance to Cuba, but stopped sending oil to ease energy shortages in the island.

Russian Aggression in Ukraine and International Sanctions

On 24 February 2022, Russia attacked Ukraine, prompting the world to apply a wide range of sanctions on the Russian regime, companies, banks and more. This led the most important Western multinational corporations, including Mexican companies, to close their operations in Russia. Travel restrictions, sports sanctions, interruption of gas deliveries to Europe and a crop crisis followed. Many countries, including the US, Western Europe and Japan, applied sanctions against Moscow and provided political, economic, military and humanitarian support to Ukraine. The UN General Assembly voted on a resolution on 2 March 2022, condemning the Russian attacks, which was approved by 141 UN members, with 35 abstentions, 5 votes against and 13 absentees.

Mexico voted in favour of this resolution. However, when it came to applying sanctions against Russia, Mexico decided not to do so. President López Obrador contested the decision of the US, Western Europe, Japan and others to impose sanctions against Russia. He found Western behaviour both hypocritical, since in the past Western states frequently meddled in the internal affairs of other states (including Mexico), and ultimately counter-productive since sanctions are unlikely to be a tool for peace. Rather, Obrador explained that he wanted peace and prosperity in the world and proposed a solution to the Russia–Ukraine war that was heavily criticised by Ukrainian authorities. López Obrador also rejected the possibility of sending arms to Ukraine. He went as far as criticising President Biden's economic support to Ukraine by claiming that, rather than buoying a distant country, the US should have provided financial support to Central American countries to contain migration pressures.

Within Mexico, López Obrador's decision was polarising. Members of the Labor Party, close to the ruling party, MORENA, established a Parliamentarian Friendship Group with Russia. This created turmoil within Congress, with the right-wing National Action Party expressing strong disagreement with this action, whereas members of other parties insisted on the importance of supporting peace and condemning Russia's invasion. Upon invitation by Ukrainian parliamentarians, Mexican federal deputies travelled to Ukraine to meet with the mayor of Kyiv and to learn more about the humanitarian consequences of the conflict (Pére 2022).

The intellectual community in Mexico also split. Some academics and social activists criticised narratives where, they claim, the Russian point of view is absent. Others grounded their views to anti-imperialism and sovereignty concerns and supported the president's view. At the same time, a large group of intellectuals criticised the arguments presented by Putin to justify the war and explained the conflict in a more elaborate fashion, including geopolitical perspectives about power dynamics between Russia, China, NATO and the US.

The US government expressed concerns about President López Obrador's views, and the US Ambassador to Mexico criticised the initiatives of Mexican parliamentarians that gave Russia a voice to justify a war widely condemned worldwide. To cool things down, the US ambassador was invited to the establishment of a Friendship Group, Mexico–US, by members of the Mexican Congress a day after the Friendship Group with Russia was created (DW 2022).

Mexico abstained from voting to suspend Russia from the UN Human Rights Council at the request of the US (Reuters 2022). When Canada called for a meeting on 5 April 2022 to raise funds for the victims of the war in Ukraine, President López Obrador excused himself by citing previous commitments and, instead, sent a video message indicating that his government would not condemn the Russian invasion of Ukraine because Mexico had been invaded in the past by Spain, France and the United States.

The fact that the López Obrador government decided not to sanction Russia was perceived as a potential challenge to Mexican companies, especially those with operations in countries that do sanction Russia. Three major Mexican companies – Bimbo, Gruma and Nemak – announced just days after the start of the Russian invasion of Ukraine that they would be closing their operations in Russia and Ukraine. Bimbo, the main supplier of McDonald's sandwich buns in Russia, announced on 14 March 2022 that it would leave the country. Gruma, a corn and flour company, stopped its operations in Russia and Ukraine. Nemak, a company that has produced auto parts for Volkswagen in Russia since 2015, stopped its operations on 3 March 2022, and shortly after announced a donation of 100,000 euros to the International Committee of the Red Cross to provide humanitarian support to Ukraine. These decisions suggest that, at least in the case of these three corporations, they do not align with López Obrador's views on the war. As multinational corporations, they are linked to the global economy and maintain operations in many different countries. While their presence in the Russian and Ukrainian markets was small before the war, the potential impacts of losing these markets were minimal. Yet, their decisions may be well received in Western markets.

Concluding Remarks

When Russia started the invasion of Ukraine on 24 February 2022, Mexico was serving as an elected member of the UN Security Council. At that time, the Security Council seemed very weak. Since the war against Iraq in March 2003, major conflicts in the world have not generated decisive actions by this body due to the threat or use of the veto by its permanent members, mostly the US, China and Russia. Indeed, since the beginning of the twenty-first century, the US has used its veto sixteen times, Russia thirty-three times and China fifteen times. France and the UK have also exercised their veto rights, but have only used it once in the same period. This is why at its annual meeting to analyse UN Security Council reform, the 78th General Assembly proposed to limit the use of the veto so that when a permanent member decides to do so, it must explain why to the UN members. Without changes to its procedures and methods being made, the UN Security Council may compromise its legitimacy.

Given this situation, international relations remain a challenge for Mexico, a country geographically positioned between the asymmetries of North America and Latin America, each of which tends to view Mexico as belonging to the other. Mexico also faces a lack of intellectual resources to debate foreign policy – there are only a couple of think tanks to discuss international affairs. Mexican foreign policy has long focused mostly on agendas such as disarmament and free trade. Today, the international agenda is much broader, involving environment, health, organised crime activities, human rights, food and energy security issues. Thus, it is time to expand the scope and views about today's world in Mexico, and for this reason, sanctions seem to be an unavoidable agenda item. The good news is that sanctions are currently being debated in Mexico and, in time, domestic legislation to regulate their application may come to light. Yet, for the time being, it is evident that the contestation of sanctions by Mexico remains intertwined with its complex bilateral relationship with the United States.

References

Bernstein, Jay. 2020. *Fighting against Imperialism: The Latin American Approach to International Sanctions*. Center on Global Energy Policy.

Brandoli, Javier. 2015. 'Los 33 fantasmas del buque norcoreano retenido en México'. *El Mundo*, 11 April.

Brice, Makini. 2019. 'Trump Threatens More Tariffs on Mexico over Part of Immigration Deal'. *Reuters*, 10 June.

Brown Solá, Carlos. 2017. 'Corea del Norte y su no tan conocida relación con México'. *Nexos*, 12 September.

Camhaji, Elías. 2023. 'Mexico and the United States Clash over Biden's Approval of More Border Wall Construction'. *El País*, 7 October.

Charron, Andrea, and Clara Portela, eds. 2022. *Multilateral Sanctions Revisited: Lessons Learned from Margaret Doxey*. McGill-Queen's University Press.

Congressional Research Service. 2023. 'U.S. Sanctions: Overview for the 188th Congress'. *Congressional Research Service*.

Council on Foreign Relations. 2007. 'Excerpt: Economic Sanctions and American Diplomacy'. Council on Foreign Relations.

Council on Foreign Relations. 2022. 'What to Know About Sanctions on North Korea'. Council on Foreign Relations.

DW. 2022. 'Diputados de México crearon "Grupo de Amistad México-Rusia"'. *Deutsche Welle*, 24 March.

Fajer Flores, Ana Luisa. 2021. 'México y Sudáfrica, 25 años construyendo diplomacia Ubuntu'. *Comercio Exterior*.

Familiar Ávalos, Jorge. 2018. 'Contradiction and Ambivalence: Mexico's Cold War and the United States'. *The Yale Review of International Studies*, 15 December.

Garay Garzón, Víctor Manuel. 2019. 'México: su lucha contra el lavado de activos y el impacto laboral'. *Revista de la Facultad de Derecho* I(273): 107–30.

Long, Colleen, and Maria Verza. 2023. 'Biden, López Obrador Open Mexico Meetings with Brusque Talk'. *Associated Press*, 9 January.

Mexico News Daily. 2022. 'Medical Community Slams AMLO for Hiring Cuban Doctors, Says There Is No Shortage'. *Mexico News Daily*, 11 May.

Montaner Peralta, Gonzalo. 2020. *Estpan con nosotros o con los terroristas. El efecto Al Qaeda y la guerra de Irak en América Latina*. Adriana Ediciones.

Palestini, Stefano. 2023. 'Why Sanctions Need to Be Seen as Legitimate'. *International Affairs*, 21 June.

Patrick, Stewart. 2016. 'Global Mexico: From Principles to Interests'. *Council on Foreign Relations*, 5 May.

PBS. 2020. 'Trump Sanctions Target Venezuela's Link to Mexico'. *Public Broadcasting Service*, 18 June.

PBS. 2023. 'Mexico's President Slams U.S. Sanctions on Venezuela and Cuba'. *Public Broadcasting Service*, 29 September.

Pellicer, Olga. 2023. 'Why Mexico Is a Quiet Presence on the World Stage'. *Americas Quarterly*, 25 April.

Peña Haller, Eduardo Patricio, and Juan Manuel Sánchez Contreras. 2017. 'La implementación en México de sanciones selectivas de las Naciones Unidas'. *Revista Mexicana de Política Exterior* 109: 125–61.

Pére, Maritza. 2022. 'Diputados de MC y PAN viajan a Ucrania'. *El Economista*, 14 July.

Plaza, Axel. 2015. 'Mu Du Bong: un barco fantasma en Veracruz'. *Contralínea*, 29 September.

Reuters. 2022. 'Mexico Declines to Impose Economic Sanctions on Russia'. *Reuters*, 1 March.

Rinna, Anthony. 2020. 'Brazil and Mexico's Relations with North Korea'. *Sino NK*, 24 September.

Rodríguez Kuri, Ariel. 2015. 'Geopolítica de la raza. Sudáfrica, Estados Unidos y boicot en los juegos olímpicos de 1968'. *Estudios de Historia Moderna y Contemporánea de México* 50: 45–62.

Rosas, María Cristina. 2017. 'México, Corea del Norte y la Doctrina Estrada'. *Etcétera*, 11 September.

Schaar, Johan. 2021. 'The Burden of the Unintended: The Humanitarian Consequences of Sanctions and the Role of the Red Cross Red Crescent'. *Swedish Red Cross.*

Scherz, Antoinette, and Alain Zysset. 2020. 'The UN Security Council, Normative Legitimacy and the Challenge of Specificity'. *Critical Review of International Social and Political Philosophy* 23(3): 371–91.

Stillman, Amy. 2021. 'Mexico Floats Restoring Diplomatic Relations with North Korea'. *BNN Bloomberg*, 17 July.

Sutherland, Manuel. 2020. *Las sanciones económicas contra Venezuela: consecuencias, crisis humanitaria, alternativas y acuerdo humanitario*. PROVEA.

United Nations. 2022. 'Haiti: Vote on Draft Resolution Establishing a Sanctions Regime'. *Security Council Report*, 21 October.

Wilkinson, James, and Christopher D. O'Sullivan. 2004. 'The UN Security Council and Iraq: Why It Succeeded in 1990, Why It Didn't in 2003, and Why the United States Should Redeem It'. *American Diplomacy* 9(1).

10

Russia under Sanctions: The Case of a 'Complex Contestation'

Intigam Mamedov and Piotr Dutkiewicz

Introduction

In February 2022, the Russian Federation invaded Ukraine. This aggression and continuing war mean the non-peaceful contestation of the West-led international rules-based order.[1] In response, many countries introduced multifaceted and multilayered sanctions.[2] Their main goal was to limit Russia's financial capacity to conduct the war. Also, the intended goal was to weaken the Russian economy and restrict some individual freedoms for the Russian elite and citizens to create – in turn – a pressure effect on the Russian decision-makers. Several waves of sanctions targeted Russia's political and economic leadership, financial system, energy sector, transportation and trade. Other restrictions also affected the broadcasting of Russian media abroad and limitations in diplomatic and consular relations with Russia.

The present chapter follows this volume's central question of '*How and why do governments, as well as citizens and the private sector, interpret and challenge sanctions and their application?*' We are focusing specifically on people's perceptions of sanctions and on how they are formed by the official narrative as well as by their own experience. We intend to respond to three research questions. First, what is the official narrative on sanctions constructed by the Russian leadership?

[1] On 2 March 2022, the UN General Assembly adopted Resolution ES-11/1, deploring Russia's aggression against Ukraine.

[2] For example, between 22 February 2022 and 11 January 2024, the total number of sanctions imposed on individuals from Russia reached more than 16,000 while entities faced more than 9,200 restrictions (see Statista 2024).

Secondly, what are the core trends in perceiving sanctions by the Russian population? And thirdly, which other factors influence general public opinion on sanctions in Russia? We will follow popular attitudes to test whether it is grounded mostly in the scale and effectiveness of state propaganda or it is a result of another set of causalities. We will be analysing such variables as structure and targets of sanctions, possibility of alternative narratives to be articulated, scale of real and potential repressions for showing discontent, and attitudes to what is called in Russia a 'Collective West' and what we call a 'Political West'.

Our approach fits simultaneously into two explanatory categories presented in this volume – reactive contestation and interpretative contestation. Russia has violated international norms on a massive scale and, basically, withdrew from the norm-based Western-led order. That fits into 'reactive contestations model', which involves actors who seek to object to or to violate norms (Wiener 2017 and Wiener and Orchard, this volume). Our chapter, however, goes beyond an official narrative to explain why and how most Russians are constructing alternative perspectives on the social/economic implications of imposed sanctions. That part fits into the 'interpretative contestation' model. The point is that Russians – taking a generally critical attitude towards the West, following the official line – 'independently' developed their negative/indifferent attitude towards sanctions that goes beyond the government narrative.

We suggest that their attitude is due to a number of reasons. First, sanctions are seen as 'mistargeted', 'unjust' and 'discredited'. Second, there is no opportunity for individuals and organisations to either perceive or articulate alternative narratives. Third, the well-being of Russian society has not radically changed after the sanctions. And fourth, having lived through several economic crises previously, Russians became more resilient to shocks. However, as Tatiana Stanovaya (2023) put it, 'Don't be fooled: this ostensible resilience to bad news and the seeming indifference to ongoing events are deceptive'. Thus, we argue that Russia presents the case of a 'complex contestation' model.

We also have an important note for the reader: this chapter covers a limited time period from February 2022 to September 2024; thus, our conclusions are based on the data harvested over that time and may have a 'temporary value' in the sense that if data collection had continued for a longer time, we may have had to correct/expand them, as in any poll-based research.

Sanctions and their Official Interpretation

Russia became a major target for sanctions in 2014 after the annexation of Crimea. However, until 2022, their volume was relatively limited. The 2019 International Monetary Fund report recorded that sanctions had slowed down the growth of the Russian economy by a modest 0.2 per cent of its GDP (Åslund 2019, 16). All changed in 2022. A new tsunami of sanctions hit Russia after the invasion of Ukraine in February 2022.

Elena Chachko and J. Benton Neath (2022, 135–6) proposed to divide them into six categories. The first category of sanctions has been imposed individually against the Russian political and economic leadership. The second category of measures aimed at the Russian financial system. The third group of sanctions targeted the energy sector at production and trade levels. A fourth group of sanctions was established in the international trade sector. The fifth category is transportation. Finally, these measures have been accompanied by an exodus of private business actors. BP, Apple, McDonald's, Mastercard and Visa, among others, have suspended operations in Russia.

The official US and EU rationale for imposing sanctions in response to the Russian invasion of Ukraine creates a picture of a massive, multi-step and coordinated political and economic engineering targeting Russia. The goal was to impose high costs on the Russian economy and – by default – on society in order to influence policymakers to be aware of the multiple costs of war, punish the political leadership and economic elite as well as make them uncertain about the future of their well-being. Regime change in Russia as a potential result of sanctions was not laid out officially, but it seems that countries imposing sanctions were informally flirting with this idea.[3]

Responding to – mainly EU/US/Canada – sanctions, Russia has begun to impose its own counter-measures (for example, on wheat exports) and develop alternative schemes of supply. Russia has also implemented strong capital controls on nationals and foreign subsidiaries to stabilise its currency and to prevent an exodus of capital (Mahlstein et al. 2022). According to a prominent Russian expert, Ivan Timofeev (2022), 'Despite the colossal damage from the sanctions, the Russian economy has shown a high threshold of stability. [. . .] Critical imports are being replaced with substitutes from friendly countries'. This optimistic evaluation is countered, however, by some influential Russian economists pointing to harm to the Russian economy made by Western sanctions (for example, Konstantin Sonin, Igor Lipsitz, Vladislav Inozemtsev and others). For our chapter, evaluating the effectiveness of imposed sanctions is less important than demonstrating the main features of the official narrative on sanctions and presenting how Russians perceive them and why.

[3] For example, Mélanie Joly, Canada's Foreign Affairs Minister, stated that Canada seeks regime change in Russia. 'The goal is definitely to do that . . . We want also to make sure that Putin and his enablers are held to account', she said (see Carment 2023).

Sweeping sanctions imposed against Russia forced its officials to create a multidimensional response. Apart from counter-measures in economy and finance, Moscow had to present a consistent explanation of the ongoing crisis that would not destabilise the existing social order and rooted beliefs. For this reason, Russian authorities needed to create and disseminate a unified narrative and ensure that it would be accepted by most citizens. To unpack such a narrative, we analysed speeches and statements of Russian officials made from February 2022 to August 2024 to identify key points in the state representation of Western sanctions. Below are a few observed trends in articulating sanctions in Russia, accompanied by President Putin's statements for greater clarity.

First of all, the official narrative circulated the idea that new sanctions were inevitable for Russia, and Ukraine was only a pretext for the West to implement them. The actual cause of sanctions was seen in the West's political ambitions and failure to force deterrence of Russia by using Ukraine as a stepping stone. Imposed sanctions were presented as a price that Russia pays for its independence and sovereignty. At the same time, the purpose of sanctions was defined as worsening the lives of ordinary people rather than exclusively the Russian political and economic elite. Putin says: 'In fact, such steps are aimed at making the lives of millions of people worse; they have all the signs of aggression, war by economic, political, information means . . .' (RIA 2022).

The extensive part of the narrative focuses on the effects of sanctions. Officials emphasise that the 'Western economic blitzkrieg' failed, and sanctions created new opportunities for Russia to increase the country's economic and financial sovereignty. The Russian economy – according to the official narrative – is getting stronger and remains open for business. The narrative discovers prospects for Russia in de-dollarisation, de-offshorisation, import substitution and strengthening technological independence. This was presented as a part of the destruction of the neo-colonial international system. Putin notes: 'objective market laws work stronger than the current political situation. This indicates that the neocolonial international system, ugly in its essence, has ceased to exist' (RBC 2023).

The Kremlin narrative also insists that sanctions were constructed by and are beneficial only to the US elites. In this context, Europe is presented as a victim of sanctions facing outflow of capital and unfavourable conditions for supplies of US weapons and liquefied natural gas. Russian officials dwell on the harmful impact of sanctions on ordinary citizens of Europe and the United States, who felt the decline in well-being. Putin admits: 'We see social and economic problems worsening in Europe, and in the US as well, food, electricity and fuel prices rising, with quality of life in Europe falling and companies losing their market edge' (Kremlin 2022).

Finally, the official explanation of sanctions illustrates risks created by the West in the global economy and international trade, particularly seen in the intensified energy crisis, food shortages, and destruction of transport and supply chains. Sanctions were articulated as depriving states of their sovereignty, harming the effectiveness of international institutions and the global legal system. Putin says: 'Sanctions largely provoke the global crisis [. . .] The blame for this lies entirely with the elites of Western countries, who, in order to maintain their global dominance, are ready to sacrifice the rest of the world' (TASS 2022).

Official representations of sanctions remain consistent and cohesive. The narrative disseminates the idea that the West has no more sanctioning mechanisms that could harm the Russian economy and Russia in general. It was widely used when the International Criminal Court issued the arrest warrant for Vladimir Putin in 2023. Russia's official narrative described the ICC as the Washington 'marionette institution' and emphasised that neither economic nor political sanctions had any legal base, but they were instead a part of the political prejudice and illegal pressure. The 2024 visit of the Russian President to Mongolia (a part of the Rome Statute, recognising ICC jurisdiction) was widely broadcast in Russian media as evidence of the ICC's 'absolute political inability'.

Official statements on sanctions are the first – albeit important – layer of constructing the 'truth'. Then, this 'truth' is filtered down to subordinated media (the only media that exist) and locked by restrictive laws and administrative regulations preventing any deviation from the Kremlin story.

Popular Perceptions of Sanctions

In this section, we will briefly analyse popular attitudes towards sanctions since the beginning of the 2022 war in Ukraine. Our research is based on sociological data provided by an independent (and designated as a 'foreign agent' in Russia) polling centre – Levada Center. We leave aside legitimate questions of the reliability of sources and whether polling on such a subject in a time of war may hide more than reveal (Volkov and Kolesnikov 2022, 5). However, it is important to note that the trends presented below were generally identified by the Kremlin-funded research centres as well. And we will sometimes use their results as concomitant evidence of the observing tendencies.

Attitudes towards sanctions were changing over time. We can distinguish five phases so far. However, the division into these phases is somewhat arbitrary since surveys were conducted with different frequencies in different periods. For the first phase (late February–May 2022), Russians faced anxiety about the expansion of Western sanctions. In March, 46 per cent of people said they felt bothered or very bothered by the imposed sanctions. This is a 14 per cent increase since the results of the poll conducted in December 2021. It is noteworthy that an impressive number of Moscow respondents – 60 per cent – expressed their concerns. However, overall, we should note that the concerns indicated didn't mean the impact of sanctions on people's lived experience and well-being. Here, 29 per cent of all the respondents and 37 per cent of the Moscow residents said sanctions created problems for them and their families. This is comparable with data from late 2014–15 (Levada Center 2022a).

This anxiety decreased slowly during the second phase (May–July 2022). In May 2022, the poll showed that 29 per cent of people were not feeling bothered at all by sanctions and further 32 per cent were 'not too much worried'. In contrast, the number of respondents who were concerned about sanctions reached 38 per cent overall and 43 per cent among Muscovites. Russians indicated that they were primarily concerned about price increases, withdrawal of international brands, blocked banking cards and travel bans. At the same time, 83 per cent of respondents said sanctions didn't create any serious problems for them and their families. The majority of people (74 per cent) believed that the key motive of Western sanctions was to weaken and humiliate Russia. A similar number of people (75 per cent) said that, in response to sanctions, Russia should continue its current policy (Levada Center 2022b).

The third phase (August 2022–early 2023) is characterised by a noticeable shift back towards the negative perception of sanctions. The number of people concerned about sanctions changed from 38 per cent in March to 41 per cent in August, with 22 per cent of respondents saying they were 'very concerned' – it is indeed the highest percentage recorded since monitoring began in 2014. Respondents in Moscow were less optimistic about the effects of sanctions than respondents in the nationwide survey: 16 per cent of all respondents and 26 per cent of the polled Moscow residents believed sanctions would damage Russia. Also, the percentage of people saying that sanctions will have no impact on Russia or even strengthen the country was 79 per cent overall against 70 per cent in the capital. The number of those stating sanctions didn't create serious problems for them and their families slightly decreased from 83 per cent in May to 80 per cent in November 2022. For the same periods, the percentage of people advocating the continuation of Russia's current politics decreased from 75 per cent to 70 per cent (Levada Center 2022c; Levada Center 2022d).

During the fourth phase (March 2023–April 2024), concerns about Western sanctions declined. In March, this figure reached its lowest for the whole period since December 2021 – 64 per cent of Russians indicated they were not at all or not much concerned about sanctions. And 81 per cent of respondents stated they didn't face serious problems caused by sanctions. These trends continued in June with 63 per cent and 87 per cent values respectively. To be more concrete, 70 per cent of Russians stated that the exodus of foreign brands did not degrade their quality of life. In July 2023, 56 per cent of respondents recognised sanctions didn't influence their lives at all and 25 per cent of people said the impact of sanctions was not very strong. Overall, society seems to have believed in the official narrative's point about the inevitability of Western sanctions. 67 per cent of respondents didn't link sanctions with the war in Ukraine and were sure that sanctions would have been imposed anyway (Levada Center 2023a; Levada Center 2023b; Public Opinion Foundation 2023a; Public Opinion Foundation 2023b).

That quite optimistic attitude developed from mid-2023 can be explained by Russia's noted economic growth on the one hand and the paradoxical effect of carpet sanctions on the other hand. Inozemtsev (2024) noted that sanctions resulted in 'an unprecedented alienation of the most pro-Western group of Russian society from the West'. He claims that the significantly increased amount of Russian tax revenues was not despite sanctions but due to them 'since wealthy people are now keeping their money in Russian banks and many large companies have returned into Russian jurisdiction'.

The fifth period covered by our analysis begins in May 2024.[4] We call the prevalent attitude toward sanctions in the current period a 'new normal'. It describes the situation in which many patterns of everyday life under sanctions (micro-life behaviour – such as food supply, health service supply, keeping lifestyle patterns and so on) changed little (if at all) within the radically changed political, social and economic environment (macro-patterns such as being at war, running a war-like economy and so on) on the national level. There are at least three main dimensions of that phenomenon that fit into a complex contestation pattern outlined earlier in this chapter.

First, concerns about sanctions weakened and stabilised at a very low level (see Figure 10.2). Only 29 per cent of people were worried about sanctions in May 2024. This is the lowest figure since the beginning of the 2022 invasion of Ukraine. 11 per cent of respondents said sanctions impacted their lives, with 88 per cent of polled stating the opposite. The number of people believing sanctions will damage Russia has reduced to a record 9 per cent (minus 5 per cent from 2023). 78 per cent think Russia must carry on with current politics, with 14 per cent advocating the search for a compromise. Both these figures have been record-breaking since at least 2015 (Levada Center 2024).

[4] It is relevant at least till now – October 2024 – the time of writing.

The second, quite contested area is the evaluation of the state of the Russian economy in 2024, which directly influences public attitudes. The majority of economists note noticeable growth in the Russian economy, even if that is due to the government's massive spending on war-related production and the human costs of conducting the war. Experts noted that 'The Russian economy has shown solid growth in many sectors while unemployment remains at a record low [. . .] Driven by military production, industrial output rose by 3.3% in July compared with a 2.7% increase the previous month, and by 4.8% since the start of the year, compared with 3.1% growth in the same period in 2023' (Bryanski 2024). Russia's economic growth relies heavily on large-scale government spending on arms production as Moscow funds its war in Ukraine, which has led to soaring wages in a tight labour market and strong consumer demand even with interest rates at 18 per cent (Korsunskaya 2024). We shall note, however, that mostly Western-based economists[5] (including Russian experts who left Russia after war started[6]) are highly critical about the reliability of Russian official data and the sustainability of such growth.[7] Nevertheless, data showing economic growth, rising salaries above the inflation level and strong consumer demand solidify our main argument that the 'new normal' has a visible economic dimension, making people worry about sanctions less than in 2022 at the first phase of the war in Ukraine.

The third dimension, a qualitative one, is a significant level of what we call 'social elasticity'. We argue (based on social media and our own conversation) that Russian society, having lived through several severe economic crises (the 1998 Russian financial crisis, the recession of 2008–9 and the Russian financial crisis in 2014–17), is (a) more resilient to absorb shocks, (b) less prone to market panic and (c) evaluating the general situation via their current personal experience.

Roots of Public Attitude

In this section, we are going to propose three basic explanations for the social indifference towards sanctions, which was clearly identified in the last two waves since at least March 2023. We believe that all the factors presented

[5] For example, see the consolidated opinion of eight European finance ministers (Svantesson et al. 2024).

[6] For example, Konstantin Sonin (Sonin 2024).

[7] We agree here with the Stockholm Institute of Transition Economics that key official economic indicators should be treated carefully as part of the Russian propaganda narrative (Stockholm School of Economics 2024).

below impacted either people's understanding of sanctions or the way they were able to get and/or articulate the alternative narratives.

1. Restrictions in Perceiving and Articulating Alternative Narratives

Our first explanation suggests that there is no space in public discourse for alternative narratives on sanctions. Since the beginning of the invasion, the Russian government has made substantial changes in the media environment. These changes have affected the number of television and radio channels broadcasting in Russia, as well as popular social networks and viewing grids on Russian TV channels. The events of the lightning war censorship described below made it almost impossible for broad social masses to hear an alternative narrative on the military operation or sanctions.

By 2 March 2022, at least eight Russian media outlets were blocked.[8] Several Ukrainian media also fell under censorship restrictions.[9] On 4 March 2022, Russian authorities blocked access to Deutsche Welle, BBC Russian, Meduza, Voice of America and Radio Free Europe/Radio Liberty. Also in March, the Russian media regulator blocked Euronews. In July, the number of websites blocked for censorship reached more than 5,000. Until autumn 2022, different media were forced to accept new rules of the game; others closed their offices or suspended their work. The broadcasting grids of the state-owned mass media were seriously revised after the beginning of the war. Political broadcasting supplanted entertainment programmes from the air of at least two main TV channels: 'Channel One' and 'Russia 1'. Many popular sources, top journalists and video bloggers were recognised as 'foreign agents' – a designation that makes their work specifically scrutinised. In September 2022, the government revoked the licence of Novaya Gazeta, whose editor-in-chief, Dmitry Muratov, won the Nobel Peace Prize in 2021. Amid all these changes, foreign media giants[10] suspended the work of their staff in Russia.

Another dimension of redesigning the infosphere in Russia has influenced popular social networks. On 4 March, Facebook was blocked after an accusation of censoring Russian pro-government media. Access to Instagram was limited on 14 March, and Twitter was slowed down in Russia after limiting more than 300 Russian government accounts. In October 2022, Meta was recognised as an extremist and terrorist organisation. At the same time,

[8] Echo of Moscow, TV Rain, Current Time, The Village, The New Times, Doxa, Taiga.Info, Krym.Realii.

[9] Such as UNIAN, Korrespondent.net, Gordon and others.

[10] For example, Bloomberg, CNN, CBS News.

TikTok suspended uploads and livestreams after Russia adopted a newly passed 'fake news law'.[11] Those who used Telegram faced the rise of pro-governmental channels there together with promoted war correspondents and a new radical phenomenon of Z-bloggers.[12] That means, when looking for an alternative narrative, people are most likely to see the extreme version of the official one.

Moreover, due to the growing oppressiveness of the regime and weak civil society, there is no safe public space for the opposition standpoint on the ongoing war and the sanctions. So, not only perceiving but also expressing alternative narratives/attitudes has become almost impossible. We observe a negative drift in tightening legal norms related to anti-government street protests. In general, since the 2000s, Russian legislation has formed a legal procedure for street protests in a permissive rather than a notification nature. Authorities have broad and, at the same time, vague grounds to refuse to hold the rally and rest upon the format, purpose, number of people, date, and so on. Such practices happen against the background of tightening punishment for unauthorised events. It shows the criminalisation of political opposition protests (Amnesty International 2021).

Then, we found a systematic crackdown on freedom of public expression in Russia. It concerns the restrictions of media examined above and, hence, the reduction of channels for disseminating opposing views. However, it is also compounded by the increased and expanded use of the so-called 'foreign agent law'. Hundreds of individuals, media and NGOs have been recognised as foreign agents. From 2022, the authorities can find a 'foreign influence' in a person's or organisation's activities and add them to the register list of 'foreign agents'.[13]

Also, we observed restrictions on academic freedom and imposing strict control over the educational process. For example, the Russian Union of Rectors publicly supported the war in Ukraine, and academic councils of many Russian universities have published similar statements. State Duma Chairman Vyacheslav Volodin said that academics working in Russian universities who condemn the 'special military operation' in Ukraine should resign (Kommersant 2022). Many higher education academic staff left Russia. Students across the

[11] In March 2022, the State Duma adopted a law criminalising the dissemination of false information about the actions of the Russian armed forces.

[12] Semi-official propagators of the war, trendy pro-war influencers connected to different sectors of Russian elites.

[13] To prove 'foreign influence' they no longer need to prove foreign financing (BBC News Russian 2022).

country are told the official narrative in extracurricular propaganda activities; those with anti-war stances were expelled from universities (Lem 2022).

As we can see, the governmental policy of suppressing political pluralism and dissent covered academia, media and social network platforms. The abovementioned changes in politics and legislation make clear that not only the organisation but also individuals were forced to follow the official narrative. Declaring alternative positions may lead to administrative or criminal prosecution, foreign agent status and subsequent restrictions.

2. Perception of Sanctions as Mistargeted, Unjust or Discredited

Our second intuitive explanation proposes that most Russian citizens see sanctions as mistargeted, unjust or discredited. This explanation is grounded on three critical aspects of the popular understanding of sanctions.

First, we witness an increasing number of areas beyond the defined sphere of economics and politics where cooperation with Russia was terminated. It appears in culture, art, education and sport. For instance, in February 2022, the West terminated cooperation with Russian academic and research institutions. It affected the EU's Research and Innovation Framework Programmes, Euratom and the Erasmus+ Programme, as well as scientific and technological cooperation with US government-affiliated organisations. Some attempts to ban Russian culture and art,[14] as well as public ultimatums imposed on world-famous Russians such as conductor Valery Gergiev or opera singer Anna Netrebko,[15] played in favour of the official narrative. Moreover, although the first restrictions on the Russian Olympic athletes were imposed for different reasons and well in advance of the 2022 invasion, they are now likely perceived as a part of the same political game of pressuring Russia. In such a perception, being Russian in the West is already grounds for discrimination.

Thus, being described by the official narrative as an element of growing Western Russophobia, sanctions and other restrictions implemented in the spheres above are likely to be perceived according to the promoted interpretation. In a similar way, while Russian propaganda impersonalises the West as a new Satan,[16] Britain's and Canada's sanctioning of the head of the Russian

[14] Russia was excluded from participating in Eurovision. Various cultural events, exhibitions and performances in Europe were cancelled (Askew 2022).

[15] They have fallen under increasing pressure because of their past contacts with Vladimir Putin. They were also delivered an ultimatum to make political statements and denounce Putin and the war in Ukraine.

[16] Such rhetoric was used by both Russian officials and famous intellectuals.

Orthodox Church, Patriarch Kirill, makes the official narrative more effective and compelling. Russians are sensitive to Orthodox faith – seven in ten Russians identified themselves as Orthodox Christians – and such actions could trigger a backlash in accusing the West of anti-religiousness and, again, of Russophobia.

Another perspective on sanctions may seem for Russians to be a part of the 'double standards' where the areas of restrictions were selected specifically not to harm some Western organised interests in Russia. For example, the European sanctions packages did not include the Russian diamond industry (Alrosa Company). Instead, from March to June 2022, Antwerp spent more than double on Russian diamonds than in the same period of 2021. The Austrian-based Raiffeisen Bank profits from operations in Russia and Belarus. At the same time, Switzerland extensively buys Russian gold, and the import volume has risen to the highest since April 2020. The same increasing dynamic we saw in importing Russian oil and gas in 2022. Some of the introduced anti-Russia measures are being reconsidered. For example, the Dutch government granted ninety-one waivers to exempt businesses from implementing EU sanctions in October 2022 (Dutch News 2022). Despite sanctions, European companies imported critical raw materials from Russia amounted to €13.7 billion between March 2022 and July 2023 (Hansens et al. 2023).

For certain periods of 2022, the EU has paid several times more for Russian energy than it allocated for Ukraine (Viner 2022). Even after introducing the embargo on Russian crude oil exports, European ships were still exporting millions of tonnes of Russian fossil fuels (Matthews et al. 2023). In October 2022, the United States imported platinum from Russia for $34.7 million and rhodium for $29.6 million. Also, the US increasingly imported unprocessed palladium from Russia. For the first half of 2023, the US paid $696.5 million (maximum since 2002) for nuclear fuel from Russia. Moreover, in 2023, Politico's investigation found out that Russia acquired hundreds of thousands of bullets from Western suppliers (see Panov et al. 2023). This constructs the perception that while sanctioning Russian culture and sport, the US cannot sacrifice Russian precious metals; and while closing entry for cars with Russian licence plates, EU countries can't abandon Russian oil and diamonds. Thus, in popular perception, anti-Russian sentiment seems to be more critical and prioritised for the West rather than financing the war through importing goods from Russia.[17]

Finally, the majority of Russian citizens liken the current wave of sanctions to the sanctions in 2014 that were imposed after the Russian annexation of

[17] Indeed, for example, sanctions on nickel, aluminium and copper of Russian origin were imposed by the United States and the UK only on 12 April 2024 – more than two years after the invasion began.

Crimea. In this case, there are two strong beliefs fortified by recent experience. The first assumes that Russia can bypass sanctions without a severe impact on everyday life. Secondly, modern sanctions seem to be just a new phase of Western efforts to devastate the Russian economy; thus, 'nothing special has happened'. And the current wave of public perception that we previously referred to as a 'new normal' makes the case for this statement.

The abovementioned issues construct a general context of how sanctions are understood in Russia. In that sense, sanctions are seen by the majority as an ongoing struggle against Russians and their culture, which lasts from the distant past and now has little correlation with someone's attitude to political regime or war. At the same time, sanctions are selective, and the West is seen as hypocritical and looking to benefit from them. If so, the belief in the official narrative is strengthened.

3. Unaffected Well-being of the Majority of Russians

Individual experience forms a strong base for shaping firm perceptions. Unless people feel the tangible and measurable effects of sanctions, they will either minimise their impact or ignore them. As we observed previously, the number of people saying sanctions didn't make a severe impact on them and their families was relatively high during all the suggested phases. The question, however, is how those individual perceptions of a limited influence of sanctions on social well-being look from the economic perspective.

Despite sanctions, Russia received significant revenues in its budget after the beginning of the war. For example, hydrocarbon supplies to foreign markets amounted to $383.7 billion in 2022 (43 per cent more than in 2021 and an absolute record for twenty-seven years). Record sales of hydrocarbons increased budget revenues by 3 trillion roubles. At the same time, Russia's foreign trade turnover grew by 8.1 per cent in 2022 – to $850.5 billion. However, budget expenditures also increased considerably. The budget deficit for 2022 (3.3 trillion roubles) has become one of the largest in the history of Russia (comparable to 4 trillion in the 2020 pandemic year), and the 2023 budget year ended with a similar deficit (around 3.2 trillion roubles). We are going to expect close results at the end of 2024. This ongoing budget deficit is overcome by withdrawing funds from Russia's National Welfare Fund.[18]

[18] It worth noting that the Central Bank assumes (among other scenarios) a risky scenario for Russia that includes falling commodity prices and the depletion of the National Welfare Fund (Bank of Russia 2024b: 57).

Nevertheless, the Russian economy has coped better with the massive sanctions than expected. Natalia Zubarevich (Forbes 2022), one of the most renowned regional economists, pointed out that government measures such as parallel imports, support for certain industries, and exports to 'friendly' countries were quite effective. Indeed, despite some gaps in the supply side (Russians were not able to find some brands/products they are used to), there was no major disruption in food supply and basic necessities. Besides, after the withdrawal of foreign companies, substitutes for many products became available. Another well-known economist, Vladislav Inozemtsev (2022) said that, unlike the crises of 2008–9 and 2014–15, the current sanctions had mostly affected specific sectors, such as equipment manufacturing, production of cars, oil and gas industry, coal mining, timber processing and freight transport. Problems in these areas – Inozemtsev argues – can be easily concealed by Russian authorities behind general macroeconomic figures, especially after the decision to classify the country's foreign trade statistics.

The survey conducted by the Russian Union of Industrialists and Entrepreneurs (RUIE) in November 2022 revealed that businesses generally felt the effects of sanctions. 48.1 per cent of polled companies believed that economic sanctions impacted their activities (38.9 per cent had the opposite opinion). The increase in prices for raw materials, equipment and components was recognised as the most critical issue for Russian businesses (Russian Union of Industrialists and Entrepreneurs 2022). Nevertheless, Russian companies demonstrated a high level of adaptability to sanctions. According to the experts of the Russian Higher School of Economics, key measures in its response to sanctions were switching to new suppliers, entering new markets and cutting costs, and, in some cases, conducting its own development of new products and technologies (Simachev et al. 2023, 20).

In 2024, however, the RUIE monitoring of the state of Russia's economy illustrates that Russian companies still witness the negative impact of sanctions. 30 per cent of companies point to the inability to get new equipment and technologies, as well as to make international payments. 20 per cent of companies indicated that Western sanctions restricted their activities. And finally, a tenth of enterprises stated they are planning to reorient their product exports to markets in friendly countries (Russian Union of Industrialists and Entrepreneurs 2024). From the presented perspective, sanctions became a challenge for Russian businesses but not an insoluble problem. A similar pattern is evident in macroeconomic figures.

In Table 10.1, we present data from the Bank of Russia macroeconomic survey, which comprises the opinion of twenty-eight economists (Bank of Russia 2024a). The survey data are from 30 August to 3 September 2024.

Table 10.1 Bank of Russia macroeconomic survey results

Variables	2021 (actual)	2022 (actual)	2023 (actual)	2024	2025	2026	2027
CPI, (%, average for the year)	6.7	13.8	5.9	8.0	5.9	4.4	4.0
GDP, %	5.9	−1.2	3.6	3.6	1.7	1.9	2.0
Unemployment rate, %	4.3	3.6	3.0	2.6	2.8	3.0	3.0
Nominal wages, %	11.5	14.1	14.6	16.0	9.0	7.0	6.6
Exports of goods and services (billion USD per year)	550	641	466	470	478	486	498
Imports of goods and services (billion USD per year)	380	347	379	369	385	397	409

It is quite clear from the presented table that a dramatic scenario of fast economic decline did not materialise. On the contrary, analysts expect the GDP growth in 2027 equal to 12 per cent of the 2021 level. According to the survey, there will be no radical change in unemployment or wages. Such an optimistic vision corresponds to some international estimations. For instance, in July 2024, the World Bank classified Russia as a high-income country (for the first time since 2015) due to the increase in the Gross National Income in 2023 (World Bank 2024). At the same time, the International Monetary Fund forecast the growth of Russia's economy by 3.2 per cent in 2024, more than some European countries, such as the UK, France and Germany (International Monetary Fund 2024).

Recognising that the Russian government succeeded in overcoming sanctions, we believe that the impact of the sanctions (and secondary sanctions) will grow with time. Among further effects that Russia is likely to face, experts name volatile rouble, divided currency market,[19] higher inflation, inequality and concentration of wealth, labour shortage and uncertainty about the federal budget revenues (Prokopenko 2024; Sinyavskaya et al. 2023; Petersen 2024; Zubarevich 2023).

At the same time, it doesn't mean that Russian society will associate potential negative consequences of sanctions with sanctions themselves, even if they will affect people's everyday activities. The indifference towards sanctions has already been based on the lasting experience of sanctions' weak impact on lifestyle and a constructed and promoted image of confident economic governance

[19] It may be divided into sanctioned and non-sanctioned segments having different currency exchange rates.

and failures of foreign sanctioning by circulating selective economic indicators. We can conclude that if sanctions were aimed at persuading people about the negative personal economic results of the war in Ukraine, they didn't work (Figure 10.1). If, in another case, sanctions were intended to quickly exclude the ability to finance the war, they also didn't work. Finally, if the purpose of sanctions was to build a social demand for changing state politics, they failed (Figure 10.3). However, what they did was they slowly made Russia turn its economy into a dependency from the war. The current equation for Russia means a direct connection between the dead-end development of the economy and financing the war.

Conclusions

Russia has violated international norms by invading Ukraine and de facto withdrew from the norm-based Western-led order. As a result, it became subject to multilayered sanctions imposed by tens of countries. Russian government reacted with complex economic, political and policy counter-measures. They have included a set of legal and administrative measures to block any popular contestation to government actions. Thus, Russian behaviour fits into 'reactive contestations model' where actors object to or violate norms (Wiener 2017 and Wiener and Orchard, this volume).

Our main goal, however, was to search for an explanation of why and how most Russians are constructing their personal perspectives on the social/economic implications of imposed sanctions. That part of our chapter fits into the 'interpretative contestation' model where those who are subject to sanctions interpret them along their perceptions of (a) the intentions of those imposing sanctions, (b) their interpretations of the utility of sanctions and, finally, (c) their consequences in their everyday life.

The point is that the majority of Russians – taking a critical attitude towards the Political West – developed their negative/indifferent attitude towards sanctions that goes beyond the government narrative but doesn't contradict it. We argue, based on accessible empirical data, that their attitude is mostly based on the perception of sanctions as 'mistargeted', 'unjust' or 'discredited'. Thus, the Russian case seems to be a hybrid of two explanatory models. We call it 'complex contestation' as it embraces and blends the state's official reaction to the sanction regime and popular reaction that seems to be quite independent of the government narrative.

Linear reaction/contestation would include the following pattern: a state violates norms and then tries to defend its behaviour by introducing a strong official narrative and securing a high level of obedience to it. As a result, most people follow it. In our findings, the pattern seems to be different (following a 'non-linear causality' – to use our term). It looks the following way. The dominant attitude – as fixed over that period by independent polls – is indifference to sanctions. Such popular indifference might be explained by two intertwined processes happening simultaneously.

On the one hand, the set of coordinated government measures, such as the tightly scripted official narrative, non-existing independent media and intense legal and administrative pressure, suppresses any private/public contestation. On the other hand, our argument in this chapter is that the Russian public is puzzled by the relative absence of visible effects of sanctions in everyday life, the apparent inconsistency of some sanctions, the appearance of double standards in their implementation and seemingly unclear explanation of their purpose by sanctioning countries – all this leads to their specific way of contesting sanctions. Those processes are ongoing within a specific Russian political culture that is highly hierarchical and state-oriented and eruption of symptoms of nationalism related to war (being part of a civic duty to withstand 'foreign-induced pressure').

But as Tatiana Stanovaya (2023) writes in *Foreign Affairs*,

> Don't be fooled: this ostensible resilience to bad news and the seeming indifference to ongoing events are deceptive – It is becoming increasingly difficult for the Kremlin to sweep unwelcome developments under the carpet. The war has begun to change Russia, and profound internal shifts are likely underway.

Appendix

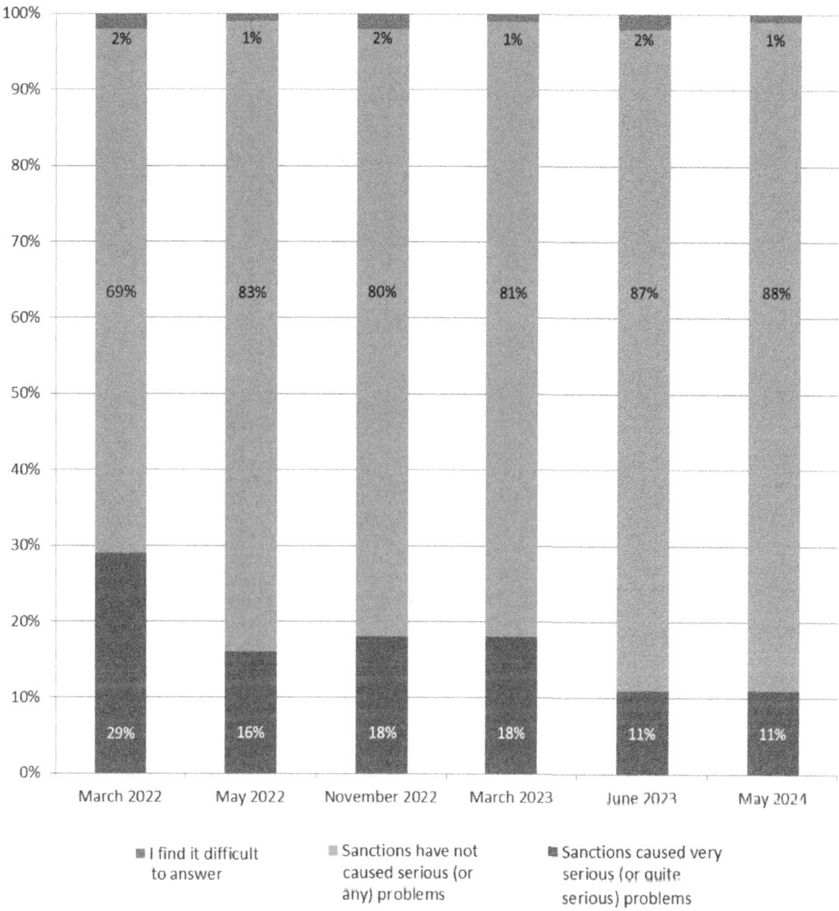

Figure 10.1 Have sanctions caused problems for you and your family? Based on the data from the polls conducted by Levada Center (designated as a 'foreign agent' in Russia)

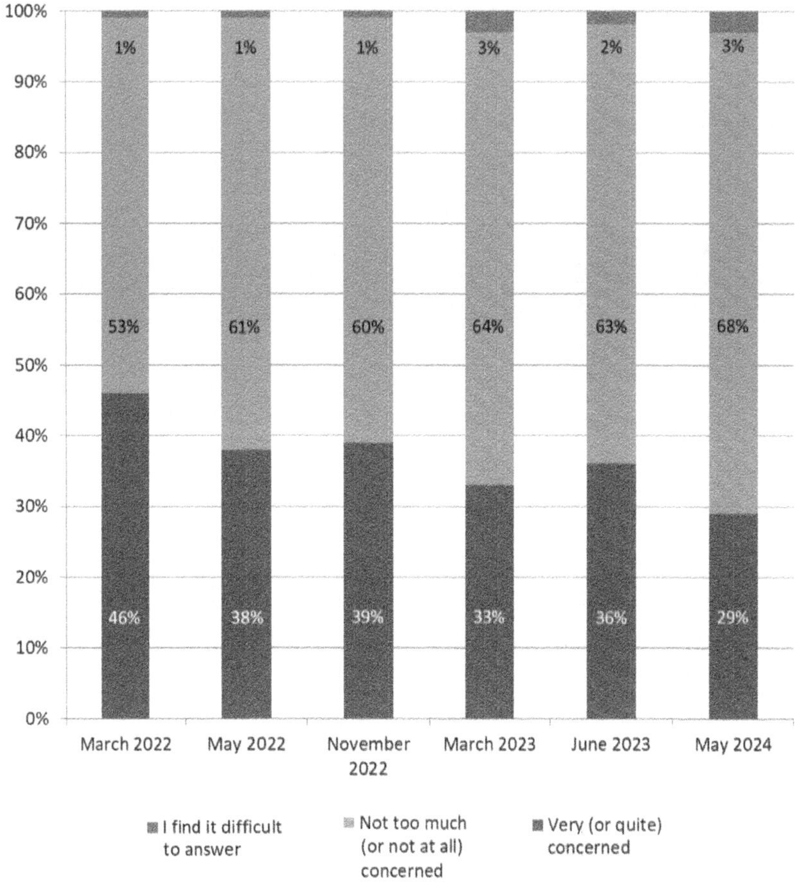

Figure 10.2 Are you concerned about the Western sanctions? Based on the data from the polls conducted by Levada Center (designated as a 'foreign agent' in Russia)

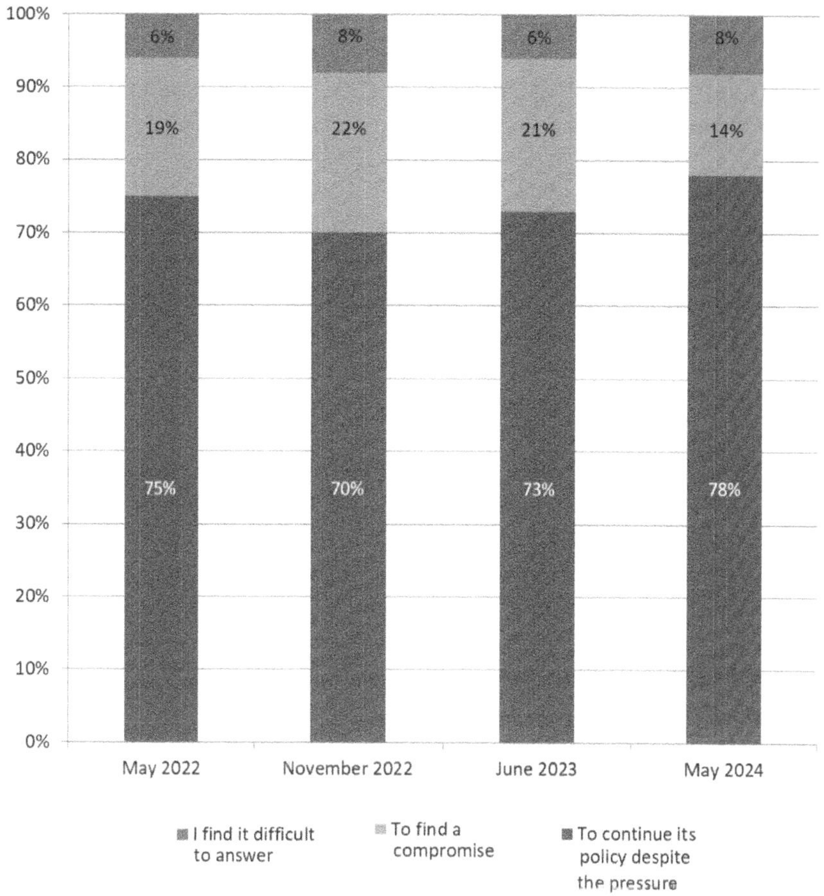

Figure 10.3 How do you think Russia should react to Western sanctions? Based on the data from the polls conducted by Levada Center (designated as a 'foreign agent' in Russia)

References

Amnesty International. 2021. *Russia: No Place for Protest.* London: Amnesty International. https://www.amnesty.org/en/documents/eur46/4328/2021/en/

Askew, Joshua. 2022. 'Should Russian Culture be "Cancelled" over Ukraine War?' *Euronews*, 30 June. https://www.euronews.com/culture/2022/06/30/should-russian-culture-be-cancelled-over-ukraine-war

Åslund, Anders. 2019. 'Western Economic Sanctions on Russia over Ukraine, 2014–2019'. *CESifo Forum* 20(4): 14–18. http://cesifo.org/DocDL/CESifo-Forum-2019-4-aslund-economic-sanctions-december.pdf

Bank of Russia. 2024a. 'Macroeconomic Survey of the Bank of Russia'. *Bank of Russia*, September. https://cbr.ru/eng/statistics/ddkp/mo_br/

Bank of Russia. 2024b. 'Основные направления единой государственной денежно-кредитной политики на 2025 год и период 2026 и 2027 годов [Main directions of the unified state monetary policy for 2025 and the period of 2026 and 2027]'. *Bank of Russia*, 27 September. https://www.cbr.ru/content/document/file/164702/on_2025(2026-2027).pdf

BBC News Russian. 2022. 'Дума приняла новый закон об 'иноагентах'. Что еще и кому будет запрещено? [The Duma adopted a new law on 'foreign agents'. What else and who will be prohibited?]'. *BBC News Russian*, 29 June. https://www.bbc.com/russian/news-61983302

Bryanski, Gleb. 2024. 'Russian Economy Shows Solid Growth despite Ukraine War Sanctions'. *Reuters*, 28 August. https://www.reuters.com/world/europe/russian-economy-shows-solid-growth-despite-ukraine-war-sanctions-2024-08-28/

Carment, David. 2023. 'Canada Should Not Support Regime Change against Russia'. *Ottawa Citizen*, 29 March. https://ottawacitizen.com/opinion/carment-canada-should-not-support-regime-change-against-russia

Chachko, Elena, and J. Benton Heath. 2022. 'A Watershed Moment for Sanctions? Russia, Ukraine, and the Economic Battlefield'. *AJIL Unbound* 116: 135–9. https://doi.org/10.1017/aju.2022.21

Dutch News. 2022. 'Dutch Government Grants 91 Waivers to Russian Sanctions'. *Dutch News*, 24 October. https://www.dutchnews.nl/news/2022/10/dutch-government-grants-91-waivers-to-russian-sanctions/

Forbes. 2022. 'Россия ведет себя как бедная страна»: главное из интервью Натальи Зубаревич ['Russia Behaves Like a Poor Country': Key Points from Natalia Zubarevich's Interview]'. *Forbes*, 19 November. https://www.forbes.ru/rubriki-kanaly/video/481333-rossia-vedet-seba-kak-bednaa-strana-glavnoe-iz-interv-u-natal-i-zubarevic

Hansens, Pascal, Sigrid Melchior, Maxence Peigné and Harald Schumann. 2023. 'Russia: Europe Imports €13 Billion of "Critical" Metals in Sanctions Blindspot'. *Investigate Europe*, 24 October. https://www.investigate-europe.eu/posts/russia-sanctions-europe-critical-raw-materials-imports

Inozemtsev, Vladislav. 2022. 'Russian Economy after Six Months of War'. *Riddle*, 30 August. https://ridl.io/russian-economy-after-six-months-of-nbsp-war/

Inozemtsev, Vladislav. 2024. 'The Shadow Side of the Sanctions'. *Delfi*, 26 August. https://www.delfi.lt/en/politics/vladislav-inozemtsev-the-shadow-side-of-the-sanctions-120045439

International Monetary Fund. 2024. 'World Economic Outlook Update'. *International Monetary Fund*, July. https://www.imf.org/en/Publications/WEO/Issues/2024/07/16/world-economic-outlook-update-july-2024

Kommersant. 2022. 'Володин призвал уволиться осуждающих спецоперацию на Украине преподавателей и ректоров вузов [Volodin called for the resignation of university teachers and rectors who condemned the special operation in Ukraine]'. *Kommersant*, 27 June. https://www.kommersant.ru/doc/5434728

Korsunskaya, Darya. 2024. 'Russia Raises Main Economic Forecasts, Sees Higher Year-End Inflation'. *Reuters*, 6 September. https://www.reuters.com/markets/europe/russia-raises-main-economic-forecasts-sees-higher-year-end-inflation-2024-09-06/

Kremlin. 2022. 'Transcript of the St Petersburg International Economic Forum Plenary session'. *Kremlin*, 17 June. http://en.kremlin.ru/events/president/news/68669

Lem, Pola. 2022. 'Russian Universities Expelling Large Numbers of Anti-war Students'. *Times Higher Education*, 12 April. https://www.timeshighereducation.com/news/russian-universities-expelling-large-numbers-anti-war-students

Levada Center. 2022a. 'Sanctions. Press-release'. *Levada Center*, 12 April. https://www.levada.ru/en/2022/04/12/sanctions-5/

Levada Center. 2022b. 'Sanctions. Press-release'. *Levada Center*, 10 June. https://www.levada.ru/en/2022/06/10/sanctions-6/

Levada Center. 2022c. 'Western Sanctions. Press-release'. *Levada Center*, 16 September. https://www.levada.ru/en/2022/09/16/western-sanctions/

Levada Center. 2022d. 'Общественное восприятие санкций Запада: Ноябрь 2022 года [Public perception of Western sanctions: November 2022]'. *Levada Center*, 15 December. https://www.levada.ru/2022/12/15/obshhestvennoe-vospriyatie-sanktsij-zapada-noyabr-2022-goda/

Levada Center. 2023a. 'Общественное восприятие санкций Запада: Июнь 2023 года [Public perception of Western sanctions: June 2023]'. *Levada Center*, 20 July. https://www.levada.ru/2023/07/20/obshhestvennoe-vospriyatie-sanktsij-zapada-iyun-2023-goda/

Levada Center. 2023b. 'Общественное восприятие санкций Запада: Март 2023 года [Public perception of Western sanctions: March 2023]'. *Levada Center*, 6 April. https://www.levada.ru/2023/04/06/obshhestvennoe-vospriyatie-sanktsij-zapada-mart-2023-goda/

Levada Center. 2024. 'Mass Perceptions about Western Sanctions'. *Levada Center*, 6 September. https://www.levada.ru/en/2024/09/06/mass-perceptions-about-western-sanctions/

Mahlstein, Kornel, Christine McDaniel, Simon Schropp and Marinos Tsigas. 2022. 'Estimating the Economic Effects of Sanctions on Russia: An Allied Trade Embargo'. *The World Economy* 45(11): 3344–83. https://doi.org/10.1111/twec.13311

Matthews, Chris, Thodoris Chondrogiannos, Sotiris Sideris and Konstantina Maltepioti. 2023. 'Europe Continues to Finance Russia's War in Ukraine with Lucrative Fossil Fuel Trades'. *Investigate Europe*, 27 January. https://www.investigate-europe.eu/en/2023/europe-continues-to-finance-russias-war-in-ukraine-with-lucrative-fossil-fuel-trades/

Panov, Sergey, Sarah Anne Aarup and Douglas Busvine. 2023. 'How US-Made Sniper Ammunition Ends Up in Russian Rifles'. *Politico*, 19 June. https://www.politico.eu/article/how-us-made-sniper-ammunition-russia-rifles-weapon-ukraine-war/

Petersen, Thieß. 2024. 'Sanctions against Russia – Limited Success, but Not Fruitless'. *Bertelsmann Stiftung*, 1 March. https://globaleurope.eu/europes-future/sanctions-against-russia-limited-success-but-not-fruitless/

Prokopenko, Alexandra. 2024. 'How the Latest Sanctions Will Impact Russia – and the World'. *Carnegie Politika*, 20 June. https://carnegieendowment.org/russia-eurasia/politika/2024/06/finance-sanctions-russia-currency?lang=en

Public Opinion Foundation. 2023a. '*Санкции против России: их цели и влияние* [Sanctions against Russia: their goals and impact]'. 10 August. https://fom.ru/Ekonomika/14907

Public Opinion Foundation. 2023b. '*Уход из России иностранных компаний* [Exit of foreign companies from Russia]'. 6 April. https://fom.ru/Ekonomika/14857

RBC. 2023. 'Путин заявил, что «неоколониальная система» прекратила существование [The 'neocolonial system' has ceased to exist, Putin said]'. *RBC*, 16 June. https://www.rbc.ru/politics/16/06/2023/648c56b69a79477cabe9222a

RIA. 2022. 'Путин назвал цель западных санкций [Putin named the purpose of Western sanctions]'. RIA, 16 March. https://ria.ru/20220316/sanktsii-1778488355.html

Russian Union of Industrialists and Entrepreneurs. 2022. 'Результаты опроса «Последствия введения санкций для российского бизнеса» [Results of the survey "Consequences of the introduction of sanctions for Russian business"]'. *Russian Union of Industrialists and Entrepreneurs*, November. https://rspp.ru/activity/analytics/rezultaty-oprosa-posledstviya-vvedeniya-sanktsiy-dlya-rossiyskogo-biznesa/

Russian Union of Industrialists and Entrepreneurs. 2024. 'Состояние российской экономики и деятельность компаний: результаты мониторинга РСПП во II квартале 2024 года [The state of the Russian economy and the activities of companies: results of the RUIE monitoring in the second quarter of 2024]'. *Russian Union of Industrialists and Entrepreneurs*, August. https://rspp.ru/activity/analytics/sostoyanie-rossiyskoy-ekonomiki-i-deyatelnost-kompaniy-rezultaty-monitoringa-rspp-vo-ii-kvartale-202/

Simachev, Yury, Andrey Yakovlev, Viktoriya Golikova, Nikolay Gorodny, Boris Kuznetsov, Mikhail Kuzyk and Anna Fedunina. 2023. 'Адаптация российских промышленных компаний к санкциям: первые шаги и ожидания [Adaptation of Russian industrial companies to sanctions: first steps and expectations]'. National Research University Higher School of Economics. https://www.hse.ru/data/2024/03/01/2082513459/Адаптация_рос.промышл.компаний_к_санкциям-доклад.pdf

Sinyavskaya, Oksana, Alina Pishnyak, Svetlana Biryukova, Svetlana Mareeva, Natalya Khalina, Elena Nazarbaeva and Darya Kareva. 2023. 'Будущее под санкциями [The future under sanctions]'. National Research University Higher School of Economics. https://iq.hse.ru/news/821709241.html

Sonin, Konstantin. 2024. 'Russia Will Suffer Decreases in Every Dimension of Prosperity'. *Atlantic Council*, 26 February. https://www.atlanticcouncil.org/in-depth-research-reports/books/russia-will-suffer-decreases-in-every-dimension-of-prosperity/

Stanovaya, Tatiana. 2023. 'Putin's Age of Chaos: The Dangers of Russian Disorder'. *Foreign Affairs* 102(5): 44–59.

Statista. 2024. 'Total Number of List-Based Sanctions Imposed on Russia by Territories and Organizations Worldwide from February 22, 2022 to January 11, 2024, by Target'. *Statista*, 11 January. https://www.statista.com/statistics/1293531/western-sanctions-imposed-on-russia-by-target/

Stockholm School of Economics. 2024. 'The Russian Economy in the Fog of War'. *Stockholm School of Economics*, September 2024. https://www.konj.se/download/18.443e2a2a19246dbc98a2c89/1727781967239/2024-10-01%20Report%20on%20the%20Russian%20economy.pdf

Svantesson, Elisabeth, Stephanie Lose, Mart Võrklaev, Riikka Purra, Arvils Ašeradens, Gintarė Skaistė, Eelco Heinen and Andrzej Domański. 2024. 'Russia Is Lying about Its Economic Strength: Sanctions Are Working – and We Need More'. *Government of Sweden*. 25 July. https://www.government.se/opinion-pieces/2024/07/russia-is-lying-about-its-economic-strength-sanctions-are-working--and-we-need-more/

TASS. 2022. 'Путин заявил, что санкции против России во многом провоцируют глобальный кризис [Putin said that sanctions against Russia are largely provoking a global crisis]'. *TAS*, 12 May. https://tass.ru/ekonomika/14607013

Timofeev, Ivan. 2022. 'Sanctions at a Bifurcation Point'. *Valdai Club*, 21 October. https://valdaiclub.com/a/highlights/sanctions-at-a-bifurcation-point/

Viner, Katharine. 2022. '€1bn for Ukraine, €35bn for Russian Energy: Top EU Diplomat Calls Out Funding Gap'. *The Guardian*, 6 April. https://www.theguardian.com/world/2022/apr/06/1bn-for-ukraine-35bn-for-russian-energy-eu-chief-calls-out-funding-gap

Volkov, Denis, and Andrei Kolesnikov. 2022. 'My Country, Right or Wrong: Russian Public Opinion on Ukraine'. *Carnegie Endowment for International Peace*, 7 September. https://carnegieendowment.org/2022/09/07/my-country-right-or-wrong-russian-public-opinion-on-ukraine-pub-87803

Wiener, Antje. 2017. 'A Theory of Contestation – A Concise Summary of Its Argument and Concepts'. *Polity* 49(1): 109–25. https://doi.org/10.1086/690100

World Bank. 2024. 'Russia Was Classified as a High-Income Country'. *The World Bank*, 2 July. https://www.worldbank.org/en/about/leadership/directors/eds23/brief/russia-was-classified-as-high-income-country

Zubarevich, Natalya. 2023. 'Special Military Economic Geography: Changes in the Russian Economy by Region'. *Re:Russia*, 13 June. https://re-russia.net/en/expertise/080/

11

Serbia and the Contestation of Sanctions against Russia

Roberto Belloni and Jasmin Ramović

Introduction

As a state striving to enter the European Union (EU), Serbia's decision not to join the EU sanctions on Russia because of its behaviour towards Ukraine can be seen as puzzling. Unlike other EU candidate states, which as a rule comply with the EU's requests to synchronise with Brussels foreign policy during their accession process, Serbia has refused to conform to this practice. Drawing from the theoretical framework developed in Chapter 1 of this volume, we examine how Serbia has contested the EU sanction regime and discuss the motivations for its actions through a discourse analysis of the two main Serbian tabloids (*Srpski Telegraf* and *Informer*) known for their political closeness to the ruling elites in Belgrade.

Following Russian occupation of Crimea in 2014, Serbia refused to apply the initial measures imposed by Brussels on Moscow. The adoption of sanctions would have gone against the basis of Serbian foreign policy, which involves the pursuit of closer ties with both the EU and Russia. De facto, this kind of reactive contestation led Belgrade to side with Moscow. With Russian full-scale aggression on Ukraine launched on 24 February 2022, Serbia not only maintained its earlier approach, but also it contested the EU sanctions regime through an interpretative contestation. Belgrade denounced the negative impact of sanctions not simply on the Russian population, but also on the very actors, above all EU member states, which engineered the sanction regime against Moscow. In addition, Serbia challenged the asymmetry of a policy process making Belgrade the passive recipient of decisions taken in Brussels, in other words, it adopted an anti-colonial argument expressing resentment for top-down decision-making coming from the European centre.

Accordingly, it criticised the sanctions sender (that is, the EU) while striving to delegitimise the use of sanctions as a policy instrument ultimately damaging the sender more than the target (on these de-legitimation strategies see Palestini, this volume).

Overall, this chapter argues that, of the three main contestation strategies discussed in this volume – reactive, interpretative and proactive – Serbia has engaged in particular in reactive and interpretative contestation. Its process of normative contestation is rooted in Belgrade's attempt to preserve a balancing act in foreign policy: as a state with deep political, cultural and religious ties with Russia, Belgrade would like to advance towards EU accession without antagonising or undermining its relationship with Moscow, which is also a key ally in its campaign against the recognition of Kosovo's independence. Accordingly, Serbia's refusal to adopt the sanction regime derives from its semi-peripheral position in the international system and its related attempt to make the most – politically, economically and in terms of status – from such a position.

The Roots of Serbia's Foreign Policy

Serbia's understanding of the pros and cons of sanctions as a foreign policy tool has been shaped by its experience during the process of Yugoslav dissolution which started in the early 1990s and, over a decade, engulfed the region in a series of vicious wars. The regime in Belgrade, led by Slobodan Milošević, fought to re-draw the borders of Yugoslavia and preserve it as a Serb-dominated entity. The resulting wars led to the death of about 130,000 people, while 2.4 million became refugees abroad and an additional 2 million internally displaced persons (Ambroso 2006).

Belgrade was widely perceived as a key villain in the Yugoslav drama and was targeted by extensive international sanctions (Licht 1995). In order to contain violence and bring the Milošević regime to the negotiating table, not only was an arms embargo imposed by the UN on Yugoslavia (which by then comprised only Serbia and Montenegro) but also painful comprehensive sanctions. Despite the initial attempt to target the regime in power, sanctions were lived by citizens as a form of collective punishment connected to actions that many of them never supported (Bianchini 2011). In practice, not only did they have a severe impact on the civilian population, hindered the search for alternatives to war and nationalism, and contributed to a 'rally around the flag' phenomenon (Woodward 1995), but also they contributed to the criminalisation of the conflict and left in their wake criminalised legacies for the post-war reconstruction period (Andreas 2004).

NATO's bombing of Serbia in 1999 left behind in the Serbian collective memory strong negative perceptions about the North Atlantic Treaty Organization (NATO) and its members, and more generally about the 'West'. NATO's intervention to defend the rights of Albanians in Kosovo set into motion a series of events that led to Kosovo's unilateral declaration of independence in February 2008, which has been perceived by both the political elites and citizens as an existential challenge to national identity and pride. Indeed, since the nineteenth century, Kosovo has been fashioned as the key geographical area that connects Serbia's past, present and future generations into an imagined community (Anderson 1991). Kosovo's declaration of independence presented Serbia with a direct challenge to its national identity and triggered very emotional reactions among citizens who consider their nation to be born in this region and thus are unwilling, for the most part, to recognise and accept the legal existence of Kosovo as an independent state. Overall, the wars of the 1990s and the related sanction regime imposed on Serbia, as well as Western support for the independence of Kosovo, contributed to preserve and even heighten the deeply rooted mistrust towards the West, described as a trait of Serbian national identity (Makrides 2014).

With the end of the Yugoslav wars of secession at the turn of the century, Serbia has committed simultaneously to Euro-Atlantic integration, which involves the pursuit of democratic and human rights norms and policy alignment with EU decisions (including on sanctions, but with the exception of Russia), and to develop political and economic ties with authoritarian and illiberal powers such as Russia and China. In 2005 the Serbian government identified accession to the EU as its main foreign policy goal and, in 2008, it ratified formal obligations with the EU by signing a Stabilization and Association Agreement – the first formal step towards accession. Since then, Serbia has struggled to proceed along the accession path, which has been hindered by Belgrade's refusal to comply with the EU's requests to 'normalise' its relationship with Kosovo, which Serbia still considers as an integral part of its national territory. At the same time, while pursuing EU integration, cosy relations with Moscow and Beijing have provided Belgrade with economic opportunities and with principled support for its stance against the recognition of Kosovo's independence.

In this context, the relationship between Serbia and Russia has been particularly close. These two states share deep fraternal ties grounded in their common Slavic and Orthodox heritage. Serbia's cultural identity is closer to that of contemporary Russia rather than compatible with European values (Patalakh 2018). The Serbian political discourse is permeated with a nineteenth-century nationalist vision focused on the importance of national sovereignty; it promotes conservative family and religious values, and involves the dream of becoming a regional power through the promotion of a 'Serbian World', understood as a 'state and political space' where 'the Serbs would live together and be united' (Popović 2021), which is reminiscent of Russia's imperial notion of asserting a 'Russian World' in its neighbourhood. Sharing strong normative affinities, Russia did not hesitate to side with Belgrade with regard to Kosovo. Russia has both protected Serbia at the UN and contributed to Belgrade's efforts to reverse Kosovo's independence.

Russia's refusal to recognise Kosovo's independence contributed to prolong the Kosovo dispute and to consign Serbia to a condition of political dependency towards Moscow (Bechev 2017). All post-2000 Serbian governments maintained and promoted their political and economic relationship with Russia. In December 2007, in anticipation of Kosovo's unilateral declaration of independence, Serbia became the only post-communist state to declare military neutrality. The government in Belgrade explained its decision to renounce its ambition to join NATO both as a response to NATO intervention in 1999 and as consequence of Serbia's special relationship with Russia (Ejdus 2014).

In sum, while identifying membership of the EU as its main foreign policy goal, the Serbian leadership has attempted to maintain both a balance between Russia and Europe and an official position of neutrality between the two (Belloni 2024). On the one hand, its political, cultural and religious ties with Russia make Moscow a reliable ally. Above all, Russia's veto power at the UN Security Council makes Kosovo's access to the world body impossible. On the other hand, Serbia's desire to access the benefits that membership of the EU entails have prompted Belgrade to commit to the reforms required to access the Union. From 2000 onwards, all governments have struggled to preserve and pursue these two apparently incompatible priorities, known as the policy of 'both Europe and Kosovo': the attempt to enter the European society of states is pursed alongside counter-secession and non-recognition of Kosovo.

This position allowed Serbia to play the two sides – the EU and Russia – against one another and thus to increase Serbia's leverage and bargaining power on foreign policy issues, including security, energy and economic matters. This strategy worked: not only has Serbia become the primary recipient of EU funding in the Western Balkans but also is the only state in the world enjoying the benefits of having signed a free trade agreement with both the EU and Russia. The menacing influence of Russia in the Western Balkans also deterred the West from criticising the worsening democratic backsliding that Serbia has been experiencing for years and which allowed President Vučić to concentrate political power increasingly in his own hands (Castaldo 2020).

When Russia annexed Crimea in 2014 the EU responded by adopting an initial set of sanctions against Moscow and asked all aspiring EU members to align their foreign policy with its decisions. While most states did, Serbia refused to comply. Even though Vučić came to power in 2012 on a pro-European agenda, Serbia's foreign policy alignment with the EU has dropped significantly, moving from 89 per cent in 2013 to 53 per cent in 2019 (Džananović 2020, 13). Pressure on authorities in Belgrade grew even more following the full-scale Russian aggression launched on Ukraine on 22 February 2022, which led to the adoption of ten sanction packages against Moscow only during the first year of war.

However, Serbian authorities maintained their balancing act between the EU and Russia. They interpreted the evolving situation in the Russo-Ukrainian war 'narcissistically', that is, through an 'excessive self-centeredness' (Hagström 2021, 334) that led them to assess the country's policy options in light of its own experience with sanctions during the 1990s, its involvement in the 1999 NATO war over Kosovo and the related scepticism about international law as a guiding principle in international relations. In practice, by refusing to adopt sanctions, Belgrade de facto sided with Moscow.

Serbian Tabloids and the Analysis of Discourse

In order to examine Serbia's contestation strategy of EU sanctions against Russia we rely on different sources, including opinion polls and source material from the Serb government. Above all, to scrutinise how the Serb political class has both interpreted the issue of sanctions against Russia and attempted to shape public opinion on this matter, we focus on the analysis of media outlets widely considered to be close to President Vučić and his affiliates. The President and his circle have almost complete control of the media, as confirmed by the fact that most tabloids in Serbia reflect, endorse and advance governmental views. Tabloid press, together with highly popular commercial pro-regime TV stations, use sensational headlines and unverified sources to cover a number of topical issues, including the war in Ukraine and EU integration. In such a context, *Informer* and *Srpski Telegraf* stand out for their relentless pro-governmental reporting. These two tabloids have continuously provided a favourable assessment of the Serbian leadership's work and contributed to produce political meaning with regard to Serbian foreign policy – including the issue of sanctions against Russia.

Informer is a particularly interesting example of the political use of media. It is led by Dragan Vučićević, who reportedly is President Vučić's favourite journalist (Živanović 2022) and who appears committed both to Vučić's glorification and to conducting brutal smear campaigns against his political rivals and those civic initiatives criticising his rule (Tomičić 2017). It is impossible to find an article in this tabloid critical of any policy, statement or action of Vučić's regime. Similarly to *Informer*, *Srpski Telegraf* is also among the group of regular recipients of public funds (Predić 2020) and is known for its strong pro-government narrative, disinformation and smear campaigns against the opposition and independent journalists, as well its active promotion of pro-Russian sentiments and anti-Western propaganda (Burazer 2021, 32).

The analysis of these tabloids' articles provides us with many interesting insights into how the ruling political class interprets and acts upon the problem of sanctions against Russia. We searched the archives of both tabloids using the combination of key words 'Russia' and 'sanctions' for the period between February 2014 to December 2023.[1] The search returned several hundred articles, sometimes only loosely connected to our research topic. Accordingly, we identified ninety-six articles from *Informer* and twenty-seven articles from *Srpski Telegraf* as the most relevant, and focused our analysis on thirty-nine articles published after the February 2022 Russian invasion of Ukraine.

In analysing this material we engaged in discourse analysis, defined by Wetherell, Taylor and Yates (2001, i) as the production of meaning through the study of talk and texts. Discourse analysis is a fruitful methodology for analysing the foreign policy of states at the periphery of the international system where countries may get stuck in multiple identity discourses (Guzzini 2022, 46). We relied primarily on critical discourse analysis – an approach which goes beyond the technical analysis of language in order to examine its political and social setting, uses and effects (Fairclough and Wodak 1997) and to uncover the naturalising/marginalising effects of discourse (Aydin-Düzgit and Rumelili 2019, 292). We centred the analysis on the four elements identified by Tonkiss as the main areas of inquiry from the perspective of critical discourse analysis: the identification of key themes and arguments used in shaping the discourse on a particular topic; patterns of association and variation between different actors and issues; the characterisations of actors, that is, how certain problems, qualities or values are associated with different political actors; and, finally, how the debate on an issue – in our case the sanction regime against Russia – emphasises particular themes while sidelining or silencing others (Tonkiss 2012, 412–17). Through this methodology we dissected the communication strategy used

[1] Due to the sheer volume of articles from the two tabloids, we will not provide internet links for each reference. Articles can be easily accessed through their titles or from the tabloids' webpages: www.informer.rs and www.telegraf.rs

by the ruling elite to shape the social meanings and forms of knowledge with regard to the issue of sanctions against Russia. This methodology shows how the Serbian contestation strategy is contingent upon the socio-political context where it emerged and leads to the suppression of normative alternatives which are understood to be inconsistent with Serbia's understanding of the issue.

Overall, our findings indicate that Serbia has grounded its opposition to sanctions on a number of different arguments which, for the most part, are based on its strategic goal of preserving its long-standing political alliance with Russia by avoiding the adoption of any initiative that would strain this alliance. To begin with, this involved the adoption of a reactive contestation strategy. As soon as Russia annexed Crimea, in late August 2014 President Vučić gave a statement to the TV channel Rosija 24, which was reported by *Srpski Telegraf*, affirming that 'Serbia has not, and will not introduce any sanctions against the Russian Federation' (Srpski Telegraf 2014b). In addition, Serbia did not contest either the legality or the legitimacy of sanctions but denounced their inappropriateness as a foreign policy tool (see Palestini, this volume) which imposes a heavy burden not only on the target state but also on the sender and on third countries.

At the same time, the Serbian elites condemned EU efforts to convince Belgrade to endorse sanctions. The Serbian president frequently expressed discomfort, widely shared by Serbian citizens, with the top-down and asymmetrical process whereby institutions in Brussels ask EU aspiring members to comply with decisions taken without their input. As Vučić explained in a January 2020 interview: 'I am fed up of being lectured by other [states] on our cooperation with [. . .] Russia . . . and I see all the others meeting Putin even more often than I do' (Euronews 2020). When commenting on EU requests to join the sanction regime, he argued that this kind of request reflected a lack of respect for both Serbia and its sovereign institutions: 'our friends do not talk to Serbia in that manner, nor will they in the future, nor will they talk to me, as the Prime Minister, like that' (Srpski Telegraf 2014a).

In brief, the outbreak of the conflict in Ukraine in 2014 has amplified the existing conflict between two identity narratives – that is, the one of brotherhood with Russia and the other of belonging to Europe. While de facto siding with Moscow, since February 2022 Belgrade has progressively begun to engage also in an interpretative type of contestation denouncing both the inappropriateness of sanctions and the perceived EU arrogance in demanding third parties to comply with norms adopted without any external input, as illustrated below.

Russian 2022 Invasion and the Contestation of Sanctions

The brutal full-scale Russian aggression against Ukraine, launched on 24 February 2022, brought about widespread condemnation around the globe. In the first year following the attack the EU introduced ten different sanction packages, asking EU aspiring members to align their foreign policy with the decisions taken in Brussels. International pressure on Serbia to endorse the wide sanction regime intensified considerably over time. The issue of sanctions became a significant source of irritation for both policymakers in Belgrade, who resented being pressured, and those in Brussels, who found Serbia's apparent uncompromising stance politically unacceptable (European Parliament 2022).

Indeed, the Serbian government maintained its earlier attitude against the possibility of endorsing the sanction regime and, thus, de facto sided with Russia. Serbian newspapers and tabloids reflected this stance. With regard to *Informer* and *Srpski Telegraf*, they maintained their pro-government interpretation of the unfolding events, and occasionally published disturbing headlines, with *Informer* getting significant attention for its claim, advanced on the first day of war, that 'Ukraine attacked Russia' (Informer 2022a). Even when media identified Russia as the aggressor, they still blamed the West for its pressure on Serbia to introduce sanctions against Russia. Serbia stood out as a victim of the war in Ukraine, President Vučić as instrumental to maintain stability despite the difficult international geopolitical situation, and the government's attempt at preserving a geopolitical balance between East and West as the best foreign policy choice.

The discourse analysis of articles published in both *Srpski Telegraf* and *Informer* after the beginning of the full-scale Russian invasion of Ukraine indicates a thematic emphasis on territorial integrity and international law, and a related endorsement of the sovereignty norm, which was manifested in Belgrade's position to support Ukraine's territorial integrity. Accordingly, Serbia voted in favour of UN resolutions condemning Russian aggression against Ukraine. On 24 February 2022 Serbia joined the EU's censure of Russian attempts to integrate parts of Ukrainian territory and rejected Moscow's recognition of the secessionist Republics of Donetsk and Lugansk.

A few days after the beginning of the Russian invasion the Serb Council for National Security, presided over by Vučić, issued a one-page document which mentioned the expression 'territorial integrity' eight times and 'international law' six times (Informer 2022b). In both this document and later policy statements, the Serbian government condemned the violation of Ukraine's territorial integrity but, at the same time, refused to join the sanction regime against Russia. Serbia's focus on territorial integrity was 'narcissistic' in nature:

Belgrade's condemnation of Russian violation of Ukrainian sovereignty reflected, first and foremost, Serbia's defence of its own territorial integrity and its related refusal to recognise Kosovo's secession. For example, on 26 February 2022, Vučić stated,

> Serbia has always led responsible and principled foreign policy, and it has heavily paid its commitment to the principles and rules of international law, including territorial integrity. While persevering to protect its territorial integrity at the end of the 20th century it was exposed not only to restrictions but also to the aggression of 19 NATO member countries (Srpski Telegraf 2022a)

In a similar vein, Prime Minister Ana Brnabić made an implicit link between the respect of Serbian territorial integrity and the situation in Ukraine: 'if you respect your territorial integrity, then you have to respect the territorial integrity of all internationally recognised states' (Dobromirović 2022). Critical discourse analysis invites us not so much to look for conclusive answers to a particular problem, but to appreciate the way in which both the problem and possible solutions are constructed (Tonkiss 2012, 409). Accordingly, Brnabić's statement not only expressed Serb grievances over the manner in which Kosovo's independence from Serbia was achieved, but also aimed at denouncing the apparent double standards of those (Western and European) states who accepted and supported Kosovo's independence against Serbian will and, in what Serbs consider a political, legal and ethical contradiction, have been pressuring Belgrade to join the sanction regime adopted against Russia because of Moscow's violation of Ukrainian territorial integrity.

The Serbian political elite used the issue of territorial integrity to expose the alleged hypocrisy of Western countries which, because of their double standards, are described as lacking principles and ideals in the conduct in international politics. This is noticeable in Vučić's statement '[f]or us territorial integrity has a somewhat different meaning than for them' (Informer 2022m) and in the words of the Minister of Interior, Aleksandar Vulin: 'Serbia will continue to conscientiously adhere to respecting the principle of territorial integrity, which definitely cannot be said for the European Union' (Informer 2022g).

Serbia's apparent respect of international principles has allowed the political elite to claim the moral high ground. For example, for Prime Minister Brnabić, Serbia is 'on the right side of history . . . We are one of the few countries in the world that respects and applies the principles of international law, as well as the UN charter' (Informer 2022k). By contrast, as Brnabić suggests, nations that joined the sanction regime presented their involvement as a moral duty emerging from the need to be 'on the correct side of history' while, in fact, their behaviour is both hypocritical and manipulative since it aims at damaging the reputation of those states who are said to be on the 'wrong side of history'.

In this context tabloids elevated the status of Serbia as one of the few free and sovereign countries in Europe: 'Western beasts are just waiting for a moment of weakness to swallow our country, which might be the only one in Europe to conduct free politics', writes *Informer* in February 2023 in its commentary on the BBC documentary about pro-Russian groups operating in Serbia (2023a). A month later the same tabloid again emphasised that Serbia is under immense pressure to adopt sanctions because it is the only remaining state in Europe to 'lead independent and free politics' (Informer 2023b). Aleksandar Vulin took the argument one step further when, in late 2022, he linked Serbia's freedom and its decision not to adopt sanctions against Russia to Vučić's leadership: '[w]e will not introduce sanctions to Russia, as long as we are led by the last free leader in Europe, President of all Serbs, Aleksandar Vučić' (Informer 2022n). The sovereignty norm, which is valued for the independence and self-determination it accords to states, is thus explicitly tied to the political leadership of President Vučić.

Another key theme raised by the tabloids involves the cost–benefit analysis in relation to the applications of sanctions. The adoption of the sanction regime is thought to be counter-productive for Serbia. At the outset of the Russian full-scale aggression on Ukraine the Council for National Security, presided by Vučić, issued a fifteen-point statement which mentioned the advantages of preserving the economic ties between Serbia and Russia (Informer 2022b). The economic rationale for not joining the sanctions regime has been explained in the press through references to 'big money' that supposedly 'comes through' as a result of the close cooperation between Serbia and Russia (Dobromirović 2023).

Rather than joining the sanction regime, Vučić capitalised on the country's links with Moscow. Since 2011 Russian gas has been imported at a discounted price. Three months after the Russian invasion Vučić reached a new agreement with President Putin that granted Serbia an additional three years of Russian gas at the 'most favourable price in Europe' (RFE 2022). He also opened Serbia's doors to Russian businesses and citizens. After the EU's ban of Russian planes and airlines from its airspace, the state-controlled Air Serbia airline doubled its direct flights between Belgrade and Moscow, thus turning Serbia into the only European air corridor left open to Russia. In 2022 more than 100,000 Russians, including highly qualified individuals working in the tech industry, took advantage of this opportunity and relocated to Serbia – in many cases bringing with them their own businesses (Savic and Jefferson 2022).

The cost–benefit analysis of sanctions has been applied also to the so-called senders, that is, those states which adopted the sanctions regime against Russia. This rhetorical device shapes the 'interpretative repertoire' (Tonkiss 2012, 413) used to delegitimise sanctions as a policy tool (Palestini, this volume). The impact of this regime is said to damage them (that is, the United States and EU member states) more than the target (Russia). The media's main focus is Germany, the state that more than any other has been pressuring Serbia to join the international sanctions. *Informer* writes that both the German agricultural and industrial sectors are heavily affected by sanctions and, as a result, German citizens are increasingly opposing their government's position on the issue (2022c). In October 2022, *Informer* explained how the situation in Germany was nearing 'a boiling point', and how 'protests against sanctions to Russia and arms delivery to Ukraine are growing in number' (2022l). In November 2023 the situation in Germany was described as 'critical'. German ministers 'announced a disaster', while 'Putin warned them, they did not listen, [and] now they are suffering the worst possible consequences' (Informer 2023k). More generally, the whole of Europe is said to be in trouble because the adoption of sanctions prevents the import of Russian gas. Combined with record prices for steel, copper and aluminium on the world market, this situation is said to impact heavily on all European states (Informer 2022d).

Serbian tabloids describe Ukraine as 'weak' and, generally, in a negative light. From the perspective of critical discourse analysis, it is important to identify how actors are characterised (Tonkiss 2012, 414–16). *Informer* takes all available opportunities to smear President Zelensky and challenge his leadership. In an issue from 14 October 2023, the tabloid writes about the corruption in Ukraine, and claims that 'most Ukrainians blame Zelensky for this problem' (Informer 2023g). A few days earlier it contends that 'Ukrainian soldiers are surrendering en masse as they cannot tolerate the tyranny of their leadership' (Informer 2023f). *Informer* also argues that American military aid to Ukraine is both unsustainable and decisive to ensure President Zelensky's political survival: 'Zelensky's end is in sight! Americans are begging in the streets while their government is sending millions to Ukraine!' (Informer 2023m). To strengthen the argument that Zelensky's political career is on the decline, and to shift the responsibility for the deaths of numerous Ukrainians from Russia to Zelensky, *Informer* published an image of Russian propaganda suggesting that Zelensky sacrificed his own people to protect the geopolitical interests of the US. The image displayed his tombstone and an epitaph reading 'The Devil of the Nation' (Informer 2023l), which is a wordplay on the title of the series *The Servant of the People* in which Zelensky was the main actor. Needless to say, this kind of metaphorical communication reveals how language is not a mirror of reality but an instrument in its construction (Aydin-Düzgit and Rumelili 2019, 291).

While the Ukrainian president is portrayed as an American puppet ultimately responsible for the loss of life in the country, Russia is glorified and represented as a strong and powerful actor. Against available evidence regarding the immense difficulties Russia's campaign has faced since the start of the aggression, *Informer* celebrated Moscow's alleged military achievements: 'The Russians wiped out entire platoons. Soviet weapons radically modernised and put in action – the result is clear!' (Informer 2023i). In addition, not only is Russia said to advance on the battlefield, but also it is thought to challenge American global hegemony: 'It has begun. Putin knocked out America. The decision of the Russian leader has shaken the world, nothing will be the same ever again!' (Informer 2023h). The tabloid adds: 'Russia does not forgive. Britain was served a uranium revenge. They didn't listen to Putin, and are now suffering the worst consequences!' (Informer 2023j) and reports the alleged destruction of a depot containing depleted uranium ammunition, which was donated by the UK to Ukraine. This occurred despite warnings from Putin advising against the donation. The report indicates that uranium particles were dispersed by the wind to southeast England, leading to heightened levels of uranium in the air quality measurements.

It is worth mentioning that tabloids' celebration of Russia is not absolute but, as mentioned above, it involves 'narcissistic' assessments of the evolving geopolitical situation. The behaviour of all main actors involved in the crisis in Ukraine is appraised in light of Serbia's own experience during the wars of Yugoslav secession in the 1990s which, to the eyes of many Serbs, provides strong empirical evidence to delegitimise this policy tool. On these grounds, *Srpski Telegraf* occasionally engaged in criticism of Russia. For instance, when Putin stated that the breakaway regions of Ukraine have a right to determine their sovereign status independently from the desiderata of the government in Kiev, and cited Kosovo's independence and the approving ruling of International Court of Justice (ICJ) as a key precedent, *Srpski Telegraf* labelled Putin's words as a 'stab in the back' (2022c). Generally, however, these kinds of allegation have been rare and they have been quickly toned down in order to avoid direct accusations against Moscow. For example, when *Informer* criticised the above-mentioned Putin's statement for 'playing the Kosovo card' (Informer 2022e) it used the opportunity to smear the opposition. In this case the focus was on Vuk Jeremić, the leader of the opposition party Narodna stranka from 2017 to 2023, and Foreign Minister at the time of Kosovo's

Declaration of Independence, who was criticised for allegedly contributing, with his actions, to the ruling of the ICJ recognising Kosovo's right to independence in violation of Serbian territorial integrity, which authorities in Belgrade consider as an unacceptable assault on national sovereignty.

Pro-European opposition parties are also targeted for their position in favour of the introduction of sanctions against Russia and, accordingly, are portrayed as traitors (Srpski Telegraf 2022c). 'What do Vučić's adversaries support? [the recognition of Serb responsibility for] genocide in Srebrenica, an independent Kosovo, sanctions against Russia' (Informer 2023d), cries one of the headlines in *Informer*. The tabloid also exaggerates the pressure that opposition parties are supposedly putting on Vučić regarding the sanction issue (Informer 2022i; Informer 2022o; Informer 2022j; Informer 2023e) in order to present Vučić as the only politician able to resist such pressure. To make this point, *Informer* quotes one of Vučić's acolytes stating in a 2023 election rally that if the opposition parties won, they would recognise Kosovo's independence 'the next day', and the day after 'they would introduce sanctions against Russia' (2023n).

Also noteworthy is what *Srpski Telegraf* and *Informer* have not reported on – in other words, what is being silenced which, explored through the tools provided by discourse analysis (Tonkiss 2012, 416–17), allows us to identify how similar instances are treated differently and thus to highlight how the rhetorical defence of the sovereignty norm is one-sided. These are topics which, if known by public opinion, may conflict with the government's narrative of a state standing up against undue foreign pressure in the name of national sovereignty and territorial integrity. Most notably, both Serbian policymakers and citizens believe that NATO intervention in 1999 broke international law because it took place without a prior mandate from the United Nations Security Council. As a result, they consider Western outrage over Russian behaviour selective and hypocritical (Devčić 2023). This belief, which is nurtured by pro-government tabloids, fails to acknowledge that NATO intervention occurred after the Yugoslav authorities (then dominated by Serbs) violated the territorial integrity of both Croatia and Bosnia and Herzegovina, whose sovereign claims to self-determination and independence had been recognised by the international community. Together with prolonged and systematic abuse of human rights of the Albanian population in Kosovo, this triggered the events culminating in the escalation of violence in Kosovo, NATO intervention and ultimately the secession of this province from Serbia.

More recently, the constant meddling of Vučić's regime in the political affairs of Montenegro and Bosnia and Herzegovina is also unreported by pro-government tabloids (Mayr 2023). Vučić and his acolytes have been supporting the President of Republika Srpska, Milorad Dodik, who has been toying with secession from Bosnia-Herzegovina and the related possibility of merging with Serbia (Radovanovic 2023). The recent introduction of the concept of the Serbian World ('Srpski svet') into public discourse by Aleksandar Vulin, a prominent figure in the Vučić's regime, is a source of concern for both Serbia's neighbours and the EU and its members (Popović 2021). This concept is reminiscent not only of Milošević's Greater Serbia project – that is, the effort to incorporate all Serbs into one state that brought years of war and suffering in the region – but also of the idea of a Russian World, which expresses Russian imperial ambitions in its neighbourhood and is linked to the ideology underpinning Russia's invasion of Ukraine. Given that the Serbian World would incorporate territories currently belonging to Montenegro, Bosnia-Herzegovina and Kosovo, the concept exposes Serbia's contradictory approach to the respect of the principle of territorial integrity and cast doubts on the inviolability of the borders of Yugoslavia's successor states (Karčić 2023). Thus, the territorial integrity of Serbia's neighbouring countries is approached in a manner completely different from the territorial integrity of Ukraine. Omission and silence envelop this aspect of Serbia's relationship with its neighbours.

In addition to the problematic stance towards territorial integrity, important voices advancing alternative normative views on the economic rationale of not adopting sanctions against Russia have been silenced and marginalised. Most notably, Zorana Mihajlović, who served as the Minister of Mining and Energy from 2012 to 2014 and, again, from 2020 to 2022, was one of the rare voices within the Serbian government in favour of joining the sanction regime against Russia. She emphasised how the ratio of trade with the EU countries, which amounted to 70 per cent, vastly outnumbered that with Russia (RTS 2022). She described the 2008 decision to grant Russia control of the energy sector in Serbia as 'irrational' and called for reversing it (Janković 2022). Even though she was a highly ranked official in Vučić's party, she was not confirmed in any ministerial position after the 2022 elections and was exposed to a brutal smear campaign in the tabloids when she left the party and established a new one (Informer 2022f; Informer 2022h; Srpski Telegraf 2022d; Informer 2023c).

By contrast, those public figures who both faithfully endorsed Vučić's political rise and adopted a pro-Russian interpretation of the events were granted prestigious ministerial posts. For example, Ivica Dačić, a former protégé of Milošević who later became an ally of Vučić, in 2024 was rewarded for his pro-Russian rhetoric with the posts of Deputy Prime Minister and Minister of Internal Affairs. Likewise, Aleksandar Vulin, known for promoting the concept of the Serbian World, was advanced to the position of Director of Security Intelligence Service in 2022. Vulin resigned from this role in July 2023 after the US imposed sanctions on him. Meanwhile, he was decorated with two medals of honour from Russia, one from the Russian Federal Security Service and the other conferred by Russian President Vladimir Putin (Vreme 2024). Despite US sanctions, in 2024 he was designated as one of the Deputy Prime Ministers in the new government of Serbia (Associated Press 2024).

Concluding Discussion

Located in the semi-periphery of the international system, and emerging on the losing side from the war against NATO in the late 1990s, Serbia has been especially concerned about issues of status and respect. The government in Belgrade resented the top-down approach involved in EU's requests to join the sanction regime and refused attempts at being 'lectured' by the West. Accordingly, Serbia implicitly endorsed a pluralist view of the international system and the related sovereign right to assess the appropriateness of Western/European demands on a case-by-case basis.

In refusing to endorse the sanction regime against Russia, Serbia adopted a reactive and interpretative contestation strategy, which made Belgrade side with Moscow, attempt to delegitimise the EU and criticise the negative impact of sanctions. In particular, Serbia has put forward arguments condemning the violation of the norm of territorial integrity of sovereign states deriving primarily from its own experience following the 1999 NATO war against the rump Yugoslavia, which resulted in Kosovo's secession from Serbia in 2008. Belgrade has condemned what it describes as Western hypocrisy – that is, the simultaneous EU defence of Ukraine's territorial integrity and its de facto endorsement of Kosovo's independence.

This condemnation has been followed by Belgrade's attempt to combine two contradictory objectives: the defence of the sovereignty norm involving territorial integrity which, if coherently pursued, should have led Belgrade to adopt sanctions against Moscow; and its own reluctance to endorse the EU-led sanction regime. This attempt has been pursued in two ways. First, Serbia has advanced doubts about the legitimacy of the norm enforcer – described by Palestini in Chapter 2 as one of the key issues which may motivate and sustain norms' contestation. The EU may have the legal right of imposing sanctions but, according to Serbia, its top-down request to adhere to policies adopted without Serbian input contradicts both the EU's rhetoric on the importance of democracy and reflects a neo-colonial attitude vis-à-vis states, like Serbia, at the periphery of the international system.

Second, Serbia has criticised sanctions themselves, whose impact on Serbian citizens during the 1990s is still vividly remembered by the population. Thus, Serbia has not only contested the legitimacy of the sender (the EU), but also rejected the utility of sanctions as tools of international politics. Serbian tabloids did not so much stress sanctions' negative consequences for Russian citizens, but rather they underscored the negative consequences for the sender(s). By stressing the counter-productive impact of sanctions on the civilian population, particularly in Germany and the UK, the tabloids adopted an argument that resonated within Serbian public opinion which, for the most part, still has vivid memories of how sanctions against Serbia during the 1990s affected citizens. This argument also served to underline the lack of strategic vision of European states who, supposedly blinded by their hostility towards Moscow, have adopted self-damaging measures.

While rejecting Western calls to join the sanction regime against Russia, at the same time Serbia approved a number of limited measures aimed at reassuring Brussels of its intention to maintain its European perspective. Serbia endorsed a declaration condemning Moscow's cyber-attacks against Ukraine, one in support of the EU's diplomatic presence in Kyiv and, finally, a declaration adopted just before the Russian invasion condemning the military build-up on the borders with Ukraine. It also joined a range of punitive measures against Moscow's proxies, including Ukraine's former President Viktor Yanukovych and Belarus President Aleksander Lukashenko (EWB 2022).

On balance, these minor steps have been useful to buy Belgrade time but have always been unlikely to lead to a full alignment. Because Serbia pursues a pragmatist foreign policy, it cannot be ruled out that Belgrade will eventually accept EU demands. Indeed, since early 2023 Vučić has begun hinting at the possibility that Serbia might introduce sanctions against Russia, if the harm of not doing so outweighs the benefits (N1 2023). With EU support, Serbia has also been seeking to reduce energy dependence on Russia and, in the long-term, on hydrocarbons.

In this evolving context, Serbia stands out in the tabloids for its heroic effort to manage a complex geopolitical context. Serbian contestation of sanctions not only attempts to de-legitimise the sender and to condemn the impact of these measures on the civilian population, but also it allows authorities in Belgrade to articulate an 'us' vs 'them' worldview which distinguishes Serbia vis-à-vis the 'morally bankrupt West' and elevates it as 'the only independent country in Europe'. President Vučić and the ruling elite emerge as the main element of stability. Vučić himself is regularly portrayed as a leader capable to guide the country through a hostile international environment and the risks associated to a war, the one between Russia and Ukraine, with potentially destabilising implications. Thus far Serbia has been able to maintain its hedging in foreign policy, but the longer the war in Ukraine continues, the more difficult Serbia's balancing act.

References

Ambroso, Guido. 2006. *The Balkans at a Crossroads: Progress and Challenges in Finding Durable Solutions for Refugees and Displaced Persons from the Wars in the Former Yugoslavia*. UNHCR, New Issues in Refugee Research.

Anderson, Benedict. 1991. *Imagined Communities: Reflection on the Origin and Spread of Nationalism*. Verso.

Andreas, Peter. 2004. 'Criminalized Legacies of War: The Clandestine Political Economy of the Western Balkans'. *Problems of Post-Communism* 51(3): 3–9.

Associated Press. 2024. 'Serbia's New Government to Include US-Sanctioned Ex-intelligence Chief with Close Ties to Russia'. 30 April. https://apnews.com/article/serbia-government-us-sanctions-russia-eb7e3e620ce3f038dddd2dbf26f5396e

Aydin-Düzgit, Senem, and Rumelili, Bahar. 2019. 'Discourse Analysis: Strengths and Shortcomings'. *All Azimuth* 8(2): 285–305.

Bechev, Dimitar. 2017. *Rival Power: Russia in Southeast Europe*. Yale University Press.

Belloni, Roberto. 2024. 'Serbia between East and West: Ontological Security, Vicarious Identity, and the Problem of Sanctions against Russia'. *European Security* 33(2): 284–302.

Bianchini, Stefano. 2011. 'The EU in the Values and Expectations of Serbia: Challenges, Opportunities and Confrontations'. In *Civic and Uncivic Values. Serbia in the Post- Milošević Era*, edited by Ola Listhaug, Sabrina P. Ramet and Dragana Dulić. CEU Press.

Burazer, Nikola. 2021. 'Media Capture – An Increasing Threat to Serbian Democracy'. *Südosteuropa Mitteilungen* (02)03: 29–38.

Castaldo, Antonino. 2020. 'Back to Competitive Authoritarianism? Democratic Backsliding in Vučić's Serbia'. *Europe-Asia Studies* 72(10): 1617–38.

Devčić, Jakov. 2023. *Serbia: Political and Social Impacts One Year after the Start of Russia's War of Aggression against Ukraine*. Belgrade: Konrad Adenauer Stiftung.

Dobromirović, M. 2022. 'Da li je ovo poslednja Šolcova ponuda?' *Informer*, 25 May.

Dobromirović, M. 2023. 'Srbijo, oteraj Ruse i Kineze! Zapad traži da se odreknemo velikih para! Novi pritisak na našu zemlju!' *Informer*, 4 March.

Džananović, Nedžma. 2020. *Foreign Policies in the Western Balkans: Alignment with the EU Common Foreign and Security Policy*. Friedrich Ebert Stiftung.

Ejdus, Filip. 2014. 'Serbia's Military Neutrality: Origins, Effects, and Challenges'. *Croatian International Relations Review* 20(71): 43–69.

Euronews. 2020. 'Serbia President Vučić "fed up of being lectured" over Ties with Russia and China'. *Euronews*, 21 January. https://www.youtube.com/watch?v=7E74Y0ylrFY

European Parliament. 2022. 'Serbia: Leading MEPs Regret Serbia's Non-Alignment with EU Sanctions Against Russia'. Press Release, 1 March.

EWB. 2022. 'Serbia Has Aligned on EU Sanctions on Belarus Over the War in Ukraine'. *European Western Balkans*, 20 May. https://europeanwesternbalkans.com/2022/05/20/serbia-has-aligned-with-eu-sanctions-on-belarus-over-the-war-in-ukraine/

Fairclough, Norman, and Wodak, Ruth. 1997. 'Critical Discourse Analysis: An Overview'. In *Discourse as Social Interaction: Discourse Studies: A Multidisciplinary Introduction*, edited by T. A. van Dijk. Sage.

Guzzini, Stefano. 2022. '"Vision of Itself" in Foreign Policy Analysis: From the Role of Ideas to Identity and Recognition'. *Teoria Polityki* 6: 33–57.

Hagström, Linus. 2021. 'Great Power Narcissism and Ontological (in)Security: The Narrative Mediation of Greatness and Weakness in International Politics'. *International Studies Quarterly* 65(2): 331–42.

Informer. 2022a. 'Ukrajina napala Rusiju!' *Informer*, 22 February.

Informer. 2022b. 'OVO JE TAČAN STAV SRBIJE O DEŠAVANJIMA U UKRAJINI! 15 tačaka Saveta za nacionalnu bezbednost koje morate pročitati!' *Informer*, 25 February.

Informer. 2022c. 'Nemačka ekonomija u šoku bez ruskog gasa, delegacija išla u Katar i UAE u potrazi za TPG!' *Informer*, 26 March.

Informer. 2022d. 'Evropa će sama upasti u jamu koju je za rusiju iskopala! Rekordne cene čelika, bakra, aluminijuma produbljuju sve težu poziciju Brisela i kompanije u odluci da se odreknu ruskog gasa'. *Informer*, 3 April.

Informer. 2022e. 'Svetski sukob preko naših leđa: Putin igra na Kosovo'. *Informer*, 28 April.

Informer. 2022f. 'ZORANA LOBIRA PO AMBASADAMA! Stranci, postavite me za premijera! Po svaku cenu želi u vrh nove vlasti!' *Informer*, 3 June.

Informer. 2022g. 'Tražiti od Srbije da uvede sankcije Rusiji i prizna nezavisnost Kosova, može samo neko ko . . . Vulin odbrusio Evropskom parlamentu!' *Informer*, 14 June.

Informer. 2022h. 'Vulin odbrusio Zorani Mihajlović: Meni ambasade ne određuju uvjerenja'. *Informer*, 12 July.

Informer. 2022i. 'Zelenović: U parlamentu cemo se boriti za sankcije Rusiji!' *Informer*, 2 September.

Informer. 2022j. 'Zelenović: Uvođenje sankcija Rusiji je naša obaveza'. *Informer*, 20 September.

Informer. 2022k. 'Ana Brnabić o pritiscima i pretnjama zbog sankcija Rusiji! Naša pozicija nije neutralna, mi smo osudili agresiju na Ukrajinu!' *Informer*, 3 October.

Informer. 2022l. 'Nemačka ključa! Sve veći protesti protiv sankcija Rusiji i isporuke oružja Kijevu, vijore se nemačke i ruske zastave!' *Informer*, 11 October.

Informer. 2022m. 'Jedini problem je što nismo uveli sankcije Rusiji! Vučić izvukao suštinu izveštaja EK: Srbija je nazadovala samo po tom pitanju usaglašenosti sa politikom EU!' *Informer*, 12 October.

Informer. 2022n. 'Recite lepo, Srbija da prizna Kosovo, napusti Srpsku i uvede sankcije Rusiji! Vulin ogolio skrivene namere Evropske komisije: Nećemo, hvala što ste pitali!' *Informer*, 12 October.

Informer. 2022o. 'Novi pritisci na Vučića, ali sada iz Srbije! Stefanović: Oni koji su protiv sankcija ugrožavaju budućnost građana!' *Informer*, 13 October.

Informer. 2023a. 'Svetski mediji po svaku cenu žele da nas uvuku u rat! BBC snimio sraman dokumentarac posvećen Srbiji, koji je prepun ekstremista sa obe strane'. *Informer*, 20 February.

Informer. 2023b. 'Raste pritisak na Srbiju! Hrvatska evroposlanica poručuje: Ako Srbija ne uvede sankcije Rusiji, ukinućemo vam evropske pare i investicije!' *Informer*, 29 March.

Informer. 2023c. 'LUDILO! Vučić kriv i što je Zorana debela!?!' *Informer*, 30 April.

Informer. 2023d. 'Evo šta zastupaju prozapadne političke partije!' *Informer*, 30 May.

Informer. 2023e. 'Ponoševac traži od Vučića da uvede sankcije Rusiji! Novi pritisci opozicije na predsednika!' *Informer*, 26 June.

Informer. 2023f. 'Šok! Ukrajinci se povlače i napuštaju ključni grad! Nešto čudno se dešava na frontu, američki oficir alarmirao javnost!' *Informer*, 10 October.

Informer. 2023g. 'Šok u SAD! Zelenski zgrozio novinara CNN-a! Skandalozne reči lidera Ukrajine munjevito se šire mrežama!' *Informer*, 14 October.

Informer. 2023h. 'Počelo je! Putin nokautirao Ameriku! Odluka lidera Rusije zatresla planetu, ništa više neće biti isto!' *Informer*, 8 November.

Informer. 2023i. 'Šta je ovo, ljudi moji?! Rusi zbrisali cele čete! Brutalno modernizovali sovjetsko oružje i bacili ga u pogon - rezultat je jasan!' *Informer*, 8 November.

Informer. 2023j. 'Rusija ne prašta! Britanija dobila uranijumsku osvetu! Nisu slušali Putina, sada trpe najstrašnije posledice!' *Informer*, 12 November.

Informer. 2023k. 'Kritično u Nemačkoj! Ministar najavio katastrofu! Putin ih je upozoravao, nisu ga slušali, sada trpe najstrašnije posledice!' *Informer*, 19 November.

Informer. 2023l. 'Hitno! Rusi poslali upozorenje Zelenskom! Amerika mu sprema nešto zastrašujuće, a onda sledi veliki preokret!' *Informer*, 21 November.

Informer. 2023m. 'Zelenskom se bliži kraj! Amerikanci prose na ulici dok njihova vlada šalje milione Ukrajini!' *Informer*, 3 December.

Informer. 2023n. 'Svi su se ujedinili protiv nas! Gujon: Ako pobede priznaće nezavisnost Kosova i uvesti sankcije Rusiji!" *Informer*, 11 December.

Janković, Marija. 2022. 'Zorana Mihajlović za BBC: "Interesi ruskih lobija su bili jači" kada se birao izvor gasa u Srbiji'. *BBC News in Serbian*, 1 June. https://www.bbc.com/serbian/lat/srbija-61609387

Karčić, Hamza. 2023. 'Serbia Is Taking a Page Out of Russia's Book'. *Foreign Policy*, 24 April. https://foreignpolicy.com/2023/04/24/serbia-balkans-expansionism-russia-montenegro-elections/

Licht, Sonja. 1995. The Use of Sanctions in Former Yugoslavia: Can They Assist in Conflict Resolution?' In *Economic Sanctions: Panacea or Peacebuilding in a Post-Cold-War World?*, edited by David Cortright and George A. Lopez. Routledge.

Makrides, Vasilios N. 2014. '"The Barbarian West": A Form of Orthodox Christian Anti-Western Critique'. In *Eastern Orthodox Encounters of Identity and Otherness*, edited by Andrii Krawchuk and Thomas Bremer. Palgrave.

Mayr, Walter. 2023. 'Serbian President Aleksandar Vučić: Playing with Fire in Belgrade'. *Der Spiegel*, 11 August. https://www.spiegel.de/international/europe/serbian-president-aleksandar-VUčić-playing-with-fire-in-belgrade-a-9adaf3c2-8e4b-4737-98b1-9761fd49828c

N1. 2023. 'Vučić: Možda ćemo morati da uvedemo sankcije Rusiji, bolje je dok ne moramo'. 2 February. https://n1info.rs/vesti/vucic-nisam-odusevljen-time-ali-mozda-cemo-morati-da-uvedemo-sankcije-rusiji

Patalakh, Artem. 2018. 'Emotions and Identity as Foreign Policy Determinants: Serbian Approach to Relations with Russia'. *Chinese Political Science Review* 3: 495–528.

Popović, Sofija. 2021. 'Call of Minister Vulin for the Creation of the "Serbian World" Provokes Condemnations'. *European Western Balkans*, 21 July. https://europeanwesternbalkans.com/2021/07/20/call-of-minister-vulin-for-the-creation-of-the-serbian-world-provokes-condemnations/

Predić, Ivana. 2020. 'Pančevo opet nagrađuje provladine medije koji krše Kodeks i zakone: Novac i za Informer, Srpski telegraf i RTV Pančevo'.

Cenzolovka.rs, 18 March. https://www.cenzolovka.rs/drzava-i-mediji/pancevo-opet-nagradjuje-provladine-medije-koji-krse-kodeks-i-zakone-novac-i-za-informer-srpski-telegraf-i-rtv-pancevo

Radovanovic, Radul. 2023. 'Separatist Bosnian Serb Leader Milorad Dodik Vows to Tear His Country Apart Despite US Warnings'. *Associated Press*, 30 December. https://apnews.com/article/bosnian-serbs-secession-threat1072c96ce29c1f118a9b5a84bbd5ff9e

RFE. 2022. 'Vučić Says Serbia Secures Gas Deal with Russia Following Phone Talks with Putin'. *Radio Free Europe*, 29 May. https://www.rferl.org/a/serbia-Vučić-gas-deal-russia/31873908.html

RTS. 2022. 'Mihajlović: Treba da razmislimo o uvođenju sankcija Rusiji'. *Radio Televizija Srbije*, 18 October. https://www.rts.rs/lat/vesti/politika/4989618/.html?email=yes

Savic, Misha, and Jefferson, Rodney. 2022. 'Russians Find Refuge from Putin in Europe's New "Casablanca"'. *Bloomberg*, 2 November.

Srpski Telegraf. 2014a. 'Vučić: Srbiju niko ne ucenjuje i neće dok sam ja na čelu Vlade Srbije'. *Srpski Telegraf*, 23 July.

Srpski Telegraf. 2014b. 'Vučić: Nema sankcija Rusiji I tacka! Srbija joj je najbolji prijatelj'. *Srpski Telegraf*, 1 September.

Srpski Telegraf. 2022a. 'Srbija između podrške teritorijalnom integritetu Ukrajine i odluke da ne uvodi sankcije Rusiji: Šta dalje?' *Srpski Telegraf*, 26 February.

Srpski Telegraf. 2022b. 'Putin zabio nož u leđa Srbiji: Trampio Kosovo za Donbas'. *Srpski Telegraf*, 28 April.

Srpski Telegraf. 2022c. 'Đilas smatra da Srbija treba da uvede sankcije Rusiji, Igor Mirović mu odgovora zbog čega to ne treba činiti'. *Srpski Telegraf*, 22 July.

Srpski Telegraf. 2022d. 'Zoranu su posebno pogodila poredjenja nje i nove ministarke'. *Srpski Telegraf*, 24 October.

Tomičić, Ladislav. 2017. 'Razgovor s vlasnikom Informera, najzloćudnijeg tabloida Balkana: Vučićeviću, jeste li vi budala?' *Novi List*, 6 February. https://www.novilist.hr/novosti/svijet/razgovor-s-vlasnikom-informera-najzlocudnijeg-tabloida-balkana-vucicevicu-jeste-li-vi-budala/

Tonkiss, Fran. 2012. 'Discourse Analysis'. In *Researching Society and Culture*, edited by Clive Seale. Sage.

Vreme. 2024. 'Vulin dobio još jedan ruski orden, sada lično od Putina'. *Vreme*, 30 January. https://vreme.com/vesti/vulin-dobio-jos-jedan-ruski-orden-sada-licno-od-putina/

Wetherell, Margaret, Stephanie Taylor and Simeon J. Yates. 2001. *Discourse Theory & Practice: A Reader*. The Open University.

Woodward, Susan L. 1995. 'The Use of Sanctions in Former Yugoslavia: Misunderstanding Political Realities'. In *Economic Sanctions: Panacea or Peacebuilding in a Post-Cold War World?*, edited by David Cortright and George A. Lopez. Westview.

Živanović, Katarina. 2022. 'Dragan J. Vučićević: Omiljeni predsednikov novinar'. *Danas*, 29 September. https://www.danas.rs/vesti/drustvo/dragan-j-vucicevic-omiljeni-predsednikov-novinar/

12

Why Are ASEAN States Not Sanctioning Russia? Sovereignty, Dependence or Vulnerability?

Matteo Dian

Introduction

Why did most ASEAN member states not impose sanctions against Russia after Moscow's invasion of Ukraine? This chapter advances three different explanations. Firstly, the non-imposition of sanction can be associated with interpretative and reactive contestation of key norms of the international order. Those states that are not imposing sanctions have a clear preference for an order rooted in the pluralist/Westphalian principles of sovereignty and non-interference (Wiener 2014, 2018; Betts and Orchard 2014). Consequently, they interpret the imposition of sanctions against Russia as a departure from those principles. It is important to notice that the same preference for sovereignty and non-interference could as well lead to the opposite interpretation: that Russia has been violating Ukraine's territorial integrity and its sovereignty.

As this chapter will further articulate below, post-colonial nationalism, critical positions on the liberal nature of the international order as promoted by Western powers, emphasis on sovereignty and the will to maintain non-alignment in disputes between great powers have had a very significant influence on the way in which ASEAN countries have positioned themselves on the issue of sanctions. This normative background has generally inspired positions of neutralism and abstentions from the sanction regime as a form of interpretative contestation.

The second explanation regards the degree of political, military and economic dependence of ASEAN countries on Russia. Some of the ASEAN member states have a history of bilateral cooperation that lasts from the Cold War era, which involves political, military and economic partnerships. This is the case, for instance, of Vietnam. Other countries, such as Myanmar, have a more recent relation, but have developed a significant degree of dependence on Russia, in particular when it comes to the defence sectors. Others depend on Russia's export in the agricultural sector and for raw materials. In some cases, interests and alignment with Russia have led some ASEAN member to engage in reactive contestation, violating the sanction regime to actively consolidate their relationship with Moscow.

A third explanation regards states' vulnerability to the global disruption created by the war, added to previous factors of disruption such as the COVID pandemic. Russia's war against Ukraine led to a global food crisis and energy crisis, and contributed to accelerate global inflation. Some of the ASEAN member states are among the most vulnerable to these trends. Consequently, their position on sanctions and more broadly their 'not taking sides' in the war stems from the effort to minimise the economic impact of the food and energy crises. Certain states, despite not being necessarily among the most vulnerable, have strong incentives to assume this same position, presenting themselves as representatives of the developing world. While interest is a key explanatory factor for foreign policy decisions, this chapter will highlight the ways in which contestation has taken place.

The decisions of each state can be traced back to a mix of the three. However, when a state does support the sanction regime, it is possible to recognise a degree of distance from these arguments, as in the case of Singapore.

The rest of the chapter proceeds as follows: the next section will discuss in more detail the three key variables determining ASEAN member states' non-participation (pluralist normative orientation; dependency on Russia; fragility to global disruption). The final section of the chapter explores the motivation that led ASEAN states to abstain from imposing sanctions on Russia.

Sovereignty, Dependence and Vulnerability

ASEAN and the International Order

ASEAN member states share several interests, economic priorities and normative principles. The main function of ASEAN itself is protecting sovereignty, independence and self-determination of member states. 'ASEAN centrality' is generally considered as an antidote to the excessive influence of great powers. These preferences reflect the legacy of the colonial past of these nations that have regained their independence and self-determination only relatively recently (Acharya 2009b, 2010; Ba 2009). The vision of regional order promoted by the ASEAN states is therefore a hybrid that combines many pluralist-Westphalian features such as respect for sovereignty, self-determination and non-interference and elements closer to a solidarist-liberal view, such as respect of international law, particularly, and the centrality of multilateralism. ASEAN promotes a unique vision of the role of great powers (Ba 2020). On the one hand, there is the recognition of the great power status of China and the United States as the determining players for the region. Occasionally Russia is included in this category. On the other hand, ASEAN's raison d'être is precisely that of preventing competition between great powers from damaging the stability and sovereignty of member states. From an economic point of view, the ASEAN states are integrated into the regional and global economic system. Therefore, they consider the stability and maintenance of free trade as key priorities. Consequently, the most common approach is that of hedging strategies, attempts to differentiate one's 'portfolio' of political and economic ties. This strategy aims to limit excessive dependence on a state, while preserving a certain degree of influence and autonomy. These strategies have led ASEAN states to cultivate a dense network of economic and security relations with the United States and China, but also with the other main regional players. Recent competition between great powers has generated a variety of similar reactions among ASEAN states. Most states in the region fear being entrapped in an escalation between great powers. Also, they are concerned about the possible consequences of geopolitical competition for regional stability and economic growth (Haacke 2019; Jones and Jenne 2022; Tan 2020).

The priorities assigned to sovereignty and self-determination are also linked to the extreme variety of internal political regimes that characterise the region, where democracies coexist with hybrid systems such as Singapore or Thailand, one-party socialist regimes such as Vietnam and absolute monarchies such as Brunei. For these reasons, the ASEAN states are against the attempts to polarise the region along strategic and ideological fault lines. The emergence of the great power competition involving the US, Russia and China and the US attempts to mobilise allies and partners for a competition between democracy and authoritarianism have been seen with apprehension. Consequently, the imposition of sanctions is often considered as part of an effort to polarise the system along ideological lines, functional to preserving the hegemonic role of the United States and the West.

Military and Economic Dependence

Recently, IR scholars have explored the 'dark side' of economic interdependence. While for decades, especially in the aftermath of the Cold War, neoliberal scholars emphasised the pacifying effect of trade and mutual dependence, lately IR scholars and policymakers have emphasised how dependence can be considered a form of vulnerability that can be leveraged by other states to exercise coercion and political influence. In the words of Daniel Drezner, states 'can weaponize networks to gather information or choke off economic and information flows, discover and exploit vulnerabilities, compel policy change, and deter unwanted actions' (Drezner, Farrell and Newman 2021; Farrell and Newman 2019). These studies returned to shed light on mechanisms that were already explained by Albert O. Hirschman, who pointed out how states can purposefully create a relationship of dependence in order to gain political influence (Hirschman 1980). These concepts provide a possible lens through which it is possible to analyse the position of ASEAN member states towards Russia after the invasion of Ukraine. Dependence on Russia in key sectors, from military equipment to raw materials, cereals or chemical fertilisers, can induce states to adopt a softer line towards Russia, to avoid compromising a necessary economic or security partnership.

General Vulnerability

Recent 'black swan' events, from the global pandemic to the re-emergence of global inflation to the shortages of food, fertilisers and fossil fuels generated by the war in Ukraine, have highlighted vulnerability to global and regional shocks. Less developed countries are clearly more vulnerable to these external shocks. Inflation and shortages do not simply translate to a generally worse economic performance but can have a significant impact on levels of unemployment, access to basic services and food. This in turn can severely affect political stability (Hellegers 2022; Ben Hassen and Bilali 2022; Bailey and Wellesley 2017; Jagtap et al. 2022). Consequently, attempts to spare their countries from the worst consequences of the economic disruption can lead policymakers to seek a position of neutrality and to avoid implementing sanctions. Very often, as the paper will discuss, governments tend to seek to maintain privileged access to the Russian market to mitigate the effects of the rise of oil, gas and food prices.

ASEAN Member States and Russia's Invasion of Ukraine

Cambodia

Cambodia's position is considered more nuanced compared with its neighbours in Indochina, Vietnam and Laos, which have clearly sided with Moscow. Cambodia has had a long-term relationship with Moscow, dating back to the Cold War era. The USSR supported Cambodia in the anti-colonial struggle

Table 12.1 Votes on UN General Assembly resolution condemning Russia's aggression against Ukraine

Country/ UN resolution	UNGA 2 March 2022	UNGA 24 March 2022 Humanitarian consequences	UNGA 7 April 2022 Suspension of Russia from Human Rights Council	UNGA 7 October 2022 Ukraine territorial integrity	UNGA 14 November 2022 Reparations to Ukraine	UNGA 26 April 2023 Condemning Russia's aggression
Brunei	Y	A	A	Y	A	Y
Cambodia	Y	Y	A	Y	A	Y
Indonesia	Y	Y	A	Y	A	Y
Laos	A	A	N	A	A	Y
Malaysia	Y	Y	A	Y	A	Y
Myanmar	Y	Y	Y	Y	Y	Y
Philippines	Y	Y	Y	Y	Y	Y
Singapore	Y	Y	A	A	Y	Y
Thailand	Y	Y	A	A	A	Y
Vietnam	A	A	N	A	A	Y

against France in the 1950s and supported the country with financial and technical aid after the end of the Khmer Rouge period.

Cambodia does not participate in UN-led sanctions. Moreover, Prime Minister Hun Sen called for a general rethinking of sanctions, considered harmful since they contribute to the ongoing food crisis and global instability (Diao, Dorosh and Ellis 2022). Nevertheless, Phnom Penh has voted to approve four of the six UNGA resolutions and has officially condemned Russia's invasion as well as the referendums in Donetsk and Lugansk, considered as dangerous violations of the principle of sovereign integrity (Storey 2022). Moreover, the Cambodian government has offered to send de-mining teams to help Ukraine in their effort to free their territory from the threat posed by landmines.

As a rotating chair of ASEAN, Cambodia has volunteered to act as a mediator between Ukraine and Russia and has offered to host bilateral talks between the two belligerents. During the ASEAN summit Cambodia's spokesperson argued that his country 'is not biased towards Russia or Ukraine', substantially conforming with the non-alignment approach promoted by most relevant ASEAN members.

Cambodia's economic relationship with Russia was not particularly developed even before the war. Its military is not dependent on Russian equipment (Associated Press 2022). Ultimately, Cambodia's approach on sanctions can be considered related to its vulnerability to global disruption, in particular in terms of food crisis, as well as by an attempt to reconcile a normative stance in favour of sovereignty and territorial integrity and the will to maintain stable relations with China.

Indonesia

Indonesia was in the spotlight in 2022, as host of the G20 and as a country willing to present itself as a leader within ASEAN. Under the leadership of President Joko Widodo, it has advocated a neutral position and has repeatedly reaffirmed its rejection of sanctions as a viable instrument of foreign policy.

On several occasions, Widodo has argued that sanctions are not conducive to a negotiated solution of the conflict and that Indonesia and ASEAN should present themselves as a mediator, and has advocated for peaceful coexistence rather than taking sides and imposing coercive measures on Russia. In March 2022, Indonesia voted in favour of the resolution condemning the invasion but emphasised that it tried to lead the other members to approve a resolution that 'contain the aspirations of all parties in a balanced manner' (Indonesian Ministry of Foreign Affairs 2022).

Widodo, as chair of the G20, promoted several efforts to mediate between Russia and Ukraine, culminated with his July trip to Kiev and to Moscow. During the trip he emphasised the necessity to stop the war as soon as possible and to re-establish the global supply chain, to alleviate the global food crisis generated by the conflict. Similarly, Minister of Foreign Affairs Marsudi underlined that securing a corridor for food and fertilisers was a key objective of Widodo's trip (Llewellyn 2022).

As chair of the G20, Widodo tried to soften the criticism of Russia expressed by the joint communiqué after the summit held in Bali. Before that, he had tried to mediate between the parts to make the participation of Putin in the summit possible.

Finally, in early June 2023, the Defence Minister Prawabo Subianto issued a 'peace proposal' that called for a ceasefire and referendums under the UN supervision in what he defined as disputed territories (as opposed to 'Ukrainian territories occupied by Russia') (Financial Times 2023). Widodo's approach to Russia's war to Ukraine is coherent with his previous foreign policy strategy and with the tradition of non-alignment of the country (Acharya 2014; Shekhar 2018; Weatherbee 2013). Even when, shortly after his election, Widodo tried to redefine Indonesia's role in the region by promoting the concept of 'Global Maritime Fulcrum', concrete priorities were always defined in terms of domestic interests, such as promoting fishing, infrastructure and economic development, as well as principles as protection of sovereignty, non-interference and non-alignment (Laksmana 2020). This foreign policy vision led Widodo to confirm an approach based on ASEAN centrality and its neutrality and autonomy. Jakarta is one of the staunchest supporters of the need to avoid permanent alignments and alliances in an environment marked by the geopolitical competition between China and the United States (Allard and Widanto 2020). For this reason, the Indonesian government was one of the major supporters of the ASEAN Outlook for the Indo-Pacific in 2019, a document that reaffirms the need to promote the centrality and neutrality of ASEAN as a tool to minimise the risks associated with rivalry between great powers, and to maintain member states' sovereignty and self-determination (Acharya 2019; Anwar 2020; Scott 2019). In this context, Indonesia has tried to nurture cooperative relations with all regional powers. China is the country's largest trading partner, representing 27 per cent of imports and 17 per cent of exports.

Many Western analysts in recent years have foreseen a more active role in terms of protection of the regional order and 'responsible middle power' capable of helping to moderate the revisionist aspects of the Chinese rise as well as confronting Russia's aggression. Indonesia's foreign policy remains firmly oriented towards the need to avoid entrapment in the competition between great powers, and to maximise the opportunities that this can offer.

Indonesia's neutral stance is also affected by a generally positive perception of Russia, seen as the inheritor of the role of the Soviet Union in the world. For many Indonesians the USSR constituted a crucial partner in the anti-colonial struggle in Southeast Asia. This view has been reinforced by Russia's recent information campaigns aiming at polishing this romanticised image of the Soviet role in post-colonial Asia. This influence is also related to the negative perception of the United States associated to the long-lasting legacy of US role in the Cold War in Southeast Asia, and to the post-2001 War on Terror. The Indonesian public tends to see the defence of Ukrainian sovereignty in the aftermath of the regime changes in Afghanistan and Iraq as hypocritical.

Beyond the will to avoid alignment, another motivating factor for Indonesia regards the perception of economic vulnerability generated by the conflict. Indonesia had significant, but not crucial economic relations with both Russia and Ukraine up to the beginning of the conflict. In 2021, Indonesia imported 1.2 billion USD worth of product from Russia and 1 billion from Ukraine. Indonesia's imports from Russia are concentrated in the fields of oil, mineral fuels and steel. Indonesia's exports to Russia are concentrated in the field of palm and coconut oil. Before the conflict Indonesia imported some 950 million USD worth of cereals from Ukraine, while exports were largely concentrated in the sector of vegetable oils. These trade patterns have significantly affected Indonesia, which has been impacted by the rising prices of oil and gas and cereals.

For Indonesia, the conflict and the sanctions have also led to positive economic developments, such as a significant increase of Russian tourists as well as men fleeing the country to avoid conscription. Up to April 2023, when the government restricted access, up to 80,000 Russians entered the country, with a peak of 20,000 in January 2023.

In the defence sectors, Indonesia has relevant relations with Moscow. It has purchased eleven Su-35 jetfighters and other equipment. However, Jakarta has promoted a very diversified set of acquisitions for defence equipment, relying especially on South Korea, France, the US and the Netherlands. Having applied the logic of hedging in the military sector, Jakarta is not dependent on any single partner. Therefore, the impact of Russian weapons sales does not appear to be a significant determinant of the country's diplomatic stance.

Laos

Laos has showcased a distinctively pro-Russian position since the outbreak of the war. It did not impose sanctions and abstained on all the UNGA resolutions, except for the resolution that expelled Russia from the Human Rights Council, which it opposed. In May 2022 the Lao state-controlled news agency has written that 'with the help of foreign countries, Ukraine has become a centre of attraction for terrorists and mercenaries' and 'the West is openly encouraging Kiev to attack Russia' (Hutt 2022). Putin himself has defined as 'satisfactory' the relations with Vientiane, defining it as a 'reliable partner'.

Warm relations between Russia and Laos date back to the Cold War. Many of the top leaders of the country were educated in the USSR, including Thongloun Sisoulith, the general secretary of the Lao People's Revolutionary Party. Despite its low level of military spending, Laos has purchased military equipment from Russia and it has also received developmental aid, especially with the removal of unexploded ordinance, a problem that has plagued the country since the Vietnam War. The general level of economic exchange between the two countries is negligible, with 0.48 per cent of Laos' import and 0.02 per cent of exports. Nevertheless, Russia is a significant source of oil and fertilisers for Laos, which has faced shortages since the beginning of 2022, largely caused by the devaluation of the local currency and soaring inflation.

Another significant factor in the Laotian position regards the relationship with China, which has developed a very significant economic influence, especially as a consequence of the launch of the Belt and Road Initiative. This has led China to invest in hydropower dams, the China–Laos railway and special economic zones (SEZ). Despite attempts by the Laotian government to hedge against an excessive Chinese influence – seeking to maintain positive relations both within ASEAN and with other powers such as Japan, Australia and, especially, Russia – Chinese political influence remains significant. From this perspective, the recent alignment between China and Russia should be considered as another key determinant of the Laotian position (Kuik and Rosli 2023).

Malaysia

Malaysia voted in favour of three UNGA resolutions that condemned Russia but did not impose any sanctions against Moscow. The two countries did not entertain significant economic or military relations before the conflict. As a consequence, the Malay response has not been influenced either by direct military dependence or strong direct economic interests.

The Malay representative at the UN during the discussion leading to the approval of the March resolution stated that it was 'in line with Malaysia's long-standing position on the need to consistently uphold the principles of sovereignty, independence and territorial integrity of States, principles which are non-negotiable to Malaysia'. He added that 'we believe that the differences and legitimate security concerns of both parties, given the complex geopolitical context, must be addressed through dialogue and peaceful means'. These statements did not translate into any policy aimed at signalling a condemnation of Russia. The Malay government repeatedly articulated its position, choosing to remain neutral to simply call for dialogue and negotiations. Analyses of the local debate showed that public opinion tends to display a pro-Russian inclination caused by several factors. The Malay political discourse is characterised by strong elements of anti-Western rhetoric, depicting the West and especially the US as imperialist and anti-Muslim. As a result, many voices tend to describe Russia as threatened by the US and NATO and provoked by Ukraine. Others tend to see Russia as a champion of the resistance against the hegemony of the West. For instance, former Prime Minister Muhathir declared that the war was generated by the 'Europeans' love of war and hegemony' (Solhi 2022).

Many political leaders in Malaysia, including Muhathir, are very critical of Israel. This criticism has intensified since the start of the Israeli military operation against Gaza in October 2023. In some cases, this has led to direct criticism against President Zelensky. The US support provided to both Ukraine, led by a president of Jewish origin, and Israel has often been interpreted as a general US and Western alignment against Muslim communities in the Middle East and globally (Loh and Mustaffa 2022). On the other hand, Putin has been considered as friendly to Muslim states, in particular for his support to Assad in Syria.

Myanmar

Myanmar is another country that has promoted a strongly pro-Russian policy. In the aftermath of the invasion, a spokesperson of the regime stated that the invasion was 'an appropriate action' and 'an attempt by Moscow to strengthen its national sovereignty'. Furthermore, state media described Russia as a 'powerful nation that plays an essential role in keeping the balance of power for world peace', while describing Zelensky as a 'puppet of the West', 'incapable' and 'lacking rationality' (International Crisis Group 2022).

The military coup of February 2021 has determined a condition of international isolation for the country. ASEAN leaders, who have historically been extremely keen to protect national self-determination and sovereignty, took the unprecedented step of denying the military junta an invitation to participate in the ASEAN summits in 2021 and 2022 (Kurlantzick 2022). Relations with China deteriorated in the short term, since Beijing had invested considerable diplomatic capital in improving relations with the democratic regime led by Aung San Suu Kyi. Moreover, China was clearly displeased with the instability generated by the coup. However, in 2022 China reopened diplomatic channels and started to economically support the country. Russia strongly backed the regime led by Min Aung Hlaing and by the military. The renewed ties with Moscow are considered functional to diversify the foreign policy relations of the new regime, seeking to decrease the overreliance on Beijing, as well as to emerge from international isolation. In this sense Moscow, having a significant leverage on other countries in ASEAN such as Vietnam, Laos and Cambodia, could help to soften the Association's stance on the junta (Thiha and Crabtree 2022).

In June 2022, Hlaing was invited to an official visit to Moscow in July and met Putin at the Eastern Economic Forum in Vladivostok in September 2022 (Zsombor 2021). Russia is also Myanmar's main supplier of weapons. This relationship has continued though the different phases of domestic politics in the country. The bilateral military links are also cemented by the fact that military personnel of Myanmar is regularly invited to participate in training activities at Russia's military academies.

This position appears at odds with the votes cast by Myanmar in the UN General Assembly, where the country's representative approved all the resolutions condemning Russia. This, however, is because Myanmar's representative to the UN, Kyaw Moe Tun, an expression of the previous democratic regime, continued to represent the country up to 2025. Ultimately, the position of Myanmar is associated with security and foreign policy ties with Russia.

The Philippines

Before the war against Ukraine, relations between the Philippines and Russia had significantly improved. Western criticisms against the government led by Rodrigo Duterte and its poor standards in terms of human rights had led the Filipino leader to upgrade its relations with Moscow. This was also helped by Duterte's personal admiration for Putin. The war changed this picture completely. The Philippines is the only country that voted in favour of all the UN resolutions condemning Russia's aggression. Moreover, during the last phase of his presidency, Duterte assumed a clearly critical stance against Moscow. Manila cancelled the purchase of Russian-made military helicopters, also for fear of being sanctioned by the US under the provisions of the Countering America's Adversaries through Sanctions Act (CAATSA).

Both Duterte and Marcos openly criticised the war. Marcos stated that 'aggression is not acceptable' (Diao, Dorosh and Pauw 2022), while Duterte stated, referring to his very controversial 'war on drugs', 'I kill criminals, Putin kills children and elderly' (Inocencio 2022). Ferdinand Marcos Jr, who has assumed a more clearly pro-US position, has described Russia's invasion of Ukraine as a violation of the principles of sovereignty and territorial integrity, considered as core norms of the international order.

The Philippines tends to see the war in Ukraine through the lenses of US–China competition and maritime and territorial disputes in the South China Sea. Consequently, Filipino fears are associated with the perceived polarisation of the international system, due to the alignment between Moscow and Beijing, alimented by the war.

Despite the statements of condemnation, and the rapprochement to Washington, Manila did not sanction Russia. The country has never been economically dependent on Russia's exports. Therefore, its position cannot be explained in those terms. In this case, the explanation relies on the other two factors: state fragility and normative orientation. The Philippines have been negatively affected by shortages of agricultural products and especially of fertilisers exported by both Ukraine and Russia and by soaring prices of fuel. Despite the modest impact in terms of GDP, the economic repercussions of the conflict have adversely affected levels of unemployment and inequality in the country. This crisis has led the country to consider buying oil from Russia, generating a debate among policymakers. So far, the government led by Marcos has refrained from doing so, due to fears of being subject to secondary sanctions and to the possibility of a 'loss of international standing' (Jose 2022).

Singapore

Singapore is the only ASEAN member state that has imposed sanctions on Russia.[1] In doing so it has significantly diverged from the approach adopted by the rest of the organisation. It has joined the so-called first wave of sanctions, put in place by US, EU and UK. Generally, the country has participated in sanctions regimes based on UN resolutions. Importantly, this is the first time that Singapore has imposed unilateral sanctions since 1978, when Vietnam invaded Cambodia.

Sanctions imposed by Singapore concern two main categories (Singapore Ministry of Foreign Affairs 2022). The first regards export controls associated with items that can be used as weapons or contribute to military operations. This category also includes electronics, computers and telecommunication systems

[1] Despite imposing sanctions Singapore abstained in the votes of three resolutions condemning the Russian invasion.

considered to be functional for military purposes. The second category regards financial measures against Russian banks and financial entities, as well as fundraising activities that can benefit the Russian government.[2]

Singapore's stance reflects a particular perspective on the international order and its key normative pillars. Singapore shares with its ASEAN partners a preference for a pluralist order, based on respect of sovereignty, non-interference, as well as multilateralism and trade openness. Overall, Singapore foreign and security policy, as for many states in the region, is based on a complex hedging strategy that has led to building a complex network of security and economic relations. Differently from other ASEAN member states, however, this normative background did not lead it to attribute priority to the principle of non-alignment, but rather to react to denounce Russia's actions as a gross violation of the principles of sovereignty and self-determination. Singaporean policymakers have also underlined how, for a small state such as Singapore, respect of territorial integrity represents a non-negotiable foundation of the international order.

Prime Minister Lee Hsien-loong clearly articulated this position during an interview with the Council of Foreign Relations, stating that:

> It [the war] [has] damaged the international framework for law and order and peace between countries. It violates the U.N. charter, it endangers the independence, sovereignty, and territorial integrity of all countries, especially small ones. And if a principle is accepted that crazy decisions and historical errors are the justification for invading somebody else, I think many of us are going to be feeling very insecure in the Asia-Pacific, but also in the rest of the world. (Council on Foreign Relations 2022)

Prime Minister Lee articulated further his perspective, stating that principles such as peaceful resolution of disputes, multilateralism and cooperation between great powers remain essential to provide small states such as Singapore with an environment in which economic openness and connectivity enable growth and development.

Importantly, Singapore is far less vulnerable to Russia's reactions compared to other regional states. Its trade with Moscow is negligible and it does not have a significant relation in the defence sector. Furthermore, Singapore, one of the richest countries in the world in terms of GDP per capita, is

[2] Singapore has targeted four main Russian banks: VTB Bank Public Joint Stock Company, The Corporation Bank for Development and Foreign Economic Affairs Vnesheconombank, Promsvyazbank Public Joint Stock Company and Bank Rossiya.

less directly impacted by inflation, food crises and other indirect economic consequences of the conflict.

Thailand

Despite voting in favour of the two UN resolutions approved in March, Thailand has not sanctioned Russia and it has sought to maintain a position of neutrality on the war in Ukraine. Thai Prime Minister Prayut Chan-o-cha and Foreign Minister Don Pramudwinai argued in favour of a position of neutrality for the country. In October the Thai representative at the UN, after declaring his abstention on the resolution on Russia's illegal annexation of the occupied provinces of Lugansk and Donetsk, stated that the resolution was counterproductive, 'provoked intransigence' and was creating obstacles for constructive dialogue. The Thai foreign ministry released a statement arguing Thailand is 'genuinely concerned about the increased politicization of international principles that have become counterproductive as the means and guidance to end the war' (Bhandari and Phaicharoen 2022).

The elections of May 2023 led to electoral success for the Move Forward Party, led by Pita Limijaroenrat. Despite this outcome, the Thai Senate, controlled by the military, blocked the nomination of Limijaroenrat as prime minister. This favoured the formation of a new coalition between military-backed parties and Pheu Thai, a party associated the Shinawatra, leading to the nomination of Paetongtarn Shinawatra as prime minister.

Many different elements contribute to explain Bangkok's position up to May 2023. A main reason concerns Thailand's own domestic problems. The Thai leadership came to power through a military coup d'état in 2014. In 2019, elections considered as not free by the international community confirmed General Prayut Chan-o-cha as prime minister. Since 2014, the Thai government has been responsible for multiple episodes of violations of human right and repression of dissent. In the aftermath of the coup, China and Russia helped Thailand to avoid international isolation and condemnation. Ultimately, the government led by Prayut seems wary of alienating great powers that offer diplomatic support in case the government return to violently repress domestic opposition.

A second considerable element of Bangkok's calculus regarding the relations with China is that, despite the continuing alliance with the US, in the last decade Thailand has promoted a hedging strategy that seeks to differentiate its foreign policy relations. China has become an increasingly central partner for Bangkok, in terms of trade relations, investments in infrastructures as well as military cooperation. Consequently, the will to preserve the relationship with

Beijing has contributed to the Thai position on Russia's war against Ukraine (Cogan 2019; Quayle 2020; Sawasdipakdi 2021).

In terms of defence industry, unlike other Southeast Asian countries, Thailand is not dependent on Russia for the acquisition of major military platforms. On the contrary, Bangkok relies on multiple partners, including the US, China, South Korea, Germany and, before the war, also Ukraine.

Economically, Russia is considered a significant partner. While trade relations are negligible, Russia is important for tourism, a fundamental pillar of the Thai economy, especially in the aftermath of the pandemic. In 2019, 1.4 million Russians visited the country. In January 2022, Russian tourists counted as 20 per cent of the total visitors in that month. Sanctions imposed on Russian airlines and banks made it very hard for Russian tourists to travel in the country. In recent months, Thai operators have sought to circumvent the sanctions using China's UnionPay and other instruments. Overall, the Thai government intends to keep the door open to them (CAN Asia 2022). Official statistics report that Thailand in 2022 received some 250,000 Russian visitors. Moreover, Thai authorities seem committed to try to normalise the access of Russian visitors in 2023.

Vietnam

Vietnam has taken a clearly pro-Russian orientation in the aftermath of the invasion. It abstained on all resolutions condemning the invasion of Ukraine and opposed the resolution banning Moscow from the Human Rights Council in the UN. The Vietnamese alignment with Russia was described by Foreign Minister Lavrov during a visit in July 2022, when he stated that 'Vietnam is a key partner in ASEAN and the two countries' relation are based on history and their common fight for justice'.

In 2021 during a state visit of the Vietnamese President Nguyen Xuan Phuc's to Moscow the two parts issued a joint statement arguing that Vietnam and Russia 'share similarity of approaches [. . .] to the majority of issues of international and regional agenda, contributing to promoting close coordination between the two countries within the framework of multilateral organisations' (Ministry of Industry and Trade, Socialist Republic of Vietnam 2021). This statement reflects the legacy of a long bilateral relationship between the two countries that dates to the Cold War and to the Vietnam War. Soviet support was essential for unification of the country under the Vietnamese Communist Party. The tradition of bilateral cooperation continued after the demise of the Soviet Union and particularly during the Putin era. In 2012, the two countries signed a strategic comprehensive partnership, considered the deepest form of diplomatic cooperation for the two countries (Baev and Tønnesson 2015; Kobelev 2015; Tsvetov 2018).

Russia is the main weapons supplier for Vietnam. The People's Army of Vietnam has acquired from Russia very sophisticated and very expensive platforms such as six kilo class submarines, four frigates and over thirty Su-30 jetfighters. SIPRI reports that Vietnam's acquisitions from Russia amount to some 9 billion USD since 1995. Up to 2014 procurement from Russia represented the near total of the Vietnamese arms import. After 2014 Vietnam imported weapons also from other partners such as Israel and South Korea, while continuing to rely on Russia for two thirds of its imports.

However, it is important to notice that Vietnam before the invasion developed significant relations also with Ukraine, partially as a result of traditional ties within the post-Soviet space, but also as a consequence of relevant diplomatic efforts that led to intense economic and cultural exchanges and to the signing of a comprehensive partnership. Despite these previous links, Vietnamese state media promoted a clearly pro-Russian narrative, censoring pro-Ukraine voices in the country, exercising a tight control on the web (Abuza 2022).

Despite the current solidity of the relations between Hanoi and Moscow, several analysts argue that the evolution of regional alignments triggered by the invasion of Ukraine might lead Vietnam to reconsider, at least partially, its position. In particular, Hanoi has always considered the alignment with Russia as an instrument to counterbalance the influence of China in Southeast Asia. The isolation generated by the war against Ukraine is likely to push Russia and China much closer, forming a cohesive, yet asymmetric block led by Beijing. This constitutes a problem for Hanoi, which has its own security problems with the PRC. For this reason, Vietnam has voted in favour of declarations that recall the necessity to respect the UN Charter, the integrity of borders. Moreover, Vietnam considers as a dangerous precedent the Russian argument that it was intervening to protect Russian ethnic minorities in Ukraine. A similar argument was used by China back in 1979 and it is still used today to legitimise China's changes in the status quo in the South China Sea.

Conclusions

Southeast Asia and ASEAN members largely abstained from imposing sanctions against Russia, with the significant exception of Singapore. This chapter provides a significant insight on patterns of norms contestation in the case of sanctions towards Russia. States that underlined their ideological opposition towards a Western-led international order, either siding with Russia or assuming a neutral position, promoted forms of applicatory contestation together with forms of validity contestation. In doing so they tended to reject sanctions as a legitimate instrument to impose costs on a norm violator (see Palestini's chapter in this volume). Consequently, they refused to apply this instrument on Russia as forms of interpretative and reactive contestation. Significantly, these forms of contestation do not coincide only with a pro-Russian strategic alignment. States that adopted a consciously neutral position, such as Indonesia or Malaysia, were among those that more clearly contested the legitimacy of sanctions as a foreign policy instrument.

Interpretative and reactive contestation shape the varied responses of Southeast Asian countries toward sanctions related to Russia, reflecting differences in historical ties, geopolitical considerations, and normative stances on international order and non-intervention.

Countries such as Indonesia, Malaysia and Thailand demonstrate interpretative contestation in their approach to sanctions. Their positions are shaped by anti-Western sentiments, adherence to norms of non-alignment and non-intervention, and perceptions of Western hypocrisy. Indonesia's and Malaysia's reluctance to openly condemn Russia reflects their normative orientation towards balancing power rather than choosing sides, consistent with their historical scepticism of Western-dominated sanctions regimes. Similarly, Thailand's cautious stance, influenced by the need to preserve political and economic relations with Russia, aligns with a broader interpretation of sovereignty and non-interference. The fragile legitimacy of the Thai government before the 2023 elections further reinforced its reluctance to criticise Russia directly, underscoring how domestic political stability interacts with normative contestation. China's increasing alignment with Russia also contributes to interpretative contestation across the region. Many ASEAN countries perceive this partnership as exacerbating global polarisation, leading to greater emphasis on neutral, non-aligned strategies championed by ASEAN. Vietnam's discomfort with the Sino-Russian partnership reflects its historical use of ties with Russia to counterbalance Chinese regional influence. In contrast, Cambodia, Myanmar, Laos and Thailand see the strengthened Beijing–Moscow relationship as a reason to keep diplomatic channels with Russia open, reinforcing a strategic interpretation that prioritises flexibility over confrontation.

Myanmar and Singapore illustrate reactive contestation in divergent ways. Myanmar, isolated after the 2021 military coup, views Russia as a crucial partner for weapons and geopolitical support. By deepening ties with Moscow, Myanmar contests Western sanctions that seek to isolate its regime, positioning its alignment with Russia as a counter-measure against international marginalisation. This reactive approach directly challenges the legitimacy of sanctions as a normative tool of international order. Singapore, on the other hand, stands as the only ASEAN country to impose unilateral sanctions against Russia, marking a significant break from regional norms of non-intervention. However, even Singapore's stance reflects cautious pragmatism; it abstained from several key UN resolutions condemning Russia in 2022, revealing hesitancy to fully align with the Western sanctions regime. The Philippines similarly condemned Russia's actions but refrained from further measures due to fears of escalating polarisation and economic vulnerability, highlighting a reactive contestation driven by national interest rather than principled opposition to sanctions.

Southeast Asia's varied responses to Russia-related sanctions illustrate a complex interplay of interpretative and reactive contestation. Interpretative contestation emerges from historical legacies of colonialism, non-alignment and scepticism towards Western norms, while reactive contestation reflects immediate geopolitical calculations and strategic partnerships. Together, these dynamics underscore the region's diverse and fluid engagement with the global sanctions regime.

References

Abuza, Zachary. 2022. 'Vietnam Placed in Awkward Position as Old Ally Russia Suffers Losses in Ukraine'. *Radio Free Asia*, 28 September. https://www.rfa.org/english/commentaries/vietnam-russia-09282022094801.html

Acharya, Amitav. 2009a. *(Re) Negotiating East and Southeast Asia: Region, Regionalism, and the Association of Southeast Asian Nations*. Stanford University Press.

Acharya, Amitav. 2009b. *Constructing a Security Community in Southeast Asia: ASEAN and the Problem of Regional Order*. Routledge.

Acharya, Amitav. 2010. *Whose Ideas Matter? Agency and Power in Asian Regionalism*. Cornell University Press.

Acharya, Amitav. 2014. *Indonesia Matters: Asia's Emerging Democratic Power*. World Scientific.

Acharya, Amitav. 2019. 'Why ASEAN's Indo-Pacific Outlook Matters'. *East Asia Forum*, 11 August. https://www.eastasiaforum.org/2019/08/11/why-aseans-indo-pacific-outlook-matters/

Allard, Tom, and Stanley Widanto. 2020. 'Indonesia to U.S., China: Don't Trap Us in Your Rivalry'. *Reuters*, 9 September.

Anwar, Dewi Fortuna. 2020. 'Indonesia and the ASEAN Outlook on the Indo-Pacific'. *International Affairs* 96(1): 111–29.

Associated Press. 2022. 'Cambodia to Send Deminers to Help Train Ukrainians'. *Associated Press*, 2 November. https://apnews.com/article/

russia-ukraine-zelenskyy-united-nations-cambodia-europe-153903b7f64956450d2ed940cca12330

Ba, Alice D. 2009. *(Re)Negotiating East and Southeast Asia: Region, Regionalism, and the Association of Southeast Asian Nations*. Stanford University Press.

Ba, Alice D. 2020. 'Multilateralism and East Asian Transitions: The English School, Diplomacy, and a Networking Regional Order'. *International Politics* 57(2): 259–77.

Baev, Pavel K., and Stein Tønnesson. 2015. 'Can Russia Keep Its Special Ties with Vietnam While Moving Closer and Closer to China?' *International Area Studies Review* 18(3): 312–25.

Bailey, Rob, and Laura Wellesley. 2017. *Chokepoints and Vulnerabilities in Global Food Trade*. Chatham House.

Ben Hassen, Tarek, and Hamid El Bilali. 2022. 'Impacts of the Russia-Ukraine War on Global Food Security: Towards More Sustainable and Resilient Food Systems?' *Foods* 11(5): 2301.

Betts, Alexander, and Philip Orchard, eds. 2014. *Implementation and World Politics: How International Norms Change Practice*. Oxford University Press.

Bhandari, Subel Rai, and Nontarat Phaicharoen. 2022. 'Vietnam and Thailand Abstain from UN Vote to Condemn Russia's Ukraine Annexation'. *Radio Free Asia*, 13 October. https://www.rfa.org/english/news/vietnam/abstention-10132022163210.html

CAN Asia. 2022. 'Thousands of Russians Stuck in Thailand as Sanctions Kick in'. *Channel News Asia*, 9 March. https://www.channelnewsasia.com/asia/russians-stuck-thailand-sanctions-ukraine-tourist-phuket-2549001

Cogan, Michael S. 2019. 'Is Thailand Accommodating China?' *Southeast Asian Social Science Review* 4(2): 24–47.

Council on Foreign Relations. 2022. 'A Conversation with Singapore Prime Minister Lee Hsien Loong'. *Council on Foreign Relations*, 30 March. https://www.cfr.org/event/conversation-singapore-prime-minister-lee-hsien-loong

Diao, Xinshen, Paul Dorosh and Karl Pauw. 2022. *The Philippines: Impacts of the Ukraine and Global Crises on Poverty and Food Security*. International Food Policy Research Institute, Country Brief 19.

Diao, Xinshen, Paul Dorosh and Mia Ellis. 2022. *Cambodia: Impacts of the Ukraine and Global Crises on Poverty and Food Security*. International Food Policy Research Institute, Country Brief 16.

Drezner, Daniel W., Henry Farrell, and Abraham L. Newman, eds. 2021. *The Uses and Abuses of Weaponized Interdependence*. Brookings Institution Press.

Farrell, Henry, and Abraham L. Newman. 2019. 'Weaponized Interdependence: How Global Economic Networks Shape State Coercion'. *International Security* 44(1): 42–79.

Financial Times. 2023. 'Indonesia Floats Ukraine Peace Plan, Triggering Sharp Western Criticism'. *Financial Times*, 3 June. https://www.ft.com/content/bf2c9186-344a-4f3a-a66a-c61244199d82

Haacke, Jürgen. 2019. 'The Concept of Hedging and Its Application to Southeast Asia: A Critique and a Proposal for a Modified Conceptual and Methodological Framework'. *International Relations of the Asia-Pacific* 19(3): 375–417.

Hellegers, Petra. 2022. 'Food Security Vulnerability Due to Trade Dependencies on Russia and Ukraine'. *Food Security* 14(6): 1503–10.

Hirschman, Albert O. 1980. *National Power and the Structure of Foreign Trade*. University of California Press.

Hutt, David. 2022. 'Will Laos Be Sanctioned for Embracing Russia?' *Los Angeles Times*, 9 July. https://asiatimes.com/2022/07/will-laos-be-sanctioned-for-embracing-russia/

Indonesian Ministry of Foreign Affairs. 2022. 'Indonesia Urges UN Member States to Pay Heed to Humanitarian Interests in the Ukraine Crisis'. *Indonesian Ministry of Foreign Affairs*. https://kemlu.go.id/portal/en/read/3369/berita/indonesia-urges-un-member-states-to-pay-heed-to-humanitarian-interests-in-the-ukraine-crisis

Inocencio, Solita Victoria. 2022. 'Marcos: Russia-Ukraine War "Unacceptable"'. *CNN Philippines*, 25 November.

International Crisis Group. 2022. *Coming to Terms with Myanmar's Russia Embrace*. Crisis Group Asia Briefing no. 173, 4 August.

Jagtap, Snehal, Holger Trollman, Floris Trollman, Gloria Garcia-Garcia, Carlos Parra-López, Lan Duong and Mouafk Afy-Shararah. 2022. 'The Russia-Ukraine Conflict: Its Implications for the Global Food Supply Chains'. *Foods* 11(14): 2098.

Jones, David Martin, and Nicole Jenne. 2022. 'Hedging and Grand Strategy in Southeast Asian Foreign Policy'. *International Relations of the Asia-Pacific* 22(2): 205–35.

Jose, Angelica E. 2022. 'Marcos Cautioned against Russian Oil Import Plan'. *BusinessWorld*, 10 October. https://www.bworldonline.com/the-nation/2022/10/10/479714/marcos-cautioned-against-russian-oil-import-plan/

Kobelev, Evgenii V. 2015. 'Russia-Vietnam Relations: Reality and Prospects'. *The Russian Journal of Vietnamese Studies* 1(5): 21–43.

Kuik, Cheng-Chwee, and Zikri Rosli. 2023. 'Laos-China Infrastructure Cooperation: Legitimation and the Limits of Host-Country Agency'. *Journal of Contemporary East Asia Studies* 12(1): 32–58.

Kurlantzick, Joshua. 2022. 'China's Support for Myanmar Further Shows the World Dividing into Autocracy Versus Democracy'. *Council on*

Foreign Relations. https://www.cfr.org/blog/chinas-support-myanmar-further-shows-world-dividing-autocracy-versus-democracy

Laksmana, Evan. 2020. 'Indonesia as "Global Maritime Fulcrum": A Post-Mortem Analysis'. *CSIS Asia Maritime Transparency Initiative*. https://amti.csis.org/indonesia-as-global-maritime-fulcrum-a-post-mortem-analysis/

Llewellyn, Aisyah. 2022. 'Widodo's Russia-Ukraine Trip Divides Critics in Indonesia'. *Al Jazeera*, 5 July. https://www.aljazeera.com/economy/2022/7/5/indonesian-leaders-russia-ukraine-trip-divides-critics-at-home

Loh, Ben, and Mohd Mustaffa. 2022. 'Social Media Discourse in Malaysia on the Russia-Ukraine Conflict: Rationales for Pro-Russia Sentiments'. *Fulcrum*. https://fulcrum.sg/social-media-discourse-in-malaysia-on-the-russia-ukraine-conflict-rationales-for-pro-russia-sentiments/

Ministry of Industry and Trade, Socialist Republic of Vietnam. 2021. *Joint Statement on 2030 Vision for Development of Viet Nam-Russia Relations*. Ministry of Industry and Trade. https://moit.gov.vn/en/news/ministerial-leaders-activities/joint-statement-on-2030-vision-for-development-of-viet-nam-russia-relations.html

Quayle, Linda. 2020. 'Southeast Asian Perspectives on Regional Alliance Dynamics: The Philippines and Thailand'. *International Politics* 57(2): 225–41.

Sawasdipakdi, Piti. 2021. 'Thailand's Engagement with China's Belt and Road Initiative: Strong Will, Slow Implementation'. *Asian Perspective* 45(2): 349–74.

Scott, David. 2019. 'Indonesia Grapples with the Indo-Pacific: Outreach, Strategic Discourse, and Diplomacy'. *Journal of Current Southeast Asian Affairs* 38(2): 194–217.

Shekhar, Vibhanshu. 2018. *Indonesia's Foreign Policy and Grand Strategy in the 21st Century: Rise of an Indo-Pacific Power*. Routledge.

Singapore Ministry of Foreign Affairs. 2022. 'Sanctions and Restrictions against Russia in Response to Its Invasion of Ukraine'. 3 March. https://www.mfa.gov.sg/Newsroom/Press-Statements-Transcripts-and-Photos/2022/03/20220305-sanctions

Solhi, Farah. 2022. 'Malaysia Supports, Votes in Favour of UN Resolution on Ukraine Crisis'. *Strait Times*, 3 March. https://www.nst.com.my/news/nation/2022/03/776512/malaysia-supports-votes-favour-un-resolution-ukraine-crisis

Storey, Ian. 2022. 'The War in Ukraine: Cambodia's Surprisingly Hard-line Stand'. *Fulcrum*, 25 May. https://fulcrum.sg/the-war-in-ukraine-cambodias-surprisingly-hard-line-stand/

Tan, See Seng. 2020. 'Consigned to Hedge: South-East Asia and America's "Free and Open Indo-Pacific" Strategy'. *International Affairs* 96(1): 131–48.

Thiha, Amara, and James Crabtree. 2022. 'Myanmar's Twin Objectives in Drawing Closer to Russia'. *International Institute Strategic Studies*, 15 September. https://www.iiss.org/blogs/analysis/2022/09/myanmars-twin-objectives-in-drawing-closer-to-russia

Tsvetov, Anton. 2018. 'Vietnam–Russia Relations: Glorious Past, Uncertain Future'. In *Vietnam's Foreign Policy under Doi Moi*, edited by Le Hong Hiep and Anton Tsvetov. De Gruyter.

Weatherbee, Donald. 2013. *Indonesia in ASEAN: Vision and Reality*. Institute of Southeast Asian Studies.

Wiener, Antje. 2014. *A Theory of Contestation*. Springer.

Wiener, Antje. 2018. *Contestation and Constitution of Norms in Global International Relations*. Cambridge University Press.

Zsombor, Peter. 2021. 'Myanmar's Junta Woos Moscow to Balance Beijing'. *VOA News*, 1 July. https://www.voanews.com/a/east-asia-pacific_myanmars-junta-woos-moscow-balance-beijing/6207695.html

Conclusions

Roberto Belloni, Thomas Biersteker and Francesco Giumelli

Drawing from the growing literature on norm contestation (Orchard and Wiener 2024) and sanctions' legitimacy (Palestini 2023), we presented a framework to guide the conceptual and empirical analysis of states' contestation of sanctions in the introduction of this volume. We also introduced a multi-perspectivist analysis of the global contestation of international sanctions and its impact on global politics, contributing to the emerging literature on global IR, with particular reference to the case of Russia following its full-scale aggression against Ukraine in February 2022.

Beginning with Orchard and Wiener's typology of three kinds of norm contestation – reactive, proactive and interpretative – we argued that *reactive contestation* challenges both the legitimacy and the standard of behaviour that a norm seeks to encourage. Sanctions against an aggressor state such as Russia express concern about the violation of the norms demanding the respect of the territorial integrity of a sovereign state and the use of armed force to settle disputes. While these norms are foundational elements of the modern international system, states may contest them nevertheless by focusing instead on other norms that are considered to be equally important or even superior. For instance, this is the case when the norm of non-intervention is invoked, which is supposedly violated by the adoption of sanctions against the aggressor, especially if sanctions are adopted unilaterally outside of the UN system. In such cases, states could be led to view sanctions as a form of 'punishment' and, from this perspective, consider them both legally and politically illegitimate. Thus, reactive contestation may reveal the existence of a debate over the hierarchy of fundamental norms that states continue to shape and reshape through their (re)actions to specific events.

Proactive contestation considers the impact of the instrument used to enforce a norm – the application of sanctions – both on the target state and its population and on other states affected by secondary sanctions or by their integration into global supply chains. This kind of contestation involves actions aimed at improving the enforcement of the norm, for example by attempting to target sanctions in order to make them less harmful for the civilian population, by strengthening due process procedures for individuals targeted by sanctions, and establishing humanitarian carve-outs to limit the unintended humanitarian consequences of targeted sanctions. In the process, not only do states accept sanctions as legitimate foreign policy instruments, but their grievances lie with the way in which sanctions are utilised rather than the instrument itself. The attempt is to make them more effective, targeted, consistent with the rule of law and compatible with regional security goals.

Interpretative contestation reveals the existence of states' different understandings of particular norms, the hierarchy of norms and/or practices employed to enforce them, like sanction regimes. States' positions within the international system, in particular whether they have experienced colonial rule and/or have been subjected to sanctions themselves, are likely to influence heavily their perception of this policy instrument. Most notably, from a post-colonial perspective, sanctions are frequently interpreted as an instrument of the strong (typically, Northern/Western/Developed states) to discipline and dominate the weak (Southern/Non-Western/Developing states). 'Western' sanctions senders are also frequently accused of selectivity and double standards which, in the eyes of states in the Global South, allegedly reveal the attempt to use sanctions in the pursuit of Western (and, within the West, especially American) interests. This is strikingly evident in the G7+ sanctions against Russia and the absence of a similar response to Israel's actions in Gaza, a point made by a number of contributors to this volume and elaborated in more detail later in this chapter.

In advancing this framework, we suggested that *reactive* contestation focuses primarily on the norms involved in the contestation process (such as territorial integrity, the prohibition of the use of force, sovereign non-interference and the protection of human rights). Building on Palestini's work on legitimacy, *proactive* contestation brings to the fore the legitimacy of the role of the actors enforcing the norm, including the UN, formal and informal regional organisations or individual states, as well as the location of contestation, which may involve states, the private sector or civil society. *Interpretative* contestation often concentrates on another of Palestini's concerns, the legitimacy and effectiveness of the instruments used in the pursuit of norm enforcement and foreign policy goals, that is, the use of sanctions, as opposed to incentives, diplomacy and the threat or use of force.

Types and Forms of Normative Contestation

Since early 2022, the Russian invasion of Ukraine has reignited a debate about international sanctions. This section elaborates in detail the various contestation forms that have been presented in the book by looking at the phenomena through a contestation over global norms, the actors enforcing them and the instruments employed to enforce them, particularly the application of international sanctions.

Contestation over Norms

Countries that have resorted to sanctions contend that they are enforcing norms against the use of force, armed aggression and in defence of the UN Charter and the principles associated with the territorial integrity of its member states or in opposition to gross violations of human rights, to name just a few. Most states would formally agree with these norms. Yet, contestation arises not because there is disagreement with the violation of these norms that led to the imposition of sanctions, but because the use of sanctions is seen as violating other norms – equal to or even more important than those invoked to justify the sanctions in the first place. In other words, states contest sanctions by engaging in a form of normative displacement, emphasising the importance of sovereign equality and non-intervention in the domestic affairs of states, while challenging both the legitimacy of those enforcing the norms and the use of sanctions as a means of enforcement.

Most states in the Global South share a commitment to the norm of sovereign equality that demands respect for their sovereignty and territorial integrity just as it is accorded to Western countries. The sovereign equality norm, which was initially put forward by non-aligned states at the Bandung Conference in 1955, involves principles such as respect for territorial integrity and sovereignty, non-aggression, non-interference in the internal affairs of sovereign states, and equality and peaceful co-existence (Basu-Mellish 2023). This broad norm is explicitly endorsed by groups like ASEAN and the BRICS, as well as by most post-colonial countries in the Global South. The norms of sovereign equality and non-intervention are prioritised by many states in their assessments of the hierarchy of global norms, a form of interpretative contestation.

Contestation over Actors Enforcing Norms

Many countries view *unilateral* restrictive measures as illegal under international law and as a violation of national sovereignty and self-determination.

Unilateral sanctions, that is, sanctions imposed by individual states or regional blocs without United Nations Security Council (UNSC) approval, are widely criticised for undermining fundamental principles of international law, particularly non-intervention and sovereign equality. In this context, the primary target of criticism is the United States, whose currency dominance and economic size allow it to enforce sanctions that often reflect its national interests. In contrast, multilateral sanctions imposed through the UNSC are viewed as both legal and more legitimate, because they result from international consensus.

While most Global South states have endorsed multilateral sanctions, they question the legitimacy of unilateral measures. African states, for example, view sanctions as policies externally imposed on them by Western powers without any consideration of their views on the appropriateness of the actions undertaken, as Agbonifo argues in Chapter 5. Similarly, Serbia's leadership has denounced what it sees as European arrogance in adopting coercive measures and then demanding compliance from states uninvolved in their formulation, as Belloni and Ramović suggest in Chapter 11.

Unilateral sanctions are widely condemned as instruments of power that interfere in the internal affairs of sovereign states, but this is also due to the view that sometimes the true 'aim' of sanctions goes beyond their stated objectives. In fact, sanctions as an instrument of foreign policy serve the strategic interests of sender nations often embedded in reproducing historical legacies and structural power asymmetries. While these critiques stem from a post-colonial perspective, the broader consensus is that these measures reinforce global power imbalances. Some African leaders, for example, argue that unilateral sanctions not only violate international law but also selectively target non-Western states to advance Western geopolitical interests. This argument could even be extended to actions of the UNSC itself, since the vast majority of resolutions applying sanctions are drafted by only three of its permanent members – the US, France and the UK. As a result, Global South nations engage in *interpretative* contestation, condemning these measures as expressions of US and EU hegemony. Given the potential for any state to fall foul of Washington or Brussels, there is a perceived need for a strong pushback (Heine 2024, 702).

While resistance to unilateral sanctions is widespread, in some cases it may be difficult to sustain in practice. Mexico, for instance, has historically opposed unilateral sanctions against Cuba and Venezuela, but in order to ease tensions with Washington, in some cases (such as that of sanctions against North Korea) ultimately adopted US-led coercive measures, as Rosas argues in Chapter 9. More generally, not only the Mexican government but also Mexican multinational corporations have adjusted their operations to comply with US sanctions to safeguard their interests in the American market. Similarly, even firms within states with very large economies, such as China, have occasionally complied with US sanctions informally to avoid secondary repercussions, illustrating a pragmatic balance between national interests and ideological opposition.

Despite these exceptions, states in the Global South are not only sceptical about the senders of sanctions as motivated by neo-colonial instincts, but they also strongly condemn the imposition of unilateral sanctions, particularly those with extra-territorial application. Especially, they reject the self-proclaimed authority of the US and the EU to adopt coercive measures unilaterally, recognising only UNSC-backed measures as valid. For instance, Iran understands such measures as direct interventions in its domestic affairs and clear threats to its sovereignty, as indicated in Chapter 5 by Alikarami and Hadian Jazy. Tehran argues further that sanctions with extra-territorial applications violate international law by prioritising the domestic legal frameworks of sanctioning states over global norms, effectively weaponising economic restrictions to interfere in the internal matters of other nations.

The BRICS echoed this sentiment in 2021, asserting that the UN is the 'sole authority to impose sanctions', reflecting broader resistance to the concentration of power in a few Western states, as Chauhan argues in Chapter 8. The BRICS countries advocate for sanctions to be imposed through multilateral frameworks, such as the UNSC, rejecting unilateral sanctions as illegitimate methods for addressing international crises. These measures not only violate the principle of non-intervention but also create an international hierarchy where powerful nations impose their will on weaker states. By contrast, the BRICS emphasise the importance of cooperation based on equality, mutual support and respect for national interests. For example, China has explicitly stated its intention to maintain normal trade relations with all countries, including Iran, as a demonstration of its commitment to these principles and its opposition to the selective, coercive nature of unilateral sanctions.

Between 2013 and 2017, Western nations increasingly targeted BRICS members and their allies, prompting strong opposition from the bloc. BRICS annual statements repeatedly condemned 'economic sanctions and the arbitrary use of unilateral coercive measures', framing them as unjust and detrimental to global cooperation. South Africa, in particular, has resisted these measures, viewing them as a tool for Western-led regime change, as seen in Iraq in 2003 and Libya in 2011. Brazil has also expressed scepticism, arguing that such sanctions are selectively applied to support or undermine specific governments. Similarly, Indian leaders denounced sanctions imposed on New Delhi after its 1998 nuclear tests, highlighting Western hypocrisy, as no comparable consequences were faced by other nuclear-armed states. This pattern of double standards reinforces the perception that unilateral sanctions serve geopolitical agendas rather than upholding international norms.

In the case of African states, the association of especially non-UN sanctions with regime change has heightened concerns about external influence. Likewise, the Non-Aligned Movement has pledged not to recognise or implement unilateral coercive measures, viewing them as violations of sovereignty and international law. The BRICS states argue that such sanctions undermine global governance by subordinating international law to the domestic policies of a few powerful states, thereby challenging the authority of the UNSC and weakening multilateral decision-making structures.

The fact that some Global South states adopt sanctions themselves is compatible with a form of proactive contestation, particularly when they attempt to justify the practice with reference to international legal norms. For instance, while the BRICS nations consistently oppose unilateral sanctions, emphasising that only those imposed 'in accordance with the provisions of the relevant UN Security Council Resolutions' are legitimate (BRICS, 2012), they justify their own sanctions as examples of counter-measures, or as Wenjie Yu describes Chinese practices in Chapter 7, as responses to perceived harms. The fifteenth BRICS summit made a different appeal to international legal norms, condemning unilateral sanctions for violating World Trade Organization (WTO) rules and disrupting global agricultural trade. These measures, particularly from Western powers, are seen as violations of international law and as tools for political interference. Alexandra Hofer's legal analysis in Chapter 4 highlights the serious challenges unilateral sanctions pose and the need for further discussion of their legitimacy.

In sum, the legitimacy of sanctions is seriously undermined by the fact that the instrument has been frequently used by states outside and beyond the action of the United Nations. The problem would be, therefore, not that sanctions have been used, but rather that they have been used either without the authorisation of the Security Council or, occasionally, without a convincing argument that would justify the utilisation of counter-measures.

Contesting the Legitimacy of the Instrument of Sanctions

Many countries question the use and effectiveness of sanctions themselves, not just the legitimacy of the actors imposing them. Their opposition to sanctions stems in part from their post-colonial experience and, in cases like Iran and

Serbia, their direct experience as targets of sanctions. As a form of interpretative contestation, the problem is not that sanctions exist, but rather that they disproportionately affect weaker countries. This is why counter-measures are undertaken to minimise this problem. The BRICS nations, for example, have promoted practices like de-dollarisation and established alternative financial institutions such as the New Development Bank and the Contingency Reserve Fund to counteract Western economic dominance and reshape global governance. China has enacted laws like the Anti-Foreign Sanctions Law to counter foreign restrictions and has attempted to redefine the legitimacy of sanctions by proactively advocating for new international norms governing their use, as Yu contends in Chapter 7.

Global South nations point to the negative impact that sanctions have on their economies and societies. Indeed, sanctions have a disproportionate effect on developing nations, stifle economic growth and can worsen humanitarian crises by increasing inflation and poverty, and by restricting access to essential goods like food and medicine. As a result, the UN General Assembly has joined the UN Human Rights Council and repeatedly condemned such measures for their negative human rights effects on civilians in target states. The GA even passed a resolution in June 2025 establishing 4 December as the International Day against Unilateral Coercive Measures (United Nations 2025).

While this negative impact on civilians is frequently noted, Russia and Serbia present unique perspectives on the issue. The Kremlin has reversed the traditional criticism of sanctions as affecting the civilian population more than the leaders of the target state by portraying European citizens – not Russian – as the primary victims of Western sanctions due to the combined influence of rising inflation and growing energy and food prices, as Mamedov and Dutkiewicz argue in Chapter 10. Similarly, in Serbia, pro-government media have not only justified the refusal to impose sanctions on Moscow but have also emphasised their negative effects on the citizens of sanctioning countries rather than on the target state, thus exposing the contradictions emerging in the application of coercive measures.

Concerns about the unintended consequences of sanctions further undermine their legitimacy, and proposals have frequently been advanced to make sanctions more targeted to enhance their legitimacy as a policy instrument. Global South nations emphasise the harm inflicted on ordinary citizens, viewing sanctions as unjust and punitive. In some cases, this focus shifts attention away from the norm violations that sanctions seek to address, as seen in Iran, where the debate centres more on the right to development and human rights than on Iran's contested nuclear and ballistic missile activities. Making sanctions 'better' or proactively arguing that only UN sanctions are legitimate has been the focus, rather than rejecting the policy instrument altogether.

Criticism of sanctions often focuses not only on their use as a foreign policy tool, but on their over-use, which can isolate targeted nations without necessarily resolving conflicts. Sanctions, in particular, have been likened to isolating the 'sick' in the 'sick room', exacerbating divisions, rather than fostering communitarian solutions, as emphasised in the chapter by John Agbonifo. Similarly, the BRICS countries consistently oppose unilateral sanctions and advocate for dialogue and cooperation. Although the BRICS states criticise unilateral sanctions, they emphasise that their position is not one of confrontation with the West, but rather an effort to promote a more balanced diplomatic approach (Reuters 2014).

In Africa, contestation of sanctions as a policy instrument combines interpretative and proactive elements, viewing Western-imposed measures as isolating and humiliating. As John Agbonifo argues in Chapter 5, the continent's response seeks an alternative approach centred on reconciliation rather than marginalisation. The African Union (AU) adopts a strategy focused on restoring stability through engagement rather than punitive measures. While acknowledging that certain behaviours warrant sanctions, the AU insists that these measures should include clear timelines for restoring constitutional order, a form of proactive contestation. Additionally, maintaining communication with sanctioned parties is considered essential to assessing their intentions and applying informal pressure for compliance. This 'communitarian' approach underscores the importance of cultural context in shaping the appropriateness of sanctions. While acknowledging the importance of adopting coercive measures, African states advocate for conflict resolution strategies that integrate, rather than isolate, sanctioned nations.

Normative Contestation over Russia's Invasion of Ukraine

Russia's invasion of Ukraine in February 2022 violated fundamental norms of the international system, including using force to resolve disputes, undermining the sovereignty and territorial integrity of a UN Member State, and abrogating commitments from 1994 that affirmed Ukrainian borders. More than thirty countries sanctioned Russia following its 2022 invasion. Most are based in the developed 'West', but they were joined by developed Asian countries like Japan, Singapore, South Korea and Taiwan. Even though a wide majority of the world's 193 countries has repeatedly condemned Russia's actions in Ukraine in resolutions passed by the UN General

Assembly,[1] the vast majority of countries in the world has opted out of sanctioning Russia.

Countries that have applied sanctions on Russia contend that they are enforcing norms against the use of force, against armed aggression and in defence of the UN Charter and principles associated with the territorial integrity of its member states. As Orchard and Wiener argue in Chapter 1, sanctioning Russia is a form of reactive contestation against Russia's claims of self-defence and its perceived threats to its security. Most states of the Global South do not endorse Russia's aggression and have condemned it in UN General Assembly resolutions. Rather, they engage in a kind of normative displacement, stressing the importance of the norm of sovereign equality and non-intervention in domestic affairs of states and challenging instead both the legitimacy of the enforcers of the norms and the use of sanctions as a means of enforcement. Those countries allied with Russia (discussed in more detail in the section on contestation over Russia that follows), in contrast, accept Russia's interpretation of security threats from NATO and have voted with it in opposition to General Assembly resolutions condemning its invasion of Ukraine.

While advancing anti-colonial arguments based on the importance of respecting the higher status non-interventionist norms of sovereignty and non-interference, Global South states have not taken these arguments to their logical conclusion. Even though they condemn violations of the territorial integrity of sovereign states, almost all countries considered in this volume – with the exception of Singapore, which considers the respect of territorial integrity a non-negotiable foundation of the international order – have censured Russian aggression against Ukraine but have refused to endorse

[1] On 2 March 2022, the UN General Assembly overwhelmingly voted to condemn Russia's 'special military operation' by a vote of 141 in favour and 5 against, with 35 abstentions (12 countries did not vote). While Brazil voted in favour of the resolution, most of the other BRICS countries at the time, India, South Africa and China, abstained, while Russia opposed it. Subsequent General Assembly resolutions condemning Russia's invasion have passed with similar majorities, particularly the February 2023 resolution condemning the invasion, though there is evidence of a decline in support for Ukraine in the UN General Assembly over time. The July 2024 resolution on nuclear safety at the Russian-occupied Zaporizhzhia nuclear power plant garnered only 99 affirmative votes. The 24 February 2025 UNGA resolution on Russia's invasion passed with only 93 affirmative votes, and notably with the opposition of the US, which joined Russia and its allies in opposition to the measure.

anti-colonial criticism of Russia as articulated by Ukraine and to adopt sanctions against Moscow.

This apparent contradiction between support for the norm of territorial integrity and the refusal to endorse sanctions trying to uphold this norm may give rise to a 'sovereignty paradox' (Verma 2024). The sovereign non-intervention principle has been mentioned by many of the authors in this volume as a key norm for many states. Some of the same countries supporting the territorial integrity norm, such as China and India, refuse to impose sanctions on Russia, citing the allegedly higher status of the norm of sovereign non-intervention. In other words, they appear to engage in normative displacement.

At the same time, while refusing to join the sanction regime, they have adopted coercive measures in the conduct of their own foreign policy, even if they justify it in defensive terms, or invoke international law to legitimise it. In a similar paradox, the UN General Assembly annually passes resolutions condemning unilateral coercive measures, yet at the same time it has long recommended that states adopt coercive measures in response to gross violations of human rights violations such as in the cases of South Africa and the Palestinian occupied territories. Rebecca Barber contends that 'unilateral coercive economic measures might be permissible if adopted "in response to a clear violation of universally accepted norms, standards or obligations" and that such measures are unilateral coercive measures, even if adopted for purposes other than subordinating state sovereignty, but they are not necessarily illegal' (Barber 2021, 364).

As Orchard and Wiener argue in Chapter 1, applying sanctions on Russia is an illustration of a reactive contestation to Russia's 'clear violation of core international norms – most notably Article 2(4) of the Charter that prohibits the aggressive use of force'. The vast majority of the countries of the world reacted by declaring their opposition to Russia's norm violation, but their reactive contestation was expressed through voting at the UN General Assembly, rather than through the application of restrictive measures. Thus, while much of the normative contestation over Russia's invasion of Ukraine supports norms against the use of force and defends principles of sovereignty and territorial integrity, much of the disagreement globally is over the means employed – the application of sanctions – to contest the norm violation, not about the norms themselves.

Stefano Palestini contends in Chapter 2 that the reluctance of African and Latin American states to sanction Russia is not indicative of support for Russia's violation of well-established norms, but rather a contestation of the practice of applying unilateral sanctions to enforce norms. He argues that unilateral sanctions are delegitimised on the grounds that they violate norms that are considered by those who contest them 'as having a higher status: sovereignty, non-intervention, and self-determination'.

From her detailed analysis of the discursive history of UN General Assembly debates about sanctions in Chapter 3, Elin Hellquist observes that sanctions against Russia did not figure prominently in UNGA debates in 2022 or 2023, and that 'disapproval with the norm violation does not consequentially lead to explicit support of sanctions'. Alexandra Hofer agrees in Chapter 4, contending that '[T]he vast majority of UNGA member states find Russia has violated international law in invading Ukraine', but while the EU, the US and aligning states 'are coordinating to impose costs on Russia . . . most countries prefer to remain neutral, and do not consider that unilateral sanctions are an appropriate method to respond to the conflict'. She goes on to say that 'many states do not believe unilateral sanctions are an appropriate means to solve disputes' and that 'when states invoke the principle of non-intervention to challenge the legality of unilateral sanctions, they are engaging in "interpretative contestation"'. Their lack of willingness to apply sanctions 'is due to the fact they don't perceive unilateral sanctions as an appropriate means to solve the conflict. They furthermore resent sanctions as a form of unlawful pressure.'

These arguments are presented in different ways in the chapters articulating perspectives from different countries and regions of the world included in the volume, which provide us with multiple perspectives on the use of sanctions against Russia. The criticism of the Russia sanctions is focused primarily on contestation over the legitimacy of the measures as highlighted by Palestini in Chapter 2, namely the illegitimacy of the senders and on the use of sanctions as a policy tool, rather than on the norms violated by Russia, on which there remains agreement amongst most countries.

The idea that senders of unilateral sanctions against Russia are illegitimate is embedded in the claim that they are a tool of Western neo-imperialism. This is articulated most clearly in the chapter on Iran by Fariba Alikarami and Nasser Hadian Jazy, as well as in the chapter on Russia by Piotr Dutkiewicz and Intigam Mamedov. Dutkiewicz and Mamedov argue in Chapter 10 that Russia has basically withdrawn from the Western-led order and that its counter-measures and efforts to circumvent the sanctions measures contribute to an anti-imperial effort to construct a more just world order based on multiple global powers, not just the Western-dominated international system. Alikarami and Hadian Jazy argue in Chapter 6 that Iran's support for Russia is based more on the logic of 'the enemy of my enemy is my friend' than it is an indication of Iranian support for Russia's norm violation and that Iran considers its support for Russia as a demonstration of opposition to the West. As they write in Chapter 6, 'Iran perceives Western sanctions against Russia as an effort by the liberal democratic order to silence dissenting voices, whether revolutionary Islam or illiberal.'

The hesitancy of resorting to sanctions, even when in agreement with the norm that triggered the adoption of sanctions for some, stems from structural inequalities and the perception of the Russia–Ukraine war as a proxy conflict between NATO and Russia. Many countries, including Iran, Serbia and several African and ASEAN states, view endorsing the G7+ (Western) sanctions as reinforcing Cold War-era divisions.

Beyond the contestation of the sources of sanctions, there is also widespread criticism of the utility and legitimacy of sanctions themselves. There is a widely held view that sanctions as policy instruments do not work. Serbian President Aleksandar Vučić declared 'we don't believe sanctions change anything', likely based in part on Serbia's experience as a target of sanctions in the 1990s. Roberto Belloni and Jasmin Ramović reiterate this point in their discussion of Serbian reactions to the Russia sanctions in Chapter 11 when they describe how Serbia denounced the 'inappropriateness of sanctions as a foreign policy tool'. In Chapter 8 on the BRICS, Rishika Chauhan argues that the BRICS had been questioning the utility of unilateral sanctions in their communiqués, even before Russia's 2022 invasion of Ukraine. Economic considerations further deter them from taking sides, as some states benefit from bypassing the sanctions regime, while others fear disruptions in global trade, particularly regarding energy and food supplies.

Many of the countries that have declined to apply sanctions on Russia have argued that there are better instruments available. This is the position of Cambodia and Indonesia in Southeast Asia, as described in Chapter 12 by Matteo Dian. Indonesian President Joko Widodo declared in 2022 that sanctions 'are not the best solution to resolve the problem'. Brazil and Mexico have similarly called for dialogue between Russia and Ukraine, rather than applying sanctions. In his survey of African reactions in Chapter 5, John Agbonifo describes how many African leaders perceived that the use of sanctions created little opportunity for dialogue and negotiation, which are necessary for bringing the war in Ukraine to an end. The imposition of sanctions on Russia did not foreground, and appears to have foreclosed, the possibility for dialogue, negotiation and use of incentives. As happened to Zimbabwe under sanctions, Russia has been abandoned in the sick room and is expected to retrace its steps as a condition for sanctions termination.

The African Union does not have a history of imposing sanctions on non-members states, and when it applies them internally to its members, prioritises engagement over isolation, a recommendation they have extended to those applying sanctions on Russia. Agbonifo argues that 'the extent to which

Western sanctions senders listen to African voices and engage with the African communitarian approach to sanctions could go a long way in determining the impact of African leaders' contestation of sanctions norms' with regard to Russia.

Calls for alternative measures (direct negotiations, a ceasefire) are common among other countries opting out of applying sanctions on Russia. Turkish Foreign Minister Mevlut Cavusoglu announced that Turkey would not join sanctions imposed on Russia, because 'sanctions will not resolve the problem' (TASS 2022). South African President Cyril Ramaphosa argued that it would not impose sanctions on Russia, as they 'may serve to prolong and intensify the conflict' (Ferreira 2022).

Another reaction to the use of sanctions against Russia is that they violate other norms and principles of international society, particularly norms associated with sovereign non-intervention in domestic affairs and the right to development. This argument was made in the chapters about the perspectives of Iran, China, Russia, Serbia and several Southeast Asian countries.

The chapters on Iran, Russia and ASEAN also indicated how the sanctions on Russia have harmed innocent populations in targeted countries through enforced shortages and high inflation and threatened global supply chains associated with food and fertiliser exports. The chapter on Serbia in particular highlighted how sanctions can be a double-edged sword that weaponises the global economy, a point also made in the chapters about views in China and Russia. As argued in the chapter on Serbia, and also in the chapter on Russia, not only the targets but the senders of sanctions can suffer from their use.

The use of sanctions against Russia is also criticised by many non-sanctioning countries as based on a double standard in the application of the policy instrument. As Belloni and Ramović argue, Western outrage over Russian behaviour is both 'selective and hypocritical'. A similar argument is made by many African countries, who question why 'Western countries condemned and imposed sanctions on Russia over the invasion of Ukraine, when they equally breached international law when they invaded and destroyed Libya (2011), Iraq (2003) and Syria (2014)'. Mexico made similar arguments, as demonstrated by María-Cristina Rosas in Chapter 9, when she observed that former Mexican President López Obrador excused himself from a meeting sponsored by Canada to raise funds for the victims of the war in Ukraine in April 2022, by citing previous commitments and, instead, sending a video message indicating that his government would not condemn the Russian invasion of Ukraine 'because Mexico had been invaded in the past by Spain, France, and the United States'.

China is generally critical of the application of unilateral sanctions, as pointed out in Chapter 8 on the BRICS, by Rishika Chauhan, and in

Chapter 7, by Wenjie Yu. China's position on the use of sanctions is a classic example of proactive contestation, in that China strives to establish an international legal justification for its use of unilateral sanctions. Thus, while China is increasingly applying unilateral sanctions of its own, it does so with reference to international law, applying restrictive measures on others only after China perceives itself to have been harmed by them. This is a classic example of proactive contestation of international norms with regard to the application of unilateral sanctions.

Mapping Contestation: What Sanctions Contestation Tells Us about Norms and Interests

The responses to Russia's invasion are complex and difficult to generalise about. However, looking at the contestation of sanctions allows us to offer an alternative lens through which governments and UN members have mediated between supporting the principle of territorial integrity of Ukraine, their material interests and their worldviews. We attempt to interpret the foreign policy attitude of various states beyond their discursive standing on sanctions, so as to consider also bilateral historical relationships, economic interests and geographical circumstances. We can, then, offer a typology of practical policy responses – ranging from self-declared and tacit allies of Russia to facilitators of circumvention, active and passive hedgers, and countries with ongoing sanctions on Russia – to show how their standing on sanctions may have been influenced by interests as well as by norms and ideas.

Allies of Russia

A small number of countries are active allies of Russia in its intervention in Ukraine. Belarus allowed its territory to be used for the initial invasion and voted against the initial UNGA resolution condemning the invasion. The DPRK also voted against the UNGA resolution and has subsequently supplied ammunition, weapons and troops in support of Russia's military efforts. Eritrea and Syria both voted against the initial UNGA resolution but were not as directly engaged as Belarus and the DPRK in their military support for Russia. Although Iran abstained from the original March 2022 UNGA resolution, it supplied drones and drone technology to Russia and, more recently, ballistic missiles to the country. Most of Russia's allies have adopted Russia's narrative of having been threatened by further NATO expansion and do not contest the invasion as a norm violation but view it as justifiable self-defence. They engage in *reactive* and *interpretative* contestation of sanctions. On the one hand, the norm of non-intervention is deemed superior to other international norms and, therefore, sanctions are viewed as a violation of a fundamental principle of the international system. On the other hand, sanctions are not legitimate, as they are not imposed by the United Nations, and they are a projection of power by a few nations of the Western-led order.

Tacit Allies

China also abstained on the UNGA resolution but, having pledged 'no limits' in its friendship with Russia in early February 2022 at the Putin/Xi summit and by benefiting from the import of lower-priced Russian petroleum exports and exporting semi-conductors to Russia, it is at least a tacit ally. Individual Chinese firms, particularly those operating in the financial sector, have walked a tightrope, trying to limit their exchanges with Russia to avoid being designated for secondary sanctions by the US. South Africa has been relatively outspoken within Africa in its support for Russia and its opposition to sanctions on the country. It abstained on the 2022 UNGA resolution and has provided moral diplomatic support from an important African country, rather than the supply of military materiel to Russia. Like Russia's allies, its tacit allies also express sympathy with Russia's strategic predicament and support its calls for a multipolar (non-Western-dominated) world order. They are concerned more with the illegitimacy of the enforcers of the norm and the policy instruments they use (sanctions), rather than with the contestation or acceptance of Russia's norm violations.

Facilitators of Russian Circumvention

A number of countries bordering Russia have become focal points for facilitating the circumvention of the G7+ restrictive measures. Kazakhstan, Armenia and Kyrgyzstan all border Russia and abstained on the 2022 UNGA resolution, while Azerbaijan, Turkmenistan and Uzbekistan did not vote on the matter. Most of these countries have historically strong trading relationships with Russia and most have shown sharp increases in imports from the EU and the US in certain goods that traditionally were exported directly to Russia. There has been a re-establishment of some of the same trading routes that were used to circumvent CoCom trade restrictions during the Cold War.[2]

[2] The Coordinating Committee for Multilateral Export Controls was established to limit exports of technology to the Warsaw Pact and China and operated from the late 1940s to the mid-1990s.

These countries have been the subject of close scrutiny and visits by delegations from both Washington and Brussels. They appear to be motivated more by the potential material advantages of circumvention than by direct engagement with the norms violated. Sanctions are not imposed because they are seen as a violation of the sovereignty principle and the view that alternative tools are likely to be more effective

Active Hedgers

The term 'active hedgers' describes the position of countries taking advantage of low oil prices and/or applying half-hearted measures to signal normatively their opposition to Russia's invasion. India abstained on the 2022 UNGA resolution and has benefited significantly from the purchase of lower-cost petroleum from Russia. It has also been historically dependent on arms exports from Russia, though their numbers are reduced today due to Russia's own military needs. Turkey voted in favour of the 2022 UNGA resolution condemning Russia, as did the United Arab Emirates, but both countries have become important locations for circumvention of the restrictive measures. Georgia also voted for the UNGA resolution, but 50 per cent of its trade remains with Russia, and the country has also been accused of circumventing the Russia sanctions even though its Central Bank issued guidelines recommending that Georgian financial institutions implement US, UK and EU sanctions. For this group of countries, the material benefits of keeping a low profile on Russia's norm violations and, especially, on sanctions outweigh the advantages of contestation.

Passive Hedgers

Most of the countries of Central and South America voted in favour of the 2022 UNGA resolution condemning Russia's invasion (with the exceptions of Bolivia, Cuba, El Salvador, Nicaragua and Venezuela, which either abstained or did not vote on the matter). Most have benefited from lower-priced petroleum from Russia, but none of the four major economic powers of the region – Brazil, Mexico, Chile or Argentina – has applied any sanctions on Russia. Drawing on their long tradition of opposition to external intervention, most have questioned the effectiveness of sanctions, raised concerns about their humanitarian consequences and articulated a preference for negotiations over sanctions, even though in practice this is not necessarily a trade-off.

Sanctioners

This group has been led historically by the US and includes all of the members of the G7, the European Union, Switzerland and a number of developed Asian countries and territories (in addition to G7 member Japan), including Singapore, South Korea and Taiwan. A total of thirty countries, regions or territories has applied sanctions on Russia over its invasion of Ukraine. They have chosen a strong form of reactive contestation, combining diplomatic condemnation with the application of sanctions that have material consequences for their populations.

Below, in Table C.1, we draw from the rich conceptual and empirical content of the chapters included in this volume in order to identify and map the different aspects of norm contestation over international sanctions and to assess the extent to which our framework represents a useful heuristic tool to analyse contemporary global dynamics.

Concluding Reflections on the Analytical Framework and the Normative Contestation of International Sanctions

Phil Orchard and Antje Wiener have made an important contribution to the literature on norm contestation through the introduction of their analytical typology distinguishing amongst different types of normative contestation. Extending their work with Stefano Palestini's consideration of the legitimacy of the enforcers of norms and the instruments they employ (sanctions) adds a dimension that yields new insights into the complexity of norm contestation as well as its practice, particularly when applied to a specific case like Russia. The analytical framework adopted in this volume has proven to be a useful heuristic device, yet its empirical application has identified notable complexities. Six key reflections emerge from this inquiry.

First, disentangling normative commitments from material interests remains a significant challenge. The Global South's preference for the principle of sovereign equality contrasts with its reluctance to impose sanctions on Moscow over its violation of the sovereignty of neighbouring Ukraine. Paradoxically, states from the Global South may also be accused of double standards and selectivity in their foreign policy conduct. While framed as a normative stance, this refusal is also driven by pragmatic considerations, such as economic ties and geopolitical alignments. Serbia's position illustrates this dynamic, as its reliance on Russian support at the UN regarding Kosovo underscores the interplay between normative contestation and strategic interests. This suggests

Table C.1 Contestation types and targets

Types of contestation	**Norms contested** Use of force Territorial integrity Sovereign non-interference Human rights	**Actors enforcing** UN Regional organisations Autonomous (G7+) sanctions Individual states *and* **Locations of contestation** States Private sectors Civil society	**Instruments employed** Sanctions Incentives Diplomacy Threats of force Use of force
Reactive	Sanctioning states normative condemnation of Russia's use of force and territorial annexation	Global South condemnations of unilateral coercive measures	Global South questions about the utility of sanctions and preferences for negotiations
Proactive	Normative displacement, giving precedence to norm of non-intervention	BRICS justifications of its sanctions as legitimate counter-measures under international law	Efforts to reform sanctions practice with greater targeting, humanitarian carve-outs and due process reforms
Interpretative	Allies of Russia defence of Russia's invasion as legitimate self-defence against NATO expansion	Global South views of unilateral sanctions as instruments of neo-colonial domination	Sanctions as violations of basic human rights to food, to health and to development

that norm adherence is often shaped by material realities, making it difficult to draw a clear distinction between the two.

Second, while the distinction between proactive, reactive and interpretative contestation is conceptually valuable, its empirical application reveals significant complexity and overlap. In responding to norm violations, actors simultaneously interpret and redefine those norms, blurring the lines between reaction and reinterpretation. For instance, African and Latin American states oppose unilateral sanctions not only as a response to Western policies, but also because they perceive such measures as violations of sovereignty. This suggests that norm contestation is inherently fluid, with reactive and interpretative dimensions often intertwining in practice. It is easier to categorise types of normative contestation, when one identifies and concentrates on a particular norm violation. Russia has been accused of simultaneously violating so many international norms that it is difficult to generalise about the reactions to its multiple violations. This may be one reason why many of our country or regional authors had difficulty selecting amongst the three types of normative contestation when attempting to characterise the types of normative contestation underway. It is very difficult to pin down the type of normative contestation without focusing on a single norm violation at a time.

Third, disagreements over the hierarchy of norms can lead to a tendency either not to engage or not to contest some norm violations. While the norms against the use of force and in favour or sovereign territorial integrity were generally reinforced by UN General Assembly voting patterns, the practice of applying sanctions to enforce norms was generally opposed due to the importance given to other norms, such as non intervention, and concerns about the human rights to development and humanitarian consequences of sanctions. Rather than address directly the norms violated by Russia's invasion of Ukraine, many countries preferred to engage in a form of norm displacement, changing the subject and talking about the violations of other norms that, for some, are arguably of equal or greater importance.

Fourth, we also encountered different practices of contestation over the use of sanctions. While many of the chapters focused on the rhetorical condemnation of sanctions at the UN Human Rights Council or in the UN General Assembly, countries subject to sanctions themselves (or potential future targets of sanctions) have engaged in forms of anticipatory strategic diversification and enhanced cooperation to minimise the effectiveness of potential future sanctions. This is particularly noteworthy amongst the BRICS countries. Thus, in addition to discursive contestation, there is behavioural contestation, where states take deliberate action to minimise the potential impact of sanctions.

Fifth, integrating multiple dimensions – reactive, proactive, interpretative, as well as the role of actors and instruments – offers a more comprehensive approach to understanding collective action and governance mechanisms. Examining patterns of cooperation and conflict through this framework highlights how disagreements over norms, institutional legitimacy and strategic interests shape international relations. Rather than viewing contestation as a binary opposition to existing norms, this perspective reveals how states navigate the tensions between principle and pragmatism.

Sixth and finally, the effort to engage scholars from multiple vantage points across the globe and to make an empathetic effort to comprehend their views on international sanctions – the pursuit of Global International Relations – is a highly rewarding exercise. We have learned a great deal from the diverse contributors to this volume, including colleagues from different disciplines, from sanctioned countries, living in exile or in countries closely associated with the application of international sanctions.

Ultimately, this volume underscores the need for a more nuanced discussion on the role of sanctions within global governance. As a central instrument of international relations, sanctions must be evaluated not only in terms of their intended objectives, but also through the broader lens of legitimacy, effectiveness and the competing interests that shape their implementation, including their long-term consequences. The complexities explored in this volume contribute to a deeper understanding of these dynamics and offer valuable insights into one of the most contested issues in contemporary global politics.

References

Barber, Rebecca. 2021. 'An Exploration of the General Assembly's Troubled Relationship with Unilateral Sanctions'. *International and Comparative Law Quarterly* 70: 343–78.

Basu-Mellish, Jack. 2023. 'UN Resolution 1514: The Creation of a New Post-Colonial Sovereignty'. *Third World Quarterly* 44(6): 1306–23.

BRICS. 2012. 'Summit: Delhi Declaration New Delhi'. New Delhi, India, 29 March. https://www.brics.unipr.it/wedit/uploads/contenuti/95/fourth-brics-summit-delhi-declaration_action-plan.pdf

Ferreira, Emsie. 2022. 'Ramaphosa Condemns War, but Not Russia Specifically'. *Mail and Guardian, Africa's Better Future*, 17 March. https://mg.co.za/news/2022-03-17-ramaphosa-condemns-war-but-not-russia-specifically/

Heine, Jorge. 2024. 'Active Non-alignment, the Sovereignty Paradox and the Russia-Ukraine War'. *Contemporary Security Policy* 45(4): 698–707.

Orchard, Philip, and Antje Wiener, eds. 2024. *Contesting the World: Norm Research in Theory and Practice.* Cambridge University Press.

Palestini, Stefano. 2023. 'The Politics of Legitimation in Combined Sanction Regimes: The Case of Venezuela'. *International Affairs* 99(3): 1087–107.

Reuters. 2014. 'BRICS Stand against Western Sanctions – Russian Foreign Minister'. *Reuters*, 15 July. https://www.reuters.com/article/south-africa-iran-oil-brics-india-idINDEE82R09U20120328

TASS. 2022. 'Turkey Will Not Join Western Sanctions against Russia – Foreign Minister'. *TASS Russia News Agency*, 13 March. https://tass.com/politics/1421411

United Nations. 2025. 'International Day against Unilateral Coercive Measures. 4 December'. https://www.un.org/en/observances/day-against-unilateral-coercive-measures

Verma, Raj. 2024. 'The Russia-Ukraine War and the Global South's Sovereignty Paradox'. *Contemporary Security Policy* 45(4): 555–69.

Index

EU Authorised Representative:
Easy Access System Europe Mustamäe tee 50, 10621 Tallinn, Estonia
gpsr.requests@easproject.com

Printed and bound by CPI Group (UK) Ltd, Croydon, CR0 4YY
07/08/2026
02189978-0001